The **Coyote** Reader

Second Edition

University of South Dakota

FOUNTAINHEAD
PRESS

As a textbook publisher, we are faced with enormous environmental issues due the large amount of paper contained in our print products. Since our inception in 2002, we have worked diligently to be as eco-friendly as possible.

Our "green" initiatives include:

Electronic Products
We deliver products in non-paper form whenever possible. This includes pdf downloadables, flash drives, & CD's.

Electronic Samples
We use a new electronic sampling system, called Xample. Instructor samples are sent via a personalized web page that links to pdf downloads.

FSC Certified Printers
All of our Printers are certified by the Forest Service Council which promotes environmentally and socially responsible management of the world's forests. This program allows consumer groups, individual consumers and businesses to work together hand in hand to promote responsible use of the world's forests as a renewable and sustainable resource.

Recycled Paper
Almost all of our products are printed on a minimum of 10-30% post consumer waste recycled paper.

Support of Green Causes
When we do print, we donate a portion of our revenue to Green causes. Listed below are a few of the organizations that have received donations from Fountainhead Press. We welcome your feedback and suggestions for contributions, as we are always searching for worthy initiatives.
Rainforest 2 Reef
Environmental Working Group

Cover designer: Doris Bruey
Book Layout: OffCenter Concept House

Copyright © 2017 Fountainhead Press

Books may be purchased for educational purposes.

For information, please call or write:

1-800-586-0030
Fountainhead Press

Southlake, TX 76092
Web site: www.fountainheadpress.com
Email: customerservice@fountainheadpress.com

ISBN: 978-1-68036-491-0

Printed in the United States of America

Contents

Contents

iv

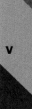

Contents

Part One
Education

What College Can Mean to the Other America

By Mike Rose

It has been nearly 50 years since Michael Harrington wrote *The Other America*, pulling the curtain back on invisible poverty within the United States. If he were writing today, Harrington would find the same populations he described then: young, marginally educated people who drift in and out of low-pay, dead-end jobs, and older displaced workers, unable to find work as industries transform and shops close. But he would find more of them, especially the young, their situation worsened by further economic restructuring and globalization. And while the poor he wrote about were invisible in a time of abundance, ours are visible in a terrible recession, although invisible in most public policy. In fact, the poor are drifting further into the dark underbelly of American capitalism.

One of the Obama administration's mantras is that we need to "out-innovate, out-educate, and out-build" our competition in order to achieve fuller prosperity. The solution to our social and economic woes lies in new technologies, in the cutting edge. This is our "Sputnik moment," a very American way to frame our problems. However, the editors of *The Economist* wrote a few months back that this explanation of our economic situation is "mostly nonsense."

Instead, the business-friendly, neoliberal magazine offered a sobering—at times almost neo-Marxist—assessment of what it considers the real danger in our economy, something at the core of Harrington's analysis: chronic, ingrained joblessness that is related to our social and economic structure. We are looking toward the horizon of innovation when we should be looking straight in front of us at the tens of millions of chronically unemployed Americans and providing comprehensive occupational, educational, and social services. Otherwise, to cite an earlier issue of *The Economist* that also dealt with American inequality, we risk "calcifying into a European-style class-based society." For people without school or work, we already have.

There are a few current policy initiatives that are aimed at helping the disadvantaged gain economic mobility, mostly through some form of postsecondary education. Sadly, the most ambitious of these—the federal American Graduation Initiative—was sacrificed during the

From *The Chronicle of Higher Education*, 2011.

health-care negotiations, although some smaller projects remained in the stimulus package and the Department of Education. Private foundations, notably Gates and Lumina, have been sponsoring such efforts as well. These efforts reach a small percentage of poor and low-income Americans and, on average, are aimed at the more academically skilled among them—although many still require remedial English and mathematics. A certificate or degree alone will not automatically lift them out of hard times—there is a bit of magic-bullet thinking in these college initiatives—but getting a decent basic education could make a significant difference in their lives. At the least, these efforts are among the few antipoverty measures that have some degree of bipartisan support.

For the last year and a half, I have been spending time at an inner-city community college that serves this population, and I have seen firsthand the effects of poverty and long-term joblessness. Although some students attend the college with the goal of transfer, the majority come for its well-regarded occupational programs. More than 90 percent must take one or more basic-skills courses; 60 percent are on financial aid. A fair number have been through the criminal-justice system.

As I have gotten to know these students, the numbers have come alive. Many had chaotic childhoods, went to underperforming schools, and never finished high school. With low-level skills, they have had an awful time in the labor market. Short-term jobs, long stretches of unemployment, no health care. Many, the young ones included, have health problems that are inadequately treated if treated at all. I remember during my first few days on the campus noticing the number of people who walked with a limp or irregular gait.

What really strikes me, though, is students' level of engagement, particularly in the occupational programs. There are a few people who seem to be marking time, but most listen intently as an instructor explains the air-supply system in a diesel engine or the way to sew supports into an evening dress. And they do and redo an assignment until they get it right. Hope and desire are brimming. Many of the students say this is the first time school has meant anything to them. More than a few talk about turning their lives around. It doesn't take long to imagine the kind of society we would have if more people had this opportunity.

10

But right at the point when opportunity is offered, it is being threatened by severe budget cuts in education and social services. For several years, the college—like so many in the United States— has been able to offer only a small number of summer classes, and classes are being cut during the year. Enrollment in existing classes is growing. Student-support services are scaled back. And all the while, more people are trying to enroll at the college; some will have to be turned away, and those who are admitted will tax an already burdened system.

Given the toll the recession has taken on state and local governments, policy makers face "unprecedented challenges" and say they "have no other choice" but to make cuts in education. Secretary of Education Arne Duncan, borrowing a now-ubiquitous phrase, has called the necessity to do more with less "the new normal."

I don't dispute the difficulty of budgeting in the recession, nor the fact that education spending includes waste that should be cut. But we need to resist the framing of our situation as inevitable and normal. This framing makes the recession a catastrophe without culpability, neutralizing the civic and moral dimensions of both the causes of the recession and the way policy makers respond to it.

The civic and moral dimensions also are diminished by the powerful market-based orientation to economic and social problems. Antigovernment, anti-welfare-state, anti-tax—this ideology undercuts broad-scale public responses to inequality.

If the editors of *The Economist* are right, the deep cuts in education— especially to programs and institutions that help poor people connect to school or work—will have disastrous long-term economic consequences that far outweigh immediate budgetary gains. And rereading *The Other America* reminds us that the stakes go beyond the economic to the basic civic question: What kind of society do we want to become? Will there be another Michael Harrington 50 years from now writing about an America that has a higher rate of poverty and even wider social divides?

Sex Ed

By Anna Quindlen

Several years ago I spent the day at a family planning clinic in one of New York City's poorest neighborhoods. I sat around a Formica table with a half-dozen sixteen-year-old girls and listened with some amazement as they showed off their knowledge of human sexuality.

They knew how long sperm lived inside the body, how many women out of a hundred using a diaphragm were statistically likely to get pregnant and the medical term for the mouth of the cervix. One girl pointed out all the parts of the female reproductive system on a placard; another recited the stages of the ovulation cycle from day one to twenty-eight. There was just one problem with this performance: although the results of their laboratory tests would not be available for fifteen more minutes, every last one of them was pregnant.

I always think of that day when someone suggests that sex education at school is a big part of the answer to the problem of teenage pregnancy. I happen to be a proponent of such programs; I think human sexuality is a subject for dispassionate study, like civics and ethics and dozens of other topics that have a moral component. I'd like my sons to know as much as possible about how someone gets pregnant, how pregnancy can be avoided, and what it means when avoidance techniques have failed.

I remember adolescence about as vividly as I remember anything, however, and I am not in the least convinced that that information alone will significantly alter the rate of teenage pregnancy. It seemed to me that day in the clinic, and on days I spent at schools and on street corners, that teenage pregnancy has a lot more to do with what it means to be a teenager than with how someone gets pregnant. When I was in high school, at the tail end of the sixties, there was a straight-forward line on sex among my friends. Boys could have it; girls couldn't. A girl who was not a virgin pretended she was. A girl who was sleeping with her boyfriend, no matter how long-playing the relationship, pretended she was not.

From *Living Out Loud,* 1987.

It is the nature of adolescence that there is no past and no future, only the present, burning as fierce, bright, and merciless as a bare light bulb. Girls had sex with boys because nothing seemed to matter except right now, not pregnancy, not parental disapprobation, nothing but those minutes, this dance, that face, those words. Most of them knew that pregnancy could result, but they assured themselves that they would be the lucky ones who would not get caught. Naturally, some of them were wrong, and in my experience they did one of three things: they went to Puerto Rico for a mysterious weekend trip; visited an aunt in some faraway state for three months and came back with empty eyes and a vague reputation; or got married, quickly, in Empire-waist dresses.

What seems to have changed most since then is that there is little philosophical counterpoint, hypocritical or not, to the raging hormones of adolescence, and that so many of the once-hidden pregnancies are hidden no more.

Not long after the day at the family planning clinic, I went to a public high school in the suburbs. In the girl's room was this graffito: Jennifer Is a Virgin. I asked the kids about it and they said it was shorthand for geek, nerd, weirdo, somebody who was so incredibly out of it that they were in high school and still hadn't had sex. If you were a virgin, they told me, you just lied about it so that no one would think you were that immature. The girls in the family planning clinic told me much the same thing—that everyone did it, that the boys wanted it, that not doing it made them seem out of it. The only difference, really, was that the girls in the clinic were poor and would have their babies, and the girls in the high school were well-to-do and would have abortions. Pleasure didn't seem to have very much to do with sex for either group. After she learned she was pregnant, one of the girls at the clinic said, without a trace of irony, that she hoped childbirth didn't hurt as much as sex had. Birth control was easily disposed of in both cases. The pill, the youngsters said, could give you a stroke; the IUD could make you sterile. A diaphragm was disgusting.

One girl told me the funniest thing her boyfriend—a real original thinker—had told her: they couldn't use condoms because it was like taking a shower with a raincoat on. She was a smart girl, and pretty, and I wanted to tell her that it sounded as if she was sleeping with a jerk who didn't deserve her. But that is the kind of basic fact of life that must be taught not in the classroom, not by a stranger, but at home by the family. It is this that, finally, I will try to teach my sons about sex, after I've explained fertile periods and birth control and all the other mechanics that are important to understand but never really go to the heart of the matter: I believe I will say that when you sleep with someone you take off a lot more than your clothes.

The Next Kind of Integration

By Emily Bazelon

JULY 20, 2008 In June of last year, a conservative majority of the Supreme Court, in a 5-to-4 decision, declared the racial-integration efforts of two school districts unconstitutional. Seattle and Louisville, Ky., could no longer assign students to schools based on their race, Chief Justice John Roberts wrote in his lead opinion in Meredith v. Jefferson County School Board (and its companion case, Parents Involved in Community Schools v. Seattle School District No. 1). Justice Stephen Breyer sounded a sad and grim note of dissent. Pointing out that the court was rejecting student-assignment plans that the districts had designed to stave off de facto resegregation, Breyer wrote that "to invalidate the plans under review is to threaten the promise of Brown." By invoking Brown v. Board of Education, the court's landmark 1954 civil rights ruling, Breyer accused the majority of abandoning a touchstone in the country's efforts to overcome racial division. "This is a decision that the court and the nation will come to regret," he concluded.

Breyer's warning, along with even more dire predictions from civil rights groups, helped place the court's ruling at the center of the liberal indictment of the Roberts court. In Louisville, too, the court's verdict met with resentment. Last fall, I asked Pat Todd, the assignment director for the school district of Jefferson County, which encompasses Louisville and its suburbs, whether any good could come of the ruling. She shook her head so hard that strands of blond hair loosened from her bun. "No," she said with uncharacteristic exasperation, "we're *already doing* what we should be."

Todd was referring to Louisville's success in distributing black and white students, which it does more evenly than any district in the country with a comparable black student population; almost every school is between 15 and 50 percent African-American. The district's combination of school choice, busing and magnet programs has brought general, if not uniform, acceptance—rather than white flight and disaffection, the legacy of desegregation in cities like Boston and Kansas City, Mo. The student population, which now numbers nearly 100,000, has held steady at about 35 percent black and 55 percent

From *The New York Times*, 2008.

white, along with a small and growing number of Hispanics and Asians.

With its decision in Meredith, the court was forcing Louisville to rethink the way it would assign elementary-school students and, in the process, to confront some tricky questions. Is the purpose of integration simply to mix students of different colors for the sake of equity or to foster greater familiarity and comfort among the races? Should integration necessarily translate into concrete gains like greater achievement for all students? If so, is mixing students by race the most effective mechanism for attaining it?

In Louisville, the achievement gap between whites and blacks is 20 percentage points at many grade levels. For Todd and her team, whatever their reservations about the decision in Meredith, coming up with an alternative assignment plan was an opportunity to think about a new kind of integration and what it might accomplish. In Louisville, integration would no longer focus solely on race but also on the barriers of class, of advantage and disadvantage. Other cities have been thinking along these lines. In the wake of the Supreme Court's decision, four other districts—Des Moines, Burlington, Vt., Omaha and Beaumont, Tex.—announced a switch to class-based integration. Seattle, too, is discussing setting aside 5 to 15 percent of the spots (a relatively small percentage) in desired high schools for low-income students.

Some of the plans go into effect this fall; others, including Louisville's, begin a year from September.

The chief justice didn't address the idea of class-based integration in his opinion. But Justice Anthony Kennedy did, in a separate concurrence. And because Kennedy cast the fifth vote for the majority, his view controls the law. Though he agreed with Roberts that public school districts should not make school assignments based on the race of individual students, he added that the court's ruling "should not prevent school districts from continuing the important work of bringing together students of different racial, ethnic and economic backgrounds."

How were schools to do this? Around the country, school-district lawyers studied Kennedy's opinion and came to a rough consensus. In its amicus brief before the court, the Bush administration cited socioeconomic integration as a "race neutral" alternative to race-based assignment plans. Kennedy picked up on this, and no other justice wrote to contradict him. As a result, the school-district lawyers concluded that districts could assign an individual child to a school based on any kind of socioeconomic measure they chose—income, assets, parental education attainment. Districts could also be "race conscious," according to Kennedy, when they drew school boundaries, chose sites for new schools and directed money to particular programs. But in these situations, they would usually be limited to taking into account the racial composition of a neighborhood rather than the race of an individual student.

In terms of the court's jurisprudence, this is a major change. Race has been the organizing principle of integration since Brown v. Board of Education. At the time of the court's ruling in Meredith, hundreds of districts were pursuing some sort of racial integration, with or without a court order, while only a few dozen at most were trying any form of socioeconomic integration. Over the years, racial integration has proved to have tangible benefits. Amy Stuart Wells, an education professor at Columbia Teachers College, has found that going to school with substantial numbers of white students helped black students to form cross-racial friendships and, by giving them access to white social networks, eventually to find work in jobs higher up the economic ladder.

However important these gains are, they are long-term and cannot be easily or quickly assessed. And increasingly, schools are held to a standard of immediately measurable outcomes. The No Child Left Behind Act, signed into law in 2002, demands student test scores that climb ever upward, with a mandate for all students to be proficient in reading and math by 2014. Test scores may not be the best way to assess the quality of a teacher or a school, but the pressure to improve scores, whatever its shortcomings, is itself on the rise. And if high test scores are the goal, it turns out, class-based integration may be the more effective tool.

Researchers have been demonstrating this result since 1966, when Congress asked James S. Coleman, a Johns Hopkins sociologist, to deliver a report on why the achievement of black students lagged far behind that of white ones. The expected answer was that more than a decade after Brown, black kids were still often going to inferior schools with small budgets. But Coleman found that the varying amount of money spent on schools didn't account for the achievement gap. Instead, the greater poverty of black families did. When high concentrations of poor kids went to school together, Coleman reported, all the students at the school tended to learn less.

How much less was later quantified. The Harvard sociologist Christopher Jencks reanalyzed Coleman's data in the 1970s and concluded that poor black sixth-graders in majority middle-class schools were 20 months ahead of poor black sixth-graders in majority low-income schools. The statistics for poor white students were similar. In the last 40 years, Coleman's findings, known informally as the Coleman Report, have been confirmed again and again. Most recently, in a 2006 study, Douglas Harris, an economist at the University of Wisconsin, found that when more than half the students were low-income, only 1.1 percent of schools consistently performed at a "high" level (defined as two years of scores in the top third of the U.S. Department of Education's national achievement database in two grades and in two subjects: English and math). By contrast, 24.2 percent of schools that are majority middle-class met Harris's standard.

There are, of course, determined urban educators who have proved that select schools filled with poor and minority students can thrive— in the right circumstances, with the right teachers and programs. But consistently good education at schools with such student bodies remains the rare exception. The powerful effect of the socioeconomic makeup of a student body on academic achievement has become "one of the most consistent findings in research on education," Gary Orfield, a UCLA education professor, and Susan Eaton, a research director at Harvard Law, wrote in their 1996 book, *Dismantling Desegregation.*

Most researchers think that this result is brought about by the advantages that middle-class students bring with them. Richard Kahlenberg of the Century Foundation lays them out in his 2001 book, *All Together Now*: more high-level classes, more parent volunteers and peers who on average have twice the vocabulary and half the behavioral problems of poor students. And, especially, more good teachers. Harris, the economist, says that poor minority students still don't have comparable access to effective teachers, measured by preparation and experience. The question, then, is whether a plan that integrates a district by class as well as by race will help win for all its schools the kind of teaching that tends to be linked to achievement. "The evidence indicates that it would," Harris says.

Ronald Ferguson, an economist at the Kennedy School of Government at Harvard, is less persuaded. His research highlights the nagging persistence of a racial achievement gap in well-off suburbs. "What happens with the achievement gap in a place like Louisville," he says, "will depend on how vigilant their leaders are to make sure high-quality instruction is delivered across the board." Such teaching is more likely in a school with a critical mass of middle-class parents, he concedes. But he stresses that to reap the benefits, poor kids have to be evenly distributed among classrooms and not just grouped together in the lowest tracks. "To the degree a district takes the kids who struggle the most academically and spreads them across different classrooms, they're making teachers' work more doable," he says. "And that may be the biggest effect."

Once they started looking for them, Todd and her colleagues saw the effects of class division and poverty in the Jefferson County schools. Thorough racial desegregation had not, it seemed, led to thorough class desegregation. At 40 of 90 elementary schools in the district, 75 percent or more of the students came from low-income homes. And the effects of these high concentrations of poverty were striking: poor students in Louisville, black and white, fared worse when they attended schools filled with other poor kids. In elementary school, 61 percent of poor students at mostly low-income schools scored proficient in reading, compared with 71 percent of poor students at majority-middle-class schools. For math, the comparative proficiency rates were 52 percent to 63 percent. Because black students were disproportionately poor, they were more likely to attend high-poverty schools, and this was contributing to the district's pronounced black-white achievement gap.

Todd and her planners wanted to tackle the problem, she says, but they were mindful of going too far in their efforts and losing the support of parents. In other districts—including Cincinnati, Evanston, Ill., Bibb County, Ga., and Madison, Wis.—the reaction to the Supreme Court's ruling had been to move to dismantle racial-integration programs. Todd and other school officials didn't want integration redefined to turn into no integration all. To get a handle on a new plan, Todd turned to an heir of James Coleman: the researcher John Powell.

In the 1960s, Powell was one of the only African-American students in his advanced high-school classes in Detroit; when he became the class valedictorian, a teacher told him he wasn't the smartest student. He now directs the Kirwan Institute for the Study of Race and Ethnicity at Ohio State University, and he says he still thinks that race is a category with singular power. But he also appreciates the stark effects of segregating poor kids. "Ever since the Coleman Report, we've seen that there's a high correlation between good schools and schools that are integrated socioeconomically as well as racially," he says. "I think everyone agrees that what we need are more good schools."

In Louisville, Powell lent his expertise to Todd and her team. They came up with a computer-generated map that shows what Powell defines as the district's areas of "low opportunity." Todd, who is 61 and taught every grade in the Louisville schools before becoming an administrator, went over the map with me one day last December. The map used two different measures of class to identify Jefferson County's areas of disadvantage: income level and the educational attainment of adults. (To gauge disadvantage, districts embarking on class-based integration often use who among their students receives free or reduced lunch; Powell, however, contends that this is a relatively crude measure.) Using census data, Todd's team identified the zones in the district in which households fall below the average income and education levels, with fewer adults who have finished high school or gone to college or beyond. Finally, the team added one more factor: a higher-than-average number of minorities, almost all of them African-Americans or Hispanics.

The map's class-plus-race formula revealed a major partition. One region, which Todd's team called Geographic Area A, is a mermaid-shaped swath of blue, with its head in Louisville's West End, just south of the Ohio River, and its tail to the south. The region encompasses the parts of the district with a higher-than-average minority population, lower-than-average median income and lower-than-average adult educational attainment. In Geographic Area A live about 30 percent of Jefferson County's students. The rest of the county, colored yellow, included everyone else—the better off, better educated and whiter Geographic Area B.

What if the district were to use this map as a guide for school integration? Instead of maintaining each school as no less than 15 percent and no more than 50 percent black, Todd's team could propose that each school have no less than 15 percent and no more than 50 percent of students from Geographic Area A. By distributing students from the district's residential zones of disadvantage, the new plan would integrate the schools by class. There would no longer be 40 elementary schools with heavily poor-student populations. There could potentially be no such schools.

Given the presumed boost to test scores resulting from distributing poor students more widely, you might wonder why Todd's team retained race as an admissions factor at all. To answer this, it's worth considering the country's existing examples of purely class-based integration. The best known is in Wake County, N.C. With 134,000 students, the Wake County school district ranks 19 among the country's 20 largest, spanning 800 square miles that include bleak tracts in the city of Raleigh, mansion-filled suburban cul-de-sacs and rural roads ending in the fresh earth of a new subdivision. The student population is about half white, one-quarter African-American and one-quarter Hispanic, Asian and multiracial. The district voluntarily pursued race-based integration in the 1980s and '90s. In 2000, after the U.S. Court of Appeals for the Fourth Circuit began to frown on the use of race in student assignment—a harbinger of the Supreme Court's stance last year—the district began assigning kids to schools based on the income level of the geographic zone they lived in. The aim was to balance the schools so that no more than 40 percent of the students at each one come from a low-income area. (This year, the district added another goal: to have no more than 25 percent of students at any one school for whom English is a second language.)

Wake County adopted class-based integration with the hard-nosed goal of raising test scores. The strategy was simple: no poor schools, no bad schools. And indeed, the district has posted striking improvements in the test scores of black and low-income students: in 1995, only 40 percent of the black students in Wake County in the third through eighth grades scored at grade level in state reading tests; by last year, the rate had almost doubled, to 82.5 percent. Statewide scores for black students also got better over the same time period, but not by as much. Wake County's numbers improve as students get older: 92 percent of all eighth graders read at or above grade level, including about 85 percent of black students and about 80 percent of low-income students. (Math scores are lower, following a statewide trend that reflects a change in the grading scale.) The district has achieved these results even as the share of low-income students overall has increased from about 30 percent a decade ago to about 40 percent today.

But the lessons of Wake County, Powell and Todd argue, don't apply everywhere. "In different districts, you have different geographic patterns," Powell says. "So you need different integration models to shop around." To begin with, Louisville is less affluent—more than 60 percent of its elementary school students receive free or reduced lunches, compared with Wake County's 40 percent. In Wake County, the vast majority of the poor students are black and Hispanic, and so mixing kids by class tightly correlates to mixing them by race. But in Jefferson County, more than a third of the kids who receive free or reduced lunches are white. As a result, redistributing students by class alone might still isolate them by race.

This is a limitation of class-based integration that holds true elsewhere. The city of San Francisco, for instance, has undergone substantial racial resegregation since retooling its diversity plan to emphasize socioeconomic factors. Even in Wake County, the fraction of students in racially segregated schools has climbed a bit over the last decade, from 25 percent to 32 percent. A 2006 paper by the education researchers Sean Reardon, John T. Yun and Michal Kurlaender crunched census data across the country and concluded that "given the extent of residential racial segregation in the United States, it is unlikely that race-neutral income-integration policies will significantly reduce school racial segregation, although there is reason to believe that such policies are likely to have other beneficial effects on schooling."

Many big cities have a different problem. Simple demographics dictate that they can't really integrate their schools at all, by either race or class. Consider the numbers for Detroit (74 percent low-income students; 91 percent black), Los Angeles (77 percent low-income; 85 percent black and Hispanic), New York City (74 percent; 63 percent), Washington (64 percent; 93 percent), Philadelphia (71 percent; 79 percent), Chicago (74 percent; 88 percent) and Boston (71 percent; 76 percent). In theory, big cities can diversify their schools by class and race by persuading many more middle-class and white parents to choose public school over private school or by combining forces with the well-heeled suburbs that surround them. But short of those developments, big cities are stuck. "The options have shrunk," says Tom Payzant, a former superintendent of schools in Boston.

Notably, there are a good many districts that have evaded this predicament. They are particularly found in the South, in part because of a historical accident. Because it was predominantly rural for longer, the South has more countywide school districts than the North. An unintended consequence was to ease the way to integration. Instead of city schools filled with poor black and Hispanic kids separated from a burgeoning ring of suburban districts stocked with affluent whites (and in some places, Asians), one district controls student assignment for the region.

Even in school districts with a mix of students of different races and income levels, however, there is no one-size-fits-all approach to socioeconomic integration, as underscored by the differences between Wake County and Jefferson County. Wake County's demographics entail that mixing kids by class, on its own, produces a fair degree of racial integration. Jefferson County's demographics don't necessarily work this way. And so civil rights lawyers suggest that districts configured like Jefferson County should continue to pursue racial diversity directly. They point to cities like Berkeley, Calif., which has an assignment plan that primarily relies on socioeconomics, but like Geography Area A also factors in the racial composition of a neighborhood to guard against resegregation along racial lines. "It's not either-or," says Anurima Bhargava, an education lawyer at the NAACP Legal Defense Fund.

In addition, there's a tacit liberal constitutional agenda at work in hybrid class-race approaches to integration: better to test Kennedy's opinion, with its support for the drawing of "race conscious" school boundaries, than to retreat further than is in fact required. "For Kennedy, there are ways of taking race into account," John Powell says. "It's just the method that's in question. How do you do it? We need to find out what's still permitted." He also points out that African-Americans are more likely than whites to be poor over generations—a bigger hurdle than a short stint in a low-income bracket.

The continuing attention to race aligns with the internal politics of Louisville and its suburbs. Many of today's parents grew up there and tend to remember and care about overcoming their county's Jim Crow legacy. In 1975, when a federal judge first ordered the city and its suburbs to desegregate, the Ku Klux Klan demonstrated, and the next day about 150 white protestors attacked eight school buses filled with black students. "We had tough times here when the buses burned," says Ann Elmore, a black member of the Jefferson County School Board. "We can still include race as a factor in our plan, and let me say I think it's important that we do."

Elsewhere in the United States, it is too soon to tell how the politics of class-based integration (Wake County) or class-plus-race (Jefferson County) will play out. Richard Kahlenberg makes the case for shifting integration policies primarily or solely to being class-based over the next decade or two. What's fair, he asks, about giving a spot in a coveted magnet program to the son of a South Asian college professor or an African-American politician over the daughter of a white waitress? Over time, such injustices threaten to sour white parents on the whole diversity enterprise, whereas giving poor kids a boost, whatever their color, is far less controversial. Polls at the time of the Supreme Court's 2003 decision in Grutter v. Bollinger, which concerned affirmative action at public universities, showed public support running 2 to 1 for giving poorer kids a leg up in going to college, as opposed to 2 to 1 against race-based preferences. In her majority opinion in the case, Justice Sandra Day O'Connor famously said she thought that racial preferences would continue only for another 25 years. Barack Obama has said, looking ahead to his daughters' college applications, that they don't deserve an admissions break—an acknowledgment that the mix of race, affirmative action and privilege is a complicated one.

To catch on nationwide, however, class-based integration would have to generate momentum that it has so far lacked. In his State of the Union address in January [2007], President Bush urged action "to help liberate poor children trapped in failing public schools." And yet a provision in the No Child Left Behind Act that theoretically allows students to transfer depends on the availability of open spaces elsewhere and has barely been utilized. The administration may have advocated class-based integration to the Supreme Court, but Bush officials haven't used their signature education law to make it happen.

If Congress were to revise No Child Left Behind to encourage more transfers of poor students to middle-class schools, would poor students drag down their better-off peers? In the end, the prospects of class-based integration will probably rise or fall on the answer to this question. Socioeconomic integration may be good for the have-nots, but if the haves think their kids are paying too great a price, they will kill it off at the polls. Richard Kahlenberg argues that the key is to ensure there is a solidly middle-class majority at as many schools as possible. That majority will then set the tone, he argues. Kahlenberg says that more research is needed to pin down the percentage of middle-class kids that a school needs to have to serve all its students well. Maybe a school can go as high as 50 percent low-income without losing ground. Or maybe it's telling that in Wake County, a proposal to increase the ceiling for low-income students from 40 percent to 50 percent died a swift death last fall after concerted protest.

Whatever the exact answer, there is some support for the view that schools can handle a substantial fraction of poor students without sacrificing performance. In Wake County, test scores of middle-class students have risen since instituting income-based integration. Additionally, Kahlenberg points out that middle-class students are generally less influenced by a school's environment because they tend to learn more at home, and that the achievement of white students has not declined in specific schools that experienced racial (and thus some class) desegregation.

Would schools need to track students by ability to protect middle-class students, who are more often higher-achieving than their low-income peers? Perhaps not. In a 2006 longitudinal study of an accelerated middle-school math program in Nassau County, N.Y., which grouped students heterogeneously, the authors found that students at all achievement levels, as well as minority and low-income students, were more likely than the students in tracked classes to take advanced math in high school. In addition, the kids who came into the program as math whizzes performed as well as other top-achievers in homogenous classes.

This study underscores Ronald Ferguson's point about the value of seating students of different backgrounds and abilities in class together, as opposed to tracking them. Still, it's worth noting that less than 15 percent of the students studied in Nassau County were low-income. So the math study doesn't tell us what happens to the high-achieving middle-class kids when close to half of their classmates aren't as well off.

At the end of February, Todd started showing the map of mermaid-shaped Geographic Area A, which she hoped to use to implement the new assignment system, to the parents of Jefferson County. Todd would start her presentation with quotes from Justice Kennedy and from Justice Breyer's dissent; she especially wanted to remind her audiences of the sentiment Breyer expressed by quoting former Justice Thurgood Marshall: "Unless our children begin to learn together, there is little hope that our people will ever learn to live together."

Todd's first stop was at a forum sponsored jointly by the Urban League and the NAACP, groups associated with Louisville's black establishment. Most of their members supported the school district, but some clergy members who worked with the city's black youth spoke against it. The Rev. John Carter, associate minister at

Green Street Baptist Church, pointed to the district's black-white achievement gap and called for a return to neighborhood schools and an earlier era of black self-reliance.

As more forums followed in high-school auditoriums across the county, white parents asked a different question: How would the new assignment plan affect their kids? Would they be forced to switch schools in second, third or fourth grade? "We like the diversity," a white parent named Niki Noe told me the next morning at her son's elementary school, St. Matthews. "But if we have to go to Chenoweth"—a school with lower test scores—"we'll pull out and go to private school."

That's a serious threat to the district's well-being, but one that Todd anticipated. She designed a grandfather clause for kids like Noe's, so that the new assignments would apply almost entirely to new students. Meanwhile, at every meeting, Todd polled parents on whether they cared about maintaining diverse schools. The University of Kentucky also conducted a telephone survey with 654 parents of elementary schoolers. In April, Todd called me, elated and relieved, with the results: 88 percent of parents supported enrollment guidelines "to ensure that students learn with students from different races and backgrounds." Todd said she had dropped Breyer's dissent in Meredith from her presentation; she was no longer feeling frustrated with the court. "It's been a personal emotional trek, but I think we've come out better for it," she said in May.

Carter, the proponent of black self-reliance, was feeling more at ease, too. He had come to see the virtue of mixing kids by income level. "Once I did the research, I was pretty impressed by the economic part of it," he said. Carter had taken note of the district's data showing that a switch to neighborhood schools, as he had first advocated, would mean that median household income would range from a high of more than $100,000 at the wealthiest school to about $8,300 at the poorest. A split between rich students and poor schools, he agreed, was the wrong path.

It is, of course, the path taken by most of the country. And yet at the end of May, the Jefferson County School Board voted unanimously to make Geographic Area A the basis for integrating elementary schools for the 2009 school year, a new chapter in the district's history. As the schools shift to the new class-plus-race formula, the district will closely watch the test scores of black students and poor students, hoping for an upsurge, and those of middle-class students, hoping to see achievement hold steady. And if they do, maybe the court's decision in Meredith will come to seem less like a cause for regret and more like an unexpected opportunity.

Unplugged: The Myth of Computers in the Classroom

By David Gelernter

Over the last decade an estimated $2 billion has been spent on more than 2 million computers for America's classrooms. That's not surprising. We constantly hear from Washington that the schools are in trouble and that computers are a godsend. Within the education establishment, in poor as well as rich schools, the machines are awaited with nearly religious awe. An inner-city principal bragged to a teacher friend of mine recently that his school "has a computer in every classroom... despite being in a bad neighborhood!"

Computers should be in the schools. They have the potential to accomplish great things. With the right software, they could help make science tangible or teach neglected topics like art and music. They help students form a concrete idea of society by displaying onscreen a version of the city in which they live—a picture that tracks real life moment by moment.

In practice, however, computers make our worst educational nightmares come true. While we bemoan the decline of literacy, computers discount words in favor of pictures and pictures in favor of video. While we fret about the decreasing cogency of public debate, computers dismiss linear argument and promote fast, shallow romps across the information landscape. While we worry about basic skills, we allow into the classroom software that will do a student's arithmetic or correct his spelling.

Take multimedia. The idea of multimedia is to combine text, sound, and pictures in a single package that you browse on screen. You don't just *read* Shakespeare; you watch actors performing, listen to songs, view Elizabethan buildings. What's wrong with that? By offering children candy-coated books, multimedia is guaranteed to sour them on unsweetened reading. It makes the printed page look even more boring than it used to look. Sure, books will be available in the classroom, too—but they'll have all the appeal of a dusty piano to a teen who has a Walkman handy.

So what if the little nippers don't read? If they're watching Olivier instead, what do they lose? The text, written word along with all

From *The New Republic*, 1994.

of its attendant pleasures. Besides, a book is more portable than a computer, has a higher-resolution display, can be written on and dog-eared and is comparatively dirt cheap.

Hypermedia, multimedia's comrade in the struggle for a brave new classroom, is just as troubling. It's a way of presenting documents on screen without imposing a linear start-to-finish order. Disembodied paragraphs are linked by theme; after reading one about the First World War, for example, or the life of Woodrow Wilson, or hemlines in the '20s. This is another cute idea that is good in minor ways and terrible in major ones. Teaching children to understand the orderly unfolding of a plot or a logical argument is a crucial part of education. Authors don't merely agglomerate paragraphs; they work hard to make the narrative read a certain way, prove a particular point. To turn a book or a document into hypertext is to invite readers to ignore exactly what counts—the story.

The real problem, again, is the accentuation of already bad habits. Dynamiting documents into disjointed paragraphs is one more expression of the sorry fact that sustained argument is not our style. If you're a newspaper or magazine editor and your readership is dwindling, what's the solution? Shorter pieces. If you're a politician and you want to get elected, what do you need? Tasty sound bites. Logical presentation be damned.

Another software species, "allow me" programs, is not much better. These programs correct spelling and, by applying canned grammatical and stylistic rules, fix prose. In terms of promoting basic skills, though, they have all the virtues of a pocket calculator.

In Kentucky, as *The Wall Street Journal* recently reported, students in grades K-3 are mixed together regardless of age in a relaxed environment. It works great, the *Journal* says. Yes, scores on computation tests have dropped 10 percent at one school, but not to worry: "Drilling addition and subtraction in an age of calculators is a waste of time," the principal reassures us. Meanwhile, a Japanese educator informs University of Wisconsin mathematician Richard Akey that in his country, "calculators are not used in elementary or junior high school because the primary emphasis is on helping students develop their mental abilities." No wonder Japanese kids blow the pants off American kids in math. Do we really think "drilling addition and subtraction in an age of calculators is a waste of time"?

If we do, then "drilling reading in an age of multimedia is a waste of time" can't be far behind.

Prose-correcting programs are also a little ghoulish, like asking a computer for tips on improving your personality. On the other hand, I ran this article though a spell-checker, so how can I ban the use of such programs in schools? Because to misspell is human; to have no idea of correct spelling is to be semiliterate.

There's no denying that computers have the potential to perform inspiring feats in the classroom. If we are ever to see that potential to perform realized, however, we ought to agree on three conditions. First, there should be a completely new crop of children's software. Most of today's offerings show no imagination. There are hundreds of similar reading and geography and arithmetic programs, but almost nothing on electricity or physics or architecture. Also, they abuse the technical capacities of new media to glitz up old forms instead of creating new ones. Why not build a time-travel program that gives kids a feel for how history is structured by zooming you backward? A spectrum program that lets users twirl a frequency knob to see what happens?

Second, computers should be used only during recess or relaxation periods. Tread them as fillips, not as surrogate teachers. When I was in school in the '60s, we all loved educational films. When we saw a movie in class, everybody won: teachers didn't have to teach, and pupils didn't have to learn. I suspect that classroom computers are popular today for the same reasons.

Most important, educators should learn what parents and most teachers already know: you cannot teach a child anything unless you look him in the face. We should not forget what computers are. Like books—better in some ways, worse in others—they are devices that help children mobilize their own resources and learn for themselves. The computer's potential to do good is modestly greater than a book's in some areas. Its potential to do harm is vastly greater, across the board.

When Bright Girls Decide That Math Is "a Waste of Time"

By Susan Jacoby

Susannah, a 16-year-old who has always been an A student in every subject from algebra to English, recently informed her parents that she intended to drop physics and calculus in her senior year of high school and replace them with a drama seminar and a work-study program. She expects a major in art or history in college, she explained, and "any more science or math will just be a waste of my time."

Her parents were neither concerned by nor opposed to her decision. "Fine, dear," they said. Their daughter is, after all, an outstanding student. What does it matter if, at age 16, she has taken a step that may limit her understanding of both machines and the natural world for the rest of her life?

This kind of decision, in which girls turn away from studies that would give them a sure footing in the world of science and technology, is a self-inflicted female disability that is, regrettably, almost as common today as it was when I was in high school. If Susannah had announced that she had decided to stop taking English in her senior year, her mother and father would have been horrified. I also think they would have been a good deal less sanguine about her decision if she were a boy.

In saying that scientific and mathematical ignorance is a self-inflicted female wound, I do not, obviously, mean that cultural expectations play no role in the process. But the world does not conspire to deprive modern women of access to science as it did in the 1930s, when Rosalyn S. Yalow, the Nobel Prize-winning physicist, graduated from Hunter College and was advised to go to work as a secretary because no graduate school would admit her to its physics department. The current generation of adolescent girls—and their parents, bred on old expectations about women's interests—are active conspirators in limiting their own intellectual development.

From *The New York Times,* 1983.

It is true that the proportion of young women in science-related graduate and professional schools, most notably medical schools, has increased significantly in the past decade. It is also true that so few women were studying advanced science and mathematics before the early 1970s that the percentage increase in female enrollment does not yet translate into large numbers of women actually working in science.

The real problem is that so many girls eliminate themselves from any serious possibility of studying science as a result of decisions made during the vulnerable period of midadolescence, when they are most likely to be influenced—on both conscious and subconscious levels— by the traditional belief that math and science are "masculine" subjects.

During the teen-age years the well-documented phenomenon of "math anxiety" strikes girls who never had any problem handling numbers during earlier schooling. Some men, too, experience this syndrome—a form of panic, akin to a phobia, at any task involving numbers—but women constitute the overwhelming majority of sufferers. The onset of acute math anxiety during the teen-age years is, as Stalin was fond of saying, "not by accident."

In adolescence girls begin to fear that they will be unattractive to boys if they are typed as "brains." Science and math epitomize unfeminine braininess in a way that, say, foreign languages do not. High-school girls who pursue an advanced interest in science and math (unless they are students at special institutions like the Bronx High School of Science where everyone is a brain) usually find that they are greatly outnumbered by boys in their classes. They are, therefore, intruding on male turf at a time when their sexual confidence, as well as that of the boys, is most fragile.

A 1981 assessment of female achievement in mathematics, based on research conducted under a National Institute for Education grant, found significant differences in the mathematical achievements of 9th and 12th graders. At age 13 girls were equal to or slightly better than boys in tests involving algebra, problem solving and spatial ability; four years later the boys had outstripped the girls.

It is not mysterious that some very bright high-school girls suddenly decide that math is "too hard" and "a waste of time." In my experience, self-sabotage of mathematical and scientific ability is often a conscious process. I remember deliberately pretending to be puzzled by geometry problems in my sophomore year in high school. A male teacher called me in after class and said, in a baffled tone, "I don't see how you can be having so much trouble when you got straight A's last year in my algebra class."

The decision to avoid advanced biology, chemistry, physics and calculus in high school automatically restricts academic and professional choices that ought to be wide open to anyone beginning college. At all coeducational universities women are overwhelmingly concentrated in the fine arts, social sciences and traditionally female departments like education. Courses leading to degrees in science- and technology-related fields are filled mainly by men.

In my generation, the practical consequences of mathematical and scientific illiteracy are visible in the large number of special programs to help professional women overcome the anxiety they feel when they are promoted into jobs that require them to handle statistics.

The consequences of this syndrome should not, however, be viewed in narrowly professional terms. Competence in science and math does not mean one is going to become a scientist or mathematician any more than competence in writing English means one is going to become a professional writer. Scientific and mathematical illiteracy— which has been cited in several recent critiques by panels studying American education from kindergarten through college—produces an incalculably impoverished vision of human experience.

Scientific illiteracy is not, of course, the exclusive province of women. In certain intellectual circles it has become fashionable to proclaim a willed, aggressive ignorance about science and technology. Some female writers specialize in ominous, uninformed diatribes against genetic research as a plot to remove control of childbearing from women, while some well-known men of letters proudly announce that they understand absolutely nothing about computers, or, for that matter, about electricity. This lack of understanding is nothing in which women or men ought to take pride.

Failure to comprehend either computers or chromosomes leads to a terrible sense of helplessness, because the profound impact of science on everyday life is evident even to those who insist they don't, won't, can't understand why the changes are taking place. At this stage of history women are more prone to such feelings of helplessness than men because the culture judges their ignorance less harshly and because women themselves acquiesce in that indulgence.

Since there is ample evidence of such feelings in adolescence, it is up to parents to see that their daughters do not accede to the old stereotypes about "masculine" and "feminine" knowledge. Unless we want our daughters to share our intellectual handicaps, we had better tell them no, they can't stop taking mathematics and science at the ripe old age of 16.

33

Two Cheers for *Brown v. Board of Education*

By Clayborne Carson

My gratuitous opinion of *Brown v. Board of Education* (1954) is somewhat ambivalent and certainly arrives too late to alter the racial policies of the past fifty years. But for those of us who practice history, hindsight offers a far more reliable kind of wisdom than does foresight. We see clearly now that while the *Brown* decision informed the attitudes that have shaped contemporary American race relations, it did not resolve persistent disputes about the nation's civil rights policies. The Supreme Court's unanimous opinion in *Brown* broke decisively with the racist interpretations of traditional American values set forth in *Scott v. Sandford* (1857) and *Plessy v. Ferguson* (1896), offering instead the optimistic "American Creed" that Gunnar Myrdal saw as the solution to "the Negro problem."[1] Like the two earlier landmark decisions, *Brown* overestimated the extent of ideological consensus among Americans and soon exacerbated racial and regional conflicts instead of resolving them. The Court's ruling against school segregation encouraged African Americans to believe that the entire structure of white supremacy was illegitimate and legally vulnerable. But the civil rights struggles *Brown* inspired sought broader goals than the decision could deliver, and that gap fostered frustration and resentment among many black Americans. In short, the decision's virtues and limitations reflect both the achievements and the failures of the efforts made in the last half century to solve America's racial dilemma and to realize the nation's egalitarian ideals.

That the *Brown* decision spurred subsequent civil rights progress seems apparent, but its impact and its significance as a source of inspiration are difficult to measure.[2] Although the Court's initial unwillingness to set firm timetables for school desegregation undercut *Brown*'s immediate impact, African Americans expanded the limited scope of the decision by individual and collective challenges to the Jim Crow system. Small-scale protests escalated during the decade after 1954, becoming a sustained mass movement against all facets of segregation and discrimination in the North as well as the South. Civil rights protests and litigation prompted Congress to pass the Civil Rights Act of 1964 and the Voting Rights

From *The Journal of American History*, 2004.

Act of 1965, both of which extended the *Brown* decision's egalitarian principles well beyond education. The historic mass struggle that followed *Brown* ultimately destroyed the legal foundations of the Jim Crow system, and their destruction prepared the way for a still more far-reaching expansion of prevailing American conceptions of civil rights and of the role of government in protecting those rights. During the past forty years, women and many minority groups, including immigrants and people with disabilities, have gained new legal protections modeled on the civil rights gains of African Americans.[3]

But the *Brown* decision also created racial aspirations that remain unrealized. Although the decision may have been predicated on the notion of a shared American creed, most white Americans were unwilling to risk their own racial privileges to bring about racial equality. The decision was neither universally accepted nor consistently enforced. "Instead, it provoked overwhelming resistance in the South and only tepid interest in the North," the historian John Higham insisted. "In the South the decision released a tidal wave of racial hysteria that swept moderates out of office or turned them into demagogues. State and local officials declined to obstruct a revival of the Ku Klux Klan. Instead, they employed every conceivable device to maintain segregation, including harassment and dissolution of NAACP chapters."[4] By the 1970s, resistance to school desegregation had become national. Northern whites in Boston and elsewhere demonstrated their unwillingness to send their children to predominantly black schools or to allow large-scale desegregation that would drastically alter the racial composition of "their" schools in "their" neighborhoods. Voters in the states of Washington and California passed initiatives to restrict the right of school boards (Washington) and state courts (California) to order busing to achieve school desegregation (the Supreme Court later held the Washington initiative unconstitutional). Nationwide, white racial resentments encouraged an enduring shift of white voters from the Democratic to the Republican party. The 1964 election would be the last presidential contest in which the majority of black voters and of white voters backed the same candidate. Since 1974, when the Supreme Court's *Milliken v. Bradley* decision set limits on busing, the legal meaning of desegregation has been scaled back to conform to American racial and political realities.[5]

African Americans generally applauded the *Brown* decision when it was announced, but the Court's failure to realize *Brown*'s bold affirmation of egalitarian ideals fueled subsequent black discontent and disillusionment. *Brown* cited studies that demonstrated the harmful psychological impact of enforced segregation on black students, reporting, "To separate them from others of similar age and qualifications solely because of their race generates a feeling of inferiority as to their status in the community that may affect their hearts and minds in a way unlikely ever to be undone." Yet the Court did not offer an effective means to correct the problem it had identified. During the decades after *Brown,* most southern black children continued to suffer the psychological consequences of segregation, while a small minority assumed the often considerable psychological and physical risks of attending newly integrated public schools. Rather than bringing large numbers of black and white students together in public schools, the *Brown* decision—and the subsequent years of litigation and social conflict—enabled a minority of black students to attend predominantly white schools. Ten years after the *Brown* decision, according to data compiled by the U.S. Department of Education, almost 98 percent of southern black students still attended predominantly black schools. Now, at the beginning of the twenty-first century, the Court's ideal of educational opportunity as "a right which must be made available to all on equal terms" is still far from being realized. American schools, both public and private, are still highly segregated. According to a recent study, the typical Latino or black student in the United States still attends a school where members of minority groups are predominant.[6]

Certainly, the *Brown* decision's most significant deficiency is its failure to address the concerns of the majority of African American students who have been unable or unwilling to seek better educational opportunities by leaving predominantly black schools for predominantly white ones. While it opened the door for the Little Rock Nine, who desegregated Central High School in 1957, the *Brown* decision offered little solace to the hundreds of students who remained at Little Rock's all-black Horace Mann High School. When Arkansas officials reacted to desegregation by closing all of Little Rock's high schools, those students were denied even segregated educational opportunities.[7] With the encouragement of the lawyers for the National Association for the Advancement of Colored People's (NAACP) Legal Defense and Education Fund, the Supreme Court largely abandoned previous efforts to enforce the separate but equal mandate in order to adopt a narrowly conceived strategy for achieving equal educational opportunity through desegregation.

The pre-*Brown* equalization effort had encouraged social scientists to develop increasingly sophisticated ways of measuring differences in the quality of schools. But during the 1950s, pro–civil rights scholars shifted their focus from the educational environment of black students in black schools to the psychological state of black students experiencing desegregation. The NAACP's initial strategy of forcing southern states to equalize facilities at all-black schools had resulted in tangible improvements, whereas the removal of racial barriers in public schools was advertised as offering intangible psychological gains.

For Thurgood Marshall, who headed the NAACP legal staff, the equalization effort had always been a means of achieving the ultimate goal of desegregation. After the Supreme Court decided in *Sweatt v. Painter* (1950) that a makeshift segregated law school at a black college could not provide educational opportunities equal to those offered by the University of Texas Law School, Marshall exulted, "The complete destruction of *all* enforced segregation is now in sight." Despite having attended predominantly black schools at every stage of his academic career, he saw segregation as a racial stigma that could not be removed by increased state appropriations for Jim Crow schools. In the early 1950s he noted that social scientists were "almost in universal agreement that segregated education produces inequality." He therefore concluded "that segregated schools, perhaps more than any other single factor, are of major concern to the individual of public school age and contribute greatly to the unwholesomeness and unhappy development of the personality of Negroes which the color caste system in the United States has produced."[8]

Few African Americans would wish to return to the pre-*Brown* world of legally enforced segregation, but in the half century since 1954, only a minority of Americans has experienced the promised land of truly integrated public education. By the mid-1960s, with dual school systems still in place in many areas of the Deep South, and with de facto segregation a recognized reality in urban areas, the limitations of *Brown* had become evident to many of those who had spearheaded previous civil rights struggles. The ideological gulf that appeared in African American politics during the period was largely the result of efforts to draw attention to the predominantly black institutions neglected in the drive for racial integration. The black power movement arose in part as an effort by African Americans to control and improve such institutions. Some black power proponents exaggerated the benefits of racial separatism, but their extremism can be best understood as a reaction against the unbalanced post-*Brown* strategy of seeking racial advancement solely through integration. Although James S. Coleman's landmark 1966 study of equality of educational opportunity found that black children attending integrated schools did better than students attending predominantly black schools, it was by no means clear that the gap was the result of interracial interactions rather than of differences in the socioeconomic backgrounds of the students involved. By the late 1960s, growing numbers of black leaders had concluded that improvement of black schools should take priority over school desegregation. In 1967, shortly before the National Advisory Commission on Civil Disorders warned that the United States was "moving toward two societies, one white, one black—separate and unequal," Martin Luther King Jr. acknowledged the need to refocus attention, at least in the short run, on "schools in ghetto areas." He also insisted that "the drive for immediate improvements in segregated schools should not retard progress toward integrated education later." Even veterans of the NAACP's legal campaign had second thoughts. "*Brown* has little practical relevance to central city blacks," Constance Baker Motley commented in 1974. "Its psychological and legal relevance has already had its effect."[9]

Black power advocates sometimes sought to replace the narrow strategy of achieving racial advancement through integration with the equally narrow strategy of achieving it through racial separatism. In both instances, claims of psychological gains often substituted for measurable racial advancements, but the continued popularity of Afrocentric educational experiments indicates that many African Americans now see voluntary segregation as psychologically uplifting. Having personally experienced the burden of desegregating numerous classrooms and having watched my son move with great success from a predominantly black college to a predominantly white law school, I am skeptical of sweeping claims about the impact of racial environment on learning. While believing that debates among African Americans during the last half century about their destiny have been useful, I regret that those debates have often exacerbated ideological conflict rather than encouraging us toward collective action. Rather than having to choose between overcoming racial barriers and improving black community institutions, we should be able to choose both.

In hindsight, the nation would have been better served if the *Brown* decision had evinced a more realistic understanding of the deep historical roots of America's racial problems—perhaps a little more familiarity with the writings of W. E. B. Du Bois and Carter G. Woodson as well as those of Myrdal and his colleagues. Rather than blandly advising that desegregation of public schools be achieved with "all deliberate speed," the Supreme Court—and the NAACP lawyers who argued before it—should have launched a two-pronged attack, not only against racial segregation but also against inferior schools, whatever their racial composition. Such an attack would have heeded the admonition that Du Bois offered in 1935, soon after his forced resignation as editor of the NAACP's journal, the *Crisis:*

> Theoretically, the Negro needs neither segregated schools nor mixed schools. What he needs is Education.... Other things being equal, the mixed school is the broader, more natural basis for the education of all youth. It gives wider contacts; it inspires great self-confidence; and suppresses the inferiority complex. But other things seldom are equal, and in that case, Sympathy, Knowledge, and the Truth, outweigh all that the mixed school can offer.[10]

Because the *Brown* decision was a decisive departure from *Plessy's* separate but equal principle, it was an important turning point in African American history. Nevertheless, fifty years later the Court's assumptions about the psychological consequences of legally enforced segregation seem dated. The Jim Crow system no longer exists, but most black American schoolchildren still attend predominantly black public schools that offer fewer opportunities for advancement than typical predominantly white public schools. Moreover, there is no contemporary civil rights movement able to alter that fact. Yet, if *Brown* represents a failed attempt to achieve comprehensive racial advancement, the opinion nonetheless still challenges us by affirming egalitarian ideals that remain relevant: "In these days, it is doubtful that any child may reasonably be expected to succeed in life if he is denied the opportunity of an education. Such an opportunity, where the state has undertaken to provide it, is a right which must be made available to all on equal terms."[11]

Notes

1. *Scott v. Sandford*, 19 How. 393 (1857); *Plessy v. Ferguson*, 163 U.S. 537 (1896); *Brown v. Board of Education*, 347 U.S. 483 (1954); Gunnar Myrdal, *An American Dilemma: The Negro Problem and Modern Democracy* (2 vols., New York, 1944).

2. On *Brown*'s direct and indirect consequences, see, for example, Michael J. Klarman, "How *Brown* Changed Race Relations: The Backlash Thesis," *Journal of American History*, 81 (June 1994), 81-118. Klarman correctly points out that *Brown* had limited impact on school desegregation, especially in the Deep South, and stimulated southern white resistance to racial reform. He concludes that the contributions of *Brown* to the broader civil rights struggle were mostly indirect.

40

3. Cf. Hugh Davis Graham, *The Civil Rights Era: Origins and Development of National Policy, 1960–1972* (New York, 1990); Hugh Davis Graham, *Collision Course: The Strange Convergence of Affirmative Action and Immigration Policy in America* (New York, 2002); and John D. Skrentny, *The Minority Rights Revolution* (Cambridge, Mass., 2002).

4. John Higham, "Introduction: A Historical Perspective," in *Civil Rights and Civil Wrongs: Black-White Relations since World War II*, ed. John Higham (University Park, 1997), 4. See also Klarman, "How *Brown* Changed Race Relations"; Numan V. Bartley, *The Rise of Massive Resistance: Race and Politics in the South in the 1950s* (Baton Rouge, 1969); and Neil McMillen, *The Citizens' Council: Organized Resistance to the Second Reconstruction, 1954–1964* (Urbana, 1971).

5. See Ronald P. Formisano, *Boston against Busing: Race, Class, and Ethnicity in the 1960s and 1970s* (Chapel Hill, 1991); and J. Anthony Lukas, *Common Ground: A Turbulent Decade in the Lives of Three American Families* (New York, 1985). *Washington v. Seattle School District*, 458 U.S. 457 (1982); *Crawford v. Los Angeles Board of Education*, 458 U.S. 527 (1982); *Milliken v. Bradley*, 418 U.S. 717 (1974). See Gary Orfield and Susan E. Eaton, *Dismantling Desegregation: The Quiet Reversal of Brown v. Board of Education* (New York, 1996).

6. *Brown v. Board of Education*, 347 U.S. at 494, 493; Gary Orfield and Chungmei Lee, "Brown at Fifty: King's Dream or Plessy's Nightmare?," Jan. 17, 2004, *The Civil Rights Project, Harvard University* http://www.%20 civilrightsproject.harvard.edu/research/reseg04/resegregation04.php (April 4, 2004). In every region of the nation, at least 30% black students still attend schools with less than 10% white enrollment. *Ibid.*

7. Cf. Melba Beals, *Warriors Don't Cry: A Searing Memoir of the Battle to Integrate Little Rock's Central High* (New York, 1995); and Melba Beals, *White Is a State of Mind: A Memoir* (New York, 1995).

8. *Sweatt v. Painter*, 339 U.S. 629 (1950); *Baltimore Afro-American*, June 17, 1950, quoted in Juan Williams, *Thurgood Marshall: American Revolutionary* (New York, 1998), 195; Thurgood Marshall, "An Evaluation of Recent Efforts to Achieve Racial Integration in Education through Resort to the Courts," *Journal of Negro Education*, 21 (Summer 1952), 316-27, esp. 322.

9. J. S. Coleman et al., *Equality of Educational Opportunity* (Washington, 1966), *passim; Report of the National Advisory Commission on Civil Disorders* (New York, 1968), 1; Martin Luther King Jr., *Where Do We Go from Here: Chaos or Community?* (New York, 1967), 228. For Constance Baker Motley's statement (quoted from *The New York Times,* May 13, 1974), see James T. Patterson, Brown v. Board of Education: *A Civil Rights Milestone and Its Troubled Legacy* (New York, 2001), 168.

10. *Brown v. Board of Education,* 349 U.S. 294 (1955); W. E. B. Du Bois, "Does the Negro Need Separate Schools?," *Journal of Negro Education,* 4 (July 1935), in *The Oxford W. E. B. Du Bois Reader,* ed. Eric J. Sundquist (New York, 1996), 431.

11. *"Brown v. Board of Education of Topeka:* Opinion on Segregation Laws," in *Civil Rights and African Americans: A Documentary History,* ed. Albert P. Blaustein and Robert L. Zangrando (Evanston, 1991), 436.

Part Two

History, Culture, and Civilization

America: The Multinational Society

By Ishmael Reed

At the annual Lower East Side Jewish Festival yesterday, a Chinese woman ate a pizza slice in front of Ty Thuan Duc's Vietnamese grocery store. Beside her a Spanish-speaking family patronized a cart with two signs: "Italian Ices" and "Kosher by Rabbi Alper." And after the pastrami ran out, everybody ate knishes.

—The New York Times *23 June 1983*

On the day before Memorial Day, 1983, a poet called me to describe a city he had just visited. He said that one section included mosques, built by the Islamic people who dwelled there. Attending his reading, he said, were large numbers of Hispanic people, forty thousand of whom lived in the same city. He was not talking about a fabled city located in some mysterious region of the world. The city he'd visited was Detroit.

A few months before, I was leaving Houston, Texas, I heard it announced on the radio that Texas's largest minority was Mexican-American, and though a foundation recently issued a report critical of bilingual education, the taped voice used to guide the passengers on the air trams connecting terminals in Dallas Airport is in both Spanish and English. If the trend continues, a day will come when it will be difficult to travel through some sections of the country without hearing commands in both English and Spanish; after all, for some western states, Spanish was the first written language and the Spanish style lives on in the western way of life.

Shortly after my Texas trip, I sat in an auditorium located on the campus of the University of Wisconsin at Milwaukee as a Yale professor—whose original work on the influence of African cultures upon those of the Americas has led to his ostracism from some monocultural intellectual circles—walked up and down the aisle, like an old-time southern evangelist, dancing and drumming the top of the lectern, illustrating his points before some serious Afro-American intellectuals and artists who cheered and applauded his performance

From *Writin' is Fightin': Thirty-Seven Years of Boxing on Paper*, 1988.

and his mastery of information. The professor was "white." After his lecture, he joined a group of Milwaukeeans in a conversation. All of the participants spoke Yoruban, though only the professor had ever traveled to Africa.

One of the artists told me that his paintings, which included African and Afro-American mythological symbols and imagery, were hanging in the local McDonald's restaurant. The next day I went to McDonald's and snapped pictures of smiling youngsters eating hamburgers below paintings that could grace the walls of any of the country's leading museums. The manager of the local McDonald's said, "I don't know what you boys are doing, but I like it," as he commissioned the local painters to exhibit in his restaurant.

Such blurring of cultural styles occurs in everyday life in the United States to a greater extent than anyone can imagine and is probably more prevalent than the sensational conflict between people of different backgrounds that is played up and often encouraged by the media. The result is what the Yale professor, Robert Thompson, referred to as a cultural bouillabaisse, yet members of the nation's present educational and cultural Elect still cling to the notion that the United States belongs to some vaguely defined entity they refer to as "Western civilization," by which they mean, presumably, a civilization created by the people of Europe, as if Europe can be viewed in monolithic terms. Is Beethoven's Ninth Symphony, which includes Turkish marches, a part of Western civilization, or the late nineteenth- and twentieth-century French paintings, whose creators were influenced by Japanese art? And what of the cubists, through whom the influence of African art changed modern painting, or the surrealists, who were so impressed with the art of the Pacific Northwest Indians that, in their map of North America, Alaska dwarfs the lower forty-eight in size?

Are the Russians, who are often criticized for their adoption of "Western" ways by Tsarist dissidents in exile, members of Western civilization? And what of the millions of Europeans who have black African and Asian ancestry, black Africans having occupied several countries for hundreds of years? Are these "Europeans" members of Western civilization, or the Hungarians, who originated across the Urals in a place called Greater Hungary, or the Irish, who came from the Iberian Peninsula?

Even the notion that North America is part of Western civilization because our "system of government" is derived from Europe is being challenged by native American historians who say that the founding fathers, Benjamin Franklin especially, were actually influenced by the system of government that had been adopted by the Iroquois hundreds of years prior to the arrival of large numbers of Europeans.

Western civilization, then, becomes another confusing category like Third World, or Judeo-Christian culture, as man attempts to impose his small-screen view of political and cultural reality upon a complex world. Our most publicized novelist recently said that Western civilization was the greatest achievement of mankind, an attitude that flourishes on the street level as scribbles in public restrooms: "White Power," "Niggers and Spics Suck," or "Hitler was a prophet," the latter being the most telling, for wasn't Adolph Hitler the archetypal monoculturalist who, in his pigheaded arrogance, believed that one way and one blood was so pure that it had to be protected from alien strains at all costs? Where did such an attitude, which has caused so much misery and depression in our national life, which has tainted even our noblest achievements, begin? An attitude that caused the incarceration of Japanese-American citizens during World War II, the persecution of Chicanos and Chinese-Americans, the near-extermination of the Indians, and the murder and lynchings of thousands of Afro-Americans.

Virtuous, hardworking, pious, even though they occasionally would wander off after some fancy clothes, or rendezvous in the woods with the town prostitute, the Puritans are idealized in our schoolbooks as "a hardy band" of no-nonsense patriarchs whose discipline razed the forest and brought order to the New World (a term that annoys Native American historians). Industrious, responsible, it was their "Yankee ingenuity" and practicality that created the work ethic. They were simple folk who produced a number of good poets, and they set the tone for the American writing style, of lean and spare lines, long before Hemingway. They worshipped in churches whose colors blended in with the New England snow, churches with simple structures and ornate lecterns.

The Puritans were a daring lot, but they had a mean streak. They hated the theater and banned Christmas. They punished people in a cruel and inhuman manner. They killed children who disobeyed their parents. When they came in contact with those whom they considered heathens or aliens, they behaved in such a bizarre and irrational manner that this chapter in the American history comes down to us as a late-movie horror film. They exterminated the Indians, who taught them how to survive in a world unknown to them, and their encounter with the calypso culture of Barbados resulted in what the tourist guide in Salem's Witches' house refers to as the Witchcraft Hysteria.

The Puritan legacy of hard work and meticulous accounting led to the establishment of a great industrial society; it is no wonder that the American industrial revolution began in Lowell, Massachusetts, but there was the other side, the strange and paranoid attitudes toward those different from the Elect.

The cultural attitudes of that early Elect continue to be voiced in everyday life in the United States: the president of a distinguished university, writing a letter to the *Times,* belittling the study of African civilizations; the television network that promoted its show on the Vatican art with the boast that this art represent "the finest achievements of the human spirit." A modern up-tempo state of complex rhythms that depends upon contacts with an international community can no longer behave as if it dwelled in a "Zion Wilderness" surrounded by beasts and pagans.

When I heard a schoolteacher warn the other night about the invasion of the American educational system by foreign curriculums, I wanted to yell at the television set, "Lady, they're already here." It has already begun because the world is here. The world has been arriving at these shores for at least ten thousand years from Europe, Africa, and Asia. In the late nineteenth and early twentieth centuries, large numbers of Europeans arrived, adding their cultures to those of the European, African, and Asian settlers who were already here, and recently millions have been entering the country from South America and the Caribbean, making Yale Professor Bob Thompson's bouillabaisse richer and thicker.

One of our most visionary politicians said that he envisioned a time when the United States could become the brain of the world, by which he meant the repository of all of the latest advanced information systems. I thought of that remark when an enterprising poet friend of mine called to say that he had just sold a poem to a computer magazine and that the editors were delighted to get it because they didn't carry fiction or poetry. Is that the kind of world we desire? A humdrum homogeneous world of all brains and no heart, no fiction, no poetry; a world of robots with human attendants bereft of imagination, of culture? Or does North America deserve a more exciting destiny? To become a place where the cultures of the world crisscross. This is possible because the United States is unique in the world: The world is here.

48

America's *Oh Sh*t* Moment: How American Civilization Can Avoid Collapse

By Niall Ferguson

Don't call me a "declinist." I really don't believe the United States—or Western civilization, more generally—is in some kind of gradual, inexorable decline.

But that's not because I am one of those incorrigible optimists who agree with Winston Churchill that the United States will always do the right thing, albeit when all other possibilities have been exhausted.

In my view, civilizations don't rise, fall, and then gently decline, as inevitably and predictably as the four seasons or the seven ages of man. History isn't one smooth, parabolic curve after another. Its shape is more like an exponentially steepening slope that quite suddenly drops off like a cliff.

If you don't know what I mean, pay a visit to Machu Picchu, the lost city of the Incas. In 1530 the Incas were the masters of all they surveyed from the heights of the Peruvian Andes. Within less than a decade, foreign invaders with horses, gunpowder, and lethal diseases had smashed their empire to smithereens. Today tourists gawp at the ruins that remain.

The notion that civilizations don't decline but collapse inspired the anthropologist Jared Diamond's 2005 book, *Collapse.* But Diamond focused, fashionably, on man-made environmental disasters as the causes of collapse. As a historian, I take a broader view. My point is that when you look back on the history of past civilizations, a striking feature is the speed with which most of them collapsed, regardless of the cause.

The Roman Empire didn't decline and fall sedately, as historians used to claim. It collapsed within a few decades in the early fifth century, tipped over the edge of chaos by barbarian invaders and internal divisions. In the space of a generation, the vast imperial metropolis of Rome fell into disrepair, the aqueducts broken, the splendid marketplaces deserted.

From *Newsweek*, 2011.

The Ming dynasty's rule in China also fell apart with extraordinary speed in the mid–17th century, succumbing to internal strife and external invasion. Again, the transition from equipoise to anarchy took little more than a decade.

A more recent and familiar example of precipitous decline is, of course, the collapse of the Soviet Union. And, if you still doubt that collapse comes suddenly, just think of how the postcolonial dictatorships of North Africa and the Middle East imploded this year. Twelve months ago, Messrs. Ben Ali, Mubarak, and Gaddafi seemed secure in their gaudy palaces. Here yesterday, gone today.

What all these collapsed powers have in common is that the complex social systems that underpinned them suddenly ceased to function. One minute rulers had legitimacy in the eyes of their people; the next they didn't.

This process is a familiar one to students of financial markets. Even as I write, it is far from clear that the European Monetary Union can be salvaged from the dramatic collapse of confidence in the fiscal policies of its peripheral member states. In the realm of power, as in the domain of the bond vigilantes, you're fine until you're not fine—and when you're not fine, you're suddenly in a terrifying death spiral.

Remember that poster that used to hang in every college dorm, of a runaway steam train that has crashed through the wall of a rail station and hit the street below, nose first? The caption was: "Oh sh*t!" I believe it's time to ask how close the United States is to the "Oh sh*t!" moment—the moment we suddenly crash downward like that train.

The West first surged ahead of the Rest after about 1500 thanks to a series of institutional innovations that I call the "killer applications":

1. *Competition.* Europe was politically fragmented into multiple monarchies and republics, which were in turn internally divided into competing corporate entities, among them the ancestors of modern business corporations.

2. *The Scientific Revolution.* All the major 17th-century breakthroughs in mathematics, astronomy, physics, chemistry, and biology happened in Western Europe.

3. *The Rule of Law and Representative Government.* An optimal system of social and political order emerged in the English-speaking world, based on private-property rights and the representation of property owners in elected legislatures.

4. *Modern Medicine.* Nearly all the major 19th- and 20th-century breakthroughs in health care were made by Western Europeans and North Americans.

5. *The Consumer Society.* The Industrial Revolution took place where there was both a supply of productivity-enhancing technologies and a demand for more, better, and cheaper goods, beginning with cotton garments.

6. *The Work Ethic.* Westerners were the first people in the world to combine more extensive and intensive labor with higher savings rates, permitting sustained capital accumulation.

For hundreds of years, these killer apps were essentially monopolized by Europeans and their cousins who settled in North America and Australasia. They are the best explanation for what economic historians call "the great divergence": the astonishing gap that arose between Western standards of living and those in the rest of the world.

In 1500 the average Chinese was richer than the average North American. By the late 1970s the American was more than 20 times richer than the Chinese. Westerners not only grew richer than "Resterners." They grew taller, healthier, and longer-lived. They also grew more powerful. By the early 20th century, just a dozen Western empires—including the United States—controlled 58 percent of the world's land surface and population, and a staggering 74 percent of the global economy.

Beginning with Japan, however, one non-Western society after another has worked out that these apps can be downloaded and installed in non-Western operating systems. That explains about half the catching up that we have witnessed in our lifetimes, especially since the onset of economic reforms in China in 1978.

Now, I am not one of those people filled with angst at the thought of a world in which the average American is no longer vastly richer than the average Chinese. Indeed, I welcome the escape of hundreds of millions of Asians from poverty, not to mention the improvements we are seeing in South America and parts of Africa. But there is a second, more insidious cause of the "great reconvergence," which I do deplore—and that is the tendency of Western societies to delete their own killer apps.

Ask yourself: who's got the work ethic now? The average South Korean works about 39 percent more hours per week than the average

American. The school year in South Korea is 220 days long, compared with 180 days here. And you don't have to spend too long at any major U.S. university to know which students really drive themselves: the Asians and Asian-Americans.

The consumer society? Did you know that 26 of the 30 biggest shopping malls in the world are now in emerging markets, mostly in Asia? Only three are in the United States. And, boy, do they look forlorn these days, as maxed-out Americans struggle to pay down their debts.

Modern medicine? Well, we certainly outspend everyone else. As a share of gross domestic product, the United States spends twice what Japan spends on health care and more than three times what China spends. Yet life expectancy in the U.S. has risen from 70 to 78 in the past 50 years, compared with leaps from 68 to 83 in Japan and from 43 to 73 in China.

The rule of law? For a real eye-opener, take a look at the latest World Economic Forum (WEF) Executive Opinion Survey. On no fewer than 15 of 16 different issues relating to property rights and governance, the United States fares worse than Hong Kong. Indeed, the U.S. makes the global top 20 in only one area: investor protection. On every other count, its reputation is shockingly bad. The U.S. ranks 86th in the world for the costs imposed on business by organized crime, 50th for public trust in the ethics of politicians, 42nd for various forms of bribery, and 40th for standards of auditing and financial reporting.

What about science? It's certainly true that U.S.-based scientists continue to walk off with plenty of Nobel Prizes each year. But Nobel winners are old men. The future belongs not to them but to today's teenagers. Here's another striking statistic. Every three years the Organization of Economic Cooperation and Development's Program for International Student Assessment tests the educational attainment of 15-year-olds around the world. The latest data on "mathematical literacy" reveal that the gap between the world leaders—the students of Shanghai and Singapore—and their American counterparts is now as big as the gap between U.S. kids and teenagers in Albania and Tunisia.

The late, lamented Steve Jobs convinced Americans that the future would be "Designed by Apple in California. Assembled in China." Yet statistics from the World Intellectual Property Organization show that already more patents originate in Japan than in the U.S., that South Korea overtook Germany to take third place in 2005, and that China is poised to overtake Germany too.

Finally, there's competition, the original killer app that sent the fragmented West down a completely different path from monolithic imperial China. Well, the WEF has conducted a comprehensive Global Competitiveness survey every year since 1979. Since the current methodology was adopted in 2004, the United States' average competitiveness score has fallen from 5.82 to 5.43, one of the steepest declines among developed economies. China's score, meanwhile, has leapt up from 4.29 to 4.90.

And it's not only that we're becoming less competitive abroad. Perhaps more disturbing is the decline of meaningful competition at home, as the social mobility of the postwar era has given way to an extraordinary social polarization. You don't have to be an Occupy Wall Street leftist to believe that the American super-rich elite—the 1 percent that collects 20 percent of the income—has become dangerously divorced from the rest of society, especially from the underclass at the bottom of the income distribution.

But if we are headed toward collapse, what would an American "Oh sh*t!" moment look like? An upsurge in civil unrest and crime, as happened in the 1970s? A loss of faith on the part of investors and a sudden Greek-style leap in government borrowing costs? How about a spike of violence in the Middle East, from Iraq to Afghanistan, as insurgents capitalize on our troop withdrawals? Or a paralyzing cyber attack from the rising Asian superpower we complacently underrate?

Is there anything we can do to prevent such disasters? Social scientist Charles Murray calls for a "civic great awakening"—a return to the original values of the American republic. He's got a point. Far more than in Europe, most Americans remain instinctively loyal to the killer applications of Western ascendancy, from competition all the way through to the work ethic. They know the country has the right software. They just can't understand why it's running so damn slowly.

What we need to do is to delete the viruses that have crept into our system: the anticompetitive quasi monopolies that blight everything from banking to public education; the politically correct pseudosciences and soft subjects that deflect good students away from hard science; the lobbyists who subvert the rule of law for the sake of the special interests they represent—to say nothing of our crazily dysfunctional system of health care, our overleveraged personal finances, and our newfound unemployment ethic.

Then we need to download the updates that are running more successfully in other countries, from Finland to New Zealand, from Denmark to Hong Kong, from Singapore to Sweden.

And finally we need to reboot our whole system.

I refuse to accept that Western civilization is like some hopeless old version of Microsoft DOS, doomed to freeze, then crash. I still cling to the hope that the United States is the Mac to Europe's PC, and that if one part of the West can successfully update and reboot itself, it's America.

But the lesson of history is clear. Voters and politicians alike dare not postpone the big reboot. Decline is not so gradual that our biggest problems can simply be left to the next administration, or the one after that.

If what we are risking is not decline but downright collapse, then the time frame may be even tighter than one election cycle.

1776 and All That

By Edward Hoagland

The country is riven and ailing, with a guns-plus-butter nuttiness in some of its governing echelons and the sort of lapsed logic implicit in the collapse of trust in money-center capitalism, which has been an undergirding theory of a good deal of the work that many people do. The tallest buildings, real profit centers, fall, as "wogs" and "ragheads" defy us, perhaps comparably to how the "gooks" in Vietnam did (from whose example Osama bin Laden may have learned that we could be defeated). But that was on foreign soil, and we believed that we had pulled our punches and beaten ourselves, and so remained triumphalist for the remainder of the twentieth century, as we had been practically since Reconstruction.

Now we're not so sure. For the first time since the War of 1812 we have been damaged in continental America by foreigners, having made other people hate us, though we had never needed to pay attention to such matters before. Proxies could fight the malcontents for us in places like Central America, and the Japanese and Germans, would-be conquerors, had not felt much real animus, becoming close, amicable allies after the war. Our first World War II hero, Colin Kelly, three days after Pearl Harbor, flew his B-17 bomber (as media myth had it) in kamikaze fashion to hit a Japanese cruiser, before the Japanese made a practice of it. To give your life for your country, like Nathan Hale, is an ideal that's since evaporated.

Obese individually and as a nation, and trying to stall the aging process, we talk instead of cars and taxes, sports and movies, cancer and entitlements, but with a half-unmentioned inkling too of what more ominously may be in store—a premonition that our righteous confidence might have served us just a bit too well. We never agonized a lot about killing off the Indians, or our slaving history either, once that was over, or being the only nuclear power ever to incinerate multitudes of people. We've hardly seemed to notice when free enterprise segues into simple greed, because our religious beginnings countenanced rapacity, as long as you tithed. Settling the seaboard in official belts of piety, whether Puritan, Anglican, Quaker or Dutch Reformed (only the frontier tended to be atheistic), we seized land

From *The Nation*, 2002.

and water with abandon, joined by Catholics, Lutherans, Methodists and what have you, westward ho. Each group encouraged its rich men to creep like a camel through the eye of the needle, and political freedoms were gradually canted away from the pure ballot box toward influence-buying.

We swallowed all of that because the New World dream envisioned everybody working hard and getting fairly rich, except when undertows of doubt pervaded our prosperity, as in the 1930s and 1960s; or now when, feeling gridlocked, we wonder if we haven't gone too far and used the whole place up. We seem to need some kind of condom invented just for greed—a latex sac where spasms of that particular vice can be ejaculated, captured and contained. Like lust, it's not going to go away. Nor will Monopoly games do the trick, any more than pornographic videos erase impulses that might result in harm. The old phrase patrons of prostitutes used to use—"getting your ashes hauled"—said it pretty well, and if we could persuade people to think of greed, as well, that way and expel its destructiveness perhaps into a computer screen, trapping the piggishness in cyberspace might save a bit of Earth. The greediest guys would not be satisfied, but greed might be looked on as slightly outré.

Some vertigo or "near death" experience of global warming may be required to trip the necessary degree of alarm. The droughts and water wars, a polar meltdown and pelagic crisis—too much saltwater and insufficient fresh. In the meantime, dried-up high plains agriculture and Sunbelt golf greens in the Republicans' heartlands will help because African famines are never enough. We need a surge of altruism, artesian decency. The oddity of greed nowadays is that it is so often solo—in the service of one ego—not ducal or kingly, as the apparatus of an unjust state. Overweening possession, such as McMansions and so on, will be loony in the century we are entering upon—ecologically, economically, morally, commonsensically. But how will we realize this, short of disastrous procrastination? Hurricanes and centrifugal violence on the home front, not to mention angry Arabs flying into the World Trade Center? That astounded us: both the anger and the technological savvy. These camel-herding primitives whom we had manipulated, fleeced, romanticized and patronized for generations, while pumping out their oil and bottling them up in monarchies and emirates that we cultivated and maintained, while jeering at them with casual racism in the meantime, when we thought of it, for not having democracies like ours. To discover that satellite TV, the Internet and some subversive preaching should suddenly provide them access to divergent opinions disconcerts if it doesn't frighten us, as does their willingness to counterpose rudimentary suicide missions to the helicopter gunships and F-16s we provide the Israelis. "Don't they value life?"

They won't be the last. The Vietcong were as culturally different from the Palestinians as we are and yet succeeded in winning a country for themselves, at a tremendous but bearable cost, which the Palestinians will also undoubtedly do. Self-sacrifice can be a match for weaponry, not because the Americans or Israelis value Asian or Arab life—at key junctures and for essentially racist reasons they have not—but because of the value they place on their own citizenry. As many as fifty Vietnamese lives were lost for every American's, but that was not a high enough ratio for us, even though, unlike some Israelis, we don't ascribe to ourselves a biblical imprimatur. So we let them have their land, and the domino calamities that had been famously predicted did not result.

To equate our own revolution with anybody else's is quite offensive to us. Mostly, in fact, we prefer to forget that we had a revolutionary past and kicked thousands of wealthy Tories into Canada, seizing their property. We were slow to condemn apartheid in South Africa, having scarcely finished abolishing our own at the time, and have been slow in general to support self-governance in the warmer climates or to acknowledge suffering among people whose skins are beiger than ours. And if our income per capita is sixty or eighty times theirs, that doesn't strike us as strange. We are a bootstrap country, after all. They should pay us heed. And the whole United Nations is "a cesspool," according to a recent New York City mayor.

But primitive notions like those of Ed Koch invite a primitive response. And box-cutters in the hands of Taliban fundamentalists are not our main problem. We have gratuitously destroyed so much of nature that the Taliban's smashing up of Buddhist statues, as comparative vandalism, will someday seem quite minuscule. We have also denatured our own nominal religions: that is, taken the bite of authenticity out of Christianity, for instance. Our real problem, I think, is a centrifugal disorientation and disbelief. There is a cost to cynicism (as in our previous activities in Afghanistan), and the systematic demonizing of communitarianism during the cold war made it harder afterward for us to reject as perverse the double-talking profiteering implicit in phenomena like Enron, when we had thought that anything was better than collective regulation and planning.

But ceasing to believe in revolutionary democracy—whether of the secular or Christian (or Emersonian) variety—has proven costly. A decent regard for the welfare of other people, in international as well as local life, is going to be more than just a matter of private virtue. In a shrinking world it may be a survival tool. Fanaticism doesn't carry as far unless catastrophic economic conditions lurk in the background, as we learned in the case of Germany between the two world wars but then, when non-Caucasians were involved, forgot. Our foreign aid budget, once the cold war ended, collapsed into spectacular stinginess, and our sole response to September 11 has been police work. This can probably erase Al Qaeda—which became after its instant victory that one morning quite superfluous anyway—but not the knowledge of our vulnerability to any handful of smart and angry plotters in this technological age. We might see an explosion of those.

Our national self-absorption (in which the focus seems more on trying to stay young than helping the young) may give capitalism a bad name. Simple hedonism and materialism was not the point of crossing the ocean. Our revolution was better than that. It was to paint the world anew.

Just Walk on By

By Brent Staples

My first victim was a woman—white, well dressed, probably in her early twenties. I came upon her late one evening on a deserted street in Hyde Park, a relatively affluent neighborhood in an otherwise mean, impoverished section of Chicago. As I swung onto the avenue behind her, there seemed to be a discreet, un-inflammatory distance between us. Not so. She cast back a worried glance. To her, the youngish black man—a broad six feet two inches with a beard and billowing hair, both hands shoved into the pockets of a bulky military jacket—seemed menacingly close. After a few more quick glimpses, she picked up her pace and was soon running in earnest. Within seconds she disappeared into a cross street.

That was more than a decade ago. I was 23 years old, a graduate student newly arrived at the University of Chicago. It was in the echo of that terrified woman's footfalls that I first began to know the unwieldy inheritance I'd come into—the ability to alter public space in ugly ways. It was clear that she thought herself the quarry of a mugger, a rapist, or worse. Suffering a bout of insomnia, however, I was stalking sleep, not defenseless wayfarers. As a softy who is scarcely able to take a knife to raw chicken—let alone hold it to a person's throat—I was surprised, embarrassed, and dismayed all at once. Her flight made me feel like an accomplice in tyranny. It also made it clear that I was indistinguishable from the muggers who occasionally seeped into the area from the surrounding ghetto. That first encounter, and those that followed signified that a vast unnerving gulf lay between nighttime pedestrians—particularly women—and me. And I soon gathered that being perceived as dangerous is a hazard in itself. I only needed to turn a corner into a dicey situation, or crowd some frightened, armed person in a foyer somewhere, or make an errant move after being pulled over by a policeman. Where fear and weapons meet— and they often do in urban America—there is always the possibility of death.

In that first year, my first away from my hometown, I was to become thoroughly familiar with the language of fear. At dark, shadowy intersections in Chicago, I could cross in front of a car stopped at a

From *The Literary Cavalcade*, 1998.

traffic light and elicit the *thunk, thunk, thunk, thunk* of the driver—black, white, male, or female—hammering down the door locks. On less traveled streets after dark, I grew accustomed to but never comfortable with people who crossed to the other side of the street rather than pass me. Then there were the standard unpleasantries with police, doormen, bouncers, cab drivers, and others whose business it is to screen out troublesome individuals *before* there is any nastiness.

I moved to New York nearly two years ago and I have remained an avid night walker. In central Manhattan, the near-constant crowd cover minimizes tense one-on-one street encounters. Elsewhere—visiting friends in SoHo, where sidewalks are narrow and tightly spaced buildings shut out the sky—things can get very taut indeed.

Black men have a firm place in New York mugging literature. Norman Podhoretz in his famed (or infamous) 1963 essay, "My Negro Problem—and Ours," recalls growing up in terror of black males; they were "tougher than we were, more ruthless," he writes—and as an adult on the Upper West Side of Manhattan, he continues, he cannot constrain his nervousness when he meets black men on certain streets. Similarly, a decade later, the essayist and novelist Edward Hoagland extols a New York where once "Negro bitterness bore down mainly on other Negroes."

Where some see mere panhandlers, Hoagland sees "a mugger who is clearly screwing up his nerve to do more than just ask for money." But Hoagland has "the New Yorker's quick hunch posture for broken-field maneuvering," and the bad guy swerves away.

I often witness that "hunch posture," from women after dark on the warren-like streets of Brooklyn where I live. They seem to set their faces on neutral and, with their purse straps strung across their chests bandolier style, they forge ahead as though bracing themselves against being stalked. I understand, of course, that the danger they perceive is not a hallucination. Women are particularly vulnerable to street violence, and young black males are drastically overrepresented among the perpetrators of that violence. Yet these truths are no solace against the kind of alienation that comes of being ever the suspect, against being set apart, a fearsome entity with whom pedestrians avoid making eye contact.

It is not altogether clear to me how I reached the ripe old age of 22 without being conscious of the lethality nighttime pedestrians attributed to me. Perhaps it was because in Chester, Pennsylvania, the small, angry industria town where I came of age in the 1960s, I was scarcely noticeable against a backdrop of gang warfare, street knifings, and murders. I grew up one of the good boys, had perhaps a half-dozen first fights. In retrospect, my shyness of combat has clear sources.

Many things go into the making of a young thug. One of those things is the consummation of the male romance with the power to intimidate. An infant discovers that random flailings send the baby bottle flying out of the crib and crashing to the floor. Delighted, the joyful babe repeats those motions again and again, seeking to duplicate the feat. Just so, I recall the points at which some of my boyhood friends were finally seduced by the perception of themselves as tough guys. When a mark cowered and surrendered his money without resistance, myth and reality merged—and paid off. It is, after all, only manly to embrace the power to frighten and intimidate. We, as men, are not supposed to give an inch of our lane on the highway; we are to seize the fighter's edge in work and in play and even in love; we are to be valiant in the face of hostile forces.

Unfortunately, poor and powerless young men seem to take all this nonsense literally. As a boy, I saw countless tough guys locked away; I have since buried several, too. They were babies, really—a teenage cousin, a brother of 22, a childhood friend in his mid-twenties—all gone down in episodes of bravado played out in the streets. I came to doubt the virtues of intimidation early on. I chose, perhaps even unconsciously, to remain a shadow— timid, but a survivor.

The fearsomeness mistakenly attributed to me in public places often has a perilous flavor. The most frightening of these confusions occurred in the late 1970s and early 1980s when I worked as a journalist in Chicago. One day, rushing into the office of a magazine I was writing for with a deadline story in hand, I was mistaken for a burglar. The office manager called security and, with an ad hoc posse pursued me through the labyrinthine halls, nearly to my editor's door. I had no way of proving who I was. I could only move briskly toward the company of someone who knew me.

Another time I was on assignment for a local paper and killing time before an interview. I entered a jewelry store on the city's affluent Near North Side. The proprietor excused herself and returned with an enormous red Doberman pinscher straining at the end of a leash.

She stood, the dog extended toward me, silent to my questions, her eyes bulging nearly out of her head. I took a cursory look around, nodded, and bade her good night. Relatively speaking, however, I never fared as badly as another black male journalist. He went to nearby Waukegan, Illinois, a couple of summers ago to work on a story about a murderer who was born there. Mistaking the reporter for the killer, police hauled him from his car at gunpoint and but for his press credentials would probably have tried to book him. Such episodes are not uncommon. Black men trade talks like this all the time.

In "My Negro Problem—And Ours," Podhoretz writes that the hatred he feels for blacks makes itself known to him through a variety of avenues—one being taken for a criminal. Not to do so would surely have led to madness—via that special "paranoid touchiness" that so annoyed Podhoretz at the time he wrote the essay.

I began to take precautions to make myself less threatening. I move about with care, particularly late in the evening. I give a wide berth to nervous people on subway platforms during the wee hours, particularly when I have exchanged business clothes for jeans. If I happened to be entering a building behind some people who appear skittish, I may walk by, letting them clear the lobby before I return, so as not to seem to be following them. I have been calm and extremely congenial on those rare occasions when I've been pulled over by the police.

And on late-evening constitutionals along streets less traveled by, I employ what has proved to be an excellent tension-reducing measure: I whistle melodies from Beethoven and Vivaldi and the more popular classical composers. Even steely New Yorkers hunching toward nighttime destinations seem to relax and occasionally they even join in the tune. Virtually everybody seems to sense that a mugger wouldn't be warbling bright, sunny selections from Vivaldi's *Four Seasons*. It is my equivalent to the cowbell that hikers wear when they know they are in bear country.

The Myth of the Latin Woman: I Just Met a Girl Named Maria

By Judith Ortiz Cofer

On a bus trip to London from Oxford University where I was earning some graduate credits one summer, a young man, obviously fresh from a pub, spotted me and as if struck by inspiration went down on his knees in the aisle. With both hands over his heart he broke into an Irish tenor's rendition of "Maria" from *West Side Story.* My politely amused fellow passengers gave his lovely voice the round of gentle applause it deserved. Though I was not quite as amused, I managed my version of an English smile: no show of teeth, no extreme contortions of the facial muscles—I was at this time of my life practicing reserve and cool. Oh, that British control, how coveted it. But Maria had followed me to London, reminding me of a prime fact of my life: you can leave the Island, master the English language, and travel as far as you can, but if you are a Latina, especially one like me who so obviously belongs to Rita Moreno's gene pool, the Island travels with you.

This is sometimes a very good thing—it may win you that extra minute of someone's attention. But with some people, the same things can make you an island—not so much a tropical paradise as an Alcatraz, a place nobody wants to visit. As a Puerto Rican girl growing up in the United States and wanting like most children to "belong," I resented the stereotype that my Hispanic appearance called forth from many people I met.

Our family lived in a large urban center in New Jersey during the sixties, where life was designed as a microcosm of my parents' casas on the island. We spoke in Spanish, we ate Puerto Rican food bought at the bodega, and we practiced strict Catholicism complete with Saturday confession and Sunday mass at a church where our parents were accommodated into a one-hour Spanish mass slot, performed by a Chinese priest trained as a missionary for Latin America.

As a girl I was kept under strict surveillance, since virtue and modesty were, by cultural equation, the same as family honor. As a teenager I was instructed on how to behave as a proper senorita.

From *The Latin Deli*, 1993.

But it was a conflicting message girls got, since the Puerto Rican mothers also encouraged their daughters to look and act like women and to dress in clothes our Anglo friends and their mothers found too "mature" for our age. It was, and is, cultural, yet I often felt humiliated when I appeared at an American friend's party wearing a dress more suitable to a semiformal than to a playroom birthday celebration. At Puerto Rican festivities, neither the music nor the colors we wore could be too loud. I still experience a vague sense of letdown when I'm invited to a "party" and it turns out to be a marathon conversation in hushed tones rather than a fiesta with salsa, laughter, and dancing—the kind of celebration I remember from my childhood.

I remember Career Day in our high school, when teachers told us to come dressed as if for a job interview. It quickly became obvious that to the barrio girls, "dressing up" sometimes meant wearing ornate jewelry and clothing that would be more appropriate (by mainstream standards) for the company Christmas party than as daily office attire. That morning I had agonized in front of my closet, trying to figure out what a "career girl" would wear because, essentially, except for Mario Thomas on TV, I had no models on which to base my decision. I knew how to dress for school: at the Catholic school I attended we all wore uniforms; I knew how to dress for Sunday mass, and I knew what dresses to wear for parties at my relatives' homes. Though I do not recall the precise details of my Career Day outfit, it must have been a composite of the above choices. But I remember a comment my friend (an Italian-American) made in later years that coalesced my impressions of that day. She said that at the business school she was attending the Puerto Rican girls always stood out for wearing "everything at once." She meant, of course, too much jewelry, too many accessories. On that day at school, we were simply made the negative models by the nuns who were themselves not credible fashion experts to any of us. But it was painfully obvious to me that to the others, in their tailored skirts and silk blouses, we must have seemed "hopeless" and "vulgar." Though I now know that most adolescents feel out of step much of the time, I also know that for the Puerto Rican girls of my generation that sense was intensified. The way our teachers and classmates looked at us that day in school was just a taste of the culture clash that awaited us in the real world, where prospective employers and men on the street would often misinterpret our tight skirts and jingling bracelets as a come-on.

Mixed cultural signals have perpetuated certain stereotypes—for example, that of the Hispanic woman as the "Hot Tamale" or sexual firebrand. It is a one- dimensional view that the media have found easy to promote. In their special vocabulary, advertisers have designated "sizzling" and "smoldering" as the adjectives of choice for describing not only the foods but also the women of Latin America. From conversations in my house I recall hearing about the harassment that Puerto Rican women endured in factories where the "boss men" talked to them as if sexual innuendo was all they understood and, worse, often gave them the choice of submitting to advances or being fired.

It is custom, however, not chromosomes, that leads us to choose scarlet over pale pink. As young girls, we were influenced in our decisions about clothes and colors by the women—older sisters and mothers who had grown up on a tropical island where the natural environment was a riot of primary colors, where showing your skin was one way to keep cool as well as to look sexy. Most important of all, on the island, women perhaps felt freer to dress and move more provocatively, since, in most cases, they were protected by the traditions, mores, and laws of a Spanish/Catholic system of morality and machismo whose main rule was: *You may look at my sister, but if you touch her I will kill you.* The extended family and church structure could provide a young woman with a circle of safety in her small pueblo on the island; if a man "wronged" a girl, everyone would close in to save her family honor. This is what I have gleaned from my discussions as an adult with older Puerto Rican women. They have told me about dressing in their best party clothes on Saturday nights and going to the town's plaza to promenade with their girlfriends in front of the boys they liked. The males were thus given an opportunity to admire the women and to express their admiration in the form *of piropos:* erotically charged street poems they composed on the spot. I have been subjected to a few piropos while visiting the Island, and they can be outrageous, although custom dictates that they must never cross into obscenity. This ritual, as I understand it, also entails a show of studied indifference on the woman's part; if she is "decent," she must not acknowledge the man's impassioned words. So I do understand how things can be lost in translation. When a Puerto Rican girl dressed in her idea of what is attractive meets a man from the mainstream culture who has been trained to react to certain types of clothing as a sexual signal, a clash is likely to take place. The line I first heard based on this aspect of the myth happened when the boy who took me to my first formal dance leaned over to plant a sloppy overeager kiss painfully on my mouth, and when I didn't respond with sufficient passion said in a resentful tone: "I thought you Latin girls were supposed to mature early"—my first instance of being thought of as a fruit or vegetable—I was supposed to *ripen*, not just grow into Womanhood like other girls.

It is surprising to some of my professional friends that some people, including those who should know better, still put others "in their place." Though rarer, these incidents are still commonplace in my life. It happened to me most recently during a stay at a very classy metropolitan hotel favored by young professional couples for their weddings. Late one evening after the theater, as I walked toward my room with my new colleague (a woman with whom I was coordinating an arts program), a middle-aged man in a tuxedo, a young girl in satin and lace on his arm, stepped directly into our path. With his champagne glass extended toward me, he exclaimed, "Evita!"

Our way blocked, my companion and I listened as the man half-recited, half-bellowed "Don't Cry for Me, Argentina." When he finished, the young girl said: "How about a round of applause for my daddy?" We complied, hoping this would bring the silly spectacle to a close. I was becoming aware that our little group I was attracting the attention of the other guests. "Daddy" must have perceived this too, and he once more barred the way as we tried to walk past him. He began to shout-sing a ditty to the tune of "La Bamba"—except the lyrics were about a girl named Maria whose exploits all rhymed with her name and gonorrhea. The girl kept saying "Oh, Daddy" and looking at me with pleading eyes. She wanted me to laugh along with the others. My companion and I stood silently waiting for the man to end his offensive song. When he finished, I looked not at him but at his daughter. I advised her calmly never to ask her father what he had done in the army. Then I walked between them and to my room. My friend complimented me on my cool handling of the situation. I confessed to her that I really had wanted to push the jerk into the swimming pool. I knew that this same man—probably a corporate executive, well educated, even worldly by most standards—would not have been likely to regale a white woman with a dirty song in public. He would perhaps have checked his impulse by assuming that she could be somebody's wife or mother, or at least *somebody* who might take offense. But to him, I was just an Evita or a Maria: merely a character in his cartoon-populated universe.

Because of my education and my proficiency with the English language, I have acquired many mechanisms for dealing with the anger I experience. This was not true for my parents, nor is it true for the many Latin women working at menial jobs who must put up with stereotypes about our ethnic group such as: "They make good domestics." This is another facet of the myth of the Latin woman in the United States. Its origin is simple to deduce. Work as domestics, waitressing, and factory jobs are all that's available to women with little English and few skills. The myth of the Hispanic menial has been sustained by the same media phenomenon that made "Mammy" from *Gone with the Wind* America's idea of the black woman for generations; Maria, the housemaid or counter girl, is now indelibly etched into the national psyche. The big and the little screens have presented us with the picture of the funny Hispanic maid, mispronouncing words and cooking up a spicy storm in a shiny California kitchen.

This media-engendered image of the Latina in the United States has been documented by feminist Hispanic scholars, who claim that such portrayals are partially responsible for the denial of opportunities for upward mobility among Latinas in the professions. I have a Chicana friend working on a Ph.D. in philosophy at a major university. She says her doctor still shakes his head in puzzled amazement at all the "big words" she uses. Since I do not wear my diplomas around my neck for all to see, I too have on occasion been sent to that "kitchen," where some think I obviously belong.

One such incident that has stayed with me, though I recognize it as a minor offense, happened on the day of my first public poetry reading. It took place in Miami in a boat-restaurant where we were having lunch before the event. I was nervous and excited as I walked in with my notebook in my hand. An older woman motioned me to her table. Thinking (foolish me) that she wanted me to autograph a copy of my brand new slender volume of verse, I went over. She ordered a cup of coffee from me, assuming that I was the waitress. Easy enough to mistake my poems for menus, I suppose. I know that it wasn't an intentional act of cruelty, yet of all the good things that happened that day, I remember that scene most clearly, because it reminded me of what I had to overcome before anyone would take me seriously. In retrospect I understand that my anger gave my reading fire, that I have almost always taken doubts in my abilities as a challenge—and that the result is, most times, a feeling of satisfaction at having won a covert when I see the cold, appraising eyes warm to my words, the body language change, the smile that indicates that I have opened some avenue for communication. That day I read to that woman and her lowered eyes told me that she was embarrassed at her little faux pas, and when I willed her to look up at me, it was my victory, and she graciously allowed me to punish her with my full attention. We shook hands at the end of the reading, and I never saw her again. She has probably forgotten the whole thing but maybe not.

Yet I am one of the lucky ones. My parents made it possible for me to acquire a stronger footing in the mainstream culture by giving me the chance at an education. And books and art have saved me from the harsher forms of ethnic and racial prejudice that many of my Hispanic *companeras* have had to endure. I travel a lot around the United States, reading from my books of poetry and my novel, and the reception I most often receive is one of positive interest by people who want to know more about my culture. There are, however, thousands of Latinas without the privilege of an education or the entree into society that I have. For them life is a struggle against the misconceptions perpetuated by the myth of the Latina as whore, domestic, or criminal. We cannot change this by legislating the way people look at us. The transformation, as I see it, has to occur at a much more individual level. My personal goal in my public life is to try to replace the old pervasive stereotypes and myths about Latinas with a much more interesting set of realities. Every time I give a reading, I hope the stories I tell, the dreams and fears I examine in my work, can achieve some universal truth which will get my audience past the particulars of my skin color, my accent, or my clothes.

I once wrote a poem in which I called us Latinas "God's brown daughters." This poem is really a prayer of sorts, offered upward, but also, through the human-to-human channel of art, outward. It is a prayer for communication, and for respect. In it, Latin women pray "in Spanish to an Anglo God/with a Jewish heritage," and they are "fervently hoping/that if not omnipotent/at least He be bilingual."

A World Not Neatly Divided

By Amartya Sen

CAMBRIDGE, England—When people talk about clashing civilizations, as so many politicians and academics do now, they can sometimes miss the central issue. The inadequacy of this thesis begins well before we get to the question of whether civilizations must clash. The basic weakness of the theory lies in its program of categorizing people of the world according to a unique, allegedly commanding system of classification. This is problematic because civilizational categories are crude and inconsistent and also because there are other ways of seeing people (linked to politics, language, literature, class, occupation or other affiliations).

69

The befuddling influence of a singular classification also traps those who dispute the thesis of a clash: To talk about "the Islamic world" or "the Western world" is already to adopt an impoverished vision of humanity as unalterably divided. In fact, civilizations are hard to partition in this way, given the diversities within each society as well as the linkages among different countries and cultures. For example, describing India as a "Hindu civilization" misses the fact that India has more Muslims than any other country except Indonesia and possibly Pakistan. It is futile to try to understand Indian art, literature, music, food or politics without seeing the extensive interactions across barriers of religious communities. These include Hindus and Muslims, Buddhists, Jains, Sikhs, Parsees, Christians (who have been in India since at least the fourth century, well before England's conversion to Christianity), Jews (present since the fall of Jerusalem), and even atheists and agnostics. Sanskrit has a larger atheistic literature than exists in any other classical language. Speaking of India as a Hindu civilization may be comforting to the Hindu fundamentalist, but it is an odd reading of India.

A similar coarseness can be seen in the other categories invoked, like "the Islamic world." Consider Akbar and Aurangzeb, two Muslim emperors of the Mogul dynasty in India. Aurangzeb tried hard to convert Hindus into Muslims and instituted various policies in that direction, of which taxing the non-Muslims was only one example. In contrast, Akbar reveled in his multiethnic court and pluralist

From *The New York Times*, 2001.

laws, and issued official proclamations insisting that no one "should be interfered with on account of religion" and that "anyone is to be allowed to go over to a religion that pleases him."

If a homogeneous view of Islam were to be taken, then only one of these emperors could count as a true Muslim. The Islamic fundamentalist would have no time for Akbar; Prime Minister Tony Blair, given his insistence that tolerance is a defining characteristic of Islam, would have to consider excommunicating Aurangzeb. I expect both Akbar and Aurangzeb would protest, and so would I. A similar crudity is present in the characterization of what is called "Western civilization." Tolerance and individual freedom have certainly been present in European history. But there is no dearth of diversity here, either. When Akbar was making his pronouncements on religious tolerance in Agra, in the 1590s, the Inquisitions were still going on; in 1600, Giordano Bruno was burned at the stake, for heresy, in Campo dei Fiori in Rome.

Dividing the world into discrete civilizations is not just crude. It propels us into the absurd belief that this partitioning is natural and necessary and must overwhelm all other ways of identifying people. That imperious view goes not only against the sentiment that "we human beings are all much the same," but also against the more plausible understanding that we are diversely different. For example, Bangladesh's split from Pakistan was not connected with religion, but with language and politics.

Each of us has many features in our self-conception. Our religion, important as it may be, cannot be an all-engulfing identity. Even a shared poverty can be a source of solidarity across the borders. The kind of division highlighted by, say, the so-called "antiglobalization" protesters—whose movement is, incidentally, one of the most globalized in the world—tries to unite the underdogs of the world economy and goes firmly against religious, national or "civilizational" lines of division.

The main hope of harmony lies not in any imagined uniformity, but in the plurality of our identities, which cut across each other and work against sharp divisions into impenetrable civilizational camps. Political leaders who think and act in terms of sectioning off humanity into various "worlds" stand to make the world more flammable—even when their intentions are very different. They also end up, in the case of civilizations defined by religion, lending authority to religious leaders seen as spokesmen for their "worlds." In the process, other voices are muffled and other concerns silenced. The robbing of our plural identities not only reduces us; it impoverishes the world.

Part Three

Media and Popular Culture

Is Facebook Linked to Selfishness? Investigating the Relationships among Social Media Use, Empathy, and Narcissism

By Tracy Alloway, Rachel Runac, Mueez Qureshi, George Kemp

Abstract

The rise of social networking sites have led to changes in the nature of our social relationships, as well as how we present and perceive ourselves. The aim of the present study was to investigate the relationship among the following in adults: use of a highly popular social networking site—Facebook, empathy, and narcissism. The findings indicated that some Facebook activities, such as chatting, were linked to aspects of empathic concern, such as higher levels of Perspective Taking in males. The Photo feature in Facebook was also linked to better ability to place themselves in fictional situations. For only the females, viewing videos was associated with the extent to which they could identify with someone's distress. The data also indicated that certain aspects of Facebook use, such as the photo feature, were linked to narcissism. However, the overall pattern of findings suggests that social media is primarily a tool for staying connected, than for self-promotion.

Keywords

Facebook, Empathy, Narcissism, Social Networking Sites

1. Introduction

Social networking sites (SNS), like Facebook, give users an opportunity to connect and interact online [1]. Since its creation in 2004, Facebook's growth has been exponential, with around 845 million active users as of February 2012 [2], 95% of college students use Facebook [3]. With this steady growth of SNS, changes in face-to-face communication have become apparent with people spending more time communicating online than in person [4]. One drawback of this increased SNS use is that individuals may isolate themselves, choosing to talk and form relationships primarily online rather than developing meaningful, face-to-face relationships [5]. Support for this

From *Social Networking,* 2014.

possibility comes from a recent report that indicated SNS users are less likely to engage or personally know their neighbors [6].

1.1. SNS Empathy

Empathy is characterized as one's ability to feel along with others, to share in their happiness and hardships [7]. In psychology, it has often been defined as a multidimensional construct, comprising both cognitive and behavioral states [8]. As with many desirable prosocial traits, individuals are not born with this innate ability, but learn to become empathic through conditioning methods [9]-[11]. Yet, if one is not exposed to the necessary nurturing to develop empathy into a habit, they may not be able to relate to others, which can impact their social aptness [7].

Current findings on the impact of SNS on empathy are mixed. A positive view is that SNS use can encourage empathy because it allows youth to widen their self-understanding and their ability to practice their empathic responses [7] [12]. SNS, like Facebook, provide accessibility to others online, which allows individuals greater opportunities to express their sympathetic feelings that they may ordinarily shy away during more personal interactions [13]. As empathy is developed over time through practice, these behaviors will become more habitual. Wright and Li found that the time spent on online activities was related to prosocial behavior, such as saying nice things, offering help, cheering someone up, and letting someone know one cares about them [14]. Thus, increased exposure to SNS could provide access to situations that foster empathic concern.

An opposing view of the impact of SNS on empathy is that increased use can lead to a desensitization of other's sentiments, resulting in a *lack* of empathy [4]. Constant SNS use can create a constant bombardment of high-level emotions and negative events in other people's lives that one would not normally be exposed to. In order to compensate, one becomes hardened to emotional experiences, which can affect face-to-face interactions. When Konrath and colleagues examined changes in empathy levels in college students between 1979 and 2009, they found a significant decrease in empathic concern and perspective taking, particularly in the last decade, which coincides with the rise in SNS use. They suggested that the shift in empathy levels could be driven by a more individualistic and self-centered attitude, as indicated by the label of "Generation Me" [15]. Support for this view comes from a survey that found only a small percentage of young adults listed helping others as their primary goal, while the majority indicated that becoming wealthy was the most important goal in their lives [16].

1.2. Empathy & Narcissism

The apparent decrease in empathy [4] coincides with a reported rise in narcissism—30% in the last 25 years, particularly in college students [17] Ritter *et al.* directly compared the relationship between narcissism and empathy and found that individuals with Narcissistic Personality Disorder (NPD) had a lower propensity for perspective taking (a construct of empathy), compared to the control group without NPD. The authors argued that a lack of empathy is a key feature of narcissism [18].

1.3. SNS & Narcissism

Narcissistic individuals are characterized by a positive and exaggerated view of themselves, including their physical attractiveness and importance [19] [20]. Although SNS like Facebook can offer a platform to engage in narcissistic behavior, the link is still unclear. Buffardi and Campbell found college students who scored higher on the Narcissistic Personality Inventory listed more Facebook friends [21]. This pattern fits with the reported high rate of social extraversion, with bonds that typically lack warmth or strong emotion, in narcissists [22] [23].

Another feature of narcissistic behavior is the practice of self-regulatory actions aimed at increasing a social perception of a positive self [24], including attention-seeking behavior [25]. However, Bergman *et al.* found that narcissism was not a strong predictor of either frequency of status updates or time spent on SNS [26]. The authors suggested that SNS use is a means of staying connected, rather than attention-seeking behavior.

1.4. Present Study

The aim of the present study was to investigate the relationship among SNS, empathy, and narcissism. We selected Facebook in light of its popularity [27]. We also extended previous research by investigating the links among narcissism, empathy, and SNS. The majority of studies to date have focused on narcissism and SNS, or empathy and SNS. However, given narcissism has been defined as a "lack of empathy" [28], it is useful to understand the relationship among these three components. There are key implications for understanding this relationship, as it can provide a useful first step in minimizing the effect of cyberbullying. Coinciding with the surge in social networking, there has been an increase in cyberbullying. In the United States, as well as Canada, Australia, and Europe, the prevalence rate of cyberbullying is between 6% and 17% [29]-[33]. Due to the anonymity of SNS, cyberbullies do not have to face the consequences of their actions, and thus may experience less empathy.

We were also interested in sex differences. There are clear patterns of higher narcissism scores for males [34], however current research is mixed regarding sex and empathic levels [35], Thus, all of the following research questions were investigated separately for male and female participants. While the majority of previous research on SNS has targeted college students, the present study included a broad range, from 18 to 50 years, to represent the increased presence of adults using social media [36]. Additionally, narcissism has been shown to decrease as people age [37]. The research questions were:

- *Question 1: How do different Facebook activities relate to empathy?*
- *Question 2: What is the relationship between empathy and narcissism?*
- *Question 3: Is Facebook usage linked to narcissism?*

2. Method

2.1. Participants

There were 410 volunteers, ranging between 18 and 50 years; 82% of participants aged 18 to 25 (male: 25%). Of the respondents, 73.6% were White, 9% were African American, 6.7% were Hispanic, and 5.2% were Asian. The majority of participants were single (82%), 11.1% were married, with the remainder classified as divorced, widowed, or separated. Most participants were college-educated (92%); the remaining 8% had completed high school.

2.2. Procedure

Volunteers were recruited over a two-month period. The study was advertised on the university research participation system. The criteria for participation was that they had to be Facebook users with English as their first language, and aged between 18 and 50. The researchers also posted a message on their Facebook wall. Individuals who chose to participate clicked on a link hosted by a third-party website, Qualtrics.

2.3. Measures

2.3.1. Facebook Usage

Participants indicated the time spent on Facebook (hours per day) and the number of friends. They also indicated whether they were in their current profile picture, how regularly they changed it, and rated their profile picture against the following criteria—physically attractive, cool, glamorous, and fashionable—on a Likert scale (1 to 5, Cronbach's alpha was 0.80). The four rating criteria questions were averaged to create a single score.

2.3.2. Facebook Activities

A Facebook questionnaire was used [38] and included the frequency of: playing games, sharing links, sending private messages, and posting, viewing, or commenting on photos or videos (Likert Scale: 0 = *Never* to 5 = *Very frequently*/100% *of the time*).

In order to confirm the reliability (internal consistency) of the survey used to measure Facebook activities, a principal-components analysis was conducted on the raw scores for all 16 questions, rotated to final solution with a Varimax rotation. Five factors emerged with eigenvalues in excess of 1.00, accounting for 66.4% of the variance (Table 1). The questions that loaded most highly on Factor 1 related to viewing and commenting on photos (FB Photos). The highest loading measures on Factor 2 related to videos and apps (FB Videos Apps). Factor 3 related to the frequency of chatting and sending private messages (FB Chat), while Factor 4 corresponded to commenting on status updates and sharing links (FB Links). Scores were averaged on this basis and used for further analyses. The question on how often they played games loaded on a separate factor (Factor 5), and the question on creating and replying to events did not load highly on any factor. Both these items were eliminated from additional analyses.

Table 1. Factor loadings on the principal components analysis (only loadings > 0.45 are shown).

Items	Photos (34%*)	Video/Apps (11%*)	Chat (9%*)	Links (7%*)	Games (3.4%*)
Posting photos of you (in a group, individual, etc.)	0.838				

Items	Photos (34%*)	Video/Apps (11%*)	Chat (9%*)	Links (7%*)	Games (3.4%*)
Posting photos in general (scenery, pets, kids etc.)	0.795				
Tagging photos	0.721				
Commenting (statuses, wall posts, pictures, etc.)	0.568				
Viewing photos	0.554				
Tagging videos		0.820			
Posting videos		0.777			
Viewing videos		0.682			
Applications (Running, Wine, Marketplace, etc.)		0.618			
Chatting on Facebook chat			0.811		
Sending private messages			0.748		
Checking to see what someone is up to	0.500		0.511		
Creating or RSVP'ing to events					
Sharing links				0.825	
Posting status updates	0.497			0.704	
Playing games (Farmville, Mafia Wars, etc.)					0.831

Note: * Proportion of variance.

2.3.3. Empathy

We used the Interpersonal Reactivity Index (IRI) [8] [39]. Cognitive empathy is measured by: the *Fantasy scale*—the tendency to identify with fictional characters and *Perspective Taking*—the ability to place oneself in another's situation. Emotional empathy is measured by: *Empathic Concern*—the sympathetic feelings for other's misfortunes and *Personal Distress*—the anguish felt during other's hardships and troubles. Each of the four subscales is comprised of seven items, which are rated on a five-point scale (A = does not describe me well to E = describes me very well). The maximum score for each subscale is 35, with higher numbers indicating higher levels of empathy.

2.3.4. Narcissism

The Narcissistic Personality Inventory-16 [40], a short form of the NPI-40 ($r = 0.90$), reflects the multiple facets of narcissism, such as self-ascribed authority, superiority, entitlement, and self-absorption [41]. NPI scores are inversely related to empathy [42]. The NPI-16 is a forced-choice questionnaire, with higher scores representing greater narcissistic tendencies (narcissism = 1; non-narcissism = 0).

3. Results

Participants used Facebook for an average of two hours per day (range: 30 minutes – 15 hours, Table 2). Facebook use for the day of testing was significantly correlated with time spent the day before ($r = 0.73$, $p < 0.001$). The average number of friends on Facebook was close to 500 for both males and females, with the majority reporting that they were in their current profile picture (89.5%).

For Facebook Usage, independent t-test confirmed that females spent more time per day on Facebook and rated their profile picture as more attractive, cool, fashionable or glamorous, compared to their male peers (Table 2). However, the females changed their profile picture more often than the males. For Facebook Activities, a MANOVA confirmed a significant sex difference (Hotelling's T-test: $F = 18.95$, $p < 0.001$). Bonferroni adjustment for multiple comparisons indicated that females reported a significantly higher frequency of viewing, posting, and tagging photos compared to their male peers.

Table 2. Descriptive statistics of Facebook questions, empathy, and narcissism, as a function of gender.

	Males	**N = 101**	**Females**	**N = 309**	**F (eta)**
Facebook Usage	**Mean**	**SD**	**Mean**	**SD**	**t**
Time spent per day (hours)	1.55	1.60	2.01	2.031	−2.04*
Number of friends	488.91	468.51	476.33	373.29	<1
Frequency of changing profile picture (days)	87.42	114.44	63.66	90.08	2.14*
Profile picture ratings	3.43	1.18	3.80	0.91	−3.19*
Facebook Activities					
FB Photos	2.73	0.73	3.22	0.74	33.45* (0.08)
FB Videos Apps	1.91	0.77	1.86	0.73	0.28
FB Chat	2.92	0.87	3.00	0.84	0.64
FB Sharing links and updates	2.79	1.02	2.78	0.88	0.05
Empathy (IRI)					
Perspective Taking	25.09	4.71	25.96	5.06	<1
Fantasy Scale	22.59	5.94	23.94	5.77	4.08* (0.01)

	Males	N = 101	Females	N = 309	F (eta)**
Facebook Usage	**Mean**	**SD**	**Mean**	**SD**	**t**
Empathic Concern	24.43	4.84	26.67	5.16	15.19* (0.04)
Personal Distress	15.89	4.72	18.68	5.01	24.64* (0.06)
Narcissism (NPI-16)	0.36	0.20	0.30	0.19	2.82* (t value)

Note: * = p < 0.05 between gender. **= F value unless otherwise stated.

Question 1: Are different Facebook activities related to empathy?

A MANOVA confirmed a sex difference in the empathy scales (Hotelling's T-test: F = 11.89, p < 0.001; Table 2). Bonferroni adjustment for multiple comparisons indicated that females scored significantly higher than males in all empathy subscales, except for Perspective Taking.

Correlation analyses were conducted to investigate the relationship between empathy and engagement with different Facebook activities, as a function of sex (Table 3). Perspective Taking was significantly related to FB Chat for males. The Fantasy Scale was significantly related to FB Photos for both males and females, and for FB Chat and FB Links for males. Empathic Control was not significantly related to any Facebook factor. Personal Distress was negatively associated with FB Chat for males and to FB Videos and Apps for females. For males, this suggests that the frequency of chatting and sending messages was related to how well they could place themselves in another's situation, as well as their ability to identify with fictional characters. However, they were less likely to feel the anguish of another's hardships. For females, viewing and commenting on photos was significantly related to their ability to identify with fictional characters, and viewing videos and apps was associated with the extent to which they could identify with someone's distress.

Question 2: What is the relationship between empathy and narcissism?

For males, empathy was not significantly related to narcissism (Table 3). However, for females, Personal Distress was significantly linked to narcissism.

Question 3: Is Facebook usage linked to narcissism?

Table 3. Correlations coefficients for the male participants in the lower half (n = 101); and for the female participants in the upper half (n = 309).

	1	2	3	4	5	6	7	8	9
1. FB Photos	1	0.49**	0.52**	0.58**	-0.003	0.16**	0.02	0.05	0.11*
2. FB Video Apps	0.57**	1	0.36***	0.34***	-0.03	-0.001	-0.10	0.14*	0.07
3. FB Chat	0.58**	0.33**	1	0.28**	0.01	0.10	-0.01	0.07	0.04
4. FB Links	0.71**	0.50**	0.37***	1	0.06	0.10	0.04	-0.03	0.15**
5. Perspective Taking (IRI)	0.11	0.001	0.31**	0.10	1	0.33**	0.59**	-0.27**	-0.02
6. Fantasy Scale (IRI)	0.26**	0.14	0.28**	0.28**	0.42**	1	0.44**	0.04	-0.05
7. Empathic Concern (IRI)	0.11	0.01	0.13	0.14	0.58**	0.47**	1	-0.14*	-0.10
8. Personal Distress (IRI)	-0.06	0.02	-0.28**	-0.09	-0.34**	0.04	-0.05	1	-0.13*
9. Narcissism (NPI-16)	0.21*	0.15	0.17	0.09	-0.12	0.11	-0.08	-0.11	1

Note: ** = p < 0.01; * = p < 0.05.

For both males and females, posting, tagging, and commenting on photos (FB Photo factor) were associated with their self-reported narcissism score (Table 3). For females only, greater frequency of sharing links and posting status updates were also linked with more narcissistic tendencies.

To order to investigate whether Facebook use was linked to narcissism, stepwise regression analyses was conducted for males and females separately (Table 4). Predictor variables were the Facebook usage questions (number of friends, time spent on Facebook per day, frequency of changing profile picture, and profile picture ratings); as well as how often they posted status updates and photos of themselves [26]. For males, only their profile picture ratings were a predictor of narcissism. For the females, both their profile picture ratings and their status update frequency predicted their narcissism score.

Table 4. Stepwise regression analyses predicting narcissism scores, as a function of gender.

	R^2 change	F	β	t
Males				
Rating of Profile Picture	0.11	10.06*	0.33	2.24*
Females				
Rating of Profile Picture	0.10	28.24*	0.28	4.76*
Frequency of updating status	0.03	8.73	0.18	2.95*

* $p < 0.05$.

4. Discussion

Question 1: How do different Facebook activities relate to empathy?

Females scored significantly higher than males in all empathy subscales, except for Perspective Taking. This is consistent with Davis' data [39], though group means are substantially higher in the present study. The pattern between Facebook and empathy also differed as a function of sex. For males, chatting on Facebook was linked to higher scores in Perspective Taking, though there were also less sensitive to another's hardships. It could be that increased social media usage provided opportunities for the males in the present study to practice such prosocial skills [13], but they aren't more likely to feel discomfort at another's distress. In contrast, for females, Personal Distress scores were linked to watching videos on Facebook. For both males and females, certain Facebook activities (chatting and commenting/

viewing photos, respectively) were related to their ability to identify with fictional characters.

Question 2: What is the relationship between empathy and narcissism?

First, it is worth noting that the NPI-16 scores in the present study were similar to previous research [41]. However, empathy levels do not appear to be declining, as IRI scores were considerably higher than those reported by Davis [39]. However, the issue of test wiseness in the participants cannot be ruled out—even though data collection was anonymous, participants may have exaggerated their responses to present themselves more favorably. An alternate explanation could be that the wider age range (18 – 50) in present study may account for the higher empathy scores, as previous samples were typically in the 18 – 25 range [4].

In the present study, the relationship between empathy and narcissism was not significant for males. For females, only narcissism was related to Personal Distress, a "self-oriented" reaction [8]. A narcissistic person would find it difficult to express emotional empathy because of their preoccupation with themselves and disinterest in others' misfortunes.

Question 3: Is Facebook usage linked to narcissism?

Looking first at Facebook activities, commenting and viewing photos was significantly related to narcissism scores for both males and females. Also, posting status updates and sharing links was associated with narcissism scores for females. As the Facebook News Feed provides notifications for comments on photos, as well as status updates and links shared, the attention received may be a key factor for why these activities are linked to narcissism. Although the present study found that commenting and viewing photos were related to narcissism, we did not investigate the nature of the comments being left by users. If future research can explore potential differences in the type of comments that male and female users receive, it may explain why narcissistic users make a more conscious effort to pursue these activities.

Next, with respect to Facebook usage, profile picture ratings predicted narcissism scores for both males and females. Narcissistic individuals are characterized by a positive and exaggerated view of themselves, especially with characteristics concerning their physical attractiveness. The profile picture is the most physical aspect of a user's online self-presentation. Facebook manages a users' attention directly by reporting changes, and therefore being very effective at increasing the spotlight on the user. Narcissistic individuals therefore may use this tool to direct attention to them.

Additionally, the female participants rated their profile pictures as more physically attractive, fashionable, glamorous, and cool, than the males. This could imply that female narcissistic users are more concerned with, and give greater value, to a profile that maintains a more physically appealing self-presentation. If women receive more compliments on their profile pictures, then updating the profile picture would give them more opportunities to receive positive reinforcement for their online self-presentation. Future research could explore this possibility.

The results showed that the act of uploading more or less photos of oneself on Facebook did not vary among any groups within the present study. This implies that managing the number of photos of oneself on Facebook is not a strategy used by narcissistic individuals.

For females, only posting status updates was a significant predictor of narcissism, which is consistent with previous findings of posting self-promoting information on SNS [21]. It is possible that for females, Facebook offers an avenue for them to present a positive "public" self and bolster self-esteem. However, the time spent on Facebook or the frequency of posting photos of themselves was not predictive of narcissism for either males or females. This pattern mirrors that found by Bergman *et al.* [26], who suggest that these activities are not attention-seeking, but rather a means of communicating.

To summarize, the present research found that some Facebook activities, such as chatting, were linked to higher levels of Perspective Taking in males. This pattern suggests that Facebook, in facilitating great social connection, may encourage some aspects of empathy in contrast to previous reports [4]. Although the photo feature was linked to narcissism, the general pattern suggests that Facebook is primarily a tool for staying connected, rather than for self-promotion.

References

[1] Murray, K.E. and Waller, R. (2007) Social Networking Goes Abroad. *International Educator*, 16, 56-59.

86

[2] Protalinski, E. (2012) Facebook Has over 845 Million Users. ZDNet. Retrieved February 4.

[3] Lampe, C., Ellison, N. and Steinfield, C. (2006) A Facebook in the Crowd: Social Searching versus Social Browsing. In: Hinds, P. and Martin, D., Eds. *Proceedings of the 2006 20th Anniversary Conference on Computer Supported Cooperative Work*, Alberta, 167-170. http://dx.doi.org/10.1145/1180875.1180901

[4] Konrath, S., O'Brien, E. and Hsing, C. (2010) Changes in Dispositional Empathy in American College Students over Time: A Meta-Analysis. *Personality and Social Psychology*, 15, 180-198. http://dx.doi.org/10.1145/1180875.1180901

[5] Putnam, R.D. (2000) Bowling Alone. Simon & Schuster, New York.

[6] Hampton, K.N., Sessions, L.F., Her, E.J. and Rainie, L. (2009) Social Isolation and New Technology. Pew Internet and American Life Project. http://www.pewinternet.org/Reports/2009/18--Social-Isolation-and-New-Technology.aspx

[7] Vallor, S. (2009) Social Networking Technologies and the Virtues. *Ethics and Information Technology*, 12, 157-170. http://dx.doi.org/10.1007/s10676-009-9202-1

[8] Davis, M.H. (1983) Measuring Individual Differences in Empathy: Evidence for Multidimensional Approach. *Journal of Personality and Social Psychology*, 44, 113–126. http://dx.doi.org/10.1037/0022-3514.44.1.113

[9] Feshbach, N.D. (1983) Learning to Care: A Positive Approach to Child Training and Discipline. *Journal of Clinical Child Psychology*, 12, 266-271. http://dx.doi.org/10.1080/15374418309533142

[10] Feshbach, N. and Cohen, S. (1988) Training Affects Comprehension in Young Children: An Experimental Evaluation. *Journal of Applied Developmental Psychology*, 9, 201-210. http://dx.doi.org/10.1016/0193-3973(88)90023-8

[11] Hatcher, S.L., Nadeau, M.S., Walsh, L.K., Reynolds, M., Galea, J. and Marz, K. (1994) The Teaching of Empathy for High School and College Students: Testing Rogerian methods with the Interpersonal Reactivity Index. *Adolescence*, 29, 961-974.

[12] Stern, S. (2008) Producing Sites Exploring Identities: Youth Online Authorship. *Youth Identity and Digital Media*, 95-117.

[13] Wandel, T.L. (2009) Online Empathy: Communicating via Facebook to Bereaved College Students. *Journal of New Communications Research*, 4, 42-53.

[14] Wright, M.F. and Li, Y. (2011) The Associations between Young Adults' Face-To-Face Prosocial Behaviors and Their Online Prosocial Behaviors. *Computers in Human Behavior*, 27, 1959-1962. http://dx.doi.org/10.1016/j.chb.2011.04.019

[15] Twenge, J.M. (2006) Generation me. Free Press, New York.

[16] Pew Research Center (2007) How Young People View Their Lives Futures and Political: A Portrait of Generation Next. http://people-press.org/reports/pdf/300.pdf

[17] Twenge, J.M., Konrath, S., Foster, J.D., Campbell, W.K. and Bushman, B.J. (2008) Ego Inflating over Time: A Cross-Temporal Meta-Analysis of the Narcissistic Personality Inventory. *Journal of Personality*, 76, 875-902. http://dx.doi.org/10.1111/j.1467-6494.2008.00507.x

[18] Ritter, K, Roepke, S., Merkl, A., Heuser, I., Fydrich, T. and Lammers, C.H. (2010) Comorbidity in Patients with Narcissistic Personality Disorder in Comparison to Patients with Borderline Personality Disorder. *Psychotherapie, Psychosomatik, Medizinische Psychologie*, 60, 14-24. http://dx.doi.org/10.1055/s-0028-1102943

[19] Campbell, W.K., Rudich, E.A. and Sedikides, C. (2002) Narcissism Self-Esteem and the Positivity of Self-Views: Two Portraits of Self-Love. *Personality and Social Psychology Bulletin*, 28, 358-368. http://dx.doi.org/10.1177/0146167202286007

[20] John, O.P. and Robins, R.W. (1994) Accuracy and Bias in Self-Perception: Individual Differences in Self-Enhancement and the Role of Narcissism. *Journal of Personality and Social Psychology*, 66, 206-219. http://dx.doi.org/10.1037/0022-3514.66.1.206

[21] Buffardi, L.E. and Campbell, W.K. (2008) Narcissism and Social Networking Web Sites. *Personality and Social Psychology Bulletin*, 34, 1303-1314. http://dx.doi.org/10.1177/0146167208320061

[22] Campbell, W.K. (1999) Narcissism and Romantic Attraction. *Journal of Personality and Social Psychology*, 77, 1254-1270. http://dx.doi.org/10.1037/0022-3514.77.6.1254

[23] Carroll, L. (1987) A Study of Narcissism Affiliation Intimacy and Power Motives among Students in Business Administration. *Psychological Reports*, 61, 355-358. http://dx.doi.org/10.2466/pr0.1987.61.2.355

[24] Campbell, W.K., Rudich, E.A. and Sedikides, C. (2002) Narcissism, Self-Esteem, and the Positivity of Self-Views: Two Portraits of Self-Love. *Personality and Social Psychology Bulletin*, 28, 358-368. http://dx.doi.org/10.1177/0146167202286007

[25] Buss, D.M. and Chiodo, L.M. (1991) Narcissistic Acts in Everyday Life. *Journal of Personality*, 59, 179-215. http://dx.doi.org/10.1111/j.1467-6494.1991.tb00773.x

[26] Bergman, S.M., Fearrington, M.E., Davenport, S.W. and Bergman, J.Z. (2011) Millennials Narcissism and Social Networking: What Narcissists Do on Social Networking Sites and Why. *Personality and Individual Differences*, 50, 706-711. http://dx.doi.org/10.1016/j.paid.2010.12.022

[27] Green, E.W. (2005) The Web of Social Networking. *US News and World Report*, 139, 58.

[28] Ritter, K., Dziobek, I., Preißler, S., Rüter, A., Vater, A., Fydrich, T. and Roepke, S. (2011) Lack of Empathy in Patients with Narcissistic Personality Disorder. *Psychiatry Research*, 187, 241-247. http://dx.doi.org/10.1016/j.psychres.2010.09.013

[29] Campbell, M.A. (2005) Cyber Bullying: An Old Problem in a New Guise? *Australian Journal of Guidance and Counseling*, 15, 68-76. http://dx.doi.org/10.1375/ajgc.15.1.68

[30] Li, Q. (2006) Cyber Bullying in Schools: A Research of Gender Differences. *School Psychology International*, 27, 157-170. http://dx.doi.org/10.1177/0143034306064547

[31] NCH. (2005) Putting U in the Picture—Mobile Phone Bullying Survey. http://wwwnchorguk/uploads/documents/Mobile_bullying_%20reportpdf/

[32] Smith, P.K., Mahdavi, J., Carvalho, M., Fisher, S., Russell, S. and Tippett, N. (2008) Cyberbullying: Its Nature and Impact in Secondary School Pupils. *Journal of Child Psychology and Psychiatry*, 49, 376-385. http://dx.doi.org/10.1111/j.1469-7610.2007.01846.x

[33] Ybarra, M. and Mitchell, K. (2004) Online Aggressor/Targets Aggressors and Targets: A Comparison of Associated Youth Characteristics. *Journal of Child Psychology and Psychiatry*, 45, 1308-1316. http://dx.doi.org/10.1111/j.1469-7610.2004.00328.x

[34] Reinhard, D.A., Konrath, S.H., Lopez, W.D. and Cameron, H.G. (2012) Expensive Egos: Narcissistic Males Have Higher Cortisol. *PLoS ONE*, 7, Article ID: e30858. http://dx.doi.org/10.1371/journal.pone.0030858

[35] Klein, K. and Hodges, S. (2001) Gender Differences, Motivation and Empathic Accuracy: When It Pays to Understand. *Personality and Social Psychology Bulletin*, 27, 720-730. http://dx.doi.org/10.1177/0146167201276007

[36] Lenhart, A., Purcell, K., Smith, A. and Zickuhr, K. (2010) Social Media and Internet Use among Teens and Young Adults. Pew Research Center.

[37] Foster, J.D., Campbell, W.K. and Twenge, J.M. (2003) Individual Differences in Narcissism: Inflated Self-Views across the Lifespan and around the World. *Journal of Research in Personality*, 7, 469-486. http://dx.doi.org/10.1016/S0092-6566(03)00026-6

[38] Junco, R. (2011) Too Much Face and not Enough Books: The Relationship between Multiple Indices of Facebook Use and Academic Performance. *Computers in Human Behavior*, 28, 187-198. http://dx.doi.org/10.1016/j.chb.2011.08.026

[39] Davis, M.H. (1980) A Multidimensional Approach to Individual Differences in Empathy. *Catalog of Selected Documents in Psychology*, 10, 85.

[40] Mehdizadeh, S. (2010) Self-Presentation 2.0: Narcissism and Self-Esteem on Facebook. *Cyberpsychology, Behavior and Social Networking*, 13, 357-364. http://dx.doi.org/10.1089/cyber.2009.0257

[41] Ames, D.R., Rose, P. and Anderson, C.P. (2006) The NPI-16 as a Short Measure of Narcissism. *Journal of Research in Personality*, 40, 440-450. http://dx.doi.org/10.1016/j.jrp.2005.03.002

[42] Watson, P.J., Grisham, S.O., Trotter, M.V. and Biderman, M.D. (1984) Narcissism and Empathy: Validity Evidence for the Narcissistic Personality Inventory. *Journal of Personality Assessment*, 48, 301-305. http://dx.doi.org/10.1207/s15327752jpa4803_12

The Dumbest Generation? Don't Be Dumb.

By Sharon Begley

Really, don't we all know by now that finding examples of teens' and twentysomethings' ignorance is like shooting fish in a barrel? If you want to exercise your eye-rolling or hand-wringing muscles, take your pick. Two thirds of high-school seniors in 2006 couldn't explain an old photo of a sign over a theater door reading COLORED ENTRANCE. In 2001, 52 percent identified Germany, Japan or Italy, not the Soviet Union, as America's World War II ally. One quarter of 18- to 24-year-olds in a 2004 survey drew a blank on Dick Cheney, and 28 percent didn't know William Rehnquist. The world's most heavily defended border? Mexico's with the United States, according to 30 percent of the same age group. We doubt that the 30 percent were boastful or delusional Minutemen.

Like professors shocked to encounter students who respond with a blank-eyed "huh?" to casual mentions of fireside chats or Antietam or even Pearl Harbor, and like parents appalled that their AP-amassing darling doesn't know Chaucer from Chopin, Mark Bauerlein sees in such ignorance an intellectual, economic and civic disaster in the making. In his provocative new book "The Dumbest Generation: How the Digital Age Stupefies Young Americans and Jeopardizes Our Future (Or, Don't Trust Anyone Under 30)," the Emory University professor of English offers the usual indicators, grand and slight. From evidence such as a decline in adult literacy (40 percent of high-school grads had it in 1992; only 31 percent did in 2003) and a rise in geographic cluelessness (47 percent of the grads in 1950 could name the largest lake in North America, compared with 38 percent in 2002), for instance, Bauerlein concludes that "no cohort in human history has opened such a fissure between its material conditions and its intellectual attainments."

He is a little late to this party, of course. The old have been wringing their hands about the young's cultural wastelands and ignorance of history at least since admirers of Sophocles and Aeschylus bemoaned the popularity of Aristophanes ("The *Frogs*," for Zeussakes?!) as leading to the end of (Greek) civilization as they knew it. The Civil War generation was aghast at the lurid dime novels of the late 1800s.

From *Newsweek,* 2008.

Victorian scholars considered Dickens, that plot-loving, sentimental ("A Christmas Carol") favorite, a lightweight compared with other authors of the time. Civilization, and culture high and low, survived it all. Can it survive a generation's ignorance of history? For those born from 1980 to 1997, Bauerlein lamented to us, "there is no memory of the past, just like when the Khmer Rouge said 'this is day zero.' Historical memory is essential to a free people. If you don't know which rights are protected in the First Amendment, how can you think critically about rights in the U.S.?" Fair enough, but we suspect that if young people don't know the Bill of Rights or the import of old COLORED ENTRANCE signs—and they absolutely should—it reflects not stupidity but a failure of the school system and of society (which is run by grown-ups) to require them to know it. Drawing on our own historical memory also compels us to note that philosopher George Santayana, too, despaired of a generation's historical ignorance, warning that "those who cannot remember the past are condemned to repeat it." That was in 1905.

A more fundamental problem is what Bauerlein has in mind by "dumbest." If it means "holding the least knowledge," then he has a case. Gen Y cares less about knowing information than knowing where to find information. (If you are reading this online, a few keystrokes would easily bring you, for the questions so far, vice president, former chief justice of the Supreme Court, North and South Korea, Lake Superior.) And it is a travesty that employers are spending $1.3 billion a year to teach basic writing skills, as a 2003 survey of managers found. But if dumb means lacking such fundamental cognitive capacities as the ability to think critically and logically, to analyze an argument, to learn and remember, to see analogies, to distinguish fact from opinion ... well, here Bauerlein is on shakier ground.

First, IQ scores in every country that measures them, including the United States, have been rising since the 1930s. Since the tests measure not knowledge but pure thinking capacity—what cognitive scientists call fluid intelligence, in that it can be applied to problems in any domain—then Gen Y's ignorance of facts (or of facts that older people think are important) reflects not dumbness but choice. And who's to say they are dumb because fewer of them than of their grandparents' generation care who wrote the oratorio "Messiah" (which 35 percent of college seniors knew in 2002, compared with 56 percent in 1955)? Similarly, we suspect that the decline in the percentage of college freshmen who say it's important to keep up with political affairs, from 60 percent in 1966 to 36 percent in 2005, reflects at least in part the fact that in 1966 politics determined whether you were going to get drafted and shipped to Vietnam. The apathy of 2005 is more a reflection of the world outside Gen-Yers' heads than inside, and one that we bet has changed tack with the historic candidacy of Barack Obama. Alienation is not dumbness.

Bauerlein is not the first scholar to pin the blame for a younger generation's intellectual shortcomings on new technology (television, anyone?), in this case indicting "the digital age." But there is no empirical evidence that being immersed in instant messaging, texting, iPods, videogames and all things online impairs thinking ability. "The jury is still out on whether these technologies are positive or negative" for cognition, says Ken Kosik of the University of California, Santa Barbara, codirector of the Neuroscience Research Institute there. "But they're definitely changing how people's brains process information." In fact, basic principles of neuroscience offer reasons to be optimistic. "We are gradually changing from a nation of callused hands to a nation of agile brains," says cognitive scientist Marcel Just of Carnegie Mellon University. "Insofar as new information technology exercises our minds and provides more information, it has to be improving thinking ability."

We think that even English professors should respect the difference between correlation and causation: just because ignorance of big lakes and oratorios got worse when the digital age dawned doesn't mean that the latter caused the former. To establish that, you need data. Alas, there isn't much. The ideal experiment is hard to pull off: to study the effect of digital technology on cognitive processing in a rigorous way, you must randomly assign groups of young people to use it a lot, a little or not at all, then follow them for years. As one 19-year-old of our acquaintance said about the chances of getting teens to volunteer for the "not at all" group, "Are you out of your [deleted] mind?"

What we do know about is multitasking: it impairs performance in the moment. If, say, you talk on a cell phone while driving, you have more trouble keeping your car within its lane and reacting to threats, Just reported earlier this year. "Multitasking forces the brain to share processing resources," he says, "so even if the tasks don't use the same regions [talking and driving do not], there is some shared infrastructure that gets overloaded." Chronic multitasking —texting and listening to your iPod and updating your Facebook page while studying for your exam on the Italian Renaissance—might also impair learning, as a 2006 study suggested. Scientists at UCLA led by Russell Poldrack scanned the brains of adults ages 18 to 45 while they learned to interpret symbols on flashcards either in silence or while also counting high-pitched beeps they heard. The volunteers learned to interpret the cards even with the distracting beeps, but when they were asked about the cards afterward, the multitaskers did worse. "Multitasking adversely affects how you learn," Poldrack said at the time. "Even if you learn while multitasking, that learning is less flexible and more specialized, so you cannot retrieve the information as easily." Difficult tasks, such as learning calculus or reading "War and Peace," will be particularly adversely affected by multitasking, says psychologist David Meyer of the University of Michigan: "When the tasks are at all challenging, there is a big drop in performance with multitasking. What kids are doing is learning to be skillful at a superficial level."

A lab experiment with cards and beeps is not real life, however. Some scientists suspect that the brain can be trained to multitask, just as it can learn to hit a fastball or memorize the Aeneid. In an unpublished study, Clifford Nass of Stanford and his student Eyal Ophir find that multitaskers do let in a great deal more information, which is otherwise distracting and attention-depleting. But avid multitaskers "seem able to hold more information in short-term memory, and keep it neatly separated into what they need and what they don't," says Nass. "The high multitaskers don't ignore [all the incoming signals], but are able to immediately throw out the irrelevant stuff." They have some kind of compensatory mechanism to override the distractions and process the relevant information effectively.

Even videogames might have cognitive benefits, beyond the hand-eye coordination and spatial skills some foster. In his 2005 book "Everything Bad Is Good for You," Steven Johnson argued that fantasy role-playing games such as Dungeons & Dragons are cognitively demanding, requiring players to build "elaborate fantasy narratives—all by rolling twenty-sided dice and consulting bewildering charts that accounted for a staggering number of variables." Players must calculate the effect of various combinations of weapon, opponent and allies "that would leave most kids weeping if you put the same charts on a math quiz," Johnson wrote. They must use deductive reasoning to infer rules as they go, such as the use of various implements, what you need to do to level-up, intermediary goals, who's friend and who's foe. The games challenge you to identify cause and effect—Johnson describes how SimCity taught his 7-year-old nephew that high tax rates in a city's industrial zone can deter manufacturers from relocating there—and to figure out nested goals, such as the need to find the tool to get the weapon to beat the enemy to cross the moat to reach the castle to (*phew*) save the princess. This is nothing if not hypothesis testing and problem solving, and games such as Final Fantasy exercise it no less than figuring out where cars traveling toward one another from 450 miles apart, one at 50mph and one at 60mph, will meet.

No one knows what kids will do with the cognitive skills they hone rescuing the princess. If they just save more princesses, Bauerlein will be proved right: Gen Y will turn out to be not just the dumbest but also the most self-absorbed and selfish. (It really aggravates him that many Gen-Yers are unapologetic about their ignorance, dismissing the idea that they should have more facts in their heads as a pre-Google and pre-wiki anachronism.) But maybe they'll deploy their minds to engineer an affordable 100mpg car, to discover the difference in the genetic fingerprints of cancers that spread and those that do not, to identify the causes and cures of intolerance and hate. Oddly, Bauerlein acknowledges that "kids these days are just as smart and motivated as ever." If they're also "the dumbest" because they have "more diversions" and because "screen activity trumps old-fashioned reading materials"—well, choices can change, with maturity, with different reward structures, with changes in the world their elders make. Writing off any generation before it's 30 is what's dumb.

Is Google Making Us Stupid?

By Nicholas Carr

"Dave, stop. Stop, will you? Stop, Dave. Will you stop, Dave?" So the supercomputer HAL pleads with the implacable astronaut Dave Bowman in a famous and weirdly poignant scene toward the end of Stanley Kubrick's *2001: A Space Odyssey*. Bowman, having nearly been sent to a deep-space death by the malfunctioning machine, is calmly, coldly disconnecting the memory circuits that control its artificial brain. "Dave, my mind is going," HAL says, forlornly. "I can feel it. I can feel it."

I can feel it, too. Over the past few years I've had an uncomfortable sense that someone, or something, has been tinkering with my brain, remapping the neural circuitry, reprogramming the memory. My mind isn't going—so far as I can tell—but it's changing. I'm not thinking the way I used to think. I can feel it most strongly when I'm reading. Immersing myself in a book or a lengthy article used to be easy. My mind would get caught up in the narrative or the turns of the argument, and I'd spend hours strolling through long stretches of prose. That's rarely the case anymore. Now my concentration often starts to drift after two or three pages. I get fidgety, lose the thread, begin looking for something else to do. I feel as if I'm always dragging my wayward brain back to the text. The deep reading that used to come naturally has become a struggle.

I think I know what's going on. For more than a decade now, I've been spending a lot of time online, searching and surfing and sometimes adding to the great databases of the Internet. The Web has been a godsend to me as a writer. Research that once required days in the stacks or periodical rooms of libraries can now be done in minutes. A few Google searches, some quick clicks on hyperlinks, and I've got the telltale fact or pithy quote I was after. Even when I'm not working, I'm as likely as not to be foraging in the Web's info-thickets—reading and writing e-mails, scanning headlines and blog posts, watching videos and listening to podcasts, or just tripping from link to link to link. (Unlike footnotes, to which they're sometimes likened, hyperlinks don't merely point to related works; they propel you toward them.)

From *The Atlantic*, 2008.

For me, as for others, the Net is becoming a universal medium, the conduit for most of the information that flows through my eyes and ears and into my mind. The advantages of having immediate access to such an incredibly rich store of information are many, and they've been widely described and duly applauded. "The perfect recall of silicon memory," *Wired*'s Clive Thompson has written, "can be an enormous boon to thinking." But that boon comes at a price. As the media theorist Marshall McLuhan pointed out in the 1960s, media are not just passive channels of information. They supply the stuff of thought, but they also shape the process of thought. And what the Net seems to be doing is chipping away my capacity for concentration and contemplation. My mind now expects to take in information the way the Net distributes it: in a swiftly moving stream of particles. Once I was a scuba diver in the sea of words. Now I zip along the surface like a guy on a Jet Ski.

I'm not the only one. When I mention my troubles with reading to friends and acquaintances—literary types, most of them—many say they're having similar experiences. The more they use the Web, the more they have to fight to stay focused on long pieces of writing. Some of the bloggers I follow have also begun mentioning the phenomenon. Scott Karp, who writes a blog about online media, recently confessed that he has stopped reading books altogether. "I was a lit major in college, and used to be [a] voracious book reader," he wrote. "What happened?" He speculates on the answer: "What if I do all my reading on the web not so much because the way I read has changed, i.e. I'm just seeking convenience, but because the way I THINK has changed?"

Bruce Friedman, who blogs regularly about the use of computers in medicine, also has described how the Internet has altered his mental habits. "I now have almost totally lost the ability to read and absorb a longish article on the web or in print," he wrote earlier this year. A pathologist who has long been on the faculty of the University of Michigan Medical School, Friedman elaborated on his comment in a telephone conversation with me. His thinking, he said, has taken on a "staccato" quality, reflecting the way he quickly scans short passages of text from many sources online. "I can't read *War and Peace* anymore," he admitted. "I've lost the ability to do that. Even a blog post of more than three or four paragraphs is too much to absorb. I skim it."

Anecdotes alone don't prove much. And we still await the long-term neurological and psychological experiments that will provide a definitive picture of how Internet use affects cognition. But a recently published study of online research habits, conducted by scholars from University College London, suggests that we may well be in the midst of a sea change in the way we read and think. As part of the five-year research program, the scholars examined computer logs documenting the behavior of visitors to two popular research sites, one operated by the British Library and one by a U.K. educational consortium, that provide access to journal articles, e-books, and other sources of written information. They found that people using the sites exhibited "a form of skimming activity," hopping from one source to another and rarely returning to any source they'd already visited. They typically read no more than one or two pages of an article or book before they would "bounce" out to another site. Sometimes they'd save a long article, but there's no evidence that they ever went back and actually read it. The authors of the study report:

It is clear that users are not reading online in the traditional sense; indeed there are signs that new forms of "reading" are emerging as users "power browse" horizontally through titles, contents pages and abstracts going for quick wins. It almost seems that they go online to avoid reading in the traditional sense.

Thanks to the ubiquity of text on the Internet, not to mention the popularity of text-messaging on cell phones, we may well be reading more today than we did in the 1970s or 1980s, when television was our medium of choice. But it's a different kind of reading, and behind it lies a different kind of thinking—perhaps even a new sense of the self. "We are not only *what* we read," says Maryanne Wolf, a developmental psychologist at Tufts University and the author of *Proust and the Squid: The Story and Science of the Reading Brain.* "We are *how* we read." Wolf worries that the style of reading promoted by the Net, a style that puts "efficiency" and "immediacy" above all else, may be weakening our capacity for the kind of deep reading that emerged when an earlier technology, the printing press, made long and complex works of prose commonplace. When we read online, she says, we tend to become "mere decoders of information." Our ability to interpret text, to make the rich mental connections that form when we read deeply and without distraction, remains largely disengaged.

Reading, explains Wolf, is not an instinctive skill for human beings. It's not etched into our genes the way speech is. We have to teach our minds how to translate the symbolic characters we see into the language we understand. And the media or other technologies we use in learning and practicing the craft of reading play an important part in shaping the neural circuits inside our brains. Experiments demonstrate that readers of ideograms, such as the Chinese, develop a mental circuitry for reading that is very different from the circuitry found in those of us whose written language employs an alphabet. The variations extend across many regions of the brain, including those that govern such essential cognitive functions as memory and the interpretation of visual and auditory stimuli. We can expect as well that the circuits woven by our use of the Net will be different from those woven by our reading of books and other printed works.

Sometime in 1882, Friedrich Nietzsche bought a typewriter—a Malling-Hansen Writing Ball, to be precise. His vision was failing, and keeping his eyes focused on a page had become exhausting and painful, often bringing on crushing headaches. He had been forced to curtail his writing, and he feared that he would soon have to give it up. The typewriter rescued him, at least for a time. Once he had mastered touch-typing, he was able to write with his eyes closed, using only the tips of his fingers. Words could once again flow from his mind to the page.

But the machine had a subtler effect on his work. One of Nietzsche's friends, a composer, noticed a change in the style of his writing. His already terse prose had become even tighter, more telegraphic. "Perhaps you will through this instrument even take to a new idiom," the friend wrote in a letter, noting that, in his own work, his "'thoughts' in music and language often depend on the quality of pen and paper."

"You are right," Nietzsche replied, "our writing equipment takes part in the forming of our thoughts." Under the sway of the machine, writes the German media scholar Friedrich A. Kittler, Nietzsche's prose "changed from arguments to aphorisms, from thoughts to puns, from rhetoric to telegram style."

The human brain is almost infinitely malleable. People used to think that our mental meshwork, the dense connections formed among the 100 billion or so neurons inside our skulls, was largely fixed by the time we reached adulthood. But brain researchers have discovered that that's not the case. James Olds, a professor of neuroscience who directs the Krasnow Institute for Advanced Study at George Mason University, says that even the adult mind "is very plastic." Nerve cells routinely break old connections and form new ones. "The brain," according to Olds, "has the ability to reprogram itself on the fly, altering the way it functions."

As we use what the sociologist Daniel Bell has called our "intellectual technologies"—the tools that extend our mental rather than our physical capacities—we inevitably begin to take on the qualities of those technologies. The mechanical clock, which came into common use in the 14th century, provides a compelling example. In *Technics and Civilization*, the historian and cultural critic Lewis Mumford described how the clock "disassociated time from human events and helped create the belief in an independent world of mathematically measurable sequences." The "abstract framework of divided time" became "the point of reference for both action and thought."

The clock's methodical ticking helped bring into being the scientific mind and the scientific man. But it also took something away. As the late MIT computer scientist Joseph Weizenbaum observed in his 1976 book, *Computer Power and Human Reason: From Judgment to Calculation*, the conception of the world that emerged from the widespread use of timekeeping instruments "remains an impoverished version of the older one, for it rests on a rejection of those direct experiences that formed the basis for, and indeed constituted, the old reality." In deciding when to eat, to work, to sleep, to rise, we stopped listening to our senses and started obeying the clock.

The process of adapting to new intellectual technologies is reflected in the changing metaphors we use to explain ourselves to ourselves. When the mechanical clock arrived, people began thinking of their brains as operating "like clockwork." Today, in the age of software, we have come to think of them as operating "like computers." But the changes, neuroscience tells us, go much deeper than metaphor. Thanks to our brain's plasticity, the adaptation occurs also at a biological level.

The Internet promises to have particularly far-reaching effects on cognition. In a paper published in 1936, the British mathematician Alan Turing proved that a digital computer, which at the time existed only as a theoretical machine, could be programmed to perform the function of any other information-processing device. And that's what we're seeing today. The Internet, an immeasurably powerful computing system, is subsuming most of our other intellectual technologies. It's becoming our map and our clock, our printing press and our typewriter, our calculator and our telephone, and our radio and TV.

When the Net absorbs a medium, that medium is re-created in the Net's image. It injects the medium's content with hyperlinks, blinking ads, and other digital gewgaws, and it surrounds the content with the content of all the other media it has absorbed. A new e-mail message, for instance, may announce its arrival as we're glancing over the latest headlines at a newspaper's site. The result is to scatter our attention and diffuse our concentration.

The Net's influence doesn't end at the edges of a computer screen, either. As people's minds become attuned to the crazy quilt of Internet media, traditional media have to adapt to the audience's new expectations. Television programs add text crawls and pop-up ads, and magazines and newspapers shorten their articles, introduce capsule summaries, and crowd their pages with easy-to-browse info-snippets. When, in March of this year, *TheNew York Times* decided to devote the second and third pages of every edition to article abstracts, its design director, Tom Bodkin, explained that the "shortcuts" would give harried readers a quick "taste" of the day's news, sparing them the "less efficient" method of actually turning the pages and reading the articles. Old media have little choice but to play by the new-media rules.

Never has a communications system played so many roles in our lives—or exerted such broad influence over our thoughts—as the Internet does today. Yet, for all that's been written about the Net, there's been little consideration of how, exactly, it's reprogramming us. The Net's intellectual ethic remains obscure.

About the same time that Nietzsche started using his typewriter, an earnest young man named Frederick Winslow Taylor carried a stopwatch into the Midvale Steel plant in Philadelphia and began a historic series of experiments aimed at improving the efficiency of the plant's machinists. With the approval of Midvale's owners, he recruited a group of factory hands, set them to work on various metalworking machines, and recorded and timed their every movement as well as the operations of the machines. By breaking down every job into a sequence of small, discrete steps and then testing different ways of performing each one, Taylor created a set of precise instructions—an "algorithm," we might say today—for how each worker should work. Midvale's employees grumbled about the strict new regime, claiming that it turned them into little more than automatons, but the factory's productivity soared.

More than a hundred years after the invention of the steam engine, the Industrial Revolution had at last found its philosophy and its philosopher. Taylor's tight industrial choreography—his "system," as he liked to call it—was embraced by manufacturers throughout the country and, in time, around the world. Seeking maximum speed, maximum efficiency, and maximum output, factory owners used time-and-motion studies to organize their work and configure the jobs of their workers. The goal, as Taylor defined it in his celebrated 1911 treatise, *The Principles of Scientific Management*, was to identify and adopt, for every job, the "one best method" of work and thereby to effect "the gradual substitution of science for rule of thumb throughout the mechanic arts." Once his system was applied to all acts of manual labor, Taylor assured his followers, it would bring about a restructuring not only of industry but of society, creating a utopia of perfect efficiency. "In the past the man has been first," he declared; "in the future the system must be first."

Taylor's system is still very much with us; it remains the ethic of industrial manufacturing. And now, thanks to the growing power that computer engineers and software coders wield over our intellectual lives, Taylor's ethic is beginning to govern the realm of the mind as well. The Internet is a machine designed for the efficient and automated collection, transmission, and manipulation of information, and its legions of programmers are intent on finding the "one best method"—the perfect algorithm—to carry out every mental movement of what we've come to describe as "knowledge work."

Google's headquarters, in Mountain View, California—the Googleplex—is the Internet's high church, and the religion practiced inside its walls is Taylorism. Google, says its chief executive, Eric Schmidt, is "a company that's founded around the science of measurement," and it is striving to "systematize everything" it does. Drawing on the terabytes of behavioral data it collects through its search engine and other sites, it carries out thousands of experiments a day, according to the *Harvard Business Review*, and it uses the results to refine the algorithms that increasingly control how people find information and extract meaning from it. What Taylor did for the work of the hand, Google is doing for the work of the mind.

The company has declared that its mission is "to organize the world's information and make it universally accessible and useful." It seeks to develop "the perfect search engine," which it defines as something that "understands exactly what you mean and gives you back exactly what you want." In Google's view, information is a kind of commodity, a utilitarian resource that can be mined and processed with industrial efficiency. The more pieces of information we can "access" and the faster we can extract their gist, the more productive we become as thinkers.

Where does it end? Sergey Brin and Larry Page, the gifted young men who founded Google while pursuing doctoral degrees in computer science at Stanford, speak frequently of their desire to turn their search engine into an artificial intelligence, a HAL-like machine that might be connected directly to our brains. "The ultimate search engine is something as smart as people—or smarter," Page said in a speech a few years back. "For us, working on search is a way to work on artificial intelligence." In a 2004 interview with *Newsweek*, Brin said, "Certainly if you had all the world's information directly attached to your brain, or an artificial brain that was smarter than your brain, you'd be better off." Last year, Page told a convention of scientists that Google is "really trying to build artificial intelligence and to do it on a large scale."

Such an ambition is a natural one, even an admirable one, for a pair of math whizzes with vast quantities of cash at their disposal and a small army of computer scientists in their employ. A fundamentally scientific enterprise, Google is motivated by a desire to use technology, in Eric Schmidt's words, "to solve problems that have never been solved before," and artificial intelligence is the hardest problem out there. Why wouldn't Brin and Page want to be the ones to crack it?

Still, their easy assumption that we'd all "be better off" if our brains were supplemented, or even replaced, by an artificial intelligence is unsettling. It suggests a belief that intelligence is the output of a mechanical process, a series of discrete steps that can be isolated, measured, and optimized. In Google's world, the world we enter when we go online, there's little place for the fuzziness of contemplation. Ambiguity is not an opening for insight but a bug to be fixed. The human brain is just an outdated computer that needs a faster processor and a bigger hard drive.

The idea that our minds should operate as high-speed data-processing machines is not only built into the workings of the Internet, it is the network's reigning business model as well. The faster we surf across the Web—the more links we click and pages we view—the more opportunities Google and other companies gain to collect information about us and to feed us advertisements. Most of the proprietors of the commercial Internet have a financial stake in collecting the crumbs of data we leave behind as we flit from link to link—the more crumbs, the better. The last thing these companies want is to encourage leisurely reading or slow, concentrated thought. It's in their economic interest to drive us to distraction.

Maybe I'm just a worrywart. Just as there's a tendency to glorify technological progress, there's a countertendency to expect the worst of every new tool or machine. In Plato's *Phaedrus*, Socrates bemoaned the development of writing. He feared that, as people came to rely on the written word as a substitute for the knowledge they used to carry inside their heads, they would, in the words of one of the dialogue's characters, "cease to exercise their memory and become forgetful." And because they would be able to "receive a quantity of information without proper instruction," they would "be thought very knowledgeable when they are for the most part quite ignorant." They would be "filled with the conceit of wisdom instead of real wisdom." Socrates wasn't wrong—the new technology did often have the effects he feared—but he was shortsighted. He couldn't foresee the many ways that writing and reading would serve to spread information, spur fresh ideas, and expand human knowledge (if not wisdom).

The arrival of Gutenberg's printing press, in the 15th century, set off another round of teeth gnashing. The Italian humanist Hieronimo Squarciafico worried that the easy availability of books would lead to intellectual laziness, making men "less studious" and weakening their minds. Others argued that cheaply printed books and broadsheets would undermine religious authority, demean the work of scholars and scribes, and spread sedition and debauchery. As New York University professor Clay Shirky notes, "Most of the arguments made against the printing press were correct, even prescient." But, again, the doomsayers were unable to imagine the myriad blessings that the printed word would deliver.

So, yes, you should be skeptical of my skepticism. Perhaps those who dismiss critics of the Internet as Luddites or nostalgists will be proved correct, and from our hyperactive, data-stoked minds will spring a golden age of intellectual discovery and universal wisdom. Then again, the Net isn't the alphabet, and although it may replace the printing press, it produces something altogether different. The kind of deep reading that a sequence of printed pages promotes is valuable not just for the knowledge we acquire from the author's words but for the intellectual vibrations those words set off within our own minds. In the quiet spaces opened up by the sustained, undistracted reading of a book, or by any other act of contemplation, for that matter, we make our own associations, draw our own inferences and analogies, foster our own ideas. Deep reading, as Maryanne Wolf argues, is indistinguishable from deep thinking.

If we lose those quiet spaces, or fill them up with "content," we will sacrifice something important not only in our selves but in our culture. In a recent essay, the playwright Richard Foreman eloquently described what's at stake:

I come from a tradition of Western culture, in which the ideal (my ideal) was the complex, dense and "cathedral-like" structure of the highly educated and articulate personality—a man or woman who carried inside themselves a personally constructed and unique version of the entire heritage of the West. [But now] I see within us all (myself included) the replacement of complex inner density with a new kind of self—evolving under the pressure of information overload and the technology of the "instantly available."

As we are drained of our "inner repertory of dense cultural inheritance," Foreman concluded, we risk turning into "'pancake people'—spread wide and thin as we connect with that vast network of information accessed by the mere touch of a button."

I'm haunted by that scene in *2001*. What makes it so poignant, and so weird, is the computer's emotional response to the disassembly of its mind: its despair as one circuit after another goes dark, its childlike pleading with the astronaut—"I can feel it. I can feel it. I'm afraid"— and its final reversion to what can only be called a state of innocence. HAL's outpouring of feeling contrasts with the emotionlessness that characterizes the human figures in the film, who go about their business with an almost robotic efficiency. Their thoughts and actions feel scripted, as if they're following the steps of an algorithm. In the world of *2001*, people have become so machinelike that the most human character turns out to be a machine. That's the essence of Kubrick's dark prophecy: as we come to rely on computers to mediate our understanding of the world, it is our own intelligence that flattens into artificial intelligence.

Jesus is a Brand of Jeans

By Jean Kilbourne

A recent ad for Thule car-rack systems features a child in the backseat of a car, seatbelt on. Next to the child, assorted sporting gear is carefully strapped into a child's carseat. The headline says: 'We Know What Matters to You.' In case one misses the point, further copy adds: 'Your gear is a priority.'

Another ad features an attractive young couple in bed. The man is on top of the woman, presumably making love to her. However, her face is completely covered by a magazine, open to a double-page photo of a car. The man is gazing passionately at the car. The copy reads, 'The ultimate attraction.'

These ads are meant to be funny. Taken individually, I suppose they might seem amusing or, at worst, tasteless. As someone who has studied ads for a long time, however, I see them as part of a pattern: just two of many ads that state or imply that products are more important than people. Ads have long promised us a better relationship via a product: *buy this and you will be loved.* But more recently they have gone beyond that proposition to promise us a relationship with the product itself: *buy this and it will love you.* The product is not so much the means to an end, as the end itself.

After all, it is easier to love a product than a person. Relationships with human beings are messy, unpredictable, sometimes dangerous. 'When was the last time you felt this comfortable in a relationship?' asks an ad for shoes. Our shoes never ask us to wash the dishes or tell us we're getting fat. Even more important, products don't betray us. 'You can love it without getting your heart broken,' proclaims a car ad. One certainly can't say that about loving a human being, as love without vulnerability is impossible.

We are surrounded by hundreds, thousands of messages every day that link our deepest emotions to products that objectify people and trivialize our most heartfelt moments and relationships. Every emotion is used to sell us something. Our wish to protect our children is leveraged to make us buy an expensive car. A long marriage simply provides the occasion for a diamond necklace. A painful reunion

From *New Internationalist*, 2016.

between a father and his estranged daughter is dramatized to sell us a phone system. Everything in the world—nature, animals, people—is just so much stuff to be consumed or to be used to sell us something.

The problem with advertising isn't that it creates artificial needs, but that it exploits our very real and human desires. Advertising promotes a bankrupt concept of *relationship*. Most of us yearn for committed relationships that will last. We are not stupid: we know that buying a certain brand of cereal won't bring us one inch closer to that goal. But we are surrounded by advertising that yokes our needs with products and promises us that *things* will deliver what in fact they never can. In the world of advertising, lovers are things and things are lovers.

It may be that there is no other way to depict relationships when the ultimate goal is to sell products. But this apparently bottomless consumerism not only depletes the world's resources, it also depletes our inner resources. It leads inevitably to narcissism and solipsism. It becomes difficult to imagine a way of relating that isn't objectifying and exploitative.

TUNED IN

Most people feel that advertising is not something to take seriously. Other aspects of the media are serious—the violent films, the trashy talk shows, the bowdlerization of the news. But not advertising! Although much more attention has been paid to the cultural impact of advertising in recent years than ever before, just about everyone still feels personally exempt from its influence. What I hear more than anything else at my lectures is: 'I don't pay attention to ads... I just tune them out... they have no effect on me.' I hear this most from people wearing clothes emblazoned with logos. In truth, we are all influenced. There is no way to tune out this much information, especially when it is designed to break through the 'tuning out' process. As advertising critic Sut Jhally put it: 'To not be influenced by advertising would be to live outside of culture. No human being lives outside of culture.'

Much of advertising's power comes from this belief that it does not affect us. As Joseph Goebbels said: 'This is the secret of propaganda: those who are to be persuaded by it should be completely immersed in the ideas of the propaganda, without ever noticing that they are being immersed in it.' Because we think advertising is trivial, we are less on guard, less critical, than we might otherwise be. While we're laughing, sometimes sneering, the commercial does its work.

Taken individually, ads are silly, sometimes funny, certainly nothing to worry about. But cumulatively they create a climate of cynicism that is poisonous to relationships. Ad after ad portrays our real lives as dull and ordinary, commitment to human beings as something to be avoided. Because of the pervasiveness of this kind of message, we learn from childhood that it is far safer to make a commitment to a product than to a person, far easier to be loyal to a brand. Many end up feeling romantic about material objects yet deeply cynical about other human beings.

UNNATURAL PASSIONS

We know by now that advertising often turns people into objects. Women's bodies—and men's bodies too these days—are dismembered, packaged and used to sell everything from chainsaws to chewing gum, champagne to shampoo. Self-image is deeply affected. The self-esteem of girls plummets as they reach adolescence partly because they cannot possibly escape the message that their bodies are objects, and imperfect objects at that. Boys learn that masculinity requires a kind of ruthlessness, even brutality.

Advertising encourages us not only to objectify each other but to feel passion for products rather than our partners. This is especially dangerous when the products are potentially addictive, because addicts do feel they are in a relationship with their substances. I once heard an alcoholic joke that Jack Daniels was her most constant lover. When I was a smoker, I felt that my cigarettes were my friends. Advertising reinforces these beliefs, so we are twice seduced—by the ads and by the substances themselves.

The addict is the ideal consumer. Ten percent of drinkers consume over sixty percent of all the alcohol sold. Most of them are alcoholics or people in desperate trouble—but they are also the alcohol industry's very best customers. Advertisers spend enormous amounts of money on psychological research and understand addiction well. They use this knowledge to target children (because if you hook them early they are yours for life), to encourage all people to consume more, in spite of often dangerous consequences for all of us, and to create a climate of denial in which all kinds of addictions flourish. This they do with full intent, as we see so clearly in the 'secret documents' of the tobacco industry that have been made public in recent years.

The consumer culture encourages us not only to buy more but to seek our identity and fulfillment through what we buy, to express our individuality through our 'choices' of products. Advertising corrupts relationships and then offers us products, both as solace and as substitutes for the intimate human connection we all long for and need.

In the world of advertising, lovers grow cold, spouses grow old, children grow up and away—but possessions stay with us and never change. Seeking the outcomes of a healthy relationship through products cannot work. Sometimes it leads us into addiction. But at best the possessions can never deliver the promised goods. They can't make us happy or loved or less alone or safe. If we believe they can, we are doomed to disappointment. No matter how much we love them, they will never love us back. Some argue that advertising simply reflects societal values rather than affecting them. Far from being a passive mirror of society, however, advertising is a pervasive medium of influence and persuasion. Its influence is cumulative, often subtle and primarily unconscious. A former editor-in-chief of *Advertising Age*, the leading advertising publication in North America, once claimed: 'Only eight percent of an ad's message is received by the conscious mind. The rest is worked and re-worked deep within, in the recesses of the brain.'

Advertising performs much the same function in industrial society as myth did in ancient societies. It is both a creator and perpetuator of the dominant values of the culture, the social norms by which most people govern their behavior. At the very least, advertising helps to create a climate in which certain values flourish and others are not reflected at all.

Advertising is not only our physical environment, it is increasingly our spiritual environment as well. By definition, however, it is only interested in materialistic values. When spiritual values show up in ads, it is only in order to sell us something. Eternity is a perfume by Calvin Klein. Infiniti is an automobile, and Hydra Zen a moisturizer. Jesus is a brand of jeans.

Sometimes the allusion is more subtle, as in the countless alcohol ads featuring the bottle surrounded by a halo of light. Indeed products such as jewellery shining in a store window are often displayed as if they were sacred objects. Advertising co-opts our sacred symbols in order to evoke an immediate emotional response. Media critic Neil Postman referred to this as 'cultural rape.'

It is commonplace to observe that consumerism has become the religion of our time (with advertising its holy text), but the criticism usually stops short of what is at the heart of the comparison. Both advertising and religion share a belief in transformation, but most religions believe that this requires sacrifice. In the world of advertising, enlightenment is achieved instantly by purchasing material goods. An ad for a watch says, 'It's not your handbag. It's not your neighbourhood. It's not your boyfriend. It's your watch that tells most about who you are.' Of course, this cheapens authentic spirituality and transcendence. This junk food for the soul leaves us hungry, empty, malnourished.

SUBSTITUTE STORIES

Human beings used to be influenced primarily by the stories of our particular tribe or community, not by stories that are mass-produced and market-driven. As George Gerbner, one of the world's most respected researchers on the influence of the media, said: 'For the first time in human history, most of the stories about people, life and values are told not by parents, schools, churches, or others in the community who have something to tell, but by a group of distant conglomerates that have something to sell.'

Although it is virtually impossible to measure the influence of advertising on a culture, we can learn something by looking at cultures only recently exposed to it. In 1980 the Gwich'in tribe of Alaska got television, and therefore massive advertising, for the first time. Satellite dishes, video games and VCRs were not far behind. Before this, the Gwich'in lived much the way their ancestors had for generations. Within 10 years, the young members of the tribe were so drawn by television they no longer had time to learn ancient hunting methods, their parents' language or their oral history. Legends told around campfires could not compete with *Beverly Hills 90210*. Beaded moccasins gave way to Nike sneakers, and 'tundra tea' to Folger's instant coffee.

As multinational chains replace local character, we end up in a world in which everyone is Gapped and Starbucked. Shopping malls kill vibrant downtown centres locally and create a universe of uniformity internationally. We end up in a world ruled by, in John Maynard Keynes's phrase, the values of the casino. On this deeper level, rampant commercialism undermines our physical and psychological health, our environment and our civic life, and creates a toxic society.

Advertising creates a world view that is based upon cynicism, dissatisfaction and craving. Advertisers aren't evil. They are just doing their job, which is to sell a product; but the consequences, usually unintended, are often destructive. In the history of the world there has never been a propaganda effort to match that of advertising in the past 50 years. More thought, more effort, more money goes into advertising than has gone into any other campaign to change social consciousness. The story that advertising tells is that the way to be happy, to find satisfaction—and the path to political freedom, as well—is through the consumption of material objects. And the major motivating force for social change throughout the world today is this belief that happiness comes from the market.

A Nation of Vidiots

By Jeffery Sachs

The past half-century has been the age of electronic mass media. Television has reshaped society in every corner of the world. Now an explosion of new media devices is joining the TV set: DVDs, computers, game boxes, smart phones, and more. A growing body of evidence suggests that this media proliferation has countless ill effects.

The United States led the world into the television age, and the implications can be seen most directly in America's long love affair with what Harlan Ellison memorably called "the glass teat." In 1950, fewer than 8% of American households owned a TV; by 1960, 90% had one. That level of penetration took decades longer to achieve elsewhere, and the poorest countries are still not there.

True to form, Americans became the greatest TV watchers, which is probably still true today, even though the data are somewhat sketchy and incomplete. The best evidence suggests that Americans watch more than five hours per day of television on average—a staggering amount, given that several hours more are spent in front of other video-streaming devices. Other countries log far fewer viewing hours. In Scandinavia, for example, time spent watching TV is roughly half the US average.

The consequences for American society are profound, troubling, and a warning to the world—though it probably comes far too late to be heeded. First, heavy TV viewing brings little pleasure. Many surveys show that it is almost like an addiction, with a short-term benefit leading to long-term unhappiness and remorse. Such viewers say that they would prefer to watch less than they do.

Moreover, heavy TV viewing has contributed to social fragmentation. Time that used to be spent together in the community is now spent alone in front of the screen. Robert Putnam, the leading scholar of America's declining sense of community, has found that TV viewing is the central explanation of the decline of "social capital," the trust that binds communities together. Americans simply trust each other less than they did a generation ago. Of course, many other factors

From *Project Syndicate*, 2011.

are at work, but television-driven social atomization should not be understated.

Certainly, heavy TV viewing is bad for one's physical and mental health. Americans lead the world in obesity, with roughly two-thirds of the US population now overweight. Again, many factors underlie this, including a diet of cheap, unhealthy fried foods, but the sedentary time spent in front of the TV is an important influence as well.

At the same time, what happens mentally is as important as what happens physically. Television and related media have been the greatest purveyors and conveyors of corporate and political propaganda in society.

America's TV ownership is almost entirely in private hands, and owners make much of their money through relentless advertising. Effective advertising campaigns, appealing to unconscious urges—typically related to food, sex, and status—create cravings for products and purchases that have little real value for consumers or society.

The same, of course, has happened to politics. American politicians are now brand names, packaged like breakfast cereal. Anybody—and any idea—can be sold with a bright ribbon and a catchy jingle.

All roads to power in America lead through TV, and all access to TV depends on big money. This simple logic has put American politics in the hands of the rich as never before.

Even war can be rolled out as a new product. The Bush administration promoted the premises of the Iraq war—Saddam Hussein's non-existent weapons of mass destruction—in the familiar colorful, fast-paced, and graphics-heavy style of television advertising. Then the war itself began with the so- called "shock and awe" bombing of Baghdad—a made-for-TV live spectacle aimed at ensuring high ratings for the US-led invasion.

Many neuroscientists believe that the mental-health effects of TV viewing might run even deeper than addiction, consumerism, loss of social trust, and political propaganda. Perhaps TV is rewiring heavy viewers' brains and impairing their cognitive capacities. The American Academy of Pediatrics recently warned that TV viewing by young children is dangerous for their brain development, and called on parents to keep children under two away from the TV and similar media.

A recent survey in the US by the organization Common Sense Media reveals a paradox, but one that is perfectly understandable. Children in poor American households today not only watch more TV than children in wealthy households, but are also more likely to have a television in their room. When a commodity's consumption falls as income rises, economists call it an "inferior" good.

To be sure, the mass media can be useful as a provider of information, education, entertainment, and even political awareness. But too much of it is confronting us with dangers that we need to avoid.

At the very least, we can minimize those dangers. Successful approaches around the world include limits on TV advertising, especially to young children; non-commercial, publicly-owned TV networks like the BBC; and free (but limited) TV time for political campaigns.

Of course, the best defense is our own self-control. We can all leave the TV off more hours per day and spend that time reading, talking with each other, and rebuilding the bases of personal health and social trust.

Supersaturation, or, The Media Torrent and Disposable Feeling

By Todd Gitlin

On my bedroom wall hangs a print of Vermeer's *The Concert*, painted around 1660. A young woman is playing a spinet. A second woman, probably her maid, holds a letter. A cavalier stands between them, his back to us. A landscape is painted on the raised lid of the spinet, and on the wall hang two paintings, a landscape and *The Procuress*, a work by Baburen, another Dutch artist, depicting a man and two women in a brothel. As in many seventeenth-century Dutch paintings, the domestic space is decorated by paintings. In wealthy Holland, many homes, and not only bourgeois ones, featured such renderings of the outer world. These pictures were pleasing, but more: they were proofs of taste and prosperity, amusements and news at once.

Vermeer froze instants, but instants that spoke of the relative constancy of the world in which his subjects lived. If he had painted the same room in the same house an hour, a day, or a month later, the letter in the maid's hand would have been different, and the woman might have been playing a different selection, but the paintings on the far wall would likely have been the same. There might have been other paintings, etchings, and prints elsewhere in the house, but they would not have changed much from month to month, year to year.

In what was then the richest country in the world, "everyone strives to embellish his house with precious pieces, especially the room toward the street," as one English visitor to Amsterdam wrote in 1640, noting that he had observed paintings in bakeries, butcher's shops, and the workshops of blacksmiths and cobblers. Of course, the number of paintings, etchings, and prints in homes varied considerably. One tailor owned five paintings, for example, while at the high end, a 1665 inventory of a lavish patrician's house in Amsterdam held two maps and thirteen paintings in one grand room, twelve paintings in his widow's bedroom, and seven in the maid's room. Still, compared with today's domestic imagery, the grandest Dutch inventories of that prosperous era were tiny. Even in the better-off households depicted

From *Media Unlimited: How the Torrent of Images and Sounds Overwhelms Our Lives,* 2002.

by Vermeer, the visual field inhabited by his figures was relatively scanty and fixed.

Today, Vernleer's equivalent, if he were painting domestic scenes, or shooting a spread for *Vanity Fair*, or directing commercials or movies, would also display his figures against a background of images; and if his work appeared on-screen, there is a good chance that he would mix in a soundtrack as well. Most of the images would be portraits of individuals who have never walked in the door—not in the flesh—and yet are recognized and welcomed, though not like actual persons. They would rapidly segue into others—either because they had been edited into a video montage, or because they appear on pages meant to be leafed through. Today's Vermeer would discover that the private space of the home offers up vastly more impressions of the larger world than was possible in 1660. In nineteenth-century Delft, painters did not knock on the door day and night offering fresh images for sale. Today, though living space has been set apart from working space, as would have been the case only for the wealthier burghers of Vermeer's time, the outside world has entered the home with a vengeance—in the profusion of media.

The flow of images and sounds through the households of the rich world, and the richer parts of the poor world, seems unremarkable today. Only a visitor from an earlier century or an impoverished country could be startled by the fact that life is now played out against a shimmering multitude of images and sounds, emanating from television, videotapes, videodiscs, video games, VCRs, computer screens, digital displays of all sorts, always in flux, chosen partly at will, partly by whim, supplemented by words, numbers, symbols, phrases, fragments, all passing through screens that in a single minute can display more pictures than a prosperous seventeenth-century Dutch household contained over several lifetimes, portraying in one day more individuals than the Dutch burgher would have beheld in the course of years, and in one week more bits of what we have come to call "information" than all the books in all the households in Vermeer's Delft. And this is not yet to speak of our sonic surroundings: the music, voices, and sound effects from radios, CD players, and turntables. Nor is it to speak of newspapers, magazines, newsletters, and books. Most of the faces we shall ever behold, we shall behold in the form of images.

Because they arrive with sound, at home, in the car, the elevator, or the waiting room, today's images are capable of attracting our attention during much of the day. We may ignore most of them most of the time, take issue with them or shrug them off (or think we are shrugging them off), but we must do the work of dispelling them—and even then, we know we can usher them into our presence whenever we like. Iconic plenitude is the contemporary condition, and it is taken for granted. To grow up in this culture is to grow into an expectation that images and sounds will be there for us on command, and that the stories they compose will be succeeded by still other stories, all bidding for our attention, all striving to make sense, all, in some sense, *ours*. Raymond Williams, the first analyst to pay attention to the fact that television is not just pictures but flow, and not just flow but drama upon drama, pointed out more than a quarter century ago, long before hundred-channel cable TV and VCRs, that

> we have never as a society acted so much or watched so many others acting....[W]hat is really new...is that drama...is built into the rhythms of everyday life. In earlier periods drama was important at a festival, in a season, or as a conscious journey to a theater; from honouring Dionysus or Christ to taking in a show. What we have now is drama as habitual experience: more in a week, in many cases, than most human beings would previously have seen in a lifetime.

Around the time Vermeer painted *The Concert*, Blaise Pascal, who worried about the seductive power of distraction among the French royalty, wrote that "near the persons of kings there never fail to be a great number of people who see to it that amusement follows business, and who watch all the time of their leisure to supply them with delights and games, so that there is no blank in it." In this one respect, today almost everyone—even the poor—in the rich countries resembles a king, attended by the courtiers of the media offering a divine right of choice.

MEASURES OF MAGNITUDE

Statistics begin—but barely—to convey the sheer magnitude of this in-touchness, access, exposure, plenitude, glut, however we want to think of it.

In 1999, a television set was on in the average American household more than seven hours a day, a figure that has remained fairly steady since 1983. According to the measurements of the A. C. Nielsen Company, the standard used by advertisers and the television business itself, the average individual watched television about four hours a day, not counting the time when the set was on but the individual in question was not watching. When Americans were asked to keep diaries of how they spend their time, the time spent actually watching dropped to a still striking three hours a day—probably an undercount. In 1995, of those who watched, the percentage who watched "whatever's on," as opposed to any specific program, was 43 percent, up from 29 percent in 1979. Though cross-national comparisons are elusive because of differences in measurement systems, the numbers in other industrialized nations seem to be comparable—France, for example, averaging three and a half hours per person. One survey of forty-three nations showed the United States ranking third in viewing hours, after Japan and Mexico. None of this counts time spent discussing programs, reading about their stars, or thinking about either.

Overall, wrote one major researcher in 1990, "watching TV is the dominant leisure activity of Americans, consuming 40 percent of the average person's free time as a primary activity [when people give television their undivided attention]. Television takes up more than half of our free time if you count...watching TV while doing something else like eating or reading...[or] when you have the set on but you aren't paying attention to it." Sex, race, income, age, and marital status make surprisingly little difference in time spent. Neither, at this writing, has the Internet diminished total media use, even if you don't count the Web as part of the media. While Internet users do watch 28 percent less television, they spend more time than nonusers playing video games and listening to the radio and recorded music—obviously a younger crowd. Long-term users (four or more years) say they go on-line for more than two hours a day, and boys and girls alike spend the bulk of their Internet time entertaining themselves with games, hobbies, and the like. In other words, the Internet redistributes the flow of unlimited media but does not dry it up. When one considers the overlapping and additional hours of exposure to radio, magazines, newspapers, compact discs, movies (available via a range of technologies as well as in theaters), and comic books, as well as the accompanying articles, books, and chats about what's on or was on or is coming up via all these means, it is clear that the media flow into the home—not to mention outside—has swelled into a torrent of immense force and constancy, an accompaniment to life that has become a central experience *of* life.

The place of media in the lives of children is worth special attention—not simply because children are uniquely impressionable but because their experience shapes everyone's future; if we today take a media-soaked environment for granted, surely one reason is that we grew up in it and can no longer see how remarkable it is. Here are some findings from a national survey of media conditions among American children aged two through eighteen. The average American child lives in a household with 2.9 televisions, 1.8 VCRs, 3.1 radios, 2.6 tape players, 2.1 CD players, 1.4 video game players, and 1 computer. Ninety-nine percent of these children live in homes with one or more TVs, 97 percent with a VCR, 97 percent with a radio, 94 percent with a tape player, 90 percent with a CD player, 70 percent with a video game player, 69 percent with a computer. Eighty-eight percent live in homes with two or more TVs, 60 percent in homes with three or more. Of the 99 percent with a TV, 74 percent have cable or satellite service. And so on, and on, and on.

The uniformity of this picture is no less astounding. A great deal about the lives of children depends on their race, sex, and social class, but access to major media does not. For TV, VCR, and radio ownership, rates do not vary significantly among white, black, and Hispanic children, or between girls and boys. For television and radio, rates do not vary significantly according to the income of the community.

How accessible, then, is the media cavalcade at home? Of children eight to eighteen, 65 percent have a TV in their bedrooms, 86 percent a radio, 81 percent a tape player, 75 percent a CD player. Boys and girls are not significantly different in possessing this bounty, though the relative usages do vary by medium. Researchers also asked children whether the television was "on in their homes even if no one is watching 'most of the time,' 'some of the time,' 'a little of the time,' or 'never.' "Homes in which television is on "most of the time" are termed *constant television households.* By this measure, 42 percent of all American households with children are constant television households. Blacks are more likely than whites or Hispanics to experience TV in their lives: 56 percent of black children live in constant television households (and 69 percent have a TV in their bedrooms, compared to 48 percent of whites).The lower the family education and the median income of the community, the greater the chance that a household is a constant television household.

As for time, the average child spent six hours and thirty-two minutes per day exposed to media of all kinds, of which the time spent reading books and magazines—not counting schoolwork—averaged about forty-five minutes. For ages two to seven, the average for total media was four hours and seventeen minutes; for ages eight to thirteen, eight hours and eight minutes, falling to seven hours and thirty-five minutes for ages fourteen to eighteen. Here, race and social class do count. Black children are most exposed, followed by Hispanics, then whites. At all age levels, the amount of exposure to all media varies inversely with class, from six hours and fifty-nine minutes a day for children in households where the median income for the zip code is under $25,000 to six hours and two minutes for children whose zip code median income is over $40,000. The discrepancy for TV exposure is especially pronounced, ranging from three hours and six minutes a day for children whose zip code incomes are under $25,000 to two hours and twenty-nine minutes for children whose zip code incomes are over $40,000. Still, these differences are not vast. Given everything that divides the rich from the poor, the professional from the working class—differences in physical and mental health, infant mortality, longevity, safety, vulnerability to crime, prospects for stable employment, and so on—the class differences in media access and use are surprisingly slender. So are the differences between American and western European children, the latter averaging six hours a day total, though in Europe only two and a quarter of those hours are spent with TV.

All such statistics are crude, of course. Most of them register the time that people *say* they spend. They are—thankfully—not checked by total surveillance. Moreover, the meaning of *exposure* is hard to assess, since the concept encompasses rapt attention, vague awareness, oblivious coexistence, and all possible shadings in between. As the images glide by and the voices come and go, how can we assess what goes on in people's heads? Still, the figures do convey some sense of the media saturation with which we live—and so far we have counted only what can be counted at home. These numbers don't take into account the billboards, the TVs at bars and on planes the Muzak in restaurants and shops, the magazines in the doctor's waiting room, the digital displays at the gas pump and over the urinal, the ads, insignias, and logos whizzing by on the sides of buses and taxis, climbing the walls of buildings, making announcements from caps, bags, T-shirts, and sneakers. To vary our experience, we can pay to watch stories about individuals unfold across larger-than-life-size movie screens, or visit theme parks and troop from image to image, display to display. Whenever we like, on foot or in vehicles, we can convert ourselves into movable nodes of communication, thanks to car radios, tape, CD, and game players, cell phones, beepers,

Walkmen, and the latest in "personal communication systems"—and even if we ourselves refrain, we find ourselves drawn willy-nilly into the soundscape that others broadcast around us.

Crucially, who we are is how we live our time—or *spend* it, to use the term that registers its intrinsic scarcity. What we believe, or say we believe, is less important. We vote for a way of life with our time. And increasingly, when we are not at work or asleep, we are in the media torrent. (Sometimes at work, we are also there, listening to the radio or checking out sports scores, pin-ups, or headlines on the Internet.) Steadily more inhabitants of the wealthy part of the world have the means, incentives, and opportunities to seek private electronic companionship. The more money we have to spend, the more personal space each household member gets. With personal space comes solitude, but this solitude is instantly crowded with images and soundtracks. To a degree that was unthinkable in the seventeenth century, life experience has become an experience in the presence of media.

VIRTUAL PLENITUDE

This is plenitude, but of a restricted sort. Though we may preserve them on videotape or in digital memory, ordinarily the images that come to us on screens are ephemeral traces. (The same goes for soundtracks.) Like the images that precede and succeed them in time, they belong to a perpetually vanishing present streaking by. As a rule, before they vanish, they offer only the most limited sense impressions. They transmit something of the look of things, but they cannot be smelled or tasted. They aren't palpable. They most commonly hang in two dimensions on a more or less flat translucent screen. This screen delivers light, gleams with availability, claims some portion of our attention, but is also apart from us. The screen is bright, brighter than ordinary reality (which is probably why it's so hard to look away), but often, for technical reasons, the picture may be a bit blurred, streaked with extraneous marks, interference patterns, or other reminders that the images are manufactured and transmitted from elsewhere.

Unless we click an off button or smash the screen, the images stream on, leaving traces in our minds but, despite the interactivity boom, strangely indifferent to us. They collect our attention but do not reciprocate. In the real time of our lives, we choose them and complete them by noticing, hearing, reading, or misreading them; yet they have no need of us. They are with us even if we are not with them. In the case of computer screens, we can alter the images—that is the very point—because they are our creatures. We buy and possess them. On the other hand, they compel a certain attention without reacting to us. They do not comment on our looks, raise no eyebrows at our choice of words or images (unless we have an up-to-date spell-checking program)—and so, to a certain degree, it is they who possess us.

Like flesh-and-blood people, the ones with whom we have "face-time," the virtual personages on-screen have identities and invite our emotions. They include, in the words of one of my students, "people who are sort of familiar and sort of not." At times they are part of the background noise and flow—part of the wallpaper, we say—and at times they loom up as something more. Sometimes we evaluate them as physical beings and moral agents. Often we find them desirable, or enviable, or in some other way they evoke the sentiments, the liking, irritation, or boredom, that flesh-and-blood individuals evoke. Yet an aura of some sort surrounds them. They take up ritual places as heroes, leaders, scapegoats, magical figures, to be admired, envied, loved, or hated; to *matter*. These familiar strangers exist *for us*, damn it. We root for them, yell at them. Fans commonly address letters to actors and confuse them with their characters. An actress on the soap opera *All My Children* once told me that she received fan letters that addressed her by name, complimented her on her performance, only to slide into addressing her character—why did you break up with your boyfriend?

Contact with the never-ending cornucopian flow of these faces, of popular culture itself, a torrent beyond us yet in some way (we think) under our control—this experience is at the core of a way of life. The familiar stranger is by no means unprecedented in history. People have long imagined a world populated with figures who were not physically at band and yet seemed somehow present. What has changed, of course, is the magnitude of the flow, the range of characters that enter our world, their omnipresence, the sheer number of stories. Inevitably, today's stories are but prologues or sequels to other stories, true and less true stories, stories that are themselves intermissions, stories without end.

Most of these stories reach us through images that reside with us—though they do so in a peculiar sense we should not be too quick to think we understand. We know, most of the time, that they are not "real" although when they grip us we don't want to tear ourselves away. Real are my family, friends, coworkers. Real is the taste of coffee, or the fly buzzing around the kitchen, or the pounding of my heart after a climb uphill. Real, in other senses, is my job, or cooking, or shopping, or organizing my routines to get to work or procure food. Images, on the other hand, depict or re-present realities but are not themselves realities. We usually know the difference. If an image depicts a place we have visited or reminds us of something that once happened to us, or something we could imagine happening, we call it *realistic*. But that is still not "real." Still less is it, in Umberto Eco's term, *hyperreal*, more real than the real, the product of an "absolute fake," like Hearst's San Simeon or a wax museum. Nor is it Jean Baudrillard's *simulacrum*, a copy of something whose original does not exist, like Disneyland's Main Street. Eco is closer to the truth when he refers to "the frantic desire for the almost real" that thrives, above all, in the United States.

Almost real: we expect a certain fidelity from images, whether fictional or "reality-based." If fictional, we expect them to be plausible, in some way *lifelike*, even if they are fantastic. We recognize them as ghosts, shadows of something substantial. They are auxiliary, virtual. No wonder that, among technophiles, the idea of virtual reality—of digitally delivered sensations that we could mistake for the actual experience of "being there"—caught on before the technology was devised, for much of our experience is already *virtual*: the sort of derivative yet riveting almost-reality that television has long delivered to us but that, until recently, has been sealed behind the screen. With virtual reality, we have the illusion of stepping inside the screen, not just attending to but being attended to *by* the images inside.

Of course, the viewer is not (ordinarily) naive. She knows that fictional beings will not step out of the screen to thrill her, as in Woody Allen's Purple Rose of Cairo, nor will the actors recognize her in the flesh, as in Neil LaBute's Nurse Betty; nor is she likely to mistake the TV image of a corpse for an actual cadaver. The adult viewer is not the infant who, psychologists assure us, cannot tell the difference between image and reality—who thinks the giraffe depicted on the TV screen is "actually" a few inches tall. But child or adult, we do demand something from our images, even if they are only "almost real." We expect them to heighten life, to intensify and focus it by being better than real, more vivid, more stark, more something. We want a burst of feeling, a frisson of commiseration, a flash of delight, a moment of recognition—so that's what it's like when your boyfriend sleeps with your sister, when you lose a patient in the emergency room, when you're voted off the Survivor island. We depend on these images to imagine the great elsewhere: "realistic" presences that point, say, to the real ruins of the World Trade Center, or fictions that gesture toward a real world where attendants wheel patients into operating rooms and police arrest suspects, or "reality-based" shows indicating that some human beings will eat a rat to win a chance at a million dollars.

All of this is so obvious and fundamental to the way we live now that to call attention to its strangeness seems banal or superfluous. Isn't the omnipresence of media simple and straightforward? But strangely, we have no language to catch precisely the unnerving, downright bizarreness of this world of images, characters, stories, jingles, sound effects, announcements, cartoons, and logos that engulfs our lives. Even words like *auxiliary*, *virtual*, and *ghostly* are poor approximations for the peculiar stream of images and sounds that winds through everyday life, so steady as to be taken for granted, so fluid as to permit us to believe that we never quite step into the same torrent twice.

HISTORICAL ORIGINS OF THE TORRENT

How did the unlimited media come to be taken for granted? Raymond Williams posed the question this way:

> Till the eyes tire, millions of us watch the shadows of shadows and find them substance; watch scenes, situations, actions, exchanges, crises. The slice of life, once a project of naturalist drama, is now a voluntary, habitual, internal rhythm; the flow of action and acting of representation and performance, raised to a new convention, that of a basic need....What is it, we have to ask, in us and in our contemporaries, that draws us repeatedly to these hundreds and thousands of simulated actions?

A good deal about the media torrent's force, its appeal, even its inescapability, remains mysterious. Respect for that mystery is not a bad place to start. We should not be too quick to say that media omnipresence is the product of runaway technology, or the quest for profits, or a drive to "escape"; or that the hunger for sensations is built into human nature or, to the contrary, is strictly a product of "late capitalism." Pat explanations blind us to the enormity of the media flow itself.

To a child growing up immersed in the culture of images, it appears the most natural thing in the world. It appears, in fact, to *be* nature.

Expecting image and sounds to appear on command (or even when uncommanded and unwanted) feels as normal as expecting the sun to rise. Because it's so easy to change channels, scan for stations, surf, graze, click, go to another source of images and sounds, you assume that if you don't like what you see or hear, you can find something better (or make your own image or soundscape). No wonder each wave of technosurprises seems somehow unsurprising—the screen hanging above an airplane seat, the car that receives e-mail and plays CDs, the watch with Internet access, the digital movie camera that switches on and off at the command of a voice. Indeed, today's inescapable hype about a brave new interconnected world has a plausible ring because a significant and growing proportion of Americans and others are already wired, or wirelessed, into numberless circuits, networks, loops of connection with images and sounds available on call. We feel about our image and sound machines as Marcel Proust once did about the telephone, "a supernatural instrument before whose miracles we used to stand amazed, and which we now employ without giving it a thought, to summon our tailor or to order an ice cream." We feel—we have no doubt—that we have the right to be addressed by our media, the right to enjoy them, the right to admit faces of our choice into our living rooms and to enter into worlds without number, to flow with them. We may not have the right to possess the beautiful faces and bodies we see there, the fortunes, celebrity, or power dangled before us, clamoring for our attention, but we have the right to want them. If we are let down, we have the right, almost the duty, to click and dip elsewhere at will.

It's easy to see how individuals grow up expecting their lives to be accompanied by image plenitude, flow, and choice. But for society as a whole, how did this blessing come to pass? Media saturation is not a gift of the gods nor of the unprovoked genius (or wickedness, or frivolity) of technological wizards. The Edisons, Marconis, Sarnoffs, De Forests, and Gateses devised and organized the media that Marshall McLuhan has called "extensions of man," but humanity came first with, its hungers and competencies. Nor are our desires the unwelcome products of vast corporations, determined to stuff human time with their commodities: with products that people would be so eager to purchase, on which they would become so dependent, that they would grant their time in exchange for money to bring these commodities home. It is that, but it is not only that. We know that Eminem's latest CD and *The Sopranos* are human creations, but it's easy to lose sight of the fact that the media flow itself is no less human in its origins, the product of millions of people who, having been molded by a mechanical way of life, have devised a seemingly endless number of ways to relieve the strains of that way of life by mechanical means.

Unlimited media result from a fusion of economic expansion and individual desire, prepared for over centuries, and nowhere more fully realized than in the United States. The pleasures of acquisition in seventeenth-century Delft led to the pleasures of consumption in twenty-first-century New York. In both, individuals matter, and therefore so do depictions of individuals. In both, individuals clothe themselves with adornments and disguises. In both, individuals claim rights—the big difference being that once exclusive rights have been expanded, including the right to think and feel as you like, and over time, the right to love, marry, move, work, sell, buy, vote, and otherwise act as you please. One thing that ever-growing numbers have the right to buy today is access to images at all hours and in extraordinary assortments, offering, at low cost except in time, a provisional combination of pleasure and some sense of mastery. People who were already interested in images and sounds won the time to consume them. An industrial apparatus arose to produce them cheaply and in profusion. The desire for pleasing windows on the world—and windows through which to escape the world—is nothing new, but only in modem society has it become possible for majorities to cultivate and live that desire, unwilling to accept anything less. Now, the desire for play, the desire for routine, the desire for diversion, the desire for orientation, the desire for representation, the desire to feel, the desire to flee from feeling— all these human desires in their complexity and contradiction are indulged in the vast circus maximus, our cultural jamboree of jamborees.

Although the media stream is modern, it draws on ancient springs. To feel accompanied by others not physically present is hardly unprecedented. We have a profound capacity to harbor images of actual or imaginary others who are not materially at hand—to remember or speculate about what they looked like, wonder what they are doing, imagine what they might think, anticipate what they might do, take part in unspoken dialogues with them. The fashioning of replicas extends across at least thirty thousand years of human history. Throughout this time people have lived, through images and simulations, "with" gods, saints, demons, kings and queens, heroes of fleet foot and sword, absent relations, clan members, friends, and enemies. The painting of a reindeer on the wall of a cave in the south of France, or the portrait of a dead ancestor in Egypt, or a cross on the wall, or the replica of a saint in the stained glass of a chapel, each opens a portal to an imagined world, beckoning us to cross a gap between the image *here* and what is, or was, or might be *there*.

None of that is new, nor is the manufacture and wide diffusion of popular culture. Poetry and song migrated across medieval Europe hand to hand, mouth to ear to mouth. Broadsheets circulated. From the second half of the fifteenth century on, Gutenberg's movable type made possible mass-printed Bibles and a flood of instructional as well as scurrilous literature. Even where literacy was rare, books were regularly read aloud. (In a scene at an inn from Cervantes's *Don Quixote*, published in 1605, farmworkers listen attentively to a reading of books found in a trunk.) In eighteenth-century England, the uplift and piety of John Bunyan's *Pilgrim's Progress*, which went through 160 editions by 1792, was supplemented by the upstart novel, that thrilling tale of individual action, which the high-minded of the time regarded as shockingly lowbrow. From then on, reading spread, especially at home alone and silently—that is, in secret. So did the imagination of what it might be like to be, or act like, somebody else: Robinson Crusoe, Moll Flanders, Tom Jones. "What sociologist David Riesman called "the stream of print" in the seventeenth, eighteenth, and nineteenth centuries opened up space for sympathy, helping to undermine theocracy and slavery. Whatever the censorious efforts of pastors and parents, Riesman wrote, "Almost always there is an underground of a more picaresque sort in which the growing boy, if not his sister, can take some refuge."

But even in Europe's most democratic outpost, America, the influx of reading matter into the household was retarded by the cost of books and the limits of literacy. The immense library of Thomas Jefferson was neither shared nor matched by his slaves or nearby tenant farmers. Still, sitting by his fire in the Kentucky wilderness, in the latter years of the eighteenth century, Daniel Boone read *Gulliver's Travels*—scarcely the popular image of the rough-tough wilderness man. The illiterate Rocky Mountain scout Jim Bridger could recite long passages from Shakespeare, which he learned by hiring someone to read the plays to him. "There is hardly a pioneer's hut that does not contain a few odd volumes of Shakespeare," Alexis de Tocqueville found on his trip through the United States in 1831-32. There were already extraordinary bursts of best-sellerdom: in a population for less literate than today's, Harriet Beecher Stowe's *Uncle Tom's Cabin* sold 300,000 copies within a year of its 1852 publication, one copy apiece for roughly 1.3 percent of the population, the equivalent of 3.6 million copies today—and then eventually ten times as many by the outbreak of the Civil War. At least in the United States, growing numbers of ordinary people had access to the "refuge" of print—and these were seldom books defending the ruling elites. As Riesman pointed out, the Bible was "the great readinghour storehouse," and it was "not one book but many, with an inexhaustible variety of messages." Slaves reading Exodus rehearsed their own freedom. Print has long sheltered those with the urge to run away, for as contemporary housewives continue to discover even while reading romance novels, "to be alone with a book is to be alone in a new way."

In the course of the nineteenth century, long before television, stories and images entered the typical household in ever-accelerating numbers. In 1865, according to literary historian Richard Ohmann, there was probably one copy of a monthly magazine for every ten Americans; in 1905, three copies for every four Americans— an increase of more than sevenfold. As for the rest of popular culture—the carnival of theater, opera, public lecture, and other live performance—its major constraint was not literacy but cost. The declining price of commercial entertainment was crucial. Sociologist Richard Butsch has calculated that in the United States of the late 1860s, about 36 million theater tickets were sold annually (about one ticket per capita, but in a population 75 percent of which was rural, and where, as Butsch writes, "the five largest markets, New York City, Boston, Philadelphia, Chicago, and San Francisco, accounted for more than half the total national box office receipts"). Compare this with the 4 billion tickets sold per year at the peak of moviegoing in the late 1940s (about twenty-seven tickets per person, roughly one purchase every two weeks). Compare that, in turn, with the nightly TV audience at any given moment of 102.5 million people age two and up, or almost 40 percent of the U.S. population, in the year 2001.

Cost-cutting goes a long way to explain this transformation. According to Butsch's computations, the costs of the *cheapest* tickets for the most popular types of performance at various times were as follows (with an update):

	Cost for laborer at proportion of daily wage
18th century (theater)	More than a full day's wage
Early 19th century (theater)	1/3
1840s-50s (minstrel show)	A little less than 1/3 (25 cents)
1870 (minstrel, variety shows)	1/6 (still 25 cents)
1880s (melodrama, vaudeville)	1/13 (10 cents)
1910 (nickelodeon)	1/40 (5 cents)
1920 (movie theater)	Less than 1/40 (10 cents)
1960s (television)	1/360 (amortizing cost of $200 black-and-white set)
1998 (cable television)	1/100 (amortizing cost of $300 color set plus basic cable)

In other words, the cost of a day of television in the 1960s was 11 percent of the cost of a nickelodeon visit fifty years earlier, and a small fraction of 1 percent of the cost of a visit to a colonial theater. Since the 1960s, the cost of a television set alone declined further in relation to (stagnant) wages, but cable bumped up the cost of the whole package.

Obviously, more popular culture can circulate partly because costs have come down precipitously. But declining cost turns out to be a more complex affair than the crisp formula "cost declines, therefore usage increases" suggests. Declining cost, growing demand, and improved technology looped into one another. Costs came down in part because technology improved, but technology improved, in part, because demand grew, or could be anticipated to grow, something producers factored in when investing in new technologies and expanding their production lines. Demand is partly a function of price, but price is a function of desire as well as of technological possibilities and the amount of time available to potential consumers. Time unencumbered by work swelled. So did money to fill time with convenient amusements.

As a consequence of the cost-demand-technology loop, popular culture is no longer a matter of the Bible and Shakespeare at home, a play once a year, or a movie every two weeks, supplemented by a magazine and a newspaper. The scale of availability has multiplied a hundredfold. An experience once reserved for exceptional occasions has become an everyday matter as continuous as—or more continuous than—one likes. But more time and lower cost are not sufficient to explain why people today spend roughly half their waking hours around and among these manufactured presences. A hunger has become part of us. Just as we gravitate toward food even when we're full or mealtimes are still far off, we're drawn toward the screen or the speaker not only when it is right over there in the living room and we have time on our hands but when we are with children, mates, coworkers, friends, lovers, and strangers, or the screen is in another room. The culture of unlimited media takes up a place in our imagination. Its language and gestures become ours, even when smuggled into our own conversation within quotation marks ("Hel*lo*?" "Dyn-o-mite!" "Just do it!"). A bizarre event reminds us of the uncanny 1950s series *The Twilight Zone*, whereupon the *dee*-dee-*dee*-dah theme will pop into the mind. We choose among our cultural furnishings but unless ensconced in a cave deep in some remote canyon, we do not choose whether to choose any more than a young man growing up in a hunter-gatherer culture chooses to hunt, or a woman to gather. These are the ways of our tribe.

DISTRACTIONS, DRUGS, AND FETISHES

The urge to grasp the totality of the media has been with us even longer than most modem media. During the centuries when popular culture had not yet grown torrential, many critics already nonetheless argued that images and performances diverted people from more constructive pursuits. Many pointed accusing fingers at the sirens of "distraction," the better to convince people to plug their ears. Some thought popular culture a distraction from a piety that ought to have been directed toward God or Church. Some saw popular culture as a pacifying circus that offered the masses some psychic compensation for their sufferings without detracting from the authorities' power. Even defenders of today's media barrage generally agree that it amounts to distraction from the burdens of industrialized life— though, unlike the critics, they celebrate it precisely for that reason, as a valuable, even a necessary remedy. Distraction cannot by itself account for the unlimited flow of today's media. But the concept deserves some exploration.

Distraction is one of those terms—like *freedom, responsibility,* and *alienation*—that requires an object to make sense. The question is, distraction from what? Mortality? God? Pain? Subjugation? Changing the world? More than one, or all, of the above? (The German Marxist critic Siegfried Kracauer, for instance, suggested in 1930: "The flight of images is the flight from revolution and death.") Your answer to the question *Distraction from what?* reveals what you value.

Distraction from mortality and distraction from God are the historical starting points for this line of thought. The Old Testament God condemned "graven images." St. Paul and St. Augustine added their own supplementary condemnations. But Blaise Pascal, the French mathematician and Augustinian devotee, was the most pungent distraction critic of early modem times. In his *Pensées* of 1657-58, Pascal declared that gambling, hunting, and womanizing were but feeble—and ultimately futile—efforts to divert ourselves from the inescapable fact of human mortality. "The only thing which consoles us for our miseries is diversion, and yet this is the greatest of our miseries." For diversion was habit-forming. Seeking excitement, we might foolishly imagine that "the possession of the objects of (our) quest would make [us] really happy," and thereby miss the only possible path to salvation—Christian devotion.

The religious strand of suspicion continues to this day. Pentacostalists disapprove of dancing, and other fundamentalists deplore televised sex. Partisans of various creeds despise "degenerate art." But over the last century and a half, secular critique and analysis have come to the fore. During the heyday of social theory, the period between 1848 and 1918 when industry, cities, bureaucracies, commerce, nationalism and empire were booming, the media flow was, by today's standards, only a rivulet. Nonetheless, some of the great social thinkers of Europe and the United States explored and tried to explain the nature of modern diversion. The founders of sociology elaborated concepts that help us understand the origins of our way of life and of the vast machinery society has devised to feed our equally vast appetite for wish fulfillment. Karl Marx called this way of life capitalism; Max Weber, rationalization; Georg Simmel, the least known but for our purposes the most helpful, intellectualism.

Marx died in 1883, four years before the first gramophone patent and twelve years before the first motion picture. Never having heard recorded music or gone to the movies, he still understood that capitalism required popular distraction. The great upender of the nineteenth century, Marx in 1843 turned Pascal on his head. For this militant atheist, religion was not what diversion diverted *from*; it was diversion itself. As the Bolivian peasant chewed coca leaves to overcome the exhaustion of a wretched life, so did the worker in a capitalist society turn to religion as "the sigh of the oppressed creature, the sentiment of a heartless world, the soul of soulless conditions. It is the *opium* of the people...the *illusory* happiness of men." Religion was mass distraction, the result of imagining man's own powers projected beyond himself into God. But according to Marx, the objects that human beings produced for the market also acquired a magical—indeed, an illusory and distracting—aspect. They became, in a sense, religious artifacts.

By 1867, in *Capital*, Marx had come to identify a new form of popular irrationality that he called "the fetishism of commodities." Commodities, he wrote, were "transcendent," "mystical," "mysterious," and "fantastic" in that they acquired value not inherent in their physical nature. Through the mysteries or the market, people assigned value to goods that they could live without. But Marx did not anticipate that capitalism, thanks to its ongoing productive success, would serve up such an abundance of transcendent mysteries with which people could compensate themselves for their sacrifices. Marx was transfixed by production, not consumption. For him, workers were wage slaves barely able to dream or becoming distracted consumers. They were condemned to growing impoverishment, not declining hours of work and increasing amounts of disposable income. He did not anticipate that the magic loaded into commodities at the production end might rub off on people at the consumption end—so much so as to create a new, enveloping way of life brimming with satisfactions.

Obsessed by the exploitative nature of production, Marx tended to think of consumption strictly as an auxiliary process that accomplished two purposes: it circulated goods and replenished the laborer's powers. It was not a fundamental, useful human act. He missed the way in which commodities didn't just "confront" people with "alien" powers in an externalized face-off but entered into people, "spoke" to them, linked them to one another, cultivated their satisfactions, and in certain ways satisfied them. As an image or sound enters the mind, one may feel oneself, at least for a moment, going to meet it, welcoming it, even melting into it—overcoming confrontation with gratification. For Marx, such satisfaction was only a distraction from the "real conditions of life." But what are those "real conditions"?

Marx was right chat markers work mysteriously, that there is magic in the way a compact disc, say, comes to be "worth" two hours of a janitor's labor or the same as a six-pack of premium beer. An act of culture produces this equation. But he underestimated the amount of magic in the world. What is going on when I walk into a music store and hold a CD in my hand? I approach not only a shiny metallic object in a plastic case whose manufacturing costs are a few cents but an aura of pleasure and a trail of resonance derived perhaps from the reputation of the band whose music it contains or from my experience of having heard a song at a party, on the radio, or downloaded onto my computer. The object of advertising is to intensify this resonance and link it with my own good feelings past and prospective. My armchair, in this sense, "produces" not only the sensation against my back and backside but a sense of comfort I may associate with my childhood. Nike sneakers produce not only a certain spongy sensation against my soles but (at least until I get into the gym) my dream of soaring like Michael Jordan.

When my friends and I shoot baskets, we aren't just compensating ourselves for what the alienation of labor has cost us; we are also forming a social relation for the purpose of play. We invest in the game some of our human powers. Why isn't our game just as real as our labor? For that matter, why isn't watching a game on TV as real and central as the labors we perform on the job?

Marx, imprisoned in the utilitarian attitude he condemned, was in this respect not radical enough. He didn't take seriously the fact that we were all children once, and all children play. They simulate and observe others simulating. Children are fascinated by mirrors and grow up impressed by games of cognition and recognition, cartoonish representations, performances in masks and disguises. Developmental psychologists point out that play has utility, increasing competencies, offering lessons in how to win and lose—but play is also gratuitous. People play "for fun," because it pleases them. Adults surrender much, but never all, of their playfulness. They do not simply put away childish things. Things promise pleasure—and not only things bought and kept for oneself. Gifts, too, are expressions of feeling, of affection, or love, or duty. Things are more than things; they are containers for love and self-love.

CALCULATION AND FEELING

In conventional usage, the media deliver an information flow. The term *information* goes with thought, cognition, knowledge. It sounds as hard (and objective and masculine) as *emotion* sounds soft (and subjective and feminine). Many commentators today think of the mind as an "information processor"; business likes to talk about IT, information technology. But what if we tease apart the notion of information? We see into our current situation more deeply if we consider information as something that happens within a human setting, something that people approach, seek, develop, employ, avoid, circulate, and resist. We do live in an "information society," but no less, if less famously, it is *a society of feeling and sensation,* toward the furtherance of which information is sometimes useful.

Marx starts with people required to live by their labor; the key modern social institution is the factory. In the standard sequence of sociological founding fathers, Marx's great successor is Max Weber (1864–1920), for whom people are required to live in power relations, and moderns, in particular, are under severe pressure to "rationalize" their social relations—to give reasons for their conduct, to think instrumentally, to calculate means toward ends. They, we, must surrender to abstract "rational-legal" rules installed by unforgiving bureaucracies. We may protest by seeking leaders tinged with grace, gifted with what Weber called "charisma," but charisma too becomes routinized in the end, and we are doomed to enclosure in the "iron cage" of modern rationality. It's easy enough to imagine why Weber's disenchanted moderns would turn to entertainment for relief, a sort of reenchantment, even though Weber did not take up the subject in particular.

For a deeper understanding of the wellsprings of the all-engulfing spectacle, we must turn to Weber's German-Jewish contemporary Georg Simmel (1858-1918), the first great modem analyst of what we take today as everyday experience. Simmel though the decisive force in people's lives is "the power and the rhythm of emotions." Desire precedes rationality, chronologically in the life of the individual but also logically, in the evolution of human conduct and institutions. The human condition begins with dependencies that are emotional (the need for love and support) as well as physical (the need for nourishment and warmth). "For man, who is always striving, never satisfied, always becoming, love is the true human condition." From the moment of birth, to live is to be and feel connected. Our cognitive and intellectual faculties rest upon foundations of feeling. The emotional linkages of childhood persist and develop in ways that make all social relations finally emotional relations, compounded of desires, satisfactions, frustrations, attachments, and antagonisms.

For Simmel, the framework in which man strives for love and connection is not so much, as with Marx, capitalist production but the money economy. "Man is a 'purposive' animal," Simmel writes. He develops goals and exercises his will to attain them through making and using tools, and increasingly through money, a means that develops psychologically into an end. People treat other people, as well as things, in a utilitarian fashion, and money is "the most extreme example of a means becoming an end." People now organize their lives to make money. They think calculatingly and categorically. They abstract calculation from sentiment. They develop the mental faculties to "size up" people, things, and situations reliably and quickly. Thus (and perhaps Simmel exaggerates the point) "money is responsible for impersonal relations between people."

The metropolis, Simmel maintains, is the most concentrated locale of the money economy, and it is here, above all, that mental life becomes "essentially intellectualistic." In the epochal movement of humanity from the village to the city, emotions were sidelined. The residents of populous cities like Berlin and Strasbourg, where Simmel lived, were required to tame their passions in favor of "calculating exactness" as a style of life. What will your trade be? For whom will you work and whom will you hire? What will you buy, where will you sell, and at what prices? Of whom will you make use? All-consuming, incessant calculation, in turn, required defenses against the assault and battery of a life in which everyone was judged according to whether he or she appeared usable, and people routinely, casually treated both persons and things with formality and "an unrelenting hardness."

Moreover, money "reduces the highest as well as the lowest values equally" to a single standard, putting them "on the same level." Money, therefore, is a school for cynicism. (In our own time, the standard of monetary worth gives us expressions like "She's a dime a dozen," "He's a loser," "You get what you pay for," and "I feel like a million bucks.") Moreover, besieged by the variety of strangers and things, people frantically categorize, cultivating an "intellectualistic quality...a protection of the inner life against the domination of the metropolis." The modern city dweller must acquire "a relentless matter-of-factness," a "blasé outlook," a kind of "reserve with its overtone of concealed aversion." The German and French languages share a word to express this sort of cultivated indifference: in German, *egal*, in French, égal. They mean "equal," but with a shrug or a somewhat depressed implication not found in English: "It doesn't matter"; "I don't care"; "It's all the same to me" (in French, expressed in the all-purpose phrase "ça *m'est* égal»).

For Simmel, "cynicism and a blasé attitude" are the direct results of "the reduction of the concrete values of life to the mediating value of money." Within the metropolis, there are special "nurseries of cynicism...places with huge turnovers," like stock exchanges, where money constantly changes hands. "The more money becomes the sole center of interest," Simmel writes, "the more one discovers that honor and conviction, talent and virtue, beauty and salvation of the soul, are exchanged against money, and so the more a mocking and frivolous attitude will develop in relation to these higher values that are for sale for the same kind of value as groceries, and that also command a 'market price.'" Cynicism is the subjective expression of a marketplace for values.

Cynicism can be enlivening, offering a momentary lift, a superior knowingness, but its dark side emerges in dismissals like "show me something I haven't seen," "been there, done that," and *so* over." At an extreme, as Simmel writes, the blasé person "has completely lost the feeling for value differences. He experiences all things as being of an equally dull and grey hue, as not worth getting excited about." Simmel is writing in 1900, before the media torrent, but he anticipates our world with his startling observation that the growth of the blasé attitude produces a paradoxical result—a culture of sensation. The cynic is content with his inner state, but the blasé person is not. Hence the latter's craving "for excitement, for extreme impressions, for the greatest speed in its change." Satisfying that craving may bring relief, but only temporarily. The more excitements, the worse. "The modern preference for 'stimulation' as such in impressions, relations and information" follows, in other words, Simmel maintains, from "the increasingly blasé attitude through which natural excitement increasingly disappears. This search for stimuli originates in the money economy with the fading of all specific values into a mere mediating value. We have here one of those interesting cases in which the disease determines its own form of the cure."

So emerges the modern individual, a role player who is also a part-time adventurer and stimulus seeker, trying frenetically to find himself by abandoning himself. This paradoxical individual is primed for unlimited media.

The money economy is not the only source of impersonal social relations. Our ordinary encounters with large numbers of unfamiliar people also drive us to calculate each other's usefulness. The members of traditional or primitive economies were dependent on small numbers of people. Modern man, Simmel argues, has many more needs. "Not only is the extent of our needs considerably wider," he writes, "but even the elementary necessities that we have in common with all other human beings (food, clothing and shelter) can be satisfied only with the help of a much more complex organization and many more hands. Not only does specialization of our activities itself require an infinitely extended range of other producers with whom we exchange products," but many of our actions require increasing amounts "of preparatory work, additional help and semi-finished products." Once upon a time, we knew the people we met at the market by name and face. "In contrast, consider how many 'delivery men' alone we are dependent upon in a money economy!" As they are functionally indistinguishable, so are they interchangeable. "We grow indifferent to them in their particularity."

Simmel is writing at the dawn of the twentieth century. Already, the calculating individual has split into parts corresponding to distinct roles (worker, parent, shopper), and he experiences most other people in equally stylized roles (coworker, shopkeeper, boss). Under the sway of calculating individualism, people must mask themselves in their roles—must appear *as* their roles—in order to be recognized by others. Yet the role never seeps into all of a person's interior crevices. The mask never melts utterly into the face. Instead, we live elaborate inner lives—which, ironically, we crave all the more intensely because of the constraints under which we operate in our outer lives. We *play* roles but *are not* the roles. Some part of us is always backstage.

For Simmel, the real person, hovering behind the strutting and fretting of everyday metropolitan life, is the one who feels. Feeling is the way a person gets personal. This obvious principle, he believes, has been disguised by "rationalistic platitudes that are entirely unpsychological." Foremost among these historic misunderstandings is that of Descartes, who, starting his chain of reasoning with reasons, proceeds, reason by reason, to the famous conclusion that he exists because he thinks.

Here, then, is the grand paradox that Simmel's thinking leads to: a society of calculation is inhabited by people who need to feel to distract themselves from precisely the rational discipline on which their practical lives rely. The calculation and reserve demanded by the money economy stimulate, by way of compensation, emotional needs and a craving for excitement and sensation. Thus does the upsurge of marketplace thinking in the eighteenth century call up its opposite, romanticism, which urges us to heed the inner voice of feeling. Real life takes place in *deep* feeling, *authentic* feeling, feeling that must be protected from social impositions, feeling that was born free and longs to go native. The idea spreads that the individual is, above all, his or her feelings.

Feeling too vigorously expressed, however, presents a management problem. Feeling too much, or expressing it too freely, would interfere with work and duty. (You do not want to give in to grief or, having fallen in love, go about walking on air while running a lathe or balancing the books.) Romanticism must be domesticated, made to fit into the niches of life. Emotions must be contained, reserved for convenient times when they may be expressed without risk to workaday life. Emotions must refresh, not drain or disrupt. They must be disposable and, if not free, at least low-cost. We are on our way here into the society of nonstop popular culture that induces limited-liability feelings on demand—feelings that do not bind and sensations that feel like, and pass for, feelings. A society consecrated to self-interest ends up placing a premium on finding life *interesting*.

What I am arguing, following Simmel, is not that human beings suddenly began to feel, but that, in recent centuries, they came to experience, and crave, particular kinds of feelings—disposable ones. It seems that, in much of the West in the seventeenth century and accelerating thereafter, feelings became associated ever more closely with the sense of an internal, subjective life set apart from the external world. By the end of the eighteenth century, the English language was teeming with new terms to describe feelings felt to be happening *in here*, within the person. During the seventeenth and eighteenth centuries, as philologist Owen Barfield pointed out, terms like *apathy, chagrin, diffidence, ennui*, and *homesickness* emerged, along with the phrase *the feelings*, while other terms for mental states, such as *agitation, constraint, disappointment, embarrassment*, and *excitement*, were relocated from the outer to the inner world. To these nouns for states of feeling were added adjectives that describe external phenomena "purely by the *effects* which they produce on human beings." Barfield's examples include *affecting, amusing, boring, charming, diverting, entertaining, enthralling, entrancing, exciting, fascinating, interesting*, and *pathetic* in its modern sense. As Barfield put it: "When a Roman spoke of events as *auspicious* or *sinister*, or when some natural object was said in the Middle Ages to be *baleful*, or *benign*, or *malign*...the activity was felt to emanate from the object itself. When we speak or an object or an event as *amusing*, on the contrary, we know that the process indicated by the word *amuse* takes place within ourselves."

So modernity, the age of calculation, produced a culture devoted to sentiment. Increasingly, the self-fashioning man or woman needed instructions in what to feel and how to express it. Philosophers wrote of "moral sentiments," sympathy foremost among them. Novels, indulging the taste for private feeling, were schools for sentiment. So were popular eighteenth-century British manuals advocating the arts of impression management. Feeling was plentiful but had to be disguised in public, lest (for example) laughing aloud damage one's ability to produce calculated impressions, or excessive enthusiasm jeopardize a woman's ability to protect herself. Middle-class strivers wished to cultivate self-control to improve their social standing and marriageability. Lord Chesterfield's volume of letters to his son on the arts of self-management, published posthumously in 1775, was a best-seller not only in England but in America. Novels conveyed not only advice about what to feel but the direct experience of feelings themselves: sympathy, surprise, recognition, satisfaction, pity, dread, and suspense; along with aesthetic pleasures in phrasing, wit, poignancy, and so on. One read, in other words, in order to feel.

By the nineteenth century, some of the main contours of present-day popular culture were evident. Entertainments like the novel filtered down from the middle class to the popular majority. It was in the United States, where the money economy and democracy developed together, that Simmel's observations about calculation and feeling prove most apropos. Usable, everyday distraction required surges of feeling and high-intensity stimuli that would be generally accessible but at the same time transitory. By the early 1830s, when Alexis de Tocqueville visited the United States—long before Times Square or Hollywood, before vaudeville or Al Jolson, Michael Jackson or Arnold Schwarzenegger, *USA Today* or the Internet—American culture was already sensational, emotional, melodramatic, and informal. Long before the remote control device, call waiting, cruise control, the car radio scan option, or the Apple mouse, before electricity, let alone the humble on-off switch, the United States was consecrated to comfort and convenience. Tocqueville accordingly wrote: "Democratic nations cultivate the arts that serve to render life easy in preference to those whose object is to adorn it." Artists in aristocratic societies perfected their craft while following established traditions, but in democracies, "What is generally sought in the productions of mind is easy pleasure and information without labor." What results, he added, are "many imperfect commodities" that "substitute the representation of motion and sensation for that of sentiment and thought....Style will frequently be fantastic, incorrect, overburdened, and loose, almost always vehement and bold. Authors will aim at rapidity of execution more than at perfection of detail. . . . There will be more wit than erudition, more imagination than profundity....The object of authors will be to astonish rather than to please, and to stir the passions more than to charm the taste."

Amusements encourage people to feel in a heightened way, to revel in familiar feelings, but also to experiment with unaccustomed ones in order to feel like somebody else without risk. The efficient production of sentiment—this has long been the essence of democratic artistry. Popular artists have the knack. Lesser ones test the waters and try to catch the wave of the moment. All of them do market research, listening for laughs and cries, looking into their audience as if into a mirror while working out their next steps. Groucho Marx wrote of his famous scoot: "I was just kidding around one day and started to walk funny. The audience liked it, so I kept it in. I would try a line and leave it in too if it got a laugh. If it didn't, I'd take it out and put in another. Pretty soon I had a character." Later, fearful that making movies insulated in a Hollywood studio had cost them their knack, the Marx brothers took a theatrical version of *A Day at the Races* out on the road. According to their publicist, Groucho's classic line "That's the most nauseating proposition I ever had" came after he had tried out *obnoxious, revolting, disgusting, offensive, repulsive, disagreeable,* and *distasteful.* "The last two of these words never got more than titters," according to the publicist. "The others elicited various degrees of ha-has. But *nauseating* drew roars. I asked Groucho why that was so. 'I don't know. I really don't care. I only know the audiences told us it was funny.'"

Tocqueville's traditional artist would have been able to say exactly why he did what he did—it was what his masters did. He belonged to a guild. His inspiration blew in from the past, not from the crowd before him. Tocqueville's democratic artist, by contrast, transmuted the popular hunger for feeling into a living manual for artwork. Cultural industries would mass-produce the results, and from a multitude of such products generate a popular culture that, given money enough and time, would come to suffuse everyday life. Thus is there a continuous upsurge from the ever-larger printings of ever more novels in the eighteenth century, to the penny press, circuses, minstrel and Wild West shows in the nineteenth, through to the Viacoms, Disneys, NBCs, and SONYS of today.

THE RISE OF THE PANOPLY

The consumption of images and sounds was an extension of the burgeoning consumption of goods. In modem society, according to Georg Simmel, a sensitive person (one senses he is describing himself) "will be overpowered and feel disorientated" by the immense spectacle of commodities. But indeed "precisely this wealth and colorfulness of over-hastened impressions is appropriate to overexcited and exhausted nerves' need for stimulation. It seems as if the modern person wishes to compensate for the one-sidedness and uniformity of what he produces within the division of labor by the increasing crowding together of heterogeneous impressions, by the increasingly hasty and colourful change in emotions."

In other words, notes Simmel's contemporary interpreter, sociologist David Frisby, "the tedium of the production process is compensated for by the artificial stimulation and amusement of consumption." One must add, since Simmel was preoccupied with the lives of men, that women at home were far less likely to be subjected to "the tedium of... production," but they had their own tedium to contend with.

Although present for the development of the motion picture, Simmel did not write much about images as such, except in the form of fashion, which he brilliantly understood as a declaration of both individuality and class distinction, of freedom and membership at one and the same time. Writing in 1904, he described fashion as a means "to combine...the tendency toward social equalization [i.e., *I look like selected others*] with the desire for individual differentiation and change [i.e., *I present to the world my unique self*]." A century ago, Simmel already grasped that fashion seized popular consciousness partly because "major, permanent, unquestioned convictions increasingly lose their force. In this way, the fleeting and changeable elements of life gain that much more free space. The break with the past...increasingly concentrates consciousness upon the present. This emphasis upon the present is clearly, at the same time, an emphasis upon change."

University trendhoppers have let themselves be convinced by French philosopher-historian Michel Foucault, with his brilliantly paranoid imagination, that the defining institution of the European nineteenth century was the Panopticon, a never-built prison designed by Jeremy Bentham in order to impose total surveillance on every waking and sleeping moment of a prisoner's life. But Simmel was more perceptive. The heart of modernity was not the Panopticon but the panoply of appearances that emerged in everyday life. He might have deployed this concept to look at the spectacle of images that already filled public spaces in the late nineteenth and early twentieth centuries: the posters and billboards conspicuously adorning the walls and vacant lots of great cities, the imagistic advertisements, the shop windows with their mannequins, the fabulous electrified signs and department store displays, the multiple sources of light and shades of color, the halftones and lithographs swarming through newspapers and magazines, all meant to be quickly superseded by new, often gaudier and more elaborate versions. Not to mention the street noises of horses, wagons, cars, children playing, musicians, and hawkers all crowding into earshot with announcements of their existence, purpose, and worth.

This sensory uproar was by no means new. A century earlier, in 1805-6, William Wordsworth heard London's "thickening hubbub" and was struck, even shocked, by the sight and sound of "pleasure whirl[ing] about incessantly," by street shows and the city's display of images, which, while composed without "subtlest craft," helped overcome human "weakness":

> Here files of ballads dangle from dead walls;
>
> Advertisements, of giant-size, from high
>
> Press forward, in all colours....

Wordsworth was perhaps the first modern poet to react viscerally to the posting of sign upon sign, the clamoring profusion of

> those sights that ape
>
> The absolute presence of reality....
>
> ...imitations, fondly made in plain
>
> Confession of man's weakness and his loves.

By Simmel's time, the clamoring confusion of posters had become a commonplace. The street shows were in decline, but the city at night had become a spectacle unto itself, for the streets were now electrified with the lamps and signs, the bright displays that promised what Theodore Dreiser called "artificial fires of merriment, the rush of profit-seeking trade, and pleasure-selling amusements," all inspiring "the soul of the toiler" to declare, "'I shall soon be free....The theatre, the halls, the parties, the ways of rest and the paths of song—these are mine in the night.'"

This vivid commotion of illuminations, images, and sounds was, in today's e-business jargon, a "push technology." The images entered into your perceptual field whether you wanted them around or not—powered, in a sense, by your own legs. Traditional signs offered useful information (repair your shoes here, buy your pork there), but the gaudier, more colossal electric displays heightened the sensational impact without adding information. To come into contact with them, you did not have to be a flâneur, Charles Baudelaire's "passionate spectator," the strolling man-about-town freed from the burdens of routine, no slave to clocks, blessed with all the time in the world to devote to the spectacle of the city. Working women and men too welcomed their strolls through the alluring streets, coming upon transitory and fragmentary surprises. The cascading images incessantly invited people to feel sensations that might not be safe or convenient in the face of flesh-and-blood human beings, who might require reciprocal relationships. Unlike palpable human beings, images offered stimuli without making demands. Strangely impersonal, displayed indifferently for everyone who might cross their path, they required nothing much—a momentary notice, a whiff of mood, a passing fancy. They stimulated sensation hut required no commitment. Encountering the profusion of signs, each clamoring for attention amid the clutter of other signs, big-city dwellers learned to take for granted the gap between the present image (the cigarette with its smoke ring) and the absent, though intimated, reality (the pleasure of filled lungs).

Writers and artists were sometimes impressed, sometimes appalled by the new concentrations of dazzle, like New York's Times Square and the center of Paris, where neon lights were first put to large-scale use. The giddy illuminations of night life sometimes jarred intellectuals, who were prone to experience the panoramic spectacle, at least at times, as a loud, attention-seizing alternative to an idealized contemplative stillness. Critics of capitalist society saw the spectacle of neon, billboards, and night-lit monuments as tricky "compensations" for the burdens of exploitation—as Siegfried

Kracauer put it with romantic overkill, "façades of light...to banish the dread of the night....a flashing protest against the darkness of our existence, a protest of the thirst for life." Such critiques did not find much resonance in a bedazzled populace. The city's hearts of brightness were staggering crowd-pleasers.

The entrepreneurs who erected these thrilling displays certainly hoped to enchant those multitudes with delirious distractions. When the lights and marquees were lit, one editorial booster wrote in 1904, Broadway was "a continuous vaudeville that is worth many times the 'price of admission'—especially as no admission price is asked." O.J. Gude—an early "broker of commercial light" who first called Broadway "the Great White Way," invented the permanent signboard, and installed the first giant electric signs in Times Square—referred to his productions in 1912 as a "phantasmagoria of...lights and electric signs." In the same year, an advertising journal that took its name, *Signs of the Times*, with a certain ironic amusement, from millennial zealots, declared: "Electrical advertising is a *picture* medium. Moreover, it is a *color* medium; still, again, electrical advertising isa medium of motion, of action, *of life*, *of light*, of compulsory attraction."

It was indeed in hopes of "compulsory attraction" that entrepreneurs of the public spectacle in New York City erected such imposing displays as a forty-five-foot-long electric Heinz pickle at Madison Square in 1900 and an illuminated Roman chariot race seventy-two feet high and nine hundred feet wide on top of a Broadway hotel in 1910. But the hope that any installation would become a "compulsory attraction" was routinely disappointed. Amid a clutter of signs, each beckoning in its own electric way, a particular sign might stimulate a shiver of enchantment, a tickle of pleasure, or a recoil of annoyance or bewilderment—a little burst of feeling—followed by a fleeting afterglow before fading, leaving, if the advertiser was lucky, a fitful remembrance of feeling touched by a trace of an image. Once the sensation passed, however, the passerby would resume his passage through the city in a state of readiness—or blaséness.

At times, there were purposive collective spectacles, too: demonstrations, parades, and, in revolutionary times, riots, and the placards, leaflets, effigies, torches, papier-mâché figures that accompanied them. As much as time permitted, men and women asserted the right to set their mood and stepped out—to saloon, club, dance hall, arcade, circus, amusement park, burlesque house, nickelodeon, vaudeville show, or "legitimate" theater.

And the public panoply had its private equivalents. By the late nineteenth century, family photographs reposed on shelves, mantels, and pianos, and not only in the homes of the prosperous. As the family shrank to nuclear scale, photographs extended it in time and space, ushering absent members into the intimate world of the here and now—once more, with feeling. Homes turned into private shrines of visual icons. Magic became domestic; one composed one's own personal spectacle.

Increasingly there were also images from beyond the family circle, the descendants of the paintings, maps, prints, and engravings of Vermeer's Dutch burghers, alongside crosses and flags, depictions of the Messiah, saints, heroes, and ancestors. Augmenting these were the images and texts delivered to the house at regular intervals: the newspapers, magazines, catalogs, sheet (and later recorded) music, and books, their numbers rising throughout the nineteenth and twentieth centuries. If income permitted, one "took" a periodical, a regular and familiar package of image and text that one liked because one approved of its formula, trusting the packagers to deliver approximately the right look, thoughts, and feelings, approving their taste, sharing their interests and curiosities, and through their formulas gaining low-risk access to a bountiful world. As during a walk down a familiar street, there might be surprises, too. Breaking with the imperatives of the time clock, one gambled—at low stakes. What would one find in this issue of the *Saturday Evening Post*? What adventure would beckon in this month's *National Geographic*? The novelty was finite; the material was new but not too new. The magazine would always be a limited liability experience. If it didn't pan out this month, one could await the next issue or subscribe to another publication with a more appealing package.

Newspapers and most magazines promised firm information, usable facts, and, at the most exalted level, knowledge, a state of comprehension. But the wonder of communications was that the carriers of information did not simply transmit faces or ideology. They occasioned a human experience—a sense of connection to the world. In a complex society, dispersed individuals had to be aware of what was going on outside their immediate milieux, in order to coordinate their activities. Thus they craved information. But this information was not pure; it arrived certified by celebrities, jostling with gossip, and, above all, accompanied by emotions. To learn what was going on elsewhere entailed some sort of mental excitement: the *wow!* of salaciousness, the *aha!* of mastery, the *click* of understanding, the *what?* of astonishment.

So not only were the factual media informative; they were diverting. The first mass newspapers, the penny press of the 1830s, as Neal Gabler has pointed out, had their origins in a working-class entertainment tradition that was already thriving.

> For a constituency being conditioned by trashy crime pamphlets, gory novels and overwrought melodramas, news was simply the most exciting, most entertaining content a paper could offer, especially when it was skewed, as it invariably was in the penny press, to the most sensational stories. In fact, one might even say that the masters of the penny press *invented* the concept of news because it was the best way to sell their papers in an entertainment environment.

Cultivating the human interest story, newspapers could be sensational yet newsy, realistic yet emotion-inspiring, vividly personal yet general in their import. They were diversions that didn't strictly divert. Or rather, they distracted readers from their immediate environs by refusing to distract them from some larger world. They cultivated curiosity, and curiosity corralled facts. Thanks to such means of delivery, the spirit of information rode high.

The money economy was accompanied by an all-embracing swirl of modernity: investments, capital flows, migrations, turnovers of taste, style, fashion, and opinion. What Simmel called "the modern soul that is so much more unstable" had a high psychic metabolism. Endlessly it regenerated boredom. "A faint sense of tension and vague longing," a "secret restlessness," a "helpless urgency" that "originates in the bustle and excitement of modern life"—all this, Simmel wrote, "impels us to search for momentary satisfaction in ever-new stimulations, sensations and external activities." Even at home, the dislodged soul needed constant replenishment, a ceaseless, streaming importation of content to play with, reflect upon, or learn from. A taste for the new ran deep, as did the economic payoff, for superficiality, replaceability, and the itch to keep up with the Joneses were good for production.

Excitements and analgesics multiplied. Modern people, led by Americans, came to expect the comfort and convenience of home access. The standard array of sensation machines grew. What could

146

more reliably cater to the volatile spirit, delivering riffs and squirts of emotion, instructions, and pleasures? New communication technologies spurred hungers by provisionally satisfying them, but as Marx had anticipated, no sooner had old needs been satisfied than new ones opened up. Entrepreneurs continually searched for the next household delivery system to feed unappeasable hungers.

For brevity's sake, I am compressing a tangled history, downplaying national differences, and exaggerating the uniformity of a process that proceeded—is still proceeding—in fits and starts. Still, the main direction has been clear enough. After newspapers and magazine came commercial radio. As costs fell, technologies that had at first been the province of the rich drifted into the middle class and then, within surprisingly few years, crossed over to the majority. With television and its auxiliaries, what had been an exclusive right to luxuriate passed into a general right to connect—and with cable, the right to connect to a channel of your own liking, the majority be damned.

The thirst for images, for music, for reverberations from the world of public affairs could be satisfied as fast as mail could be delivered and vacuum tubes warmed up. But availability did not quench the thirst for images and sounds. To the contrary: the more technologies, the more images and sounds they could carry, the greater the thirst—and the desire to please one's private self. Boredom was a crime against plenitude. Who could say, "Stop, I have enough"? Technology came to the aid of fragmented tastes. Media conglomerates spun out multiple channels for distinct demographic niches. Why not establish your own mood, create your personalized top ten from the ever-expanding menu of entertainment and information that flows through the living room? Why stop at the living room? Why not pipe the bounty into the bedroom? Yet always there is the threat of tedium and the persistent shrug. A century after Georg Simmel wrote about "nurseries of cynicism," we find them in the household, where the bountiful screen offers access indiscriminately to an episode of fictional domestic anguish, a tennis match, a sports utility vehicle driving over a mountain, a soccer score, a salad preparation, an animal cartoon, a futurist dystopia, a murder headline, a joke, a poker-faced policeman, a nude, a hurricane victim shivering in the cold, a jewelry advertisement...

In George Orwell's classic *1984*, Big Brother was the ultimate coercive broadcaster, the sole controller of propaganda. But Big Brother had no chance against niche media and personal choice. In the West, at least, he was no more than a hollow bogeyman. In the widening torrent available to all-consuming humanity, you rode your own current. Why not revel in the pursuit of such happiness? Why fear engulfment?

NOMADICITY

Increasingly, you could carry your private current anywhere. The home entertainment center was, after all, a luxury for which you had to confine yourself. Images and manufactured sounds came home but you had to be home to greet them. So why not render your private amusements portable? Why not, like Pascal's well-served if pitiable monarch, have it all wherever and whenever you like?

Self-sufficiency, that most tempting and expansive of modern motifs, feels like a sort of liberation—until it becomes banal and we have need of the next liberation. People gravitate toward portability and miniaturization—each a kind of freedom—in everyday life. The mountaineer's backpack evolved into the hippie traveler's aluminum-framed pack, which in turn evolved into the contemporary frameless version, which in turn gave rise to the utilitarian but waistline-disturbing fanny pack, the bulky monster sticking out horizontally, and the trim designer variety that is, in effect, a purse that leaves the hands free. Portable nourishment is another sign of the nomadic thrust toward self-sufficiency: the Hershey bar (1894), the ice-cream cone (1904), Life Savers (1913), trail mix (1970s), the portable water bottle (1990s). The tendency has been toward performing as many functions as possible in the course of one's movements—"multitasking"—so that as we move, new accessories become mandatory. The indented tray inside the glove compartment and the cup holder next to the front seat have become standard equipment.

Not only must material provisions be available on demand; so must sustenance for the senses, not least the ears. After the portable battery-powered radio, the car radio, and the transistorized radio, the logic of individualism pointed toward that exemplary little machine for musical transport, Sony's Walkman. The theme is well enunciated in a London billboard of 2001 that does not even bother to indicate any particular product: "Give today a soundtrack."

The Walkman story shows how the convenience of a single powerful man could generate a marketing triumph. Before a transoceanic flight in 1979, Sony chairman Masaru Ibuka asked company engineers to create a stereo music player so he could hear classical favorites of his choice. Airlines already provided passengers with earphones and canned musical loops, but Ibuka did not want anyone overriding his personal taste, so Sony engineers connected headphones to an advanced tape recorder for him. Ibuka was delighted with the results, and his partner Akio Morita realized that this jury-rigged contraption might have sales potential among teenagers, who were already accustomed to carrying portable radios. The Walkman was born. What had begun as a toy for Ibuka was promptly sold to consumers less accustomed to indulging their personal whims. Supply proceeded to trigger demand. By the end of 1998, without much advertising, Sony had sold almost 250 million Walkmen worldwide, not to mention the Discmen and all the specialized spinoff players for joggers, swimmers, and skiers.

Throughout the twentieth century, supply and demand looped together in an unceasing Möbius strip, technology always increasing the radius of contact: the pay phone, car radio, battery-powered radio, transistor radio, remote-accessible answering machine, fax machine, car phone, laptop computer, Walkman, airplane and train phone, portable CD player, beeper, mobile phone, Palm Pilot, Internet access, PCD, GPD, and so on ad acronym. Once "interactivity" by machine became feasible, the hallmark of so many communication inventions was *nomadicity*, which, according to the Internet pioneer who coined the term, "means that wherever and whenever we move around, the underlying system always knows who we are, where we are, and what services we need." Actually, not *we* so much as *I*, for more and more often the contemporary nomad travels alone, detribalized—or rather, in the company of that curious modern tribe each of whose members seeks to travel alone while being technologically connected to others. Equipped for accessibility, he may encroach upon the right of others to control their own private space: the battery-powered boom box blaring music or narrating a ball game (even the one taking place before one's eyes in the stadium itself); the cell phone trilling during the play or the concert; the caller shouting into his phone on the train, in the restaurant, at the park, or on the street.

Charles Baudlelaire once lamented: "They left one right out of the Declaration of the Rights of Man and Citizen: the right to leave." Now, for hours each day, the right to leave is secure, though doubtless not in the way Baudelaire had in mind. In fact, the right to leave has merged with the right to be *somewhere else.* For a growing proportion of the population, and for a growing number of hours per day, you can, after a fashion, break the limits of space, choosing from your private menu of activities, amusements, and contacts. You are not exactly alone, because you are with others, their music, their games, their voices. Commuting or washing the floors, you are a movable node, never wholly abandoned. Even in extremis—but who could have imagined such extremity?—your voice can reach out to a loved one from the inferno of the World Trade Center about to collapse or the cabin of a hijacked plane. The horrific emergencies of September 11, 2001, put to extraordinary ends what have become the ordinary means to overcome distance.

How shall we understand the appeal of these ordinary means? Consider the humdrum experience of waiting for a bus, which Jean-Paul Sartre took as a metaphor for modern alienation. Sartre called this ordinary condition serialization, by which he meant losing one's individuality and being reduced to a function—waiting. The immobilized man on line cannot pursue his own ends because he has lost control of his time in favor of the bus company's schedule, the pileup of fellow travelers, the traffic that has delayed the bus. He is the creature of a routine that demands self-suppression. Now imagine this man on line equipped with a personal stereo. His ears project him, at least partially, elsewhere—or rather, elsewhere enters him, corporeal, immediate, intimate. He stands in the line but leaves it behind for a chosen communion. He blocks out unwanted contact. Now he is, paradoxically, an individual because he has company— music, familiar music at that. He feels little spurts of emotion. Music rubs up against him, gets inside him. He nods along with the beat. Against the pressures of work and environment—even against his own unpleasant obsessions—he has a compensation: he has enveloped himself in a sort of mobile bubble. He has—to quote from Walkmanned Londoners interviewed in one study—"shut everything out" and "squashed thoughts." The music, turned up loud enough to drown out ambient noise, "takes over his senses." "It's like living in a movie." Availing himself of "a life-support machine," he has taken charge of his mood.

Now imagine this man still in line or trapped in some other serialized reality—in an elevator, on the train, or stuck in a traffic jam—and equip him with escape implements in the form of today's proliferating mobile equipment: the cellular phone, the Game Boy, the personal communication system with text messaging and Internet access, feeding him sports scores and stock quotes, eventually cartoons, jokes, slot machines, card games, and pornographic images, asking him at all hours: "Where would you like to go?" Take charge of your mood! Possessing an "arsenal of mobile technology," he comes to feel that he has the right to them. He is, to some degree, shielded from urban fear.

Some admirers of our present-day electronic efflorescence are carried away with promises of the technological sublime. One recent enthusiast heralds *techgnosis*. But nomadic access raised to the level of gods and angels rings sublimely ridiculous. Usually, the very point of dot-communion is banality. Through the most mundane act of emailing about the weather or instant-messaging a "buddy" about nothing at all except that you're stuck in a boring lecture, or that you exist and affirm the other's existence ("Whassup?" "Not much"), or phoning your loved one from the air to report that your plane is late or from the street to report that you are just now emerging from the subway, you have, in a sense, spun off a filament of yourself to conduct your business, secure your network, greet your friend, discharge your duty, arrange your pleasure. Intellectuals may scoff, but it is the relatively trivial mercy that most people in a consumerist culture seek much of the time.

But the freedom to be even incidentally connected is not uncomplicated. It goes with being incidentally accessible, which amounts to being on call and interruptible everywhere by your boss, your nurse, your patient, your anxious parent, your client, your stockbroker, your baby-sitter, as well as your friend whose voice, even electronically, you welcome even if you have just seen each other face-to-face. Friendship makes intrusion welcome—perhaps that is part of its definition—and nomadicity, no question, is a boon to certain kinds of friendship. In a suburb where nothing seems to happen, *something* can happen—again and again. You can send along jokes, photos, shopping recommendations, references smart and dumb. It was probably America Online's "buddy lists" for instant messaging that made that huge Internet portal so popular.

Wireless handheld devices with Internet access carry the instantaneous buddy principle out into public space. Having been launched in Japan with considerable success, they are galloping through the United States and Europe. Sony's mobile Internet device, no doubt to be called Webman, is set to go into American circulation shortly. "We believe that the mobile terminal will be a very...strategic product for Sony," the company's president, Kunitake Ando, told the *Asian Wall Street Journal.* "Just like we created a Walkman culture, we'll have a sort of mobile culture," he said, adding that sooner or later Sony was planning to pipe on-line music and even movies through a new generation of mobile phones. Such prognostications may be hype, but Sony's have a way of turning out accurate.

At this writing, though, the principle of instantaneous access is most firmly at work with nomad-friendly mobile phones. In the year 2000, 53 percent of Americans owned mobile phones, up from 24 percent in 1995. So did 63 percent of British adults, about as many as in Japan though not so many as in Italy, Sweden, and Finland. Their diffusion rate is tremendous, comparable to television's, exceeding that of telephones, radios, and VCRs, and more visible in public, of course, than any of those.

The mobile phone radically transforms the soundscape. Like the servant's bell, its chime or ditty is a summons, but also a claim that you have the right to conduct your business willy-nilly wherever you are, whether you're a day-trader in New York or a Hong Kong youngster chatting away in a subway car (that city has wired its tunnels). Private practices open out into public spaces. So if the Webbed-up, wired, or wirelessed nomad rarely gets to relish full-bodied freedom, there is still the pleasure of knowing one is wanted *right now.*

The new technonomadicity comes with this paradox: the fully-equipped nomad, seeking freedom of access at will, becomes freely accessible to other people's wills. The sender also receives. The potential for being intruded upon spurs technological fixes; with caller ID, for example, you can block calls from old boyfriends, or screen calls to see who wants contact, or defer contact by dumping a call into voicemail. As in a military arms race, the dialectic of offense and defense ratchets up. There is a second paradox: those who hope to control their moods when they go out in public find themselves invaded by alien noises. In theaters, concerts, conferences, parks, and churches, the trill of the cell phone is not an angelic visitation. The commons explodes with private signals. Again, the defense also improves. Theaters announce, before the curtain goes up, that ringers should be turned off—with uneven success. Devices to block mobile phones are already being marketed to restaurants and theater owners.

So communication comes at a price—not just the monetary price, which falls year after year; nor just the invasion of solitude; no, the third inevitable price of nomadicity is surveillance. This is not just the risk of being overheard in a public place. After all, the mobile phoner who wishes to preserve privacy in the face of proximity can still do so, for the new devices amplify the lowered human voice with wondrous fidelity. But cellular conversations are peculiarly capable of being intercepted, not only by public agencies but by interested private parties, whether by accident or deliberately.

Still, the new nomad, intent on living out a dream of personal power, seems willing to pay the price. The omnicommunicative utopia appeals to a centuries-old passion to control one's circumstances without renouncing social bonds. This is the version of freedom that drives the civilization that American (but not only American) enterprise and power carry to the ends of the earth. It is an omnivorous freedom, freedom to behold, to seek distraction, to seek distraction *from* distraction (in T. S. Eliot's words), to enjoy one's rootlessness, to relish the evanescent. But as the Canadian songwriter Leonard Cohen once wrote, "Where do all these highways go now that we are free?"

SOUNDTRACKING

The new nomad may not have bargained on finding himself so frequently prey to interruption. Not only does his cell phone trill when he may not find it so welcome, but the common world is increasingly soundtracked. Whatever the rhetoric of networked individualism, individuals are not the only communicators in public. Institutions routinely use sound to orchestrate a collective mood, to "brand" space, exploiting the fact that we can choose not to see far more easily than we can choose not to hear. Looking away from a screen may be psychologically difficult, but it can be done: you crane your head or simply walk away. But the ear is less discriminating than the eye. Human beings lack earlids. Your head need not be cocked toward a sound source for the sound to command your attention.

Most of the soundscape is not summoned up by junior Nietzsches just as they like. It is administered. Now, imposed sound is not necessarily noxious. When the community at large caters the sound-surround, few people within earshot experience it as an imposition. Performers at fairs, on street corners or subway station platforms, festivals in public parks, brass bands in parades, street dances, even boom boxes on beaches or stoops—these arc, in varying degrees, fell to be "expressions of the community." Living in a heavily Appalachian neighborhood in Chicago in the mid-1960s, I could follow the same country-western song down the block as it wafted out of window after window, all the apartments tuned to the same radio station.

But increasingly, our desire for diversion is appropriated, packaged, and radiated back at us by an organization that has figured out how to dovetail our desire with its desire to profit from the pleasure principle. Access to the popular ear is purchased. The capacity to make oneself heard—in other words, the capacity to interrupt— becomes a dimension of social power. Mall shops and restaurants get to entertain—or exercise sonic power over—everyone within earshot. Moods have monetary value. Organizing moods is good business. And so, in Milan Kundera's words, "The acoustic image of ecstasy has become the everyday decor of our lassitude." Bathed in the "trivialized ecstasy" of public soundtracks, we are prompted to feel as the music commands us to feel.

Industry was the first institution to be soundtracked. In 1937, industrial psychologists in Great Britain proposed (in a report to the British Industrial Health Research Board titled *Fatigue and Boredom in Repetitive Work*) that music had charms to soothe the savage worker at his repetitive job when he might otherwise be absent, or going home early, or goofing off, or otherwise heeding an unorchestrated drummer. During World War II, the BBC heightened productivity in arms factories with radio programs like *Music While You Work*. Americans were not far behind, piping music into war plants and shipyards beginning in 1942. Mood management tested in war proved no less useful in peace. Convinced that the methods of sonic satisfaction had proved themselves, private industry began to avail itself of the output of the Muzak Corporation. "By 1946," according to communications scholars Simon C. Jones and Thomas G. Schumacher, "Muzak was installed in the workplaces of most major American firms, with separate programs for offices and factories." Muzak researchers went beyond the canning of comforting strains; they developed the principle of "stimulus progression," having found that a staged sequence of tunes, gradually boosting tempo, rhythm, and orchestra size on a scale from 1 ("slow and mellow") to 5 ("bright and upbeat"), boosted productivity. Psychological lifts could be scientifically programmed. However tedious the work, the music was smooth, for the original recordings had been cleansed of any lurches of rhythm or melody. This was domesticated music, laced with "a hint of nostalgia and fantasy but contained within a rational, orderly structure," its "stylistic regularity and harmonic simplicity" suggesting a "secure, private, domestic world that signifies the comfort and security of home." If you could not be coaxed to "whistle while you work," the sound system would do the whistling for you.

If music to work by, why not music to shop by or wait by? In the 1950s, the Muzak Corporation began to orchestrate for retail establishments, aiming to induce a buying mood. Muzak filled supermarkets with languorous rhythms, meant to relax shoppers and coax them into spending more time in the aisles. Other sequences built up the rhythms, the volume inching up, producing psychic tension—to be relieved by pulling something off the shelves. By the 1980s, scarcely a public space lacked a soundtrack: shops, malls, airports, airplanes, cruise ships, stadiums, hospitals, restaurants, doctors' and dentists' offices, gyms, banks, hotel lobbies, theme parks, elevators, bathrooms, waiting rooms of all kinds. An airliner now signaled arrival, contact with the mother-pod, by locking into its soundtrack. Airports spawned the musical subgenre of "ambient sound," known derisively as "elevator music," and half mocked, half indulged in the contemporary postmodernist manner by the droll Brian Eno in a series of records called "Music for Airports."

Meanwhile, shops catering to the young led a shift to so-called foreground music—sounds promoting an upbeat atmosphere in an age when electrified music is normal, and normally loud. Muzak and other corporations now bounce signals off extraterrestrial satellites to beam "storecasting" music to particular "consumption environments" for distinct demographic groups, even programmed for specific times of day. At clothing and restaurant chains, malls, and (of course) music stores catering to a youthful clientele, the sound pulsates loudest, often accompanied by music video screens. Even the network news has its theme songs, broadcasting a sense of urgency along with reliability. Restaurants that "skew" older, as the marketers say, are partial to the relaxed piano tinkles of the Windham Hill label, which are to the more rarefied palettes of upscale baby boomers what Mantovani's cloying strings were to their down-market aunts and uncles. But the auditory wraparound is not always popular with customers, let alone staff. A New York Pottery Barn employee tells me he winces at the pounding of the soundtrack operating nonstop in his department. Still, it must not be an automatic irritant that at many a metropolitan restaurant or bar catering to younger-thanforty clientele the acoustics are managed so as to amplify the roar and enforce the sense that this is where things are happening. (At the same time, *buzz* has become the commonplace term for public repute.) Meanwhile, other restaurants market themselves to the middle-aged by installing acoustic baffles, turning down the ambient sound to make conversation more discernible to ears that have lost acuity, the process often speeded a long by years of attending concerts in front of gigantic speakers. To every niche, a sound.

In Europe, as in the United States, wraparound sound has become a normal accompaniment to everyday life. The Beatles' "Let It Be" resounds from a Swissair flight. At a Thai restaurant in Berlin, the soundtrack features "Over the Rainbow." Evidently, many people prefer mood music, however unsubtle, to what would otherwise be their own private improvisations. At worst, they are indifferent. "Perhaps," as J. Bottum writes, "it was Hollywood that taught us to expect life to come with background music, a constant melodic commentary on the movie of our lives." The Muzak Corporation and its imitators are thoughtful enough to provide variety, so that it never seems that Big Brother or the Wizard of Noise is in charge. So, passing through the world, modem individuals hear a corporate-produced pastiche. We hear it, in Bottum's words, "in snippets, as we cross from one stereo zone to another—the radio suddenly blaring out as the car starts up, the jukebox suddenly cut off as the door to the diner closes....We've all been damned to a perpetual quarter-final round of *Name That Tune*."

Yet the private resists the public in this realm as well, fighting technology with technology. Wired, nomadic individuals play defense against institutional auditory control, drowning out the public soundtrack with their own Walkman or Discman, and while it would be silly to see them as heroes of a sonic class struggle, fighting back against the capitalist appropriation of the soundscape, the headphones surely do screen out unwelcome noise by substituting a personal soundtrack. In fact, they protect not only from Muzak and woofer-heavy hip-hop car stereos passing by but from miscellaneous motors, truck, bus, airplane, and motorcycle engines, honking horns, cracked mufflers, sirens, chain saws, and pneumatic drills—not to mention the steady drones, rumbles, whirrs, and hums emitted by fluorescent lights, refrigerators, heaters, computers, fans, air conditioners, microwave ovens, dial tones, and the rest of the apparatus of everyday electrified life. In an age of scattered urban din, the rhythmic pulsation of hip-hop may be, for its partisans, the loud intrusion that erases the minor rackets. The upbeat, tweeter-heavy, violin-drenched soundtrack may be electricity's shelter—against electricity itself.

PAYING, AND PAYING FOR, ATTENTION

A teenager in a Berkeley theater, chatting amiably with her friend during the movie, growls at a complaining patron: "What's the matter, man? It's only a movie!" At a multiplex in Greenwich Village, a woman on her cell phone during the trailer insists, "I want to see this movie just as much as you do!" No matter that theaters run "Please let us know if anything interferes with your enjoyment of this show" announcements along with the popcorn and soft drink promotions before the feature. In recent years, I've heard a baby cry at a classical concert (and the usher refuse to tell the mother to tend to her child outside). I've heard mobile phones go off in the middle of plays, though signs urge customers to turn off their phones, beepers, and other electronic equipment, and announcements to that effect are made. I've heard phones trill in seminar rooms, lecture halls, libraries and in the otherwise hushed galleries of museums. Public life is a place where private transactions go on—this is the assumption. Private life in public converges with public life in private. For growing numbers of people, the world is a multiplex, chock-full of electronics: an arcade of amusements.

It is easy to cast a rosy glow over the sacrosanctness of private space, yet even spaces that are literally sanctified are seldom places of unswerving attention. I once attended a Christmas Eve mass in Florence and, standing in the back, was startled to hear the fairly continuous rumble of Italians gossiping. During much of theatrical history, audiences have chatted, yelled, and otherwise expressed themselves as vigorously as they dared. Although Shakespeare's Elizabethan audiences were probably attentive—at least judging from the fact that the most frequent complaints about disturbing noises during performances refer to nutcracking—antebellum Americans were not. The folks in the balcony frequently made their displeasure known by pelting both the actors and the fancy people below with pennies, rotten fruit, eggs, apples, nuts, and gingerbread. In 1832, the English traveler Frances Trollope observed at a theater in Cincinnati "coatless men with their sleeves rolled up, incessantly spitting, reeking 'of onions and whiskey.'" She enjoyed the Shakespeare but abhorred the "perpetual" noises. Crowds often demanded instant encores and chimed in to recite long stretches of dialogue they had committed to memory. A New York journalist found the cheers and jeers of theater crowds a "merry and riotous chorus," adding that "compared with the performances in the audience, the ranting and bellowing and spasmodic galvanism of the actors on the stage are quite tame and commonplace." A French reporter attending a Shakespeare performance in California in 1851 noted that "the more [the spectators] like a play, the louder they whistle, and when a San Francisco audience bursts into shrill whistles and savage yells, you may be sure they are in raptures of joy." On occasion, members of the audience jumped onto the stage to examine the props. In Albany, a canal boatman screamed at Iago, "You damned lying scoundrel, I would like to get hold of you after the show and wring your infernal neck!"

Intellectuals cherish the act of attention, believing that attention is not something that happens to you but something you undertake. You contemplate, or immerse yourself and experience a sort of communion, whether with nature or a work of art. You actively *attend* to it. In this spirit, even the humble movie theater ought to be a sort of sacralized space for connection and concentration, not an amplified jukebox with up-tempo music and Hollywood trivia quizzes to fill the time before trailers.

The art historian Jonathan Crary maintains that the act of attention acquired fresh importance and virtue toward the end of the nineteenth century. It was then that what had been more or less a common culture broke in half. The great temples of culture—the opera, the symphony, the grand museums—insisted on decorum so that the act of spiritual elevation could take place uninterrupted. Elevated people wanted attention to be paid; indeed, you demonstrated your elevation *by* paying attention. The working classes moved to vaudeville, burlesque, dance halls, pool halls, and later nickelodeons. Their neighborhood movie theaters were more raucous than those of the middle class. As the high arts demanded sustained attention, psychologists began to treat inattention as a flaw. Attention was associated with willpower, craft, and love. Without attention, "the bringing of the consciousness to a focus in some special direction," warned a British psychologist in 1886, "meaningless reverie will take the place of coherent thought." A German psychologist wrote in 1893 that without the capacity for attention, "consciousness would be at the mercy of external impressions . . . thinking would be made impossible by the noisiness of our surroundings." Modern distraction, then, so frequently decried, "was *not* a disruption of stable or 'natural' kinds of sustained" perception but "an *effect*, and in many cases a constituent element, of the many attempts" to make people pay attention. People were not naturally attentive but became so. Amid the everyday buzz of what William James called "the stream of consciousness," attention was an interlude of concentration seized from an everyday life of "permanent low-level attentiveness," itself a reaction to the "relentless colonization of 'free' or leisure time."

Intellectuals, who love to cultivate attention and do it for a living, have long been indignant about intrusions upon their solitude and communion. If it wasn't the locomotive piercing the silence of the bucolic idyll, it was the menace of urban chaos: the turmoil of horsedrawn carriages, the mud, the excrement of horses, not to mention the neon, the flamboyant designs and banner headlines, the intrusive photos and garish posters of the yellow press, which in 1890 occasioned the first legal defense of the right to privacy. What the clutter of advertising did to the urban scene, billboards did to the surrounding countryside. Already more than a century ago, we were on our way to the contemporary sense of supersaturation—the overflow that seems to pour out of an overfilled atmosphere of signs and signals, generating grumpy reactions to "information overload."

But for all the refinement of their reactions, intellectuals have been paying attention, though not necessarily as the cultural industry intends. And attention is precisely the commodity that advertisers buy. "Eyeballs" and "impressions" are what the proprietors of media sell—what all the television and radio stations, billboard owners, and Internet sites market to advertisers. No space today is safe. Ads are placed on the backs of airplane seats, at eyeball height over urinals, on the backs of stall doors in women's bathrooms. In 2000, ABC installed motion-sensitive talking ads in a thousand public urinals in New York and Los Angeles to promote a new sitcom. Anyone with a screen or a surface wants to rent it out—the side of a bus or a gas pump, the top and sides of a taxi, even its hubcaps.

And today, you need not step out of doors to be poked and prodded by corporate sales bureaus, for there are the push technologies of phone solicitations, now frequently mechanized to improve the efficiency of the callers. (Answer the phone at your peril between 6 and 7 P.M., but no time is safe.) The stars of ABC's full 2000 season called random numbers to leave messages about the new shows on answering machines. There are the banner and pop-up ads on the Internet, increasingly wiggly and obtrusive—though users have learned to ignore even these, occasioning trouble for Internet finance. There are ads on rented videos, on sports scoreboards and sports equipment, and—in the form of product placement—in movies and TV shows. My New York University identification card carries an advertisement from AT&T. This is not to mention the theme songs and jingles that aim to attach themselves to everyday consciousness like replicable viruses.

In fact, the ironic challenge for all cultural entrepreneurs, all advertisers, studios, movie and music distributors, publishing companies, newspapers, magazines, toy companies, television networks, Internet providers, and so on is to "break through the clutter." But of course the clutter is not a force of nature; it is an artifact of the frenzy of competition. The clutter consists of nothing but the sum of all prior attempts to break through the clutter. So the clutter of images and manufactured sounds is the engine that drives ads into hitherto virgin spaces.

Where is the commercial presence *not* taken for granted? Eight million students in the United States and Canada attend schools whose administrations accept free TV sets from Channel One on the condition that the students watch its daily news broadcasts, complete with youth-targeted commercials. A company called YouthStream posts advertisement boards in 7,200 high school locker rooms, reaching (according to the company's promotions) some 70 percent of American high school students. Company hype about the merits of public advertising to children is extravagant. Consider, for example, this rapturous promise from Mike Searles, former president of KidsR-Us, a children's clothing chain: "If you own this child at an early age, you, can own this child for years to come. Companies are saying, 'Hey, I want to own the kid younger and younger.'"

Branding—of companies, not of cattle—is the *cri du jour* in marketing and public relations, but it is more than that. It is integral to a way of life. Many kids want to be "owned," cheerfully trading in one set of "owners" for others as they grow up. When companies speak of branding, they mean two things: landing a symbol in front of you repeatedly and in multiple venues, hoping to attract attention, and building a ladder in the imagination from attention to belief (Prudential is rock-solid; Coke, effervescent; Apple, cool). The magic of imaginative association is nothing new; the practice of hiring celebrities to infuse goods with meaning and stoke up desire for them ballooned in the course of the twentieth century. To these testimonials have been added the symbols and logos, the typographies and labels, the long-playing theme ads and public relations campaigns that establish "corporate identity," radiating a feeling about a company's style, offering a "unique selling proposition" that links a company to a mood and a social type.

On signs, T-shirts, caps, coffee mugs, key chains, shopping bags, and posters, in shops, private and public museums, arenas, theaters, and tourist sites, branding is now normal. Companies invest grandly in state-of-the-art designers to acquire the right logos, for in a prosperous society people have so much time to pay attention and so much discretionary income with which to indulge their desires that branding rewards investment. But the most extraordinary thing is the extent to which branding is voluntary, even enthusiastic, a fashion statement of affiliation. Labels affirm membership. The United States has reached an unprecedented degree of brand saturation, so many are the volunteers ready and eager to pay for the privilege of displaying their logos in public. In the 1930s, the down-and-out felt humiliated when compelled to wear sandwich boards to make ends meet, but children today gladly turn themselves into walking billboards. Once it was the working and farming classes who branded themselves by wearing Caterpillar Tractor and John Deere caps. But then came Lacoste's little alligators, followed by a flood of other insignia, to the point where in the 1970s it became almost impossible to buy an unbranded polo shirt. Calvin Klein, Ralph Lauren, Donna Karan, Tommy Hilfiger, and other designers branded jeans, socks, and other garments galore, each cornering a status-specific market. Marlboro did the same, selling clothing and gear from specialized shops in Europe.

But conspicuous collaboration, the desire to be branded, was not simply manufactured from on high. In an era of ever-renewed self-reinvention, when religion, region, and trade fail to provide deep identities, a brand can be a declaration, like a preprinted greeting card. The consumer has not chosen to choose, exactly, but from among the range of images on offer, has consented to choose. And why not? For the price of the artifact, you buy a statement: *I am my logo. I have this glamour, or power, or smoothness, or (fill in style) behind me.* While some stragglers proudly go without logos, the path of least resistance now is to surrender and embrace them or wear them ironically.

Those who fight profit-making corporations promote their own anticorporate logos. Greenpeace has its own, as do campaigners against capitalist globalization. Critics may try to make the media torrent swerve, but cannot imagine drying it up. In the country of the branded, even the opponents brand themselves.

Escape from Wonderland: Disney and the Female Imagination

By Deborah Ross

In 1989, Disney's little mermaid first asked the musical question, "When's it my turn?" She asked it again in 1996, when her movie was re-released in theaters, and she continues to ask it, frequently, in many of our living rooms. Never has a protagonist had so many turns to demand a turn: yet, seemingly, she remains unsatisfied. If even the heroine in a Disney "girls' movie" does not enjoy being a girl, how must the girls watching her feel about it?

Behind this gender question lurks a larger political one. If Ariel's feminist rhetoric is undercut by more conservative elements in her movie, so is the environmentalism of *The Lion King*, the multiculturalism of *Pocahontas*, the valuing of difference in *The Hunchback of Notre Dame*—in short, all the quasi-liberal sentiments that focus groups have no doubt caused to grace the surface of the last decade's Disney features. Ideology in Disney is a much vexed question, and I will not attempt here to untangle a knot which began forming for critics when Walt first denied having any politics back in the thirties, and which has only grown in mass and complexity since his death, as his corporation's management style has evolved to cope with a burgeoning staff of artists and technicians, changing public tastes, and changing perceptions of those tastes.

One generalization I do suggest, however, is that Disney the man and the corporation are known for a belief in control. The top-down management style Disney epitomizes—Auschwitz (Giroux 55), or Mouschwitz (Lewis 88), is a frequent analogy—thrives on homogeneity and rigid adherence to rules. These are features often decried in Disney production and product, both by critics of capitalism, such as Benjamin and Adorno,[1] and by far less radical proponents of individualism and open debate, from early Disney biographer Richard Schickel to educator Henry Giroux. Yet imagination, the company's major commodity, does not easily lend itself to a program of control. To encourage imagination in artists, and arouse it in viewers, is to invite unique self-expression rather than homogeneity, and spontaneity rather than predictability. Link

From *Marvels & Tales: Journal of Fairy-tale Studies*, 2004.

imagination to the animated cartoon, an art form with roots in dada, surrealism, and radical politics, and matters could well get out of hand.[2]

I believe that this conflict between control and imaginative freedom is visible in the animated features that have come out of the Disney studios, from *Snow White and the Seven Dwarfs* to *Lilo and Stitch.* Of course, ambiguity is rarely viewed now as either a moral or an aesthetic flaw, and the presence of elements that contradict each other may well be preferable to consistent, monologic disapproval of imagination. Neither, however, do conflict and contradiction in themselves necessarily create a space for viewers to question values and exercise judgment. Much depends on how the elements relate to each other, or how an audience is likely to relate them. An audience even partially looking for guides to behavior along with entertainment will have to resolve apparent ambiguities into one suggested course of action. Giroux's attack on Disney rests on the contention that for children, these movies, however apparently bland, do have a didactic effect (18). For them, ambiguity at its best ultimately resolves into a connected but complex world view that embraces difference and spontaneity; at its worst, it can produce confusion and anxiety.

I wish to explore the overall impressions these films may give children about the value of their own imaginations, and thus about their own value as unique individuals able to envision, and eventually to enact, change. In particular, to get back to Ariel, I am concerned about what girls may learn about this potentially explosive aspect of their characters that could so easily burst the bounds of traditional femininity. To help answer this question, I have chosen to examine the way various elements of image, story, and dialogue interact to influence the valuation of imagination in three of Disney's girls' movies: *Alice in Wonderland* (1951), *The Little Mermaid* (1989), and *Beauty and the Beast* (1991, re-released 2001).

I have chosen these three because, although one might be called "prefeminist" and the other two "post-," all specifically concern young women who fantasize about a life more vivid and exciting than their reality. I will suggest that some of these films' discomfort with female imagination has roots far back in didactic narrative for girls by looking at Charlotte Lennox's 1759 novel, *The Female Quixote,* which concerns the fortunes of a young woman who might be considered the great-grandmother, or prototype, of the Disney heroine. Then, comparing the three Disney movies with their written fairy-tale sources, l will show how much more confusing a many-tongued message can become when it is told in pictures as well as words.

Girls have been learning from stories where to draw the line between fantasy and reality probably since the first story was told, but one sees this didactic purpose especially clearly beginning in the seventeenth century, when romances and literary fairy tales were first written specifically for, about, and even by women. Samuel Johnson was greatly concerned about the effects of fiction on "the young, the ignorant, and the idle," and Paul Hunter has shown that there was indeed a class of new readers early in the eighteenth century who were socially displaced and looking to novels for moral and social guidance as well as entertainment (Hunter 271-72). From that time till the present, conservative authors have used romances and novels to teach girls that their dreams are dangerous and of little relevance to their daily lives. Progressive or feminist authors, on the other hand, have encouraged young women readers' belief in fantasy to help them visualize what they want, perhaps as a first step toward going after it. For example, it can be argued (as I have done elsewhere) that European women's experience with romantic fiction gradually gained them the right, first, to refuse to cooperate in arranged marriages, and eventually, to choose husbands for themselves.[3]

Charlotte Lennox's *The Female Quixote* illustrates both these conservative and progressive plot patterns, for it both draws upon and criticizes earlier romances, which themselves often both celebrated and punished female imagination and expressiveness.[4] Therefore, like Disney's movies today, which also use material from the romance and fairy-tale tradition, Lennox's novel can be more muddling than enlightening to young people seeking instruction on the conduct of real life. As the title suggests, the premise is that a young girl is at least as likely to have her head turned by reading romances as Cervantes's knight-errant had been over a century before. Appropriately, the romances devoured by this quixote, Arabella, are the largely female-centered French romances of d'Urfé and Scudéry, which focus more on love than on questing, and in which males are present mainly either to carry off or rescue heroines. A reader who takes too literally stories in which women wield such power, albeit of a limited kind, will not adjust well to woman's lot: being ignored, submitting always to others' convenience, like Jane Austen in her letters, perpetually waiting to be "fetched" by a male relative (Austen 9-10). Thus Arabella's reading sets her up to make many ridiculous mistakes, and ultimately to be humbled, or humiliated, when she learns her own real unimportance.

The novel shows its author's ambivalence about Arabella's fantasy in several ways. Overtly, she presents it as an adolescent error the heroine must grow out of in order to find happiness. Yet her very frank satire of the world to which Arabella's cure forces her to conform leaves readers wondering, along with the heroine, whether the world of romance might not be preferable. Romances also receive implicit support from the central "real" narrative's resemblance to romance: beautiful heroine, beloved by the perfect man, whom after trials and separations she marries, presumably to live happily ever after. If the novel presents a romantic story under the guise of realism, then perhaps Arabella is not so quixotic after all.

The Female Quixote thus presents contradictory impressions about the worthiness of the heroine's desires, the degree to which those desires are ultimately fulfilled or frustrated, and the amount of satisfaction with the outcome the tone directs the reader to feel. Critics of our own time naturally enjoy this ambivalence (the novel has had a comeback of sorts in the last decades and is available in paperback), which particularly lends itself to feminist approaches of the *Madwoman in the Attic,* conformist text-radical subtext variety. Yet the fact that this novel might well make a madwoman out of any young female reader looking for a framework for understanding life should also be part of our critical awareness. Critics may find it a useful model for highlighting similar constellations of ideological paradox in other stories about women's imagination, stories which also leave their audiences struggling to integrate contradictory messages.

Disney's female quixotes are at least as sorely beset by ambiguity as Arabella. The heroines' fantasies reveal desires for many things, including novelty, excitement, power, sex, and knowledge. Some of these desires are ridiculed, others respected; some are fulfilled, others surrendered. And the paradoxes in the plots are further complicated by words and images that seem at times to be telling stories of their own.

The presence of conservative elements in Disney's *Alice in Wonderland* is not surprising, considering that it was released in 1951, when "Hollywood's dark prince" was still very much alive, fighting unions, castigating the League of Women Voters, and exerting strong control over the studio's output.[5] One would perhaps not expect, though, to find an American movie of the midtwentieth century so much more stereotypically Victorian than its nineteenth-century British source.

Of course, Lewis Carroll's *Alice's Adventures in Wonderland* and *Through the Looking Glass* are not typical of Victorian children's literature. In particular, most girls' stories of this era promoted humility, devotion, punctuality, and tidiness, implying that adventure (as a countess once told Lennox's Arabella) is something a nice girl would be wise to avoid (Lennox 365). The Alice stories, on the other hand, present adventure as positive: whether wondrous or frightening, it leads the heroine in the direction of personal growth and control over her surroundings. Alice learns how to manage her size, how to talk back to a queen, and, finally, how to wear the crown of adulthood. Carroll celebrates childhood as a brief, fleeting time in which even girls may follow talking rabbits before being overtaken by the "dull reality" (115) of womanhood.

The Disney movie begins with the same positive message about girls' fantasies. In her opening conversation, Disney's Alice, like Carroll's, expresses the usual quixotic desires: to escape boredom (with lessons), to satisfy curiosity (about the white rabbit), and above all, to exert power. Things would be different "in my world," she notes, though her sister ridicules her ambition. Books, for one thing, would all have pictures—a remark given to Alice by Carroll in a way that almost invites someone to make an Alice movie. The first few minutes of the movie do seem to deliver what Alice wants by introducing such pictorial wonders as singing flowers and surrealistic insects.

Soon, however, the plot darkens, signaled by small but significant cuts and alterations in the original dialogue. Speaking with the Cheshire Cat, who tells her everyone in the neighborhood is mad, Alice speaks Carroll's line, "But I don't want to go among mad people" (63). The cat responds that everyone in Wonderland is mad, but he does not go on to say that Alice too is mad, so that already Disney's Alice is presented as out of her element, the lone sane and rational creature among lunatics.

After the mad tea party, in a section of plot invented for the movie, Disney's Alice has had enough craziness and wants to go home. Overjoyed to find what looks like a path—symbolic of her now acknowledged need for order and direction—she is reduced to helpless tears when it is erased by a fanciful broom creature. She then passively sits down to wait to be rescued, all the while lecturing herself about the importance of reason and patience, and berating herself for the curiosity that once again has led her into trouble. The movie takes a line from early in the story, "She generally gave herself very good advice (though she very seldom followed it)" (23), puts it in the first person, and makes it the center of a self-lacerating musical lament in which Alice abandons for good her fantasy of excitement and power to dwindle into a tiny, forlorn figure in the center of a large, dark frame. In the end of the movie, the defiance and assertiveness of the line, "You're only a pack of cards," are lost, as she utters it while fleeing for her life from the menacing gang of wonders she has created. She is saved, not by facing them down with dawning maturity and confidence, like the "real" Alice, but by waking up.[6]

British reviewers at the time of the movie's release, when the militantly innocuous Enid Blyton held sway over English children's imaginations, objected to Disney's "anarchic" alteration of what they saw as a serene and placid children's tale (Allan 137). But Carroll's story is in fact far more tolerant of anarchy, in the sense of irrationality, than the Disney version. The images used to tell the story further support this rationalist message. Despite Disney artist Claude Coats's comment that the staff had "let [them]selves go with some wild designs" (Allan 138), the visuals in fact are rather staid and restrained, mainly literal, representational renderings of the story done in the highly finished, realistic style for which the studio was famous. The fall down the rabbit hole, for example, which marks Alice's entry into the dream state, might have lent itself to surrealistic treatment like that of *Dumbo's* "Pink Elephants on Parade" sequence, but instead it is simply a serial listing in images of the objects Carroll mentions that Alice sees on her way down.

Surrealism does appear, briefly, in the visual puns formed by the caterpillar's smoke (as he asks "why [k]not"), and in the wild proliferation of crockery at the tea party, the cups and saucers truly "animated" and seeming to breed like, well, rabbits. Yet the story-line ensures that just as this style reaches its climax, Alice is reaching the limits of her fear of imagination. What might have been delightful Daliesque creatures—telephone-ducks, drum-frogs—function rather to frighten the heroine at a point in the plot when she has rejected all this "nonsense" and is anxious to get home to write a book about it.[7] Writing a story, she has decided, is much safer than living one.

Thus all elements combine to entrap the unwary viewer: to entice her to fantasize—even to pay money for the privilege—and then to make her feel, like Alice, guilty and ashamed.

Contrasting Alice's defeated whining with Ariel's anthem of independence in *The Little Mermaid*, one is apt to feel girls have come a long way. Here, as Laura Sells and Marina Warner observe, the tale on which the movie is based is ostensibly more conservative than Disney's retelling (Sells 176, 177, 181; Warner 397, 403).[8] Hans Christian Andersen's story is a tragic celebration of feminine self-sacrifice. His mermaid fantasizes about becoming human partly because, like Alice, she is curious about a world she has only glimpsed (here, from below rather than from above). But that world interests her mainly because in it dwells a man who resembles a handsome statue she already adores. Her love is partly sexual, of course, since she needs to be human from the waist down to win the hero. But her ultimate desire is spiritual, for only by marrying a human can a mermaid, who normally lives three hundred years and then turns into sea foam, gain a soul and eternal life.

In pursuit of this desire Andersen's mermaid is willing to spend all she has: her voice, her health, and eventually her life. She buys her new legs, from which blood oozes with every agonizing step, by letting the sea witch cut out her tongue. The permanent loss of her voice means playing dumb in more ways than one, as she can only listen demurely as the prince lectures her about her own world, the sea (166).[9] Failing to bring the prince to a proposal, she could save her own life by killing him, but she chooses instead to die. Her many acts of self-torture earn her a slight reprieve as she is turned into a spirit of the air, instead of sea-foam, and given a chance to gain a soul by performing more selfless deeds. Andersen gives her this reward, not for having a dream, but for desiring martyrdom. No real authorial punishment is needed for a female quixote so intent on punishing herself.

Naturally in the Disney version the mutilation and blood would have to go. But much more would have to be altered to make this tragic story look and sound so convincingly like a triumph of adolescent self-will and entitlement, as befit the close of the "me decade." (Warner comments on how often, while she can speak, Ariel utters the verb "want" [403].) For example, instead of making the mermaid love the human world because she loves a human, the movie has Ariel love a human mainly because she is already curious enough about his world to have collected a cave full of human souvenirs (in Andersen's story this collection belongs to a mermaid sister). Like Alice before her initiation, Ariel imagines this other world as in a sense more her own than her actual world. She believes it to be a utopia of free movement: she dreams of legs first for "jumping" and "dancing" and "strolling," and only secondarily for marrying.

There is nothing masochistic about this mermaid's fantasy; nor is she willing to sacrifice herself to fulfill it, though she is willing to gamble. Her voice, for example, is not permanently lost but poured into a shell, ready to be returned to her if she succeeds, and she has every intention of succeeding. Eighties heroine that she is, she means to have it all: voice, soul, legs, and husband.

170

For the most part, the movie seems to present this female quixote's fantasy positively and reward her with her desire, as the older generation, in the person of her father, learns to abandon prejudice and let teenagers live their own lives. But there are undercurrents here, so to speak, that work against the theme of imaginative freedom. The odd thing about Ariel's quixotism—what makes the audience recognize it *as* quixotism—is that the exotic world of her fantasy is, to us, boring and commonplace. Even a two-year-old viewer knows, as the heroine does not, that forks are not used to comb hair, and that human fathers do indeed "reprimand their daughters," just like old King Triton. Thus we laugh at Ariel's naive reveries, as Andersen's listeners must have laughed at his mermaid's amazed reaction to birds (150). In the end, it seems ludicrous that Ariel should put so much rebellious energy into becoming the girl next door.

The visual style of the movie makes Andersen's painful story seem oddly encouraging by comparison. Andersen shifts points of view back and forth between the mermaids, who see our world as exotic, and his own audience, who glamorize the unknown world below. He provides lavish descriptions of the shore as well as the sea in order to reawaken his listeners' sense of wonder at their own city lights, sunsets, forests, and hills (151-52). An outsider's desire to live here thus becomes quite understandable. The movie contains no such balance, for beauty and splendor are mainly found "Under the Sea," the title of the dizzying production number in which Sebastian the crab tries to convince Ariel that there's no place like home. Here creatures and objects are surrealistically combined and transformed into an underwater orchestra. Here in abundance are the magical bubbles that have signaled fun with physics in Disney movies from *Snow White* to *Dumbo* to *Cinderella*. The world of humans, in contrast, though picturesque, is static and finite. When Ariel takes a bath at Eric's palace, while mundane, gossiping laundresses wash her clothes, one is forced to notice that bubbles here just don't *do* anything. Similarly, Grimsby's pipe, which Ariel mistakes for a musical instrument, produces more soot than smoke—nothing approaching the punning puffs from the caterpillar's hookah in *Alice*, or even the smoky ink that billows about in the sea witch's cave. Clearly, Sebastian is right: it is "better down where its wetter."

The images the movie uses to tell the story thus give its trendy feminism a reverse spin. Whatever Ariel might *say*, or sing, what we see her *do* is flee a world of infinite possibility to settle in the land of the banal. Her fantasy is a sort of anti-fantasy. Yes, she gets her legs, she makes her stand, she marches—but only down the aisle, to marry some guy named Eric.

Many fairy tales, and many more movies, end with a wedding, and for this reason they often draw censure from critics, such as Janet Wasko (116) and Elizabeth Bell (114, 155), who would like to see our daughters presented with other options. Without question there ought to be more than one girls' story out there, relentlessly repeated with minor variations. I would also argue, however, that just as in life there are marriages and marriages, so in fiction living happily ever after is not always a euphemism for dying. When the marriage seems to grant the heroine true personal fulfillment and possibilities for further growth, the ending may actually seem like the beginning of a new life. Such is the case with *Beauty and the Beast,* a tale endowed by ancient archetypes with a feminine power that resists the attempts of individual authors, such as Madame Leprince de Beaumont in 1757, to tie its heroine down to mediocrity. With *The Little Mermaid* behind us, we might expect Disney's version to dole out a similarly dull and didactic message, clothed in mock-progressive nineties clichés of gender equality. But in Disney's *Beauty and the Beast,* thanks in part to the screenplay by Linda Woolverton (the first woman writer of a Disney animated feature), imagination flows freely in the words and the images, allowing the tale to work its magic.[10]

One problem with the plot that ends in marriage, of course, is its reduction of the heroine to an object of desire, and therefore a heroine actually named Beauty would not, on the face of it, seem like a good role model. In this tale, however, with its roots penetrating beyond the Cupid and Psyche tale from Apuleius's *The Golden Ass* to very old stories about beast bridegrooms (Warner 275; Zipes 24-25), the heroine is more subject than object because her quest for a desirable mate drives the plot. (Apuleius intensifies the female point or view by having the tale narrated by an old woman [Warner 275]). Of course, the whole question of the story's sexual politics hinges on whether the heroine's desire can be consciously controlled, by herself or by others; whether, as is often said in Christian wedding ceremonies, love is an act or will rather than a feeling; whether, therefore, she can make herself love the one she "ought." Conservative versions of *Beauty and the Beast* do tend to assume such schooling of the will is possible, as Jack Zipes emphasizes (29-40). Nevertheless, an important feature even in such versions is that the beast, though he may be dutifully or even cheerfully endured, cannot become a handsome prince until the heroine actively wants him, truly chooses him for reasons of her own. The young female audience is thus reassured that sex in conjunction with love is pleasant rather than frightening (Bettelheim 306; Warner 312-13); in other words, the beast of one's choice is not a beast at all.

At about the same time Charlotte Lennox was composing *The Female Quixote,* Madame Leprince de Beaumont, with similar concerns about young women's imaginations, was dressing this ancient tale in anti-romance, turning to her own purpose a Scudérian vocabulary of love that, to her readers, would be all too familiar. Beauty feels "esteem" for the Beast because of his "great service" to her, and eventually she comes to feel "tenderness" for him as she wants to care for him and ease his distress (Beaumont 37). Out of this tenderness comes a desire to marry him—including, one supposes, some sexual feeling. The romance code word for active sexual desire—"inclination"—never appears.[11] By telling her young readers that esteem and tenderness are the best basis for marriage, Beaumont warns them not to wait for the handsome, witty lover of their fantasies; in the closing words of the rewarding fairy: "You have preferred virtue before either wit or beauty, and you deserve to find one in whom all these are united" (47). In this way, the author joins the tradition of conservative writers who urge girls to face reality and, to the very limited extent they will be permitted to choose, to choose wisely.[12] Still, while schooling the reader in what she ought to desire, Beaumont cannot avoid conveying the importance of the heroine's will, for until Beauty desires the Beast, a beast he will remain.

The Disney movie reaches past Beaumont to draw upon older strains of the story. For example, here, as in some older versions, including that of Beaumont's immediate predecessor, Madame de Villeneuve (Warner 290-91), it is the Beast rather than Beauty who is supposed to learn self-control. The heroine is therefore permitted—even encouraged—to fantasize to her heart's content. Where Beaumont only noted that Beauty liked to read, Disney enlarges on Belle's taste in books, which turns out to be just like Arabella's: fairy tales and romances about swordfights, magic, a prince in disguise, and above all, a "she" at the center of the action. Nor is she content just to read about "adventure in the great wide somewhere." Given the chance to tour the Beast's library—ordinarily for Belle the greatest of temptations—she chooses instead to explore the forbidden west wing of his castle, as if somehow aware that she will find there the escape from "provincial life" she has been longing and singing for. For all her quixotism, however, Belle, unlike Arabella, is seen as "rather odd" only by her neighbors, not by her audience.

Certainly, as several commentators observe, the movie has its share of politically correct modern touches to underscore the heroine's self-determination (Warner 316-17; Zipes 46). Interestingly, however, each apparent innovation in fact draws on the French romance tradition that Belle and Arabella revere. Most notably, the movie makes contemporary-sounding statements about gender stereotypes by introducing a new character as foil to the Beast, the hypermasculine Gaston, who boasts in a Sigmund Romberg-ish aria, "I'm especially good at expectorating," "I use antlers in all of my decorating," and "every last inch of me's covered with hair." He is the real beast, of course, an animal who sneers at the Beast for being so openly in touch with his feminine side, "the Male Chauvinist Pig [. . .] that would turn the women of any primetime talkshow audience into beasts themselves" (Jeffords 170). But Gaston is not really new. He dates back, beyond the Cocteau movie often cited as his source, to the French romance villain who loves the heroine selfishly, determined to possess her by force: by winning her in a duel, carrying her off, or scheming to get her parents to give her to him. Gaston arranges to have Belle's eccentric father locked in a madhouse unless she agrees to marry him. Then he nearly kills the beast under the illusion that the winner gets Belle as prize. The Beast, in contrast, is the romance hero who fights the villain to win the heroine's freedom, not her hand, which he will accept only as her gift. In fact, he would rather die than oppress her. By choosing the Beast over Gaston, Belle helps this ancient story confirm the value of a woman's equal right to a will of her own.

Gaston also helps this movie make another observation mistakenly thought of as modern: that men and women aren't nearly as different as some men would like them to be. This idea is found in women's romantic writing from the seventeenth century on,[13] and it reverberates in Belle's opening song as she wishes for someone who understands her and shares her interests. Naturally she chooses to marry the gentleman who gives her the key to his extensive library, not the "positively primeval" clod who throws her book in the mud with a warning about what happens to society when women are taught to read. And in the end, when the spell is broken and the Beast resumes his original shape, he markedly resembles Belle, unruly bangs and all. By marrying a man who can help her get what she wants, and who wants the same things, symbolically she is marrying an aspect of herself.[14]

The Beast's oddly familiar new face is not the only image in the movie that makes one feel the heroine's fantasy is a worthy one. Much creativity was lavished on the look of the castle that provides the atmosphere of old romance. Although for most of the movie it resembles a Gothic ruin, and Belle comes here at first as a prisoner, it is really a house of magic in which every object is alive, or "animated"—most famously the dinnerware that dances and sings "Be Our Guest." And the enchantment does not quite end with the breaking of the spell, but is rather replaced with a different kind of magic as the castle comes into its original baroque splendor with a seeming infinity of detail, something new around every corner, and always a new corner for the eye to explore. As Belle waltzes with her Prince around that gorgeous marble hall, the title tune welling up around them, one may see as well as feel that she's getting not just a husband, but more books than she can read in a lifetime, and a home as big and beautiful as her imagination.

Neither age, divorce, nor parenthood has yet made me cynical enough to see the ending of this movie without a sob of satisfaction. But then Disney did begin training me to react in just that way from a very early age (the first movie I ever saw, at the age of five, was *Sleeping Beauty*). Critics have been warning the public for decades about the Disney program to bring about the complete "invasion and control of children's imaginations" (Schickel 18), as well as the silencing of fairy tales' originally female voice (Warner 416-17); no doubt I am a cipher in the company's success. How much more complete the Disney conquest will become for our children and grandchildren, with the constant replay made possible by video and DVD, is definitely cause for concern.

The market forces that drive Disney today are dangerous, to be sure, as is the ideology of the market-place the movies promote, as Giroux and others warn. Fortunately, however, because the overriding goal is self-promotion—because Disney will absorb and use whatever works, or whatever sells the product—the movies lack the philosophical consistency of propaganda.[15] Thus films like *Beauty and the Beast,* which pays more than lip-service to the liberating potential of fantasy, can sometimes appear.

Nevertheless, the fact that many Disney movies implant seeds of guilt and fear to spring up along with children's developing imaginations is a serious problem. The mixed messages noticeable in *Alice* are present in earlier movies such as *Dumbo* and "The Sorcerer's Apprentice" in *Fantasia.* They continue in more recent examples such as *Hercules* and *The Hunchback of Notre Dame,* in which only evil and terrifying characters wield the transformative power that is, in essence, the animator's art; thus these movies almost identify themselves as products of black magic.[16] Some recent films seem almost to reject the notion of animation altogether, striking the eye most forcibly with stills such as the battlefield in *Mulan* or the cathedral of Notre Dame—breathtaking, to be sure, but unlike the Beast's castle, completely static. Clearly the reluctance to embrace imagination with both arms is still present among the many and shifting ideas that make up the Disney ethos.

The inconsistencies found in these movies do not lighten either the parent's burden of guiding the young in their adventures with the media, or the critic's task of understanding the various manifestations of culture. On the contrary, they oblige us to do more than count the number of profane words or violent acts or exposed body parts; and also to do more than catalogue plots, count the numbers of males and females and quantify relative levels of aggression. Instead, we must watch carefully the interplay of elements within the films and notice how many stories are going on at one time. Watching the faces of our children as they watch, we will often find that imagination, in these movies, is like Alice's garden—just beyond a little locked door, the key to which is tantalizingly, frustratingly, out of reach.

Notes

1. Miriam Hansen discusses Benjamin's and Adorno's objections to Disney in some detail. Jack Zipes's critique of Disney also occurs within a larger argument about the "freezing" of fairy tales into myths to perpetuate bourgeois, patriarchal values (see his Introduction and Chapter 3).

2. Janet Wasko notes that Disney deliberately avoided the more "anarchistic and inventive" styles of animation employed at other studios (115). My own belief, on which my approach to Disney is based, is that where there is animation, anarchy can never be wholly suppressed. For discussion of the roots of animation in surrealism and dada, see Inez Hedges.

3. I develop this argument in *The Excellence of Falsehood*. Marina Warner (169, 277-78) and Jack Zipes (21-23, 28) discuss the seventeenth-century *précieuses'* preoccupation with the issue of forced marriage.

4. Warner discusses ambivalence about the old woman or "Mother Goose" figure who narrates fairy tales throughout the first half of *From the Beast to the Blonde*, and more specifically the power of the female voice in her discussion of "The Little Mermaid" (394).

5. I refer here to the title of Marc Eliot's Disney biography. Holly Allen and Michael Denning discuss politics at the Disney studio during the 1940s. For a full discussion of Disney's rather complex politics, see Steven Watts.

6. Donald Britton comments that in the Disney cartoon universe, "children don't become adults; rather, adults kill children" (120).

7. Dali had been at the studio in 1946, and Robin Allan believes his influence was still apparent in *Alice* (137).

8. See also Wasko 134.

9. See Warner's discussion on the significance of this silence, and of the blood which in Anderson's tale connects pain with the dawning of female sexuality (387-408).

10. See Bell 114; Murphy 133-34; Warner 313.

11. See the Map of Tender in Scudéry's *Clelia* (1: 42).

12. See Warner 292-94.

13. See for example the pastoral lyrics of Aphra Behn.

14. See Clarissa Pinkola Estes for an interpretation of the Beast as an aspect of the heroine's own personality (272–73). Warner also discusses how the beast in modern versions of the tale, including Disney's, functions to help the heroine get in touch with her own inner beast, or sexuality (307–13).

15. Giroux notes inconsistent values among elements in the films (5, 91). Wasko emphasizes consistent elements that make "classic Disney" a recognizable "brand" (3, 152) but does not explore tensions among the elements she lists as consistent, such as "work ethic" vs. "escape fantasy" (114).

16. A notable exception is *The Emperor's New Groove*, in which magic transformative portions intended as evil by the villain turn positive and bring about both the narrative and visual climax of the movie.

Works Cited

Alice in Wonderland. Dir. Clyde Geronimi, Hamilton Luske, and Wilfred Jackson. Walt Disney Company. 1951.

Allan, Robin. "Alice in Disneyland," *Sight and Sound* 54 (Spring 1985): 136–38.

Allen, Holly, and Michael Denning. "The Cartoonists' Front." *South Atlantic Quarterly* 92.1 (1993): 89–117.

Andersen, Hans Christian. "The Little Mermaid." *Hans Christian Andersen: His Classic Fairy Tales.* Trans. Erik Haugaard. Garden City, NY: Doubleday, 1978. 149–70.

Apuleius. *Transformations of Lucius Otherwise Known as the Golden Ass.* Trans. Robert Graves. New York: Noonday, 1998.

Austen, Jane. *Selected Letters.* Oxford: Oxford UP, 1985.

Beaumont, Madame Leprince de. *Beauty and the Beast.* Trans. P. H. Muir. New York: Knopf. 1968.

Beauty and the Beast. Dir. Gary Trousdale and Kirk Wise. Walt Disney Company, 1991.

Behn, Aphra. *The Works of Aphra Behn: Poetry.* Ed. Janet Todd. Columbus: Ohio UP, 1992.

Bell, Elizabeth. "Somatexts at the Disney Shop." Bell, Haas, and Sells 107-24.

Bell, Elizabeth, Lynda Haas, and Laura Sells, eds. *From Mouse to Mermaid: The Politics of film, Gender, and Culture.* Bloomington: Indiana UP, 1995.

Bettelheim, Bruno. The *Uses of Enchantment.* New York: Vintage, 1977.

Britton. Donald. "The Dark Side of Disneyland." *Mythomania: Fantasies, Fables, and Sheer Lies in Contemporary American Popular Art.* By Bernard Welt. Los Angeles: Art Issues, 1996. 113–26.

Carroll, Lewis. *Alice's Adventures* in *Wonderland and Through the Looking-Glass.* New York: New American Library, 1960.

Cinderella. Dir. Hamilton Luske and Wilfred Jackson. Walt Disney Company, 1950.

Dumbo. Dir. Ben Sharpsteen. Walt Disney Company, 1941.

Eliot, Marc. *Walt Disney: Hollywood's Dark Prince.* New York: Birch lane, 1993.

The Emperor's New Groove. Dir. Mark Dindal. Walt Disney Company, 2000.

Estes, Clarissa Pinkola. *Women Who Run with the Wolves.* New York: Ballantine, 1992.

Fantasia. Dir. Ford Beebe and Bill Roberts. Walt Disney Company, 1942.

Gilbert, Sandra, and Susan Gubar. *The Madwoman* in *the* Allie. New Haven: Yale UP, 1979.

Giroux, Henry. The *Mouse that Roared: Disney and the End of Innocence.* Lanham, M D: Rowman, 1999.

Hansen, Miriam. "Of Mice and Ducks: Benjamin and Adorno on Disney." *South Atlantic Quarterly* 92.1 (1993): 27-61.

Hedges, lnez. *Languages of Revolt: Dada and Surrealist Literature and Film.* Durham: Duke UP, 1983.

Hercules. Dir. Ron Clements and John Musker. Walt Disney Company, 1997.

The Hunchback of Notre Dame. Dir. Gary Trousdale and Kirk Wise. Walt Disney Company. 1996.

Hunter, J. Paul. " 'The Young, the Ignorant, and the Idle': Some Notes on Readers and the Beginnings of the English Novel." *Anticipations of the Enlightenment in England, France, and Germany.* Ed. Alan Charles Kors and Paul J. Korshin. Philadelphia: U of Pennsylvania P, 1987. 259-82.

Jeffords, Susan. "The Curse of Masculinity." Bell, Haas, and Sells 161-72.

Johnson, Samuel. *The Rambler.* Ed. W.J. Bate and Albrecht B. Strauss. New Haven: Yale UP, 1969.

Lennox, Charlotte. *The Female Quixote.* 1759. Boston: Pandora. 1986.

Lewis, Jon. "Disney after Disney." *Disney Discourse: Producing the Magic Kingdonl.* Ed. Eric Smoodin. New York: Routledge, 1994.

Lilo and Stitch. Dir. Dean DeBlois and Chris Sanders (Ill). Walt Disney Company, 2002.

The Lion King. Dir. Rob Minkoff and Roger Allers. Walt Disney Company, 1994.

The Little Mermaid. Dir. John Musker and Ron Clements. Walt Disney Company, 1989.

Mulan. Dir. Tony Bancroft and Barry Cook. Walt Disney Company, 1998.

Murphy, Patrick D. " 'The Whole Wide World Was Scrubbed Clean': The Androcentric Animation of Denatured Disney." Bell, Haas, and Sells, 125–36.

Pocahontas. Dir. Mike Gabriel and Eric Goldberg. Walt Disney Company, 1995.

Ross, Deborah. *The Excellence of Falsehood.* Lexington: UP of Kentucky, 1991.

Schickel, Richard. The *Disney Version.* New York: Simon, 1968.

Scudéry, Madeleine de. *Clelia.* Trans. John Davies. London: Herringman, 1678.

Sells, Laura. " 'Where Do the Mermaids Stand?' Voice and Body in *The Little Mermaid.*" Bell, Haas, and Sells, 175–92.

The Sleeping Beauty. Dir. Clyde Geronimi. Walt Disney Company, 1959.

Snow White and the *Seven Dwarfs.* Dir. David Hand. Walt Disney Company, 1938.

Warner, Marina. *From the Beast to* the *Blonde: On Fairy Tales and Their Tellers.* New York: Noonday, 1994.

Wasko, Janel. *Understanding Disney.* Cambridge, UK: Polity, 2001.

Watts, Steven. "Walt Disney: Art and Politics in the American Century." *Journal of American History* 82.1 (June 1995): 84–110.

Zipes, Jack. *Fairy Tale as Myth/Myth as Fairy Tale.* Lexington: UP of Kentucky, 1994.

Part Four

Religion and Belief

Religion: What's God Got to Do with It?

By Karen Armstrong

The activity that we call religion is complex. Religious and non-religious people alike often share the same misperceptions. Today in the west, it is often assumed that religion is all about the supernatural and that it is inseparable from belief in an external, personalised deity. Critics claim that religion encourages escapist fantasies that cannot be verified. The explosion of terrorism (which is often given a religious justification) has convinced many people that religion is incurably violent. I have lost count of the number of times a taxi driver has informed me that religion has been the cause of all the wars in history.

Yet we find something very different when we look back to the period that the German philosopher Karl Jaspers called the "Axial Age" (c.900 to 200BCE) because it proved to be pivotal to the spiritual development of humanity. In this era, in four distinct regions of the world, the traditions that have continued to nourish humanity either came into being or put down roots. Hinduism, Buddhism and Jainism emerged in India; Confucianism and Taoism in China; monotheism was born in Israel; and philosophical rationalism developed in Greece. It was a period of astonishing creativity; we have never really succeeded in going beyond the insights of such sages as the Buddha, the mystics of the Upanishads, Confucius, Lao-tzu, and the great Hebrew prophets. Rabbinic Judaism, Christianity and Islam, for example, can be seen as a later flowering of the religion that had developed in Israel during the Axial Age.

Despite interesting and revealing differences in emphasis, these traditions all reached remarkably similar solutions. They can, perhaps, tell us something important about the structure of our humanity. The God of Israel was an important symbol of transcendence, but in the other Axial faiths the gods were not very important. Confucius discouraged speculation about spirits and the afterlife: how could you talk about other-worldly phenomena, when there was so much that you did not understand about earthly matters?

During the Indian Axial Age, the ancient Vedic deities retreated from the religious imagination. They were seen as unsatisfactory

From *New Statesman,* 2006.

expressions of the sacred, and were either demoted to human status or seen as aspects of the psyche. Many of the Axial sages were reaching beyond the gods to a more impersonal transcendence—to Brahman, Nirvana or the Tao—that was also inseparable from humanity. Yogins and Taoists did not believe that their ecstatic trances represented an encounter with the supernatural, but regarded them as entirely natural to humanity. Later, the more sophisticated theologians in all three of the monotheistic religions would make similar claims about the experience of the reality that they called God.

None of these sages was interested in dogma or metaphysics. A person's theological opinions were a matter of total indifference to a teacher like the Buddha. He insisted that nobody should ever take any religious teaching, from however august a source, on faith or at second hand. One of the Buddha's disciples pestered him continuously about metaphysics: was there a God? Who created the world? He was so preoccupied with these matters that he neglected his yoga and ethical practice. The Buddha told him that he was like a man who had been shot with a poisoned arrow but refused to have any medical treatment until he discovered the name of his assailant and what village he came from: he would die before he got this perfectly useless information.

The Taoists were also wary of dogmatic conformity; they believed that the kind of certainty that many seek in religion was unrealistic and a sign of immaturity. Eventually, the Chinese preferred to synthesise the schools which had developed during their Axial Age, because no single tradition could have the monopoly of truth. In all four regions, when a sage started to insist upon strict orthodoxy, this was usually a sign that the Axial Age was drawing to a close.

The prophets of Israel were more like political commentators than theologians; they found the divine in analysis of current events rather than metaphysics. Jesus, as far as we know, spent no time discussing the trinity or original sin, which would later become so important to Christians; and the Koran dismisses theological dogmatism as *zannah*, self-indulgent guesswork that makes people stupidly quarrelsome and sectarian.

Religion was not about believing credal propositions, but about behaving in a way that changed you at a profound level. Human beings have always sought what the Greeks called *ekstasis*, a "stepping out" of the mundane, in moments when we feel deeply touched within and lifted momentarily beyond ourselves. The Axial sages all believed that if we stepped outside of our egotism and greed, we would transcend ourselves and achieve an enhanced humanity. Yoga, for instance, one of the great spiritual technologies of the Axial Age, was a formidable assault on the ego, designed to take the "I" out of the practitioner's thinking.

But the safest way to achieve this *ekstasis* was by the practice of compassion. Compassion—the ability to feel with another—was not simply the litmus test of any true religiosity, but the chief way of encountering the ineffable reality of Nirvana, Brahman, God and Tao. For the Buddha, compassion brought about *ceto-vimutti*, the "release of the mind" that was a synonym for the supreme enlightenment of Nirvana, a sacred realm of peace in the core of one's being.

All the Axial religions, in different ways, regarded what has been called the Golden Rule as the essence of religion: "Do not do to others what you would not like them to do to you." Confucius was the first to formulate this maxim. It was, he said, the thread that pulled all his teachings together and should be practised all day and every day. Five hundred years later, Rabbi Hillel was asked to sum up the whole of Jewish teaching while he stood on one leg. He replied: "That which is hateful to you, do not do to your neighbour. That is the Torah. The rest is commentary. Go and study it."

The Chinese sage Mo-tzu (c.480-390) insisted that we had to have *jian ai*, "concern for everybody." The priestly authors of Leviticus urged the Israelites to love and honour the stranger; the Buddha taught layfolk and monks alike a method of meditation called "the Immeasurables," in which they systematically extended benevolent thoughts to the four corners of the world. Jesus told his disciples to love their enemies. This impartial sympathy would break down the barricades of egotism, because it was offered with little hope of any return.

If a ruler practised *jian ai*, Mo-tzu taught, war would be impossible. The Axial religions all developed in regions that were convulsed by violence on an unprecedented scale. Iron weaponry meant that warfare had become more deadly; states had become more coercive; in the market place, merchants preyed on each other aggressively. In every case, throughout the Axial Age, the catalyst for religious change was always a disciplined revulsion towards this violence.

In the 9th century, the ritualists of India systematically extracted all the violence from the sacrificial ritual, and in seeking the cause of aggression in the psyche, discovered the inner self. Renouncers, Buddhists and Jains all insisted that *ahimsa*, "harmlessness," was an indispensable prerequisite to enlightenment. In the Tao Te Ching, Lao-tzu pointed out that violence could only elicit more violence. The sage-ruler must always seek to bring a military campaign to a speedy end: "Bring it to a conclusion, but do not intimidate." Some of the gospels present Jesus as a man of *ahimsa* who taught his followers to turn the other cheek.

Socrates, one of the greatest figures of the Axial Age, also condemned retaliation as evil. In general, however, the Greeks did not eschew violence. Ultimately, they did not have a religious Axial Age. Their great transformation was philosophical, scientific and mathematical, and pagan religion continued to flourish in Greece until it was forcibly replaced by Christianity in the fifth century CE.

Compassion is an unpopular virtue. All too often, religious people have preferred to be right rather than compassionate. They have shielded themselves from the demands of empathy by making secondary and peripheral goals—such as theological correctness or sexual orthodoxy—central to their faith. As the Chinese sages pointed out, vehement professions of belief were essentially egotistic, a pompous trumpeting of self, and, therefore, they impeded enlightenment. Denominational chauvinism, like nationalism, should also be seen as a form of collective egotism or, in monotheistic terms, idolatry.

Nevertheless, in our torn, conflicted world, we need to revive the Axial ethos. This does not require orthodox belief and need not involve the supernatural. In the Axial Age, individualism was beginning to supersede the older tribal or communal expressions of identity. The sages were trying to moderate the clash of competing egos and they were all concerned about the plight of society. We are still rampant, chronic individualists, but our technology has created a global village, which is interconnected electronically, militarily, politically and economically. If we want to survive, it makes practical sense to cultivate *jian ai*. We need to apply the Golden Rule politically, and learn that other nations, however remote from our own, are as important as ours.

Yes, This Is About Islam

By Salman Rushdie

"This isn't about Islam." The world's leaders have been repeating this mantra for weeks, partly in the virtuous hope of deterring reprisal attacks on innocent Muslims living in the West, partly because if the United States is to maintain its coalition against terror it can't afford to suggest that Islam and terrorism are in any way related.

The trouble with this necessary disclaimer is that it isn't true. If this isn't about Islam, why the worldwide Muslim demonstrations in support of Osama bin Laden and Al Qaeda? Why did those 10,000 men armed with swords and axes mass on the Pakistan-Afghanistan frontier, answering some mullah's call to jihad? Why are the war's first British casualties three Muslim men who died fighting on the Taliban side?

Why the routine anti-Semitism of the much-repeated Islamic slander that "the Jews" arranged the hits on the World Trade Center and the Pentagon, with the oddly self-deprecating explanation offered by the Taliban leadership, among others, that Muslims could not have the technological know-how or organizational sophistication to pull off such a feat? Why does Imran Khan, the Pakistani ex-sports star turned politician, demand to be shown the evidence of Al Qaeda's guilt while apparently turning a deaf ear to the self-incriminating statements of Al Qaeda's own spokesmen (there will be a rain of aircraft from the skies, Muslims in the West are warned not to live or work in tall buildings)? Why all the talk about American military infidels desecrating the sacred soil of Saudi Arabia if some sort of definition of what is sacred is not at the heart of the present discontents?

Of course this is "about Islam." The question is, what exactly does that mean? After all, most religious belief isn't very theological. Most Muslims are not profound Koranic analysts. For a vast number of "believing" Muslim men, "Islam" stands, in a jumbled, half-examined way, not only for the fear of God—the fear more than the love, one suspects—but also for a cluster of customs, opinions and prejudices that include their dietary practices; the sequestration or near-sequestration of "their" women; the sermons delivered by their mullahs of choice; a loathing of modern society in general, riddled

From *The New York Times*, 2001.

as it is with music, godlessness and sex; and a more particularized loathing (and fear) of the prospect that their own immediate surroundings could be taken over—"Westoxicated"—by the liberal Western-style way of life.

Highly motivated organizations of Muslim men (oh, for the voices of Muslim women to be heard!) have been engaged over the last 30 years or so in growing radical political movements out of this mulch of "belief." These Islamists—we must get used to this word, "Islamists," meaning those who are engaged upon such political projects, and learn to distinguish it from the more general and politically neutral "Muslim"—include the Muslim Brotherhood in Egypt, the blood-soaked combatants of the Islamic Salvation Front and Armed Islamic Group in Algeria, the Shiite revolutionaries of Iran, and the Taliban. Poverty is their great helper, and the fruit of their efforts is paranoia. This paranoid Islam, which blames outsiders, "infidels," for all the ills of Muslim societies, and whose proposed remedy is the closing of those societies to the rival project of modernity, is presently the fastest growing version of Islam in the world.

This is not wholly to go along with Samuel Huntington's thesis about the clash of civilizations, for the simple reason that the Islamists' project is turned not only against the West and "the Jews," but also against their fellow Islamists. Whatever the public rhetoric, there's little love lost between the Taliban and Iranian regimes. Dissensions between Muslim nations run at least as deep, if not deeper, than those nations' resentment of the West. Nevertheless, it would be absurd to deny that this self-exculpatory, paranoiac Islam is an ideology with widespread appeal.

Twenty years ago, when I was writing a novel about power struggles in a fictionalized Pakistan, it was already de rigueur in the Muslim world to blame all its troubles on the West and, in particular, the United States. Then as now, some of these criticisms were well-founded; no room here to rehearse the geopolitics of the cold war and America's frequently damaging foreign policy "tilts," to use the Kissinger term, toward (or away from) this or that temporarily useful (or disapproved-of) nation-state, or America's role in the installation and deposition of sundry unsavory leaders and regimes. But I wanted then to ask a question that is no less important now: Suppose we say that the ills of our societies are not primarily America's fault, that we are to blame for our own failings? How would we understand them then? Might we not, by accepting our own responsibility for our problems, begin to learn to solve them for ourselves?

Many Muslims, as well as secularist analysts with roots in the Muslim world, are beginning to ask such questions now. In recent weeks Muslim voices have everywhere been raised against the obscurantist hijacking of their religion. Yesterday's hotheads (among them Yusuf Islam, a.k.a. Cat Stevens) are improbably repackaging themselves as today's pussycats.

An Iraqi writer quotes an earlier Iraqi satirist: "The disease that is in us, is from us." A British Muslim writes, "Islam has become its own enemy." A Lebanese friend, returning from Beirut, tells me that in the aftermath of the attacks on Sept. 11, public criticism of Islamism has become much more outspoken. Many commentators have spoken of the need for a Reformation in the Muslim world.

I'm reminded of the way noncommunist socialists used to distance themselves from the tyrannical socialism of the Soviets; nevertheless, the first stirrings of this counterproject are of great significance. If Islam is to be reconciled with modernity, these voices must be encouraged until they swell into a roar. Many of them speak of another Islam, their personal, private faith.

The restoration of religion to the sphere of the personal, its depoliticization, is the nettle that all Muslim societies must grasp in order to become modern. The only aspect of modernity interesting to the terrorists is technology, which they see as a weapon that can be turned on its makers. If terrorism is to be defeated, the world of Islam must take on board the secularist-humanist principles on which the modern is based, and without which Muslim countries' freedom will remain a distant dream.

The Rival Conceptions of God

By C. S. Lewis

I have been asked to tell you what Christians believe, and I am going to begin by telling you one thing that Christians do not need to believe. If you are a Christian you do not have to believe that all the other religions are simply wrong all through. If you are an atheist you do have to believe that the main point in all the religions of the whole world is simply one huge mistake. If you are a Christian, you are free to think that all these religions, even the queerest ones, contain at least some hint of the truth. When I was an atheist I had to try to persuade myself that most of the human race have always been wrong about the question that mattered to them most; when I became a Christian I was able to take a more liberal view. But, of course, being a Christian does mean thinking that where Christianity differs from other religions, Christianity is right and they are wrong. As in arithmetic—there is only one right answer to a sum, and all other answers are wrong: but some of the wrong answers are much nearer being right than others.

The first big division of humanity is into the majority, who believe in some kind of God or gods, and the minority who do not. On this point, Christianity lines up with the majority—lines up with ancient Greeks and Romans, modern savages, Stoics, Platonists, Hindus, Mohammedans, etc., against the modern Western European materialist.

Now I go on to the next big division. People who all believe in God can be divided according to the sort of God they believe in. There are two very different ideas on this subject. One of them is the idea that He is beyond good and evil. We humans call one thing good and another thing bad. But according to some people that is merely our human point of view. These people would say that the wiser you become the less you would want to call anything good or bad, and the more clearly you would see that everything is good in one way and bad in another, and that nothing could have been different. Consequently, these people think that long before you got anywhere near the divine point of view the distinction would have disappeared altogether. We call a cancer bad, they would say, because it kills a man; but you might

From *Mere Christianity*, 1952.

just as well call a successful surgeon bad because he kills a cancer. It all depends on the point of view. The other and opposite idea is that God is quite definitely "good" or "righteous." a God who takes sides, who loves love and hates hatred, who wants us to behave in one way and not in another. The first of these views—the one that thinks God beyond good and evil—is called Pantheism. It was held by the great Prussian philosopher Hagel and, as far as I can understand them, by the Hindus. The other view is held by Jews, Mohammedans and Christians.

And with this big difference between Pantheism and the Christian idea of God, there usually goes another. Pantheists usually believe that God, so to speak, animates the universe as you animate your body: that the universe almost is God, so that if it did not exist He would not exist either, and anything you find in the universe is a part of God. The Christian idea is quite different. They think God invented and made the universe—like a man making a picture or composing a tune. A painter is not a picture, and he does not die if his picture is destroyed. You may say, "He's put a lot of himself into it," but you only mean that all its beauty and interest has come out of his head. His skill is not in the picture in the same way that it is in his head, or even in his hands expect you see how this difference between Pantheists and Christians hangs together with the other one. If you do not take the distinction between good and bad very seriously, then it is easy to say that anything you find in this world is a part of God. But, of course, if you think some things really bad, and God really good, then you cannot talk like that. You must believe that God is separate from the world and that some of the things we see in it are contrary to His will. Confronted with a cancer or a slum the Pantheist can say, "If you could only see it from the divine point of view, you would realize that this also is God." The Christian replies, "Don't talk damned nonsense." (*)

[*] One listener complained of the word damned as frivolous swearing. But I mean exactly what I say—nonsense that is damned is under God's curse, and will (apart from God's grace) lead those who believe it to eternal death.

For Christianity is a fighting religion. It thinks God made the world—that space and time, heat and cold, and all the colours and tastes, and all the animals and vegetables, are things that God "made up out of His head" as a man makes up a story. But it also thinks that a great many things have gone wrong with the world that God made and that God insists, and insists very loudly, on our putting them right again.

And, of course, that raises a very big question. If a good God made the world why has it gone wrong? And for many years I simply refused to listen to the Christian answers to this question, because I kept on feeling "whatever you say, and however clever your arguments are, isn't it much simpler and easier to say that the world was not made by any intelligent power? Aren't all your arguments simply a complicated attempt to avoid the obvious?" But then that threw me back into another difficulty.

My argument against God was that the universe seemed so cruel and unjust. But how had I got this idea of just and unjust? A man does not call a line crooked unless he has some idea of a straight line. What was I comparing this universe with when I called it unjust? If the whole show was bad and senseless from A to Z, so to speak, why did I, who was supposed to be part of the show, find myself in such violent reaction against it? A man feels wet when he falls into water, because man is not a water animal: a fish would not feel wet.

Of course I could have given up my idea of justice by saying it was nothing but a private idea of my own. But if I did that, then my argument against God collapsed too—for the argument depended on saying that the world was really unjust, not simply that it did not happen to please my private fancies. Thus in the very act of trying to prove that God did not exist—in other words, that the whole of reality was senseless—I found I was forced to assume that one part of reality—namely my idea of justice—was full of sense.

Consequently atheism turns out to be too simple. If the whole universe has no meaning, we should never have found out that it has no meaning: just as, if there were no light in the universe and therefore no creatures with eyes, we should never know it was dark. Dark would be without meaning.

The Allegory of the Cave

By Plato

SOCRATES: Next, said I [Socrates], compare our nature in respect of education and its lack to such an experience as this.

PART ONE: SETTING THE SCENE: THE CAVE AND THE FIRE

The cave

SOCRATES: Imagine this: People live under the earth in a cavelike dwelling. Stretching a long way up toward the daylight is its entrance, toward which the entire cave is gathered. The people have been in this dwelling since childhood, shackled by the legs and neck. Thus they stay in the same place so that there is only one thing for them to look that: whatever they encounter in front of their faces. But because they are shackled, they are unable to turn their heads around.

A fire is behind them, and there is a wall between the fire and the prisoners

SOCRATES: Some light, of course, is allowed them, namely from a fire that casts its glow toward them from behind them, being above and at some distance. Between the fire and those who are shackled

[i.e., behind their backs] there runs a walkway at a certain height. Imagine that a low wall has been built the length of the walkway, like the low curtain that puppeteers put up, over which they show their puppets.

The images carried before the fire

SOCRATES: So now imagine that all along this low wall people are carrying all sorts of things that reach up higher than the wall: statues and other carvings made of stone or wood and many other artifacts that people have made. As you would expect, some are talking to each other [as they walk along] and some are silent.

GLAUCON: This is an unusual picture that you are presenting here, and these are unusual prisoners.

SOCRATES: They are very much like us humans, I [Socrates] responded.

---

c.a. 514–520 C.E.

What the prisoners see and hear

SOCRATES: What do you think? From the beginning people like this have never managed, whether on their own or with the help by others, to see anything besides the shadows that are [continually] projected on the wall opposite them by the glow of the fire.

GLAUCON: How could it be otherwise, since they are forced to keep their heads immobile for their entire lives?

SOCRATES: And what do they see of the things that are being carried along [behind them]? Do they not see simply these [namely the shadows]?

GLAUCON: Certainly.

SOCRATES: Now if they were able to say something about what they saw and to talk it over, do you not think that they would regard that which they saw on the wall as beings?

GLAUCON: They would have to.

SOCRATES: And now what if this prison also had an echo reverberating off the wall in front of them [the one that they always and only look at]? Whenever one of the people walking behind those in chains (and carrying the things) would make a sound, do you think the prisoners would imagine that the speaker were anyone other than the shadow passing in front of them?

GLAUCON: Nothing else, by Zeus!

SOCRATES: All in all, I responded, those who were chained would consider nothing besides the shadows of the artifacts as the unhidden.

GLAUCON: That would absolutely have to be.

PART TWO: THREE STAGES OF LIBERATION

FREEDOM, STAGE ONE

A prisoner gets free

SOCRATES: So now, I replied, watch the process whereby the prisoners are set free from their chains and, along with that, cured of their lack of insight, and likewise consider what kind of lack of insight must be if the following were to happen to those who were chained.

Walks back to the fire

SOCRATES: Whenever any of them was unchained and was forced to stand up suddenly, to turn around, to walk, and to look up toward the light, in each case the person would be able to do this only with pain and because of the flickering brightness would be unable to look at those things whose shadows he previously saw.

Is questioned about the objects

SOCRATES: If all this were to happen to the prisoner, what do you think he would say if someone were to inform him that what he saw before were [mere] trifles but that now he was much nearer to beings; and that, as a consequence of now being turned toward what is more in being, he also saw more correctly?

The answer he gives

SOCRATES: And if someone were [then] to show him any of the things that were passing by and forced him to answer the question about what it was, don't you think that he would be a wit's end and in addition would consider that what he previously saw [with his own eyes] was more unhidden than what was now being shown [to him by someone else].

GLAUCON: Yes, absolutely.

Looking at the fire-light itself

SOCRATES: And if someone even forced him to look into the glare of the fire, would his eyes not hurt him, and would he not then turn away and flee [back] to that which he is capable of looking at? And would he not decide that [what he could see before without any help] was in fact clearer than what was now being shown to him?

GLAUCON: Precisely.

FREEDOM, STAGE TWO

Out of the cave into daylight

SOCRATES: Now, however, if someone, using force, were to pull him [who had been freed from his chains] away from there and to drag him up the cave's rough and steep ascent and not to let go of him until he had dragged him out into the light of the sun...

Pain, rage, blindness

SOCRATES: ...would not the one who had been dragged like this feel, in the process, pain and rage?

And when he got into the sunlight, wouldn't his eyes be filled with the glare, and wouldn't he thus be unable to see any of the things that are now revealed to him as the unhidden?

GLAUCON: He would not be able to do that at all, at least not right away.

Getting used to the light

SOCRATES: It would obviously take some getting accustomed, I think, if it should be a matter of taking into one's eyes that which is up there outside the cave, in the light of the sun.

Shadows and reflections

SOCRATES: And in this process of acclimatization he would first and most easily be able to look at (1) shadows and after that (2) the images of people and the rest of things as they are reflected in water.

Looking at things directly

SOCRATES: Later, however, he would be able to view (3) the things themselves [the beings, instead of the dim reflections]. But within the range of such things, he might well contemplate what there is in the heavenly dome, and this dome itself, more easily during the night by looking at the light of the stars and the moon, [more easily, that is to say,] than by looking at the sun and its glare during the day.

GLAUCON: Certainly.

FREEDOM, STAGE THREE: THE SUN

Looking at the sun itself

SOCRATES: But I think that finally he would be in the condition to look at (4) the sun itself, not just at its reflection whether in water or wherever else it might appear, but at the sun itself, as it is in and of itself and in the place proper to it and to contemplate of what sort it is.

GLAUCON: It would necessarily happen this way.

Thoughts about the sun: its nature and functions

SOCRATES: And having done all that, by this time he would also be able to gather the following about the sun: (1) that it is that which grants both the seasons and the years; (2) it is that which governs whatever there is in the now visible region of sunlight; and (3) that it is also the cause of all those things that the people dwelling in the cave have before their eyes in some way or other.

GLAUCON: It is obvious that he would get to these things—the sun and whatever stands in its light—after he had gone out beyond those previous things, the merely reflections and shadows.

Thoughts about the cave

SOCRATES: And then what? If he again recalled his first dwelling, and the "knowing" that passes as the norm there, and the people with whom he once was chained, don't you think he would consider himself lucky because of the transformation that had happened and, by contrast, feel sorry for them?

GLAUCON: Very much so.

What counts for "wisdom" in the cave

SOCRATES: However, what if among the people in the previous dwelling place, the cave, certain honors and commendations were established for whomever most clearly catches sight of what passes by and also best remembers which of them normally is brought by first, which one later, and which ones at the same time? And what if there were honors for whoever could most easily foresee which one might come by next?

What would the liberated prisoner now prefer?

SOCRATES: Do you think the one who had gotten out of the cave would still envy those within the cave and would want to compete with them who are esteemed and who have power? Or would not he or she much rather wish for the condition that Homer speaks of, namely "to live on the land [above ground] as the paid menial of another destitute peasant"? Wouldn't he or she prefer to put up with absolutely anything else rather than associate with those opinions that hold in the cave and be that kind of human being?

GLAUCON: I think that he would prefer to endure everything rather than be that kind of human being.

PART THREE: THE PRISONER RETURNS TO THE CAVE

The return: blindness

SOCRATES: And now, I responded, consider this: If this person who had gotten out of the cave were to go back down again and sit in the same place as before, would he not find in that case, coming suddenly out of the sunlight, that his eyes were filled with darkness?

GLAUCON: Yes, very much so.

The debate with the other prisoners

SOCRATES: Now if once again, along with those who had remained shackled there, the freed person had to engage in the business of asserting and maintaining opinions about the shadows—while his eyes are still weak and before they have readjusted, an adjustment that would require quite a bit of time—would he not then be exposed to ridicule down there? And would they not let him know that he had gone up but only in order to come back down into the cave with his eyes ruined—and thus it certainly does not pay to go up.

And the final outcome:

SOCRATES: And if they can get hold of this person who takes it in hand to free them from their chains and to lead them up, and if they could kill him, will they not actually kill him?

GLAUCON: They certainly will.

End

Grief Beyond Belief—How Atheists Are Dealing With Death

By Greta Christina

In a society that reflexively copes with death by using religion, grieving atheists are turning to each other.

How do you deal with death—your own, or that of people you love—when you don't believe in God or an afterlife?

Especially when our culture so commonly handles grief with religion... in ways that are so deeply ingrained, people often aren't aware of it?

A new online faith-free grief support group, Grief Beyond Belief, is grappling with that very question. And the launch of the group—along with its rapid growth—presents another compelling question: Why do so many atheists need and want a separate godless sub-culture... for grief support, or anything else?

Grief Beyond Belief was launched by Rebecca Hensler after the death of her three-month-old son. Shortly after Jude's death, she discovered Compassionate Friends, an online network of parents grieving the deaths of their children. But even though Compassionate Friends is not a religious organization, she says, "I often felt alienated by assurances from other members that my son was in heaven or by offers to pray for me, comforts that were kindly meant but that I do not believe and cannot accept." And she knew there were others who felt the same way. (Conflict of interest alert: Hensler and I are friends, and I actively encouraged and supported her in launching this group.)

So about a year later, she started a Facebook page, Grief Beyond Belief. And the group grew and flourished far beyond her expectations. Once the atheist blogosphere heard about the group, news about it spread like wildfire, and membership in the group grew rapidly, rising to over a thousand in just the first couple of weeks. The group is open to atheists, agnostics, humanists, and anyone without belief in a higher power or an afterlife, to share memories, photos, thoughts, feelings or questions, and to give others support, perspective, empathy, or simply a non-judgmental ear. And it's also open to believers who are

From *Freethoughtsblog.com*, 2011.

questioning, struggling with, or letting go of their beliefs. As long as you don't offer prayers, proselytize for your religious beliefs, or tell other members that their dead loved ones are in a better place with the angels, you're welcome to join.

So why do atheists need this?

Salt in the Wound

For some grieving non-believers, the comforts offered by religious believers are neutral, and can even be positive. These atheists don't agree that their dead loved ones are still alive and that they'll see them again someday; but they can accept the intent behind the sentiments, and can feel connected with and supported by believers even though they don't share the beliefs.

But for many non-believers, these comforts are actively upsetting. They are the antithesis of comforting. They rub salt in the wound.

For many grieving non-believers, the "comforts" of religion and religious views of death present a terrible choice: Either pretend to agree with ideas they reject and in many cases actively oppose... or open up about their non-belief, and start a potentially divisive argument at a time when they most need connection and comfort. As GBB member William Farlin Cain said, "I was still very much in the atheist closet at the time [my mom] passed away, and I was surrounded by believers saying all the things believers say, and I had to say them too just to keep the peace. It was hard."

Religious ideas about death can also make atheists feel alienated: hyper-aware of their marginalized status, and of the ways that atheists in our culture are invisible at best. As I've told believers who were pressing their religious "comforts" on me even though I'd explicitly said I didn't want that: If you wouldn't tell a Jewish person that their dead loved one is in the arms of Jesus Christ, why would you think it's appropriate to tell a non-believer that their dead loved one is in Heaven? And yet many believers do think this is appropriate... to the point where they not only offer nonbelievers the "comfort" of their opinion that death is not final, but persist in doing so even when specifically asked not to. They're so steeped in the idea of religion as a comfort, they seem unable to think of any other way to comfort those in need. And they seem unable to see that their beliefs aren't universally shared by everyone.

200

But these beliefs aren't universally shared. And they aren't seen as universally comforting, either. In fact, religious ideas about death can be profoundly upsetting to people who don't believe them. Sentiments that many believers find comforting —such as Heaven and Hell, or God's plan for life and death—are, for many non-believers, more than just ideas they don't agree with. They are ideas they find distressing, hurtful, and repugnant. As GBB member Lisa M. Lilly said, "After my parents were killed by a drunk driver, people said things to me that I found extremely difficult to hear, such as that their deaths were God's plan or God's will. While I'm sure the speakers thought they were offering comfort, the idea that God wanted my mother to be run over and die in the street and my father to suffer 6 1/2 weeks with severe injuries, only to die after several surgeries, was appalling to me." And as GBB member Karen Vidrine commented, "Even when believers don't say it, I know they are thinking of Hell and how to tell me my children [who committed suicide] are there." Even though atheists don't agree with these ideas, they're still disturbing—and they're the last thing they want to hear about when they're struggling with their grief.

This isn't just true for non-believers, either. It's often true for grieving believers as well. In fact, as Hensler points out, the death of a loved one is often a trigger for questioning or abandoning religious faith— especially if that death is particularly painful or unjust. (This is a big reason why Hensler created the group to welcome not only atheists, but believers who are questioning their faith.) The idea that death is part of God's plan, for instance, is comforting to some—but for many, this idea either makes them angry at God, or guilt-ridden about what they or their loved ones did wrong to bring on his wrath. And the idea of Heaven or another perfectly blissful afterlife is often comforting only when you don't think about it very carefully. When you consider the idea of a spiritual "place" where we somehow are ourselves and yet magically don't change or grow, don't experience any conflict, don't have the freedom to screw up, and are untroubled by the suffering of others (either living or in Hell)... this idea can become more and more disturbing the more carefully you consider it. And many people find that they cope with death and grief far better without it.

But the reality is that spiritual beliefs permeate grief support—so much so that it's invisible to believers, who often perpetuate it without even thinking. As GBB founder Hensler pointed out, even in the non-religious Compassionate Friends group, "so many of their members are religious or spiritual that there is no real way to participate without being constantly exposed to comments about god, angels and signs. And when I posted about my son and my grief on the page, commenters frequently projected those beliefs onto me, with offers to pray or reassurances that Jude is in heaven. Half the time I felt understood and supported, and half the time I felt like screaming." GBB member Kevin Millham echoes this sentiment. "The hospice in which my wife died has a wonderful bereavement program, and I now belong to a grief support there. Everyone tries to be supportive and not proselytize, but the other members are Christians without exception, and we often hear in group meetings how their faith is helping them get through (though I notice they're having every bit as hard a time as I am...). What helps them does not help me, however, and I find that talk of an afterlife I do not believe in is a way of minimizing my attempts to deal with the finality of my wife's death, however well-intentioned the 'better place' comments may be."

And planning funerals and memorials with religious content is so common that, even when non-believers explicitly request secular ceremonies upon their death, these wishes frequently get ignored. Said GBB member Julie Downing Wirtz, "When my mom died, she left explicit instructions for her funeral. It was to be in the funeral home, not the church, she wanted 2 songs played, and she named them clearly. Well, some of my siblings chose not to honor her wishes, went to the Catholic church my mother no longer attended, somehow got the pastor there to allow the funeral service, but he would not allow the songs that my mom felt would give us comfort, since they were not religious songs." This also happened to GBB member Kevin Millham when his wife died: "The memorials we had discussed and agreed upon before her death were pretty much hijacked by local religious and spiritual types."

Even supposedly secular memorials often get infused with religious or spiritual content. And this tendency is so deeply ingrained, the people planning these events aren't even aware that the content is religious, and might be unwelcome to non-believers. Hensler tells the story of a memorial held for a number of children, including her son—a memorial that was explicitly described as non-religious. "A book was read to all the children in attendance," she says, "who were mostly grieving siblings. The book was written from the point of view of a dead child, describing 'where I am now' in vague, stars-and-rainbows sorts of terms. It disturbed me, particularly because my late son was one of the children honored at the ceremony. How can they say an event will be non-religious and then teach the children who attend about a version of afterlife?" And before you ask... this didn't happen in a small town in the Midwest, or the deeply religious South. It happened in San Francisco—one of the most secular, least traditionally religious, most diversity-supportive cities in the country. As Hensler noted, "A whole lot of people seem to think that as long as you aren't talking about Jesus, any support you provide is universally welcome.

This latter point cannot be emphasized enough. There's an all-too-common assumption that "non-religious" means "not adhering to the tenets of a specific religious sect." If you aren't talking about Jesus, or Allah, or reincarnation—if all you're talking about is non-specific ideas of some sort of higher power or some sort of afterlife—that's typically seen to be "non-religious." Atheism—or indeed, any sort of non-belief in any supernatural beings or forces—is still so invisible in our culture that the possibility simply isn't considered. So even supposedly inclusive, secular events end up with religious or spiritual content that leaves non-believers out in the cold.

But even if none of this were the case—even if grieving atheists were never confronted with religious ideas about death in upsetting or alienating ways, or even if no atheists were upset or alienated by these ideas—the need for non- faith- based grief support would still be powerful.

Because in a time of grief, the need for others who understand, others with a similar outlook on life and death, is powerful.

Secular and religious views of life—and death—can be radically different. The view that life and death are deliberately guided by a conscious supernatural being is radically different from the view that life and death are entirely natural processes, guided by physical cause and effect. The view that consciousness is a metaphysical substance with the ability to survive death is radically different from the view that consciousness is a biological process created by the brain, and that it ends when the brain dies. The view that life is permanent is radically different from the view that life is ephemeral.

And the forms of comfort and perspective that we find helpful in grief can also be radically different. The idea that life is eternal and we'll see our loved ones again someday is radically different from the idea that life is transitory and therefore ought to be intensely treasured. The idea that life and death are part of God's benevolent plan is radically different from the idea that life and death are part of natural cause and effect, and that we and our loved ones are part of the physical universe and are intimately connected with it. The idea that our dead loved ones are no longer suffering because they're in a blissful Heaven is radically different from the idea that our dead loved ones are no longer suffering because they no longer exist, and that being dead is no more painful or frightening than not having been born yet. The idea that death is an illusion is radically different from the idea that death is necessary for life and change to be possible. The idea that the soul will live forever is radically different from the idea that things don't have to be permanent to be valuable and meaningful. The idea that there will be a final judgment in which the bad are punished and the good are rewarded is radically different from the idea that we were all phenomenally, astronomically lucky to have been born at all. The idea that our loved ones will always live on in an afterlife is radically different from the idea that we keep our loved ones alive in our memories, and that they live on in the ways they changed us and the world. Believers and non-believers have many things in common, and much of what we find comforting during grief is the same—but much of it is seriously different, and even contradictory.

So for many grieving non-believers, the comfort offered by religious believers is, at best, not particularly comforting. Even if it isn't actively upsetting, it simply doesn't connect. And so the comfort, perspective, practical guidance, support, and simple "I've been there and know what you're going through" offered by the Grief Beyond Belief network has been intensely welcomed. As Hensler says, "One of the hardest parts about the first few days of Grief Beyond Belief was the number of people who said, "I wish this had existed when..."

GBB member Nita-Jane Grigson: "I get a sense of support from other people going through what I'm going through, that my friends don't understand." GBB member William Farlin Cain: "Other grief groups more or less insist I indulge my 'spiritual side,' and I just want something of the rational as I revisit the grieving process these years later." GBB member Karen Vidrine: "I like being able to comment and vent about my children's deaths, suicides, without fear of judgment." GBB member James Sweet: "I look for the same things I think just about anyone is looking for in a grief support group: To know other people are going through the same things; to vent; to share; to find hope in loss, to see that no matter how terrible the tragedy, life still goes on. I just don't need to worry so much about having to bite my tongue." GBB member Lisa M. Lilly: "I am grateful to Grief Beyond Belief for providing a forum where feelings of loss are acknowledged and shared without anyone insisting that somehow the tragedy is a good thing or fits with religious views held by others." GBB member Kevin Millham: "I come here to be with kindred spirits who will understand what it is I'm going through even if we do not often respond directly to each other's posts. Just knowing that I'm not alone in my (lack of) beliefs is a comfort when in my hometown I feel so alienated."

Even people who currently aren't grieving are finding Grief Beyond Belief valuable —because it helps them support the bereaved non-believers in their lives. GBB member Julie Downing Wirtz says, "As a trained Funeral Celebrant, and Life Tribute Specialist, serving only non-religious families, I find the posts at GBB help me to serve my clients with a better understanding of the various thoughts that go through people's minds when they are grieving, many of which are very different from my own experiences." And GBB member Christine M. Pedro-Panuyas concurs. " I haven't lost anyone close to me, but what Grief Beyond Belief has really done for me is it helped me know what to say to those who have lost someone. It helped me learn the words to say that are comforting and are comforting in a powerful way because they are true."

When The Trump Card Fails

It's commonly assumed that death is religion's trump card. No matter what atheism has to offer—a better sex life, freedom from religion's often random taboos, the embrace of reality over wishful thinking, etc.—many people automatically assume that, when it comes to death and grief, the comfort of believing in an afterlife will always win out. They assume that any argument for atheism being, you know, true, will ultimately crumble in the face of our desire for death to not be the end.

Many atheists reject this assumption passionately. We point out that many religious beliefs about death are far from comforting—Hell being the most obvious—and that many former believers welcome atheism as a profound relief. We point out that religious beliefs about death are only comforting when you don't think about them very carefully. We point out that a philosophy that accepts reality is inherently more comforting than a philosophy based on wishful thinking... since it doesn't involve cognitive dissonance and the unease of self-deception. And we point out that there are many godless philosophies of death that offer comfort, meaning, and hope—with complete acceptance of the permanence of death, and without any belief in any sort of afterlife.

But it's one thing to face the general idea of death with a godless philosophy. It's another thing entirely when someone you love dies, and you're dealing with the immediate and painful reality of grief.

I'm Right, You're Wrong, Go to Hell: Religions and the Meeting of Civilization

By Bernard Lewis

For a long time now it has been our practice in the modern Western world to define ourselves primarily by nationality, and to see other identities and allegiances—religious, political, and the like—as subdivisions of the larger and more important whole. The events of September 11 and after have made us aware of another perception—of a religion subdivided into nations rather than a nation subdivided into religions—and this has induced some of us to think of ourselves and of our relations with others in ways that had become unfamiliar. The confrontation with a force that defines itself as Islam has given a new relevance—indeed, urgency—to the theme of the "clash of civilizations."

At one time the general assumption of mankind was that "civilization" meant us, and the rest were uncivilized. This, as far as we know, was the view of the great civilizations of the past—in China, India, Greece, Rome, Persia, and the ancient Middle East. Not until a comparatively late stage did the idea emerge that there are different civilizations, that these civilizations meet and interact, and—even more interesting—that a civilization has a life-span: it is born, grows, matures, declines, and dies. One can perhaps trace that latter idea to the medieval Arab historian-philosopher Ibn Khaldun (1332-1406), who spoke in precisely those terms, though what he discussed was not civilizations but states—or, rather, regimes. The concept wasn't really adapted to civilizations until the twentieth century.

The first writer to make the connection was the German historian Oswald Spengler. Perhaps influenced by the horrors of World War I and the defeat of imperial Germany, he looked around him and saw civilization in decline. He built a philosophy on this perception, captured in the phrase "the decline of the West"—*Der Untergang des Abendlandes*. His two volumes under this title were published in 1918 and 1922. In these he discussed how different civilizations meet, interact, rise and decline, and fall. His approach was elaborated by Arnold Toynbee, who proceeded with a sort of wish list of civilizations—and, of course, also a hit list. Most recently Samuel

From *The Atlantic*, 2003.

Huntington, of Harvard University, has argued that the clash of civilizations, more than of countries or governments, is now the basic force of international relations. I think most of us would agree, and some of us have indeed said, that the clash of civilizations is an important aspect of modern international relations, though probably not many of us would go so far as to imply, as some have done, that civilizations have foreign policies and form alliances.

There have been a number of different civilizations in human history, and several are extant, though not all in the same condition. Mustafa Kemal, later known as Atatürk, dealt with the relative condition of civilizations in some of the speeches in which he urged the people of the newly established Turkish Republic to modernize. He put the issue with military directness and simplicity. People, he said, talked of this civilization and that civilization, and of interaction and influence between civilizations; but only one civilization was alive and well and advancing, and that was what he called modernity, the civilization "of our time." All the others were dying or dead, he said, and Turkey's choice was to join this civilization or be part of a dying world. The one civilization was, of course, the West.

Only two civilizations have been defined by religion. Others have had religions but are identified primarily by region and ethnicity. Buddhism has been a major religious force, and was the first to try to bring a universal message to all mankind. There is some evidence of Buddhist activities in the ancient Middle East, and the possibility has been suggested of Buddhist influence on Judaism and, therefore, on the rise of Christianity. But Buddhism has not expanded significantly for many centuries, and the countries where it flourishes—in South, Southeast, and East Asia—are defined, like their neighbors, by culture more than by creed. These other civilizations, with the brief and problematic exception of communism, have lacked the ideological capacity—and for the most part even the desire—for indefinite expansion.

Christianity and Islam are the two religions that define civilizations, and they have much in common, along with some differences. In English and in most of the other languages of the Christian world we have two words, "Christianity" and "Christendom." Christianity is a religion, a system of belief and worship with certain ecclesiastical institutions. Christendom is a civilization that incorporates elements that are non-Christian or even anti-Christian. Hitler and the Nazis, it may be recalled, are products of Christendom, but hardly of

Christianity. When we talk of Islam, we use the same word for both the religion and the civilization, which can lead to misunderstanding. The late Marshall Hodgson, a distinguished historian of Islam at the University of Chicago, was, I think, the first to draw attention to this problem, and he invented the word "Islamdom." Unfortunately, "Islamdom" is awkward to pronounce and just didn't catch on, so the confusion remains. (In Turkish there is no confusion, because "Islam" means the civilization, and "Islamiyet" refers specifically to the religion.)

In looking at the history of civilization we talk, for example, of "Islamic art," meaning art produced in Muslim countries, not just religious art, whereas the term "Christian art" refers to religious or votive art, churches and pious sculpture and painting. We talk about "Islamic science," by which we mean physics, chemistry, mathematics, biology, and the rest under the aegis of Muslim civilization. If we say "Christian science," we mean something totally different and unrelated.

Does one talk about "Jewish science"? I don't think so. One may talk about Jewish scientists, but that's not the same thing. But then, of course, Judaism is not a civilization—it's a religion and a culture. Most of Jewish history since the Diaspora has taken place within either Christendom or Islam. There were Jews in India, there were Jews in China, but those communities didn't flourish. Their role was minimal, both in the history of the Jews and in the history of India and China. The term "Judeo-Christian" is a new name for an old reality, though in earlier times it would have been equally resented on both sides of the hyphen. One could use an equivalent term, "Judeo-Islamic," to designate another cultural symbiosis that flourished in the more recent past and ended with the dawn of modernity.

To what extent is a religiously defined civilization compatible with pluralism—tolerance of others within the same civilization but of different religions? This crucial question points to a major distinction between two types of religion. For some religions, just as "civilization" means us, and the rest are barbarians, so "religion" means ours, and the rest are infidels. Other religions, such as Judaism and most of the religions of Asia, concede that human beings may use different religions to speak to God, as they use different languages to speak to one another. God understands them all. I know in my heart that the English language is the finest instrument the human race has ever devised to express its thoughts and feelings, but I recognize in my mind that others may feel exactly the same way about their languages, and I have no problem with that. These two approaches to religion may conveniently be denoted by the terms their critics use to condemn them—"triumphalism" and "relativism." In one of his sermons the fifteenth-century Franciscan Saint John of Capistrano, immortalized on the map of California, denounced the Jews for trying to spread a "deceitful" notion among Christians: "The Jews say that everyone can be saved in his own faith, which is impossible." For once a charge of his against the Jews was justified. The Talmud does indeed say that the righteous of all faiths have a place in paradise. Polytheists and atheists are excluded, but monotheists of any persuasion who observe the basic moral laws are eligible. The relativist view was condemned and rejected by both Christians and Muslims, who shared the conviction that there was only one true faith, theirs, which it was their duty to bring to all humankind. The triumphalist view is increasingly under attack in Christendom, and is disavowed by significant numbers of Christian clerics. There is little sign as yet of a parallel development in Islam.

Tolerance is, of course, an extremely intolerant idea, because it means "I am the boss: I will allow you some, though not all, of the rights I enjoy as long as you behave yourself according to standards that I shall determine." That, I think, is a fair definition of religious tolerance as it is normally understood and applied. In a letter to the Jewish community of Newport, Rhode Island, that George Washington wrote in 1790, he remarked, perhaps in an allusion to the famous "Patent of Tolerance" promulgated by the Austrian Emperor Joseph II a few years previously, "It is now no more that toleration is spoken of, as if it was by the indulgence of one class of people that another enjoyed the exercise of their inherent natural rights." At a meeting of Jews, Christians, and Muslims in Vienna some years ago the Cardinal Archbishop Franz Koenig spoke of tolerance, and I couldn't resist quoting Washington to him. He replied, "You are right. I shall no more speak of tolerance; I shall speak of mutual respect." There are still too few who share the attitude expressed in this truly magnificent response.

For those taking the relativist approach to religion (in effect, "I have my god, you have your god, and others have theirs"), there may be specific political or economic reasons for objecting to someone else's beliefs, but in principle there is no theological problem. For those taking the triumphalist approach (classically summed up in the formula "I'm right, you're wrong, go to hell"), tolerance is a problem.

Because the triumphalist's is the only true and complete religion, all other religions are at best incomplete and more probably false and evil; and since he is the privileged recipient of God's final message to humankind, it is surely his duty to bring it to others rather than keep it selfishly for himself.

Now, if one believes that, what does one do about it? And how does one relate to people of another religion? If we look at this question historically, one thing emerges very clearly: whether the other religion is previous or subsequent to one's own is extremely important. From a Christian point of view, for example, Judaism is previous and Islam is subsequent. From a Muslim point of view, both Judaism and Christianity are previous. From a Jewish point of view, both Christianity and Islam are subsequent—but since Judaism is not triumphalist, this is not a problem.

But it is a problem for Christians and Muslims—or perhaps I should say for traditional Christians and Muslims. From their perspective, a previous religion may be regarded as incomplete, as superseded, but it is not necessarily false if it comes in the proper sequence of revelation. So from a Muslim point of view, Judaism and Christianity were both true religions at the time of their revelation, but they were superseded by the final and complete revelation of Islam; although they are out-of-date—last year's model, so to speak—they are not inherently false. Therefore Muslim law, sharia, not only permits but requires that a certain degree of tolerance be accorded them.

It is, of course, a little more complicated: Jews and Christians are accused of falsifying their originally authentic scriptures and religions. Thus, from a Muslim point of view, the Christian doctrine of the Trinity and of the divinity of Jesus Christ are distortions. The point is made in several Koranic verses: "There is no God but God alone, He has no companion," and "He is God, one, eternal. He does not beget, He is not begotten, and He has no peer." These and similar verses appear frequently on early Islamic coins and in inscriptions, and are clearly polemical in intent. They are inscribed, notably, in the Dome of the Rock, in Jerusalem—a challenge to Christianity in its birthplace. Jews are accused of eliminating scriptural passages foretelling the advent of Muhammad. Anything subsequent to Muhammad, "the Seal of the Prophets," is, from the Muslim perspective, necessarily false. This explains the harsh treatment of post-Islamic religions, such as the Bahai faith and the Ahmadiya movement, in Islamic lands.

Muslims did not claim a special relationship to either of the predecessor religions, and if Jews and Christians chose not to accept Muhammad, that was their loss. Muslims were prepared to tolerate them in accordance with sharia, which lays down both the extent and the limits of the latitude to be granted those who follow a recognized religion: they must be monotheists and they must have a revealed scripture, which in practice often limited tolerance to Jews and Christians. The Koran names a third qualified group, the Sabians; there is some uncertainty as to who they were, and at times this uncertainty provided a convenient way of extending the tolerance of the Muslim state to Zoroastrians or other groups when it was thought expedient. On principle, no tolerance was extended to polytheists or idolaters, and this sometimes raised acute problems in Asian and African lands conquered by the Muslims.

Tolerance was a much more difficult question for Christians. For them, Judaism is a precursor of their religion, and Christianity is the fulfillment of the divine promises made to the Jews. The Jewish rejection of that fulfillment is therefore seen as impugning some of the central tenets of the Christian faith. Tolerance between different branches of Christianity would eventually become an even bigger problem. Of course, the outsider is more easily tolerated than the dissident insider. Heretics are a much greater danger than unbelievers. The English philosopher John Locke's famous *A Letter Concerning Toleration*, written toward the end of the seventeenth century, is a plea for religious tolerance, still a fairly new idea at that time. Locke wrote, "Neither pagan, nor Mahometan, nor Jew, ought to be excluded from the civil rights of the commonwealth, because of his religion." Someone is of course missing from that list: the Catholic. The difference is clear. For Locke and his contemporaries, the pagan, the Muslim, the Jew, were no threat to the Church of England; the Catholic was. The Catholic was trying to subvert Protestantism, to make England Catholic, and, as Protestant polemicists at the time put it, to make England subject to a foreign potentate—namely, the Pope in Rome.

Muslims were in general more tolerant of diversity within their own community, and even cited an early tradition to the effect that such diversity is a divine blessing. The concept of heresy—in the Christian sense of incorrect belief recognized and condemned as such by properly constituted religious authority—was unknown to classical Islam. Deviation and diversity, with rare exceptions, were persecuted only when they offered a serious threat to the existing order. The very notion of an authority empowered to rule on questions of belief was alien to traditional Islamic thought and practice. It has become less alien.

212

A consequence of the similarity between Christianity and Islam in background and approach is the long conflict between the two civilizations they defined. When two religions met in the Mediterranean area, each claiming to be the recipient of God's final revelation, conflict was inevitable. The conflict, in fact, was almost continuous: the first Arab-Islamic invasions took Islam by conquest to the then Christian lands of Syria, Palestine, Egypt, and North Africa, and, for a while, to Southern Europe; the Tatars took it into Russia and Eastern Europe; and the Turks took it into the Balkans. To each advance came a Christian rejoinder: the Reconquista in Spain, the Crusades in the Levant, the throwing off of what the Russians call the Tatar yoke in the history of their country, and, finally, the great European counterattack into the lands of Islam, which is usually called imperialism.

During this long period of conflict, of *jihad* and crusade, of conquest and reconquest, Christianity and Islam nevertheless maintained a level of communication, because the two are basically the same kind of religion. They could argue. They could hold disputations and debates. Even their screams of rage were mutually intelligible. When Christians and Muslims said to each other, "You are an infidel and you will burn in hell," each understood exactly what the other meant, because they both meant the same thing. (Their heavens are differently appointed, but their hells are much the same.) Such assertions and accusations would have conveyed little or no meaning to a Hindu, a Buddhist, or a Confucian.

Christians and Muslims looked at each other and studied each other in strikingly different ways. This is owing in part, at least, to their different circumstances. Christian Europeans from the start had to learn foreign languages in order to read their scriptures and their classics and to communicate with one another. From the seventh century onward they had a further motive to look outward—their holy places, in the land where their faith was born, were under Muslim rule, and could be visited only with Muslim permission. Muslims had no comparable problems. Their holy places were in Arabia, under Arab rule; their scriptures were in Arabic, which across their civilization was the language also of literature, of science and scholarship, of government and commerce, and, increasingly, of everyday communication, as the conquered countries in Southwest Asia and North Africa were Arabized and forgot their ancient languages and scripts. In later times other Islamic languages emerged, notably Persian and Turkish; but in the early, formative centuries Arabic reigned alone.

This difference in the experiences and the needs of the two civilizations is reflected in their attitudes toward each other. From the earliest recorded times people in Europe tried to learn the languages of the Islamic world, starting with Arabic, the language of the most advanced civilization of the day. Later some, mostly for practical reasons, learned Persian and more especially Turkish, which in Ottoman times supplanted Arabic as the language of government and diplomacy. From the sixteenth century on there were chairs of Arabic at French and Dutch universities. Cambridge University had its first chair of Arabic in 1632, Oxford in 1636. Europeans no longer needed Arabic to gain access to the higher sciences. Now they learned it out of intellectual curiosity—the desire to know something about another civilization and its ways. By the eighteenth century Europe boasted a considerable body of scholarly literature regarding the Islamic world—editions of texts and translations of historical and literary and theological works, as well as histories of literature and religion and even general histories of Islamic countries, with descriptions of their people and their ways. Grammars and dictionaries of Arabic, Persian, and Turkish were available to European scholars from the sixteenth century onward. It is surely significant that far more attention was given to Arabic, the classical and scriptural language of Islam, than to Persian and Turkish, the languages of the current rulers of the world. In the course of the nineteenth century European and later also American scholars set to work to disinter, decipher, and interpret the buried and forgotten languages and writings of antiquity, and thus to recover an ancient and glorious chapter in history. These activities were greeted with incomprehension and then with suspicion by those who did not share and there-fore could not understand this kind of curiosity.

The Islamic world, with no comparable incentives, displayed a total lack of interest in Christian civilization. An initially understandable, even justifiable, contempt for the barbarians beyond the frontier continued long after that characterization ceased to be accurate, and even into a time when it became preposterously inaccurate.

It has sometimes been argued that the European interest in Arabic and other Eastern languages was an adjunct—or, given the time lag, a precursor—of imperialism. If that is so, we must acquit the Arabs and the Turks of any such predatory intent. The Arabs spent 800 years in Spain without showing much interest in Spanish or Latin. The Ottomans ruled much of southeastern Europe for half a millennium, but for most of that time they never bothered to learn Greek or any Balkan or European language—which might have been useful. When they needed interpreters, they used converts and others from these various countries. There was no Occidentalism until the expanding West forced itself on the attention of the rest of the world. We may find similar attitudes in present-day America.

Today we in the West are engaged in what we see as a war against terrorism, and what the terrorists present as a war against unbelief. Some on both sides see this struggle as one between civilizations or, as others would put it, between religions. If they are right, and there is much to support their view, then the clash between these two religiously defined civilizations results not only from their differences but also from their resemblances—and in these there may even be some hope for better future understanding.

Part Five

Health
and
Medicine

"This Is the End of the World": The Black Death

By Barbara Tuchman

In October 1347, two months after the fall of Calais[1], Genoese trading ships put into the harbor of Messina in Sicily with dead and dying men at the oars. The ships had come from the Black Sea port of Caffa (now Feodosiya) in the Crimea, where the Genoese maintained a trading post. The diseased sailors showed strange black swellings about the size of an egg or an apple in the armpits and groin. The swellings oozed blood and pus and were followed by spreading boils and black blotches on the skin from internal bleeding. The sick suffered severe pain and died quickly within five days of the first symptoms. As the disease spread, other symptoms of continuous fever and spitting of blood appeared instead of the swellings or buboes. These victims coughed and sweated heavily and died even more quickly, within three days or less, sometimes in 24 hours. In both types everything that issued from the body—breath, sweat, blood from the buboes and lungs, bloody urine, and blood-blackened excrement—smelled foul. Depression and despair accompanied the physical symptoms, and before the end "death is seen seated on the face."

The disease was bubonic plague, present in two forms: one that infected the bloodstream, causing the buboes and internal bleeding, and was spread by contact; and a second, more virulent pneumonic type that infected the lungs and was spread by respiratory infection. The presence of both at once caused the high mortality and speed of contagion. So lethal was the disease that cases were known of persons going to bed well and dying before they woke, of doctors catching the illness at a bedside and dying before the patient. So rapidly did it spread from one to another that to a French physician, Simon de Covino, it seemed as if one sick person "could infect the whole world." The malignity of the pestilence appeared more terrible because its victims knew no prevention and no remedy.

The physical suffering of the disease and its aspect of evil mystery were expressed in a strange Welsh lament which saw "death coming

---

1 After a year-long siege, the French citizens of Calais surrendered to Edward III, king of England and self-declared King of France.

From *A Distant Mirror: The Calamitous 14th Century*, 1978.

into our midst like black smoke, a plague which cuts off the young, a rootless phantom which has no mercy for fair countenance. Woe is me of the shilling in the armpit! It is seething, terrible...a head that gives pain and causes a loud cry...a painful angry knob...Great is its seething like a burning cinder...a grievous thing of ashy color." Its eruption is ugly like the "seeds of black peas, broken fragments of brittle sea-coal...the early ornaments of black death, cinders of the peelings of the cockle weed, a mixed multitude, a black plague like halfpence, like berries...."

Rumors of a terrible plague supposedly arising in China and spreading through Tartary (Central Asia) to India and Persia, Mesopotamia, Syria, Egypt, and all of Asia Minor had reached Europe in 1346. They told of a death toll so devastating that all of India was said to be depopulated, whole territories covered by dead bodies, other areas with no one left alive. As added up by Pope Clement VI at Avignon, the total of reported dead reached 23,840,000. In the absence of a concept of contagion, no serious alarm was felt in Europe until the trading ships brought their black burden of pestilence into Messina while other infected ships from the Levant carried it to Genoa and Venice.

By January 138 it penetrated France via Marseille, and North Africa via Tunis. Shipborne along coasts and navigable rivers, it spread westward from Marseille through the ports of Languedoc to Spain and northward up the Rhône to Avignon, where it arrived in March. It reached Narbonne, Montpellier, Carcassone, and Toulouse between February and May, and at the same time in Italy spread to Rome and Florence and their hinterlands. Between June and August it reached Bordeaux, Lyon, and Paris, spread to Burgundy and Normandy, and crossed the Channel from Normandy into southern England. From Italy during the same summer it crossed the Alps into Switzerland and reached eastward to Hungary.

In a given area the plague accomplished its kill within four to six months and then faded, except in the larger cities, where, rooting into the close-quartered population, it abated during the winter, only to reappear in spring and rage for another six months.

In 1349 it resumed in Paris, spread to Picardy, Flanders, and the Low Countries, and from England to Scotland and Ireland as well as to Norway, where a ghost ship with a cargo of wool and a dead crew drifted offshore until it ran aground near Bergen. From there the plague passed into Sweden, Denmark, Prussia, Iceland, and as far as Greenland. Leaving a strange pocket of immunity in Bohemia, and Russia unattacked until 1351, it had passed from most of Europe by mid-1350. Although the mortality rate was erratic, ranging from one fifth in some places to nine tenths or almost total elimination in others, the overall estimate of modern demographers has settled—for the area extending from India to Iceland—around the same figure expressed in Froissart's casual words: "a third of the world died." His estimate, the common one at the time, was not an inspired guess but a borrowing of St. John's figure for mortality from plague in Revelation, the favorite guide to human affairs of the Middle Ages.

A third of Europe would have meant about 20 million deaths. No one knows in truth how many died. Contemporary reports were an awed impression, not an accurate count. In crowded Avignon, it was said, 400 died daily; 7,000 houses emptied by death were shut up; a single graveyard received 11,000 corpses in six weeks; half the city's inhabitants reportedly died, including 9 cardinals or one third of the total, and 70 lesser prelates. Watching the endlessly passing death carts, chroniclers let normal exaggeration take wings and put the Avignon death toll at 62,000 and even at 120,000, although the city's total population was probably less than 50,000.

When graveyards filled up, bodies at Avignon were thrown into the Rhône until mass burial pits were dug for dumping the corpses. In London in such pits corpses piled up in layers until they overflowed. Everywhere reports speak of the sick dying too fast for the living to bury. Corpses were dragged out of homes and left in front of doorsteps. Morning light revealed new piles of bodies. In Florence the dead were gathered up by the Compagnia della Misericordia—founded in 1244 to care for the sick—whose members wore red robes and hoods masking the face except for the eyes. When their efforts failed, the dead lay putrid in the streets for days at a time. When no coffins were to be had, the bodies were laid on boards, two or three at once, to be carried to graveyards or common pits. Families dumped their own relatives into the pits, or buried them so hastily and thinly "that dogs dragged them forth and devoured their bodies."

Amid accumulating death and fear of contagion, people died without last rites and were buried without prayers, a prospect that terrified the last hours of the stricken. A bishop in England gave permission to laymen to make confession to each other as was done by the Apostles, "or if no man is present then even to a woman," and if no priest could be found to administer extreme unction, "then faith must suffice." Clement VI found it necessary to grant remissions of sin to all who died of the plague because so many were unattended by priests. "And no bells tolled," wrote a chronicler of Siena, "and nobody wept no matter what his loss because almost everyone expected death....And people said and believed, 'This is the end of the world.'"

In Paris, where the plague lasted through 1349, the reported death rate was 800 a day, in Pisa 500, in Vienna 500 to 600. The total dead in Paris numbered 50,000 or half the population. Florence, weakened by the famine of 1347, lost three to four fifths of its citizens, Venice two thirds, Hamburg and Bremen, though smaller in size, about the same proportion. Cities, as centers of transportation, were more likely to be affected than villages, although once a village was infected, its death rate was equally high. At Givry, a prosperous village in Burgundy of 1,200 to 1,500 people, the parish register records 615 deaths in the space of fourteen weeks, compared to an average of thirty deaths a year in the previous decade. In three villages of Cambridgeshire, manorial records show a death rate of 47 percent, 57 percent, and in one case 70 percent. When the last survivors, too few to carry on, moved away, a deserted village sank bank into the wilderness and disappeared from the map altogether, leaving only a grass-covered ghostly outline to show where mortals once had lived.

In enclosed places such as monasteries and prisons, the infection of one person usually meant that of all, as happened in the Franciscan convents of Carcassone and Marseille, where every inmate without exception died. Of the 140 Dominicans at Montpellier only seven survived. Petrarch's[2] brother Gherardo, member of a Carthusian monastery, buried the prior and 34 fellow monks one by one, sometimes three a day, until he was left alone with his dog and fled to look for a place that would take him in. Watching every comrade die, men in such places could not but wonder whether the strange peril that filled the air had not been sent to exterminate the human race. In Kilkenny, Ireland, Brother John Clyn of the Friars Minor, another monk left alone among dead men, kept a record of what had happened lest "things which should be remembered perish with time and vanish from the memory of those who come after us." Sensing "the whole world, as it were, placed within the grasp of the Evil One," and waiting for death to visit him too, he wrote, "I leave parchment to continue

2 Francesco Petrarch (1304–1374), Italian writer whose sonnets to "my lady Laura" influenced a tradition of European love poetry for centuries.

this work, if perchance any man survive and any of the race of Adam escape this pestilence and carry on the work which I have begun." Brother John, as noted by another hand, died of the pestilence, but he foiled oblivion.

The largest cities of Europe, with populations of about 100,000, were Paris and Florence, Venice and Genoa. At the next level, with more than 50,000, were Ghent and Bruges in Flanders, Milan, Bologna, Rome, Naples, and Palermo, and Cologne. London hovered below 50,000, the only city in England except York with more than 10,000. At the level of 20,000 to 50,000 were Bordeaux, Toulouse, Montpellier, Marseille, and Lyon in France, Barcelona, Seville, and Toledo in Spain, Siena, Pisa, and other secondary cities in Italy, and the Hanseatic trading cities of the Empire. The plague raged through them all, killing anywhere from one third to two thirds of their inhabitants. Italy, with a total population of 10 to 11 million, probably suffered the heaviest toll. Following the Florentine bankruptcies, the crop failures and workers' riots of 1347-47, the revolt of Cola di Rienzi that lunged Rome into anarchy, the plague came as the peak of successive calamities. As if the world were indeed in the grasp of the Evil One, its first appearance on the European mainland in January 1348 coincided with a fearsome earthquake that carved a path of wreckage from Naples up to Venice. Houses collapsed, church towers toppled, villages were crushed, and the destruction reached as far as Germany and Greece. Emotional response, dulled by horrors, underwent a kind of atrophy, epitomized by the chronicler who wrote, "And in these days was burying without sorrowe and wedding without friendschippe."

In Siena, where more than half the inhabitants died of the plague, work was abandoned on the great cathedral, planned to be the largest in the world, and never resumed, owing to loss of workers and master masons and "the melancholy and grief" of the survivors. The cathedral's truncated transept still stands in permanent witness to the sweep of death's scythe. Agnolo di Tura, a chronicler of Siena, recorded the fear of contagion that froze every other instinct. "Father abandoned child, wife, husband, one brother another," he wrote, "for this plague seemed to strike through the breath and sight. And so they died. And no one could be found to bury the dead for money or friendship....And I, Agnolo di Tura, called the Fat, buried my five children with my own hands, and so did many others likewise."

There were many to echo his account of inhumanity and few to balance it, for the plague was not the kind of calamity that inspired mutual help. Its loathsomeness and deadliness did not herd people together in mutual distress, but only prompted their desire to escape each other. "Magistrates and notaries refused to come and make the wills of the dying," reported a Franciscan friar of Piazza in Sicily; what was worse, "even the priests did not come to hear their confessions." A clerk of the Archbishop of Canterbury reported the same of English priests who "turned away from the care of their benefices from fear of death." Cases of parents deserting children and children their parents were reported across Europe from Scotland to Russia. The calamity chilled the hearts of me, wrote Boccacio[3] in his famous account of the plague in Florence that serves as introduction to the *Decameron*, "One man shunned another...kinsfolk held aloof, brother was forsaken by brother, oftentimes husband by wife; nay, what is more, and scarcely to be believed, fathers and mothers were found to abandon their own children to their fate, untended, unvisited as if they had been strangers." Exaggeration and literary pessimism were common in the 14th century, but the Pope's physician, Guy de Chauliac, was a sober, careful observer who reported the same phenomenon: "A father did not visit his son, nor the son his father. Charity was dead."

Yet not entirely. In Paris, according to the chronicler Jean de Venette, the nuns of the Hôtel Dieu or municipal hospital, "having no fear of death, tended the sick with all sweetness and humility." New nuns repeatedly took the places of those who died, until the majority "many times renewed by death now rest in peace with Christ as we may piously believe."

When the plague entered northern France in July 1348, it settled first in Normandy and, checked by winter, gave Picardy a deceptive interim until the next summer. Either in mourning or warning, black flags were flown from church towers of the worst-stricken villages of Normandy. "And in that time," wrote a monk of the abbey of Fourcarment, "the mortality was so great among the people of Normandy that those of Picardy mocked them." The same unneighborly reaction was reported of the Scots, separated by a winter's immunity from the English. Delighted to hear of the disease that was scourging the "southrons," they gathered forces for an

---

3 Giovanni Boccaccio (1313-1375), Italian writer best known for his collection of stories, *The Decameron*, in which seven young ladies and three young men flee from Florence to escape the Black Death and tell stories to while away the time.

invasion, "laughing at their enemies." Before they could move, the savage mortality fell upon them too, scattering some in death and the rest in panic to spread the infection as they fled.

In Picardy in the summer of 1349 the pestilence penetrated the castle of Coucy to kill Enguerrand's[4] mother, Catherine, and her new husband. Whether her nine-year-old son escaped by chance or was perhaps living elsewhere with one of his guardians is unrecorded. In nearby Amiens, tannery workers, responding quickly to losses in the labor force, combined to bargain for higher wages. In another place villagers were seen dancing to drums and trumpets, and on being asked the reason, answered that, seeing their neighbors die day by day while their village remained immune, they believed they could keep the plague from entering "by the jollity that is in us. That is why we dance." Further north in Tournai on the border of Flanders, Gilles li Muisis, Abbot of St. Martin's, kept one of the epidemic's most vivid accounts. The passing bells rang all day and all night, he recorded, because sextons were anxious to obtain their fees while they could. Filled with the sound of mourning, the city became oppressed by fear, so that the authorities forbade the tolling of bells and the wearing of black and restricted funeral services to two mourners. The silencing of funeral bells and of criers' announcements of deaths was ordained by most cities. Siena imposed a fine on the wearing of mourning clothes by all except widows.

Flight was the chief recourse of those who could afford it or arrange it. The rich fled to their country places like Boccaccio's young patricians of Florence, who settled in a pastoral palace "removed on every side from the roads" with "wells of cool water and vaults of rare wines." The urban poor died in their burrows, "and only the stench of their bodies informed neighbors of their death." That the poor were more heavily afflicted than the rich was clearly remarked at the time, in the north as in the south. A Scottish chronicler, John of Fordun, stated flatly that the pest "attacked especially the meaner sort and common people—seldom the magnates." Simon de Covino of Montpellier made the same observation. He ascribed it to the misery and want and hard lives that made the poor more susceptible, which was half the truth. Close contact and lack of sanitation was the unrecognized other half. It was noticed too that the young died in greater proportion than the

---

4 Enguerrand de Coucy, a French nobleman, is the historical figure around whom Tuchman constructs her account of the fourteenth century.

old; Simon de Covino compared the disappearance of youth to the withering of flowers in the fields.

In the countryside peasants dropped dead on the roads, in the fields, in their houses. Survivors in growing helplessness fell into apathy, leaving ripe wheat uncut and livestock untended. Oxen and asses, sheep and goats, pigs and chickens ran wild and they too, according to local reports, succumbed to the pest. English sheep, bearers of the precious wool, died throughout the country. The chronicler Henry Knighton, canon of Leicester Abbey, reported 5,000 dead in one field alone, "their bodies so corrupted by the plague that neither beast nor bird would touch them," and spreading an appalling stench. In the Austrian Alps wolves came down to prey upon sheep and then, "as if alarmed by some invisible warning, turned and fled back into the wilderness." In remote Dalmatia border wolves descended upon a plague-stricken city and attacked human survivors. For want of herdsmen, cattle strayed from place to place and died in hedgerows and ditches. Dogs and cats fell like the rest.

The dearth of labor held a fearful prospect because the 14th century lived close to the annual harvest both for food and for next year's seed. "So few servants and laborers were left," wrote Knighton, "that no one knew where to turn for help." The sense of a vanishing future created a kind of dementia of despair. A Bavarian chronicler of Neuberg on the Danube recorded that "Men and women...wandered around as if mad" and let their cattle stray "because no one had any inclination to concern themselves about the future." Fields went uncultivated, spring seed unknown. Second growth with nature's awful energy crept back over cleared land, dikes crumbled, salt water reinvaded and soured the lowlands. With so few hands remaining to restore the work of centuries, people felt, in Walsingham's words, that "the world could never again regain its former prosperity."

Though the death rate was higher among the anonymous poor, the known and the great died too. King Alfonso XI of Castile was the only reigning monarch killed by the pest, but his neighbor King Pedro of Aragon lost his wife, Queen Leonora, his daughter Marie, and a niece in the space of six months. John Cantacuzene, Emperor of Byzantium, lost his son. In France the lame Queen Jeanne and her daughter-in-law Bonne de Luxemburg, wife of the Dauphin, both died in 1349 in the same phase that took the life of Enguerrand's mother. Jeanne, Queen of Navarre, daughter of Louis X, was another victim. Edward III's second daughter, Joanna, who was on her way to marry Pedro, the heir of Castile, died in Bordeaux. Women appear to have been more vulnerable than men, perhaps because, being more housebound, they were more exposed to fleas. Boccaccio's mistress Fiammetta, illegitimate daughter of the King of Naples, died, as did Laura, the beloved—whether real or fictional—of Petrarch. Reaching out to use in the future, Petrarch cried, "Oh happy posterity who will not experience such abysmal woe and will look upon our testimony as a fable."

In Florence Giovanni Villani, the great historian of his time, died at 68 in the midst of an unfinished sentence: "...*e dure questo pistolenza fino a...* (on the midst of this pestilence there came to an end...)." Siena's master painters, the brothers Ambrogio and Pietro Lorenzetti, whose names never appear after 1348, presumably perished in the plague, as did Andrea Pisano, architect and sculptor of Florence. William of Ockham and the English mystic Richard Rolle of Hampole both disappear from mention after 1349. Francisco Datini, merchant of Prato, lost both his parents and two siblings. Curious sweeps of mortality afflicted certain bodies of merchants in London. All eight wardens of the Company of Cutters, all six wardens of the Hatters, and four wardens of the Goldsmiths died before July 1350. Sir John Pulteney, master draper and four times Mayor of London, was a victim, likewise Sir John Montgomery, Governor of Calais.

Among the clergy and doctors the mortality was naturally high because of the nature of their professions. Out of 24 physicians in Venice, 20 were said to have lost their lives in the plague, although, according to another account, some were believed to have fled or to have shut themselves up in their houses. At Montpellier, site of the leading medieval medical school, the physician Simon de Covino reported that, despite the great number of doctors, "hardly one of them escaped." In Avignon, Guy de Chauliac confessed that he performed his medical visits only because he dared not stay away for fear of infamy, but "I was in continual fear." He claimed to have contracted the disease but to have cured himself by his own treatment; if so, he was one of the few who recovered.

Clerical mortality varied with rank. Although the one-third toll of cardinals reflects the same proportion as the whole, this was probably due to their concentration in Avignon. In England, in strange and almost sinister procession, the Archbishop of Canterbury, John Stratford, died in August 1348, his appointed successor died in May 1349, and the next appointee three months later, all three within a year. Despite such weird vagaries, prelates in general managed to sustain a higher survival rate than the lesser clergy. Among bishops the deaths have been estimated at about one in twenty. The loss of priests, even if many avoided their fearful duty of attending the dying, was about the same as among the population as a whole.

Government officials, whose loss contributed to the general chaos, found, on the whole, no special shelter. In Siena four of the nine members of the governing oligarchy died, in France one third of the royal notaries, in Bristol 15 out of the 52 members of the Town Council or almost one third. Tax-collecting obviously suffered, with the result that Philip VI was unable to collect more than a fraction of the subsidy granted him by the Estates in the winter of 1347-48.

Lawlessness and debauchery accompanied the plague as they had during the great plague of Athens of 430 B.C., when according to Thucydides, men grew bold in the indulgence of pleasure: "For seeing how the rich died in a moment and those who had nothing immediately inherited their property, they reflected that life and riches were alike transitory and they resolved to enjoy themselves while they could." Human behavior is timeless. When St. John had his vision of plague in Revelation, he knew from some experience or race memory that those who survived "repented not of the work of their hands....Neither repented they of their murders, nor of their sorceries, nor of their fornication, nor of their thefts."

Ignorance of the cause augmented the sense of horror. Of the real carriers, rats and fleas, the 14th century had no suspicion, perhaps because they were so familiar. Fleas, though a common household nuisance, are not once mentioned in contemporary plague writings, and rats only incidentally, although folklore commonly associated them with pestilence. The legend of the Pied Piper arose from an outbreak of 1284. The actual plague bacillus, *Pasturella pestis*, remained undiscovered for another 500 years. Living alternately in the stomach of the flea and the bloodstream of the rat who was the flea's host, the bacillus in its bubonic form was transferred to humans and animals by the bite of either rat or flea. It traveled by virtue of *Rattus rattus*, the small medieval black rat that lived on ships, as well as by the heavier brown or sewer rat. What precipitated the turn of the bacillus from innocuous to virulent form is unknown, but the occurrence is now believed to have taken place not in China but somewhere in central Asia and to have spread along the caravan routes. Chinese origin was a mistaken notion of the 14th century based on real but belated reports of huge death tolls in China from drought, famine, and pestilence which have since been traced to the 1330s, too soon to be responsible for the plague that appeared in India by 1346.

The phantom enemy had no name. Called the Black Death only in later recurrences, it was known during the first epidemic simply as the Pestilence or Great Mortality. Reports from the East, swollen by fearful imaginings, told of strange tempests and "sheets of fire" mingled with huge hailstones that "slew almost all," or a "vast rain of fire" that burned up men, beasts, stones, trees, villages, and cities. In another version, "foul blasts of wind" from the fires carried the infection to Europe "and now as some suspect it cometh round the seacoast." Accurate observation in this case could not make the mental jump to ships and rats because no idea of animal- or insect-borne contagion existed.

The earthquake was blamed for releasing sulfurous and foul fumes from the earth's interior, or as evidence of a titanic struggle of planets and oceans causing waters to rise and vaporize until fish died in masses and corrupted the air. All these explanations had in common a factor of poisoned air, of miasmas and thick, stinking mists traced to every kind of natural or imagined agency from stagnant lakes to malign conjunction of the planets, from the hand of the Evil One to the wrath of God. Medical thinking, trapped in the theory of astral influences, stressed air as the communicator of disease, ignoring sanitation or visible carriers. The existence of two carriers confused the trial, the more so because the flea could live and travel independently of the rat for as long as a month and, if infected by the particularly virulent septicemic form of the bacillus, could infect humans without reinfecting itself from the rat. The simultaneous presence of the pneumonic form of the disease, which was indeed communicated through the air, blurred the problem further.

The mystery of the contagion was "the most terrible of all the terrors," as an anonymous Flemish cleric in Avignon wrote to a correspondent in Bruges. Plagues had been known before, from the plague of Athens (believed to have been typhus) to the prolonged epidemic of the 6th century A.D., to the recurrence of sporadic outbreaks in the 12th and 13th centuries, but they had left no accumulated store of understanding. That the infection came from contact with the sick or with their houses, clothes, or corpses was quickly observed but not comprehended. Gentile da Foligon, renowned physician of Perugia and doctor of medicine at the universities of Bologna and Padua, came close to respiratory infection when he surmised that poisonous material was "communicated by means of air breathed out and in." Having no idea of microscopic carriers, he had to assume that the air was corrupted by planetary influences. Planets, however, could not explain the ongoing contagion. The agonized search for an answer gave rise to such theories as transference by sight. People fell ill, wrote Guy de Chauliac, not only by remaining with the sick but "even by looking at them." Three hundred years later Joshua Barnes, the 17th century biographer of Edward III, could write that the power of infection had entered into beams of light and "darted death from the eyes."

227

Doctors struggling with the evidence could not break away from the terms of astrology, to which they believed all human physiology was subject. Medicine was the one aspect of medieval life, perhaps because of its links with the Arabs, not shaped by Christian doctrine. Clerics detested astrology, but could not dislodge its influence. Guy de Chauliac, physician to three popes in succession, practiced in obedience to the zodiac. While his *Cirurgia* was the major treatise on surgery of its time, while he understood the use of anesthesia made from the juice of opium, mandrake, or hemlock, he nevertheless prescribed bleeding and purgatives by the planets and divided chronic from acute diseases on the basis of one being under the rule of the sun and the other of the moon.

In October 1348 Philip VI asked the medical faculty of the University of Paris for a report on the affliction that seemed to threaten human survival. With careful thesis, antithesis, and proofs, the doctors ascribed it to a triple conjunction of Saturn, Jupiter, and Mars in the 40th degree of Aquarius said to have occurred on March 20, 1345. They acknowledged, however, effects "whose cause is hidden from even the most highly trained intellects." The verdict of the masters of Paris became the official version. Borrowed, copied by scribes, carried abroad, translated from Latin into various vernaculars, it was everywhere accepted, even by the Arab physicians of Cordova and Granada, as the scientific if not the popular answer. Because of the terrible interest of the subject, the translations of the plague tracts stimulated use of national languages. In that one respect, life came from death.

To the people at large there could be but one explanation—the wrath of God. Planets might satisfy the learned doctors, but God was closer to the average man. A scourge so sweeping and unsparing without any visible cause could only be seen as Divine punishment upon mankind for its sins. It might even be God's terminal disappointment in his creature. Matteo Villani compared the plague to the Flood in ultimate purpose and believed he was recording "the extermination of mankind." Efforts to appease Divine wrath took many forms, as when the city of Rouen ordered that everything that could anger God, such as gambling, cursing, and drinking, must be stopped. More general were the penitent processions authorized at first by the Pope, some lasting as long as three days, some attended by as many as 2,000, which everywhere accompanied the plague and helped to spread it.

Barefoot in sackcloth, sprinkled with ashes, weeping, praying, tearing their hair, carrying candles and relics, sometimes with ropes around their necks or beating themselves with whips, the penitents wound through the streets, imploring the mercy of the Virgin and saints at their shrines. In a vivid illustration for the *Très Riches Heures* of the Duc de Berry, the Pope is shown in a penitent procession attended by four cardinals in scarlet from hat to hem. He raises both arms in supplication to the angel on top of the Castel Sant' Angelo, while white-robed priests bearing banners and relics in golden cases turn to look as one of their number, stricken by the plague, falls to the ground, his face contorted with anxiety. In the rear, a gray-clad monk falls beside another victim already on the ground as the townspeople gaze in horror.

(Nominally the illustration represents a 6th century plague in the time of Pope Gregory the Great, but as medieval artists made no distinction between past and present, the scene is shown as the artist would have seen it in the 14th century.) When it became evident that these processions were sources of infection, Clement VI had to prohibit them.

In Messina, where the plague first appeared, the people begged the Archbishop of neighboring Catania to lend them the relics of St. Agatha. When the Catanians refused to let the relics go, the Archbishop dipped them in holy water and took the water himself to Messina, where he carried it in a procession with prayers and litanies through the streets. The demonic, which shared the medieval cosmos with God, appeared as "demons in the shape of dogs" to terrify the people. "A black dog with a drawn sword in his paws appeared among them, gnashing his teeth and rushing upon them and breaking all the silver vessels and lamps and candlesticks on the altars and casting them hither and thither....So the people of Messina, terrified by this prodigious vision, were all strangely overcome by fear."

The apparent absence of earthly cause gave the plague a supernatural and sinister quality. Scandinavians believed that a Pest Maiden emerged from the mouth of the dead in the form of a blue flame and flew through the air to infect the next house. In Lithuania the Maiden was said to wave a red scarf through the door or window to let in the pest. One brave man, according to legend, deliberately waited at his open window with drawn sword and, at the fluttering of the scarf, chopped off the hand. He died of his deed, but his village was spared and the scarf long preserved as a relic in the local church.

Beyond demons and superstition the final hand was God's. The Pope acknowledged it in a Bull of September 1348, speaking of the "pestilence with which God is afflicting the Christian people." To the Emperor John Cantacuzene it was manifest that a malady of such horrors, stenches, and agonies, and especially one bringing the dismal despair that settled upon its victims before they died, was not a plague "natural" to mankind but "a chastisement from Heaven." To Piers Plowman[5] "these pestilences were for pure sin."

The general acceptance of this view created an expanded sense of guilt, for if the plague were punishment there had to be terrible sin to have occasioned it. What sins were on the 14th century conscience? Primarily greed, the sin of avarice, followed by usury, worldliness, adultery, blasphemy, falsehood, luxury, irreligion. Giovanni Villani, attempting to account for the cascade of calamity that had fallen upon Florence, concluded that it was retribution for the sins of avarice and usury that oppressed the poor. Pity and anger about the condition of the poor, especially victimization of the peasantry in war, was often expressed by writers of the time and was certainly on the conscience of the century. Beneath it all was the daily condition of medieval life, in which hardly an act or thought, sexual, mercantile, or military, did not contravene the dictates of the Church. Mere failure to fast or attend mass was sin. The result was an underground lake of guilt in the soul that the plague now tapped.

That the mortality was accepted as God's punishment may explain in part the vacuum of comment that followed the Black Death. An

---

5 The main character (and title) of a fourteenth-century poem by the English poet William Langland (c. 1330-c. 1386).

investigator has noticed that in the archives of Périgord references to the war are innumerable, to the plague few. Froissart mentions the great death but once, Chaucer gives it barely a glance. Divine anger so great that it contemplated the extermination of man did not bear close examination.

It's Spreading: Outbreaks, Media Scares, and the Parrot Panic of 1930

By Jill Lepore

On December 14, 1929, during a holiday shopping season darkened by the greatest stock-market crash in American history, Simon S. Martin bought a parrot for his wife, Lillian, at a pet shop on North Eutaw Street, in Baltimore. It was not, as it happened, a well parrot. Hoping to surprise his wife, Martin seems to have asked his daughter, Edith, and her husband, Lee Kalmey, the owner of an auto repair shop, to take care of the bird and bring it over to his house in Annapolis in ten days' time. By Christmas Eve, the parrot must have shown signs of illness: puffy eyes, a drooping head, and feathers as ruffled as if it had flown through a squall. Come Yuletide, the Martins had a dead parrot on their hands.

The pet-shop owner, who may have been wise to the fact that Simon Martin was secretary of the Annapolis Chamber of Commerce, at first offered a replacement, although by New Year's, when Lillian Martin and Edith and Lee Kalmey fell dangerously ill, he was backpedalling, denying that he had ever sold Martin a bird. Meanwhile, the Kalmeys were getting sicker and sicker, showing symptoms of both pneumonia and typhoid.

On January 6th, a local doctor examined the patients. He had just read a newspaper article about something called parrot fever: it had shown up in Argentina months earlier, when an actor playing a sailor had caught it from his stage parrot. The disease, also called psittacosis, had since spread through South America and Europe. No one seemed to know much about it except that it was deadly. The doctor sent a telegram to the U.S. Public Health Service, in Washington: "CAN YOU PLACE SUPPLY PARROT FEVER SERUM OUR DISPOSAL IMMEDIATELY." Unfortunately, there was no serum, or any known treatment. The mayor alerted the governor. Within forty-eight hours, epidemiologists from the Baltimore City Health Department, the Maryland Department of Health, the United States Navy and Army, and the Public Health Service, including a team of men from the Hygienic Laboratory in Washington, arrived on the scene. Someone called the newspaper.

From *The New Yorker*, 2009.

" 'PARROT' DISEASE BAFFLES EXPERTS" the Washington *Post* reported in an issue that went to press the night of January 8th, thrilling readers with a medical mystery that would capture the nation's attention with the prospect of a parrot-fever pandemic. Reports, cabled and wired and radioed across land and sea, were printed in the daily paper or broadcast, within minutes, on the radio: tallies, theories, postmortems, more to fear. Before it was over, an admiral in the U.S. Navy ordered sailors at sea to cast their pet parrots into the ocean. One city health commissioner urged everyone who owned a parrot to wring its neck. People abandoned their pet parrots on the streets. Every sneeze seemed a symptom. As the story grew, it took on certain familiar—and, as it turned out, durable—features, features that borrow as much from pulp fiction as from public health: super scientists fight super bugs in race to defeat foreign menace invading American homes, beneath the very Christmas tree.

Epidemics follow patterns because diseases follow patterns. Viruses spread; they reproduce; they die. Epidemiologists study patterns in order to combat infection. Stories about epidemics follow patterns, too. Stories aren't often deadly but they can be virulent: spreading fast, weakening resistance, wreaking havoc. During the recent swine-flu panic, Joe Biden warned Americans not to ride the subway or fly on an airplane, and pharmacies ran out of surgical masks. Why was it so hard to tell, as the story was breaking, if a flu outbreak of pandemic proportions was under way? The world is a far better place for the work epidemiologists do. Maybe, though, we could do with a few more narratologists.

The stories about epidemics that are told in the American press— their plots and tropes—date to the nineteen-twenties, when modern research science, science journalism, and science fiction were born. The germ theory of disease dates to the mid-eighteen-hundreds. Pasteur developed a rabies vaccine in 1885, launching a global battle against infectious illness. By the nineteen- twenties, scientists had developed a vaccine for diphtheria; other vaccines, like the one for polio, would take decades, but hopes ran high. In "The Conquest of Disease" (1927), Thurman B. Rice, a professor of sanitary science, predicted the eradication of sickness itself.

Meanwhile, ordinary people learned to blame germs, not God, for catastrophes like the pandemic of 1918, when at least fifty million people, including nearly seven hundred thousand Americans, died of influenza. Germ theory, which secularized infectious disease, had a side effect: it sacralized epidemiology. The nineteen-twenties witnessed the inauguration of what the historian of medicine Nancy Tomes has called the "epidemic exposé," the hair-raising account of a disease that threatens to destroy the human race. The genre's master was a bacteriologist turned journalist named Paul de Kruif. He had taught at the University of Michigan and worked for the U.S. Sanitary Corps, studying the gangrene bacillus. After the war, he turned to writing. In 1925, his collaboration with Sinclair Lewis led to the publication of "Arrowsmith," a novel about a young doctor fighting bubonic plague—an early medical thriller, for which de Kruif received twenty-five per cent of the royalties. In 1926, de Kruif turned to nonfiction, publishing "Microbe Hunters," a book of profiles of scientists, starting with Leeuwenhoek, who can see tiny things the rest of us can't, things that are trying to kill us.

"Microbe Hunters," which inspired a generation of young readers to pursue careers in science, appeared a month before the first issue of Hugo Gernsback's *Amazing Stories*, the first magazine of what is now called science fiction. Many of its stories concern the work of laboratory scientists; the issue of July, 1929, included "The Purple Death," the story of a young doctor who keeps a copy of "Microbe Hunters" on his desk.

The coming plague was Paul de Kruif's bread and butter. Three months before Simon Martin bought his wife a parrot for Christmas, de Kruif issued a warning in the lead article of *Ladies' Home Journal*: "In American milk today there lurks a terrible, wasting fever, that may keep you in bed for a couple of weeks, that may fasten itself on you for one, or for two, or even for seven years—that might culminate by killing you." What was this dread malady? Undulant fever. "At least 50,000 people are sick with it at this very moment," their ailment virtually unknown to "their baffled doctors." De Kruif's article, titled "Before You Drink a Glass of Milk," scared a lot of people and sold a lot of magazines. Boasting of its success, the editor of *Ladies' Home Journal* explained, "Nobody had ever heard of undulant fever before."

The experts who descended on Annapolis in early January, 1930, weren't half as baffled as the Washington *Post* made them out to be, but the reading public must have been at least twice as confused. Was parrot fever really something to worry about? Reading the newspaper, it was hard to say. "NOT CONTAGIOUS IN MAN," the *Times* announced. "Highly contagious," the Washington *Post* said. Who knew? Nobody had ever heard of it before. It lurked in American homes. It came from afar. It was invisible. It might kill you. It made a very good story. In the late hours of January 8th, editors at the Los Angeles *Times* decided to put it on the front page: "TWO WOMEN AND MAN IN ANNAPOLIS BELIEVED TO HAVE 'PARROT FEVER.' "

The next day, in Toledo, Mrs. Percy Q. Williams, whose husband had just returned from Cuba with two parrots, died in Mercy Hospital; in Baltimore, Mrs. Louise Schaeffer succumbed to what had at first appeared to be pneumonia. (Women, many of them widows, constituted the majority of the outbreak's victims. There were suggestions that lonely old women had got the disease by feeding their parrots mouth to mouth. Some called the disease "old maid's pneumonia.") Those deaths would normally have been unremarkable: two older women fading away in the cold of winter. Not this week. On learning that Schaeffer "had been in contact with a parrot several days before she became ill," physicians suspected parrot fever and ordered an autopsy, whereupon the Surgeon General, Dr. Hugh Smith Cumming (a eugenicist best known to history for launching the Tuskegee syphilis experiment, that same year), warned Americans to stay away from recently imported parrots. He insisted that he "did not fear an epidemic," but that, of course, only got people talking about one. Although the results of Schaeffer's autopsy were not yet available, "BALTIMORE WOMAN DIES" made it onto the front page of the Chicago *Daily Tribune* on January 11th and "PARROT FEVER KILLS 2 IN THIS COUNTRY" appeared on page 3 of the *Times*. That paper also reported on efforts to trace deadly Argentine parrots that had come to the United States through what were called, as if they were criminals, "two suspected New York dealers."

Some people were worried about more than parrots. On January 11th, after several clerks in the poultry department of a Toledo store started coughing, the city's Health Department launched an investigation into "incipient cases" of psittacosis. Two days later, in a story that appeared on the front page of William Randolph Hearst's San Francisco *Examiner*, the Associated Press announced that the country's scientists had declared war: "The disease-fighting armament of the nation today was directed against a new and mysterious enemy." The microbe hunters had taken out their microscopes.

In the years following the First World War, a great many American scientists were looking for sources to fund their vital research. The nation's scientific organizations hired publicity firms.

In 1926, a coalition of scientists launched a campaign to raise "A National Fund for the Support of Research in Pure Science." Half the battle, though, had to do with winning over the public, and de Kruif 's work made clear that stories were powerful ammunition. Before the First World War, journalists didn't generally report on science, and they certainly didn't profile scientists.

After the war, scientists tried writing for newspapers and magazines, attempting to explain the value of their work, but, year by year, the number of scientists writing for a popular audience fell while the number of journalists specializing in science writing rose. Perhaps the era's most effective pro-science publicity machine was the Science Service, a wire service founded in 1920 and edited by a chemist named Edwin E. Slosson. Its purpose was to promote scientific research by feeding stories to newspapers. The service, Slosson said, would not "indulge in propaganda unless it be propaganda to urge the value of research and the usefulness of science." Financed by the newspaper publisher E. W. Scripps, and later by the American Association for the Advancement of Science and the National Research Council, the Science Service reached a fifth of the American reading public by the mid-nineteen-thirties.

What a microbe hunter needed to do to get funding was to hunt and kill a microbe, preferably a lethal one that nobody had ever heard of before. On January 6, 1930, when that family doctor sent his telegram to the U.S. Public Health Service, the message was sent on to the Hygienic Laboratory, where Dr. Charles Armstrong, a forty-five-year-old pathologist, was charged with heading the investigation. Armstrong wanted to contain the outbreak, urgently; he also wanted to develop a serum, to save the lives of people already infected. Doing so would require experiments; those experiments required infected parrots and infected people. To gather subjects, Armstrong needed to spread the word about psittacosis. What Armstrong needed was a parrot-fever panic.

As Armstrong arrived in Annapolis, a team of public-health officials was sent to that North Eutaw Street pet shop in Baltimore—where four employees were now sick—to track down the purchasers of all the recently imported parrots. Not all those parrots had stayed in town. Mrs. Hugh Lett bought a parrot in Baltimore on December 18th; the bird died on New Year's Eve; Mrs. Lett took sick on January 7th, by which time she was in Cambridge. Armstrong wired messages to public-health officials across the country, asking them to be on the lookout for psittacosis. In city after city, parrot dealers handed over to investigators sick parrots and lists of the people who had bought parrots for Christmas. Dead birds, some of which were exhumed, were shipped to Washington. Cases of suspected psittacosis cropped up in Providence and Chicago, New Haven and Los Angeles. The home of an Ohio family was quarantined after yet another Christmas parrot died. Inevitably, there were cases merely "simulating psittacosis," like the parents of fifteen-year-old Lillian Muller, of the Bronx, who had bought their daughter a parrot, imported from Argentina, at a pet shop in Harlem. The *Times* offered reassurance: "The Mullers' parrot has been eating regularly and has exhibited no signs of drooping." [One constabulary note: The A.P. reported from North Adams, Massachusetts, on January 13th, "A parrot in a local family, whose name was not given out, recently died." Polly?]

By January 15th, the *Times* reported fifty cases nationwide, including eleven in New York City, and seven deaths, including one in Queens and one in Yonkers. Doctors insisted, in vain, that "there was no occasion for general alarm," and "stressed the fact that in none of the cases reported so far in New York has the diagnosis been definitely established as psittacosis." Later that day—after the *Times* went to press with the death count—authorities revealed that blood tests on the New York dead had all come out negative. The *Times*, whose coverage of parrot fever was, all things considered, a model of restraint and clarity, made a point of announcing those negative tests. Elsewhere, though, autopsies and blood cultures that came out negative for psittacosis didn't make it into the papers. By now, Lillian Martin and Edith and Lee Kalmey were fast improving; this was not widely reported, either. People who got better simply fell out of the news.

The nationwide sweep for psittacosis soon supplied Armstrong with enough samples—parrots, healthy, sick, and dead; the blood from infected humans; and even the scrapings from Lillian Martin's birdcage—to begin his work, which he conducted in two basement rooms in the Hygienic Laboratory, aided by his technician, Henry (Shorty) Anderson. "Those parrots were sure mean bastards," Armstrong said. Armstrong and Anderson wore rubber gloves, put trays filled with cresol in the doorways, and covered the birds' cages with disinfectant-soaked curtains. They were not, however, especially fastidious. "The only thing hygienic about the Hygienic Laboratory was its name," one researcher there said. Armstrong explained, "If we'd got too careful, we'd have spent all our time being careful and how could we have found out anything about it?"

This was yet another hallmark of the swashbuckling microbe hunter, who lacked the fussiness of the housewife. "Germ" became a household word in the nineteen-teens. By the twenties, Americans, and especially housewives, lived in fear of germs. Not only did newspapers and magazines run almost daily stories about newly discovered germs like undulant fever but their pages were filled with advertisements for hygiene products, like Listerine (first sold over the counter in 1914 and, in many ways, the granddaddy of Purell), Lysol (marketed, in 1918, as an anti-flu measure), Kotex ("feminine hygiene," the first menstrual pad, introduced in 1920, a postwar conversion of a surgical dressing developed by Kimberly-Clark), Cellophane (1923), and Kleenex (1924; another Kimberly-Clark product, sold as a towel for removing makeup until a consumer survey revealed that people were using it to blow their noses). Perhaps because kitchens and laboratories have much in common, journalists like de Kruif strove to underscore the manliness of the microbe hunter. Armstrong, de Kruif wrote, "was definitely not the kind of man who would even own a parrot, let alone kiss it."

Armstrong and Anderson and other government scientists worked night and day. On January 13th, the Chicago *Daily Tribune* reported a landmark success: "PARROT FEVER GERM ISOLATED."

The parrot-fever story made the malady out to be virulent, mysterious, and exotic, despite these facts: the disease was not baffling; it had been identified in the nineteenth century; it was known to infect members of the Psittacidae family, which includes parrots, parakeets, macaws, and cockatoos; in the nineteen-thirties, the only birds likely to be contagious were those brought to the United States during the last months of 1929; it is possible to catch the disease only from an infected bird (people can't spread it); it infected then, and continues to infect today, between one and two hundred Americans every year. There was a danger, to be sure. Psittacosis is now easily treated with antibiotics like doxycycline, but that wasn't the case in 1930, when one in five people infected with the disease died. Nevertheless, the only people who had much to worry about were people who had been in quite close contact with certain tropical birds very recently imported from South America.

Psittacosis incited, if briefly, a sizable panic among people who, by any reasonable measure, had nothing to fear. That was dangerous. Even as the story unfolded, what to make of parrot fever and just how much responsibility the press or the scientific community bore for the panic proved matters of dispute. But what happened next seems nearly as dangerous as the panic itself: people suddenly started insisting that parrot fever didn't exist.

"U.S. ALARM OVER PARROT DISEASE NOT WARRANTED," the Chicago *Daily Tribune* declared, on January 15th. Less than two weeks into the story, parrot fever looked, suddenly, silly. Parrot fever became a national joke. A Washington correspondent for the *Times* filed a story about a parrot owned by Secretary of State Henry Stimson. The parrot, named the Old Soak, had been locked in the basement of the Pan-American Building, "not because he has psittacosis" but because he had a habit of swearing. The *Wall Street Journal* ran this joke: what did the janitor say when the professor at the Polytechnic Institute asked him why he was cleaning the lab with carbolic acid? " 'So none of de Poly students gets dis new parrot fever.' " Even the straight stories weren't taken seriously. "A parrot foundling made its appearance early yesterday morning when a green bird with a chipped beak was discovered in the vestibule of John Schreyer's home, 25-27 Humphreys Street, East Elmhurst, Queens," the *Times* reported, whereupon jailbirds at Sing Sing offered asylum for all unwanted parrots; the warden said, "The inmates here think this talk about parrot fever is nonsense."

A pro-parrot lobby formed. On January 17th, six of the country's leading importers of winged pets, including the Odenwald Bird Company, the Imperial Pet Shop, and the Dahle Bird Company of Philadelphia, gathered at the Hotel Commodore in New York, where they founded the Bird Dealers' Association of America. Prussia and Bavaria, suffering from their own outbreaks, had already instituted parrot embargoes. The bird business was in a bad way. The Bird Dealers fought back by claiming that the disease did not exist, had never existed in human beings, "and that the scare over 'parrot fever' had been chiefly brought about by the active imagination of a Baltimore newspaper man."

Exaggeration breeds exaggeration. The counter-story spread as wildly as the story had. And the Bird Dealers had a point about the imagination of newspapermen. The first American doctor to believe he had seen psittacosis had read about it in the newspaper. The Martins' doctor probably read Hearst's Baltimore *American*. Every Sunday, Hearst produced for his papers a supplement called the *American Weekly*. Edited by Morrill Goddard, the *American Weekly* was something between *Parade* and the *National Enquirer*. Goddard knew how to sell a plague and knew, too, that selling plagues was good for his advertising accounts with hygiene-product manufacturers. In March, 1930, Goddard was interviewed by the staff of the J. Walter Thompson Company, one of the nation's most influential advertising agencies. "There is a lot of interest now in parrot fever," the interviewer observed, asking, "How far will the research on parrot fever have to go before you print something about it?" Goddard took umbrage at the suggestion that he had not already covered parrot fever—that he had not, in fact, *scooped* parrot fever. "We were the first newspaper to present it to the American public," he claimed, not quite accurately, "to warn them that parrots might be deadly in the home." As to how he had come by the story, Goddard explained that he spent his evenings reading obscure scientific journals, where he read about the outbreak in Buenos Aires:

I sent down to our man there and he sent me a wretched story without details and I cabled him and he sent me a second story with further details and pictures and that story was printed about four or five weeks before the first case developed in New York. It gave all the details of what is known as "psittacosis." Now, it is a matter of dispute whether it is a germ or a virus but it is a matter of no consequence as far as making a feature out of it.

Goddard had no real interest in the science. He wanted to run a story about a danger lurking in American homes: "The fact that the parrot in the cage at your house may put you in the cemetery is enough for me."

On January 16th, just over one week after the Washington *Post* printed its first parrot-fever piece, the *Times* ran a story radioed in by a correspondent in Austria: A Viennese scientist believed that Americans were suffering from "mass suggestion." Dr. Julius Bauer said, "Psittacosis has been known to science since 1892. Now for some reason it has assumed in the public mind the dimensions of a plague." The next day, the Science Service, reporting on an article in the *Journal of the American Medical Association*, reminded Americans that "the possibility of unusual disorders must be ever present in the medical mind." Who knew what might infect us next? Parrot fever ought to serve as proof that "it is no longer possible for any person or any nation to live in isolation." The world, in short, was a dangerous place.

Or was it just a gullible one? "Every winter, America has to have a new malady, and this year it is Parrot Fever," a columnist for the *Post* wrote. "People are getting all worked up over this new 'parrot-fever,'

" a writer for *Life* scoffed, "but Lord! it's been endemic at the Capitol since Polly was an egg." E. B. White figured that the country was suffering from nothing so much as a bad case of the heebie-jeebies, brought on by extended exposure to newspapers that were forever issuing warnings about sharks infesting the beaches of New Jersey, anthrax spores contaminating unsterilized shaving brushes, and noxious gases escaping from iceboxes in the middle of the night. In an issue that went to press on January 20th, *The New Yorker's* Talk of the Town included a piece by White calling parrot fever merely "the latest and most amusing example of the national hypochondria":

There have been hundreds of national menaces, keeping us all on tenterhooks, keeping the populace feeling the national pulse and applying the national stethoscope. Psittacosis is one of the best, because one of the most picturesque. What will probably happen will be that some reporter will invent a disease traceable to something that happens to everybody: "Otis heart" from riding in elevators, maybe, or "corn-flakes itch" from eating breakfast food, and we'll all die of autosuggestion.

That hasn't happened quite yet, but we still can't tell whether we are all about to die or whether we are being sold a bill of goods. This condition is chronic.

On January 22, 1930, the *Post* reported that Lillian Martin and Edith and Lee Kalmey had recovered. Herbert Hoover prepared to sign an executive order banning the importation of parrots. The story seemed more or less wrapped up. But then, terribly, scientists starting dying. On January 23rd, Dr. Daniel S. Hatfield, the chief of the bureau of communicable diseases of the Baltimore City Health Department, succumbed to psittacosis. Hatfield's colleague Dr. William Stokes died on February 10th. Shorty Anderson died on February 8th. That same day, Charles Armstrong was admitted to the U.S. Naval Hospital with a fever of 104 degrees.

The director of the Hygienic Laboratory, George McCoy, insisted on taking over Armstrong's work himself. He took blood from a patient who had recovered from psittacosis and injected it into Armstrong's veins. Armstrong improved, and eventually recovered. Afterward, he wrote up his report, according to which there had been a total of a hundred and sixty-nine cases of psittacosis nationwide, and thirty-three fatalities. In his report, Armstrong credited the press, without which, he believed, "this outbreak would largely have escaped detection." Armstrong's work earned him a place in de Kruif's 1932 sequel to "Microbe Hunters," a book titled "Men Against Death."

In February and early March of 1930, while Armstrong was still recovering, nine other people at the Hygienic Laboratory became sick. Psittacosis seemed to have contaminated the whole building. On March 15th, McCoy ordered the building evacuated. Alone, he walked down the stairs to Armstrong's basement laboratory. He killed, with chloroform, every parrot, mouse, pigeon, guinea pig, rat, and monkey that had been used in the psittacosis experiments. "He murdered and murdered and made a slick and clean job of it," de Kruif wrote. He burned the bodies in the building's incinerator. He sealed all the windows. The fumigation squad arrived at 2 P.M. and began spraying the building with cyanide. Sparrows flying fifty feet over the building froze, mid-flight, and fell to earth. The next day, the headline in the *Post* read, "PARROT FEVER PANIC SEIZES LABORATORY." Two months later, on May 26, 1930, Congress rewarded the Hygienic Laboratory by expanding it and granting it a new name: the National Institute of Health.

Topic of Cancer

By Christopher Hitchens

I have more than once in my time woken up feeling like death. But nothing prepared me for the early morning last June when I came to consciousness feeling as if I were actually shackled to my own corpse. The whole cave of my chest and thorax seemed to have been hollowed out and then refilled with slow-drying cement. I could faintly hear myself breathe but could not manage to inflate my lungs. My heart was beating either much too much or much too little. Any movement, however slight, required forethought and planning. It took strenuous effort for me to cross the room of my New York hotel and summon the emergency services. They arrived with great dispatch and behaved with immense courtesy and professionalism. I had the time to wonder why they needed so many boots and helmets and so much heavy backup equipment, but now that I view the scene in retrospect I see it as a very gentle and firm deportation, taking me from the country of the well across the stark frontier that marks off the land of malady. Within a few hours, having had to do quite a lot of emergency work on my heart and my lungs, the physicians at this sad border post had shown me a few other postcards from the interior and told me that my immediate next stop would have to be with an oncologist. Some kind of shadow was throwing itself across the negatives.

The previous evening, I had been launching my latest book at a successful event in New Haven. The night of the terrible morning, I was supposed to go on *The Daily Show* with Jon Stewart and then appear at a sold-out event at the 92nd Street Y, on the Upper East Side, in conversation with Salman Rushdie. My very short-lived campaign of denial took this form: I would not cancel these appearances or let down my friends or miss the chance of selling a stack of books. I managed to pull off both gigs without anyone noticing anything amiss, though I did vomit two times, with an extraordinary combination of accuracy, neatness, violence, and profusion, just before each show. This is what citizens of the sick country do while they are still hopelessly clinging to their old domicile.

The new land is quite welcoming in its way. Everybody smiles encouragingly and there appears to be absolutely no racism. A

From *Vanity Fair*, 2010.

generally egalitarian spirit prevails, and those who run the place have obviously got where they are on merit and hard work. As against that, the humor is a touch feeble and repetitive, there seems to be almost no talk of sex, and the cuisine is the worst of any destination I have ever visited. The country has a language of its own—a lingua franca that manages to be both dull and difficult and that contains names like ondansetron, for anti-nausea medication—as well as some unsettling gestures that require a bit of getting used to. For example, an official met for the first time may abruptly sink his fingers into your neck. That's how I discovered that my cancer had spread to my lymph nodes, and that one of these deformed beauties—located on my right clavicle, or collarbone—was big enough to be seen and felt. It's not at all good when your cancer is "palpable" from the outside. Especially when, as at this stage, they didn't even know where the primary source was. Carcinoma works cunningly from the inside out. Detection and treatment often work more slowly and gropingly, from the outside in. Many needles were sunk into my clavicle area—"Tissue is the issue" being a hot slogan in the local Tumorville tongue—and I was told the biopsy results might take a week.

Working back from the cancer-ridden squamous cells that these first results disclosed, it took rather longer than that to discover the disagreeable truth. The word "metastasized" was the one in the report that first caught my eye, and ear. The alien had colonized a bit of my lung as well as quite a bit of my lymph node. And its original base of operations was located—had been located for quite some time—in my esophagus. My father had died, and very swiftly, too, of cancer of the esophagus. He was 79. I am 61. In whatever kind of a "race" life may be, I have very abruptly become a finalist.

In whatever kind of a "race" life may be, I have very abruptly become a finalist.

The notorious stage theory of Elisabeth Kübler-Ross, whereby one progresses from denial to rage through bargaining to depression and the eventual bliss of "acceptance," hasn't so far had much application in my case. In one way, I suppose, I have been "in denial" for some time, knowingly burning the candle at both ends and finding that it often gives a lovely light. But for precisely that reason, I can't see myself smiting my brow with shock or hear myself whining about how it's all so unfair: I have been taunting the Reaper into taking a free scythe in my direction and have now succumbed to something so predictable and banal that it bores even me. Rage would be beside the point for the same reason. Instead, I am badly oppressed by a gnawing sense of waste. I had real plans for my next decade and felt I'd worked hard enough to earn it. Will I really not live to see my children married? To watch the World Trade Center rise again? To read—if not indeed write—the obituaries of elderly villains like Henry Kissinger and Joseph Ratzinger? But I understand this sort of non-thinking for what it is: sentimentality and self-pity. Of course my book hit the best-seller list on the day that I received the grimmest of news bulletins, and for that matter the last flight I took as a healthy-feeling person (to a fine, big audience at the Chicago Book Fair) was the one that made me a million-miler on United Airlines, with a lifetime of free upgrades to look forward to. But irony is my business and I just can't see any ironies here: would it be less poignant to get cancer on the day that my memoirs were remaindered as a box-office turkey, or that I was bounced from a coach-class flight and left on the tarmac? To the dumb question "Why me?" the cosmos barely bothers to return the reply: Why not?

The *bargaining* stage, though. Maybe there's a loophole here. The oncology bargain is that, in return for at least the chance of a few more useful years, you agree to submit to chemotherapy and then, if you are lucky with that, to radiation or even surgery. So here's the wager: you stick around for a bit, but in return we are going to need some things from you. These things may include your taste buds, your ability to concentrate, your ability to digest, and the hair on your head. This certainly appears to be a reasonable trade. Unfortunately, it also involves confronting one of the most appealing clichés in our language. You've heard it all right. People don't have cancer: they are reported to be battling cancer. No well-wisher omits the combative image: You can beat this. It's even in obituaries for cancer losers, as if one might reasonably say of someone that they died after a long and brave struggle with mortality. You don't hear it about long-term sufferers from heart disease or kidney failure.

Myself, I love the imagery of struggle. I sometimes wish I were suffering in a good cause, or risking my life for the good of others, instead of just being a gravely endangered patient. Allow me to inform you, though, that when you sit in a room with a set of other finalists, and kindly people bring a huge transparent bag of poison and plug it into your arm, and you either read or don't read a book while the venom sack gradually empties itself into your system, the image of the ardent soldier or revolutionary is the very last one that will occur to you. You feel swamped with passivity and impotence: dissolving in powerlessness like a sugar lump in water.

It's quite something, this chemo-poison. It has caused me to lose about 14 pounds, though without making me feel any lighter. It has cleared up a vicious rash on my shins that no doctor could ever name, let alone cure. (Some venom, to get rid of those furious red dots without a struggle.) Let it please be this mean and ruthless with the alien and its spreading dead-zone colonies. But as against that, the death-dealing stuff and life-preserving stuff have also made me strangely neuter. I was fairly reconciled to the loss of my hair, which began to come out in the shower in the first two weeks of treatment, and which I saved in a plastic bag so that it could help fill a floating dam in the Gulf of Mexico. But I wasn't quite prepared for the way that my razorblade would suddenly go slipping pointlessly down my face, meeting no stubble. Or for the way that my newly smooth upper lip would begin to look as if it had undergone electrolysis, causing me to look a bit too much like somebody's maiden auntie. (The chest hair that was once the toast of two continents hasn't yet wilted, but so much of it was shaved off for various hospital incisions that it's a rather patchy affair.) I feel upsettingly de-natured. If Penélope Cruz were one of my nurses, I wouldn't even notice. In the war against Thanatos, if we must term it a war, the immediate loss of Eros is a huge initial sacrifice.

These are my first raw reactions to being stricken. I am quietly resolved to resist bodily as best I can, even if only passively, and to seek the most advanced advice. My heart and blood pressure and many other registers are now strong again: indeed, it occurs to me that if I didn't have such a stout constitution I might have led a much healthier life thus far. Against me is the blind, emotionless alien, cheered on by some who have long wished me ill. But on the side of my continued life is a group of brilliant and selfless physicians plus an astonishing number of prayer groups. On both of these I hope to write next time if—as my father invariably said—I am spared.

Between a Woman and Her Doctor: A Story About Abortion You Will Never Forget

By Martha Mendoza

I could see my baby's amazing and perfect spine, a precise, pebbled curl of vertebrae. His little round skull. The curve of his nose. I could even see his small leg floating slowly through my uterus.

My doctor came in a moment later, slid the ultrasound sensor around my growing, round belly and put her hand on my shoulder. "It's not alive," she said.

She turned her back to me and started taking notes. I looked at the wall, breathing deeply, trying not to cry.

I can make it through this, I thought. I can handle this.

I didn't know I was about to become a pariah.

I was 19 weeks pregnant, strong, fit and happy, imagining our fourth child, the newest member of our family. He would have dark hair and bright eyes. He'd be intelligent and strong—really strong, judging by his early kicks.

And now this. Not alive?

I didn't realize that pressures well beyond my uterus, beyond the too bright, too-loud, too-small ultrasound room, extending all the way to boardrooms of hospitals, administrative sessions at medical schools and committee hearings in Congress, were going to deepen and expand my sorrow and pain.

On November 6, 2003, President Bush signed what he called a "partial birth abortion ban," prohibiting doctors from committing an "overt act" designed to kill a partially delivered fetus. The law, which faces vigorous challenges, is the most significant change to the nation's abortion laws since the U.S. Supreme Court ruled abortion legal in Roe v. Wade in 1973. One of the unintended consequences of this new law is that it put people in my position, with a fetus that is already dead, in a technical limbo.

From *Ms. Magazine*, 2004.

Legally, a doctor can still surgically take a dead body out of a pregnant woman. But in reality, the years of angry debate that led to the law's passage, restrictive state laws and the violence targeting physicians have reduced the number of hospitals and doctors willing to do dilations and evacuations (D&Es) and dilations and extractions (intact D&Es), which involve removing a larger fetus, sometimes in pieces, from the womb.

At the same time, fewer medical schools are training doctors to do these procedures. After all, why spend time training for a surgery that's likely to be made illegal?

At this point, 74 percent of obstetrics and gynecology residency programs do not train all residents in abortion procedures, according to reproductive health researchers at the National Abortion Federation. Those that do usually teach only the more routine dilation and curettage—D&C, the 15-minute uterine scraping used for abortions of fetuses under 13 weeks old.

Fewer than 7 percent of obstetricians are trained to do D&Es, the procedure used on fetuses from about 13 to 19 weeks. Almost all the doctors doing them are over 50 years old.

"Finding a doctor who will do a D&E is getting very tough," says Ron Fitzsimmons, executive director of the National Coalition of Abortion Providers.

My doctor turned around and faced me. She told me that because dilation and evacuation is rarely offered in my community, I could opt instead to chemically induce labor over several days and then deliver the little body at my local maternity ward. "It's up to you," she said.

I'd been through labor and delivery three times before, with great joy as well as pain, and the notion of going through that profound experience only to deliver a dead fetus (whose skin was already starting to slough off, whose skull might be collapsing) was horrifying.

I also did some research, spoke with friends who were obstetricians and gynecologists, and quickly learned this: Study after study shows D&Es are safer than labor and delivery. Women who had D&Es were far less likely to have bleeding requiring transfusion, infection requiring intravenous antibiotics, organ injuries requiring additional surgery or cervical laceration requiring repair and hospital readmission.

A review of 300 second-trimester abortions published in 2002 in the American Journal of *Obstetrics & Gynecology* found that 29 percent of women who went through labor and delivery had complications, compared with just 4 percent of those who had D&Es.

The American Medical Association said D&Es, compared to labor and delivery, "may minimize trauma to the woman's uterus, cervix and other vital organs."

There was this fact, too: The intact D&E surgery makes less use of "grasping instruments," which could damage the body of the fetus. If the body were intact, doctors might be able to more easily figure out why my baby died in the womb.

I'm a healthy person. I run, swim and bike. I'm 37 years old and optimistic. Good things happen to me. I didn't want to rule out having more kids, but I did want to know what went wrong before I tried again.

We told our doctor we had chosen a dilation and evacuation.

"I can't do these myself," said my doctor. "I trained at a Catholic hospital."

My doctor recommended a specialist in a neighboring county, but when I called for an appointment, they said they couldn't see me for almost a week.

I could feel my baby's dead body inside of mine. This baby had thrilled me with kicks and flutters, those first soft tickles of life bringing a smile to my face and my hand to my rounding belly. Now this baby floated, limp and heavy, from one side to the other, as I rolled in my bed.

And within a day, I started to bleed. My body, with or without a doctor's help, was starting to expel the fetus. Technically, I was threatening a spontaneous abortion, the least safe of the available options.

I did what any pregnant patient would do. I called my doctor. And she advised me to wait.

I lay in my bed, not sleeping day or night, trying not to lose this little baby's body that my own womb was working to expel. Wait, I told myself. Just hold on. Let a doctor take this out.

I was scared. Was it going to fall out of my body when I rose, in the middle of the night, to check on my toddler? Would it come apart on its own and double me over, knock me to the floor, as I stood at the stove scrambling eggs for my boys?

On my fourth morning, with the bleeding and cramping increasing, I couldn't wait any more. I called my doctor and was told that since I wasn't hemorrhaging, I should not come in. Her partner, on call, pedantically explained that women can safely lose a lot of blood, even during a routine period.

I began calling labor and delivery units at the top five medical centers in my area. I told them I had been 19 weeks along. The baby is dead. I'm bleeding, I said. I'm scheduled for a D&E in a few days. If I come in right now, what could you do for me, I asked.

Don't come in, they told me again and again. "Go to your emergency room if you are hemorrhaging to avoid bleeding to death. No one here can do a D&E today, and unless you're really in active labor you're safer to wait."

More than 66,000 women each year in the U.S. undergo an abortion at some point between 13 and 20 weeks, according to the Centers for Disease Control and Prevention.

The CDC doesn't specify the physical circumstances of the women or their fetuses. Other CDC data shows that 4,000 women miscarry in their second trimester. Again, the data doesn't clarify whether those 4,000 women have to go through surgery.

Here's what is clear: Most of those women face increasingly limited access to care. One survey showed that half of the women who got abortions after 15 weeks of gestation said they were delayed because of problems in affording, finding or getting to abortion services.

No surprise there; abortion is not readily available in 86 percent of the counties in the U.S.

Although there are some new, early diagnostic tests available, the most common prenatal screening for neural tube defects or Down syndrome is done around the 16th week of pregnancy. When problems are found—sometimes life-threatening problems—pregnant women face the same limited options that I did.

At last I found one university teaching hospital that, at least over the telephone, was willing to take me.

"We do have one doctor who can do a D&E," they said. "Come in to our emergency room if you want."

But when I arrived at the university's emergency room, the source of the tension was clear. After examining me and confirming I was bleeding but not hemorrhaging, the attending obstetrician, obviously pregnant herself, defensively explained that only one of their dozens of obstetricians and gynecologists still does D&Es, and he was simply not available.

Not today. Not tomorrow. Not the next day.

No, I couldn't have his name. She walked away from me and called my doctor.

"You can't just dump these patients on us," she shouted into the phone, her high-pitched voice floating through the heavy curtains surrounding my bed. "You should be dealing with this yourself."

Shivering on the narrow, white exam table, I wondered what I had done wrong. Then I pulled back on my loose maternity pants and stumbled into the sunny parking lot, blinking back tears in the dazzling spring day, trying to understand the directions they sent me out with: Find a hotel within a few blocks from a hospital. Rest, monitor the bleeding. Don't go home—the 45-minute drive might be too far.

The next few days were a blur of lumpy motel beds, telephone calls to doctors, cramps. The pre-examination for my D&E finally arrived. First, the hospital required me to sign a legal form consenting to terminate the pregnancy. Then they explained I could, at no cost, have the remains incinerated by the hospital pathology department as medical waste, or for a fee have them taken to a funeral home for burial or cremation.

They inserted sticks of seaweed into my cervix and told me to go home for the night. A few hours later—when the contractions were regular, strong and frequent—I knew we needed to get to the hospital. "The patient appeared to be in active labor," say my charts, "and I explained this to the patient and offered her pain medication for vaginal delivery."

According to the charts, I was "adamant" in demanding a D&E. I remember that I definitely wanted the surgical procedure that was the safest option. One hour later, just as an anesthesiologist was slipping me into unconsciousness, I had the D&E and a little body, my little boy, slipped out.

Around his neck, three times and very tight, was the umbilical cord, source of his life, cause of his death.

This past spring, as the wild flowers started blooming around the simple cross we built for this baby, the Justice Department began trying to enforce the Bush administration's ban and federal courts in three different cities heard arguments regarding the new law.

Doctors explained that D&Es are the safest procedure in many cases, and that the law is particularly cruel to mothers like me whose babies were already dead.

In hopes of bolstering their case, prosecutors sent federal subpoenas to various medical centers, asking for records of D&Es. There's an attorney somewhere, someday, who may poke through the files of my loss.

I didn't watch the trial because I had another appointment to keep— another ultrasound. Lying on the crisp white paper, watching the monitor, I saw new life, the incredible spine, tiny fingers waving slowly across my uterus, a perfect thigh.

Best of all, there it was, a strong, four-chamber heart, beating steady and solid. A soft quiver, baby rolling, rippled across my belly.

"Everything looks wonderful," said my doctor. "This baby is doing great."

Naked

By Atul Gawande, M.D., M.P.H.

There is an exquisite and fascinating scene in *Kandahar,* a movie set in Afghanistan under the Taliban regime, in which a male physician is asked to examine a female patient. They are separated by an opaque screen. Behind it, the woman is covered from head to toe by her burka. The two do not talk directly to each other. The patient's young son serves as the go-between. She has a stomachache, he says.

"Does she throw up her food?" the doctor asks.

"Do you throw up your food?" the boy asks.

"No," the woman says, perfectly audibly, but the doctor waits as if he has not heard.

"No," the boy tells him.

For the exam, the doctor has cut a two-inch circle in the screen. "Tell her to come closer," he says. The boy does. She brings her mouth to the opening, and through it he looks inside. "Have her bring her eye to the hole," he says. And so the exam goes. Such, apparently, can be the demands of decency.

When I started my surgical practice two years ago, I was not at all clear about what my own etiquette of examination should be. Expectations are murky; we have no clear standards in the United States; and the topic can be fraught with hazards. Physical examination is deeply intimate, and the way a doctor deals with the naked body—particularly when the doctor is male and the patient female—inevitably raises questions of propriety and trust.

No one anywhere seems to have discovered the ideal approach. A surgical colleague who practices in Iraq told me about the customs of physical examination there. He said he feels no hesitation about examining female patients completely when necessary, but because a doctor and a patient of opposite sex cannot be alone together without eyebrows being raised, a family member will always accompany them for the exam. Women do not remove their clothes or change into a gown for the exam, and only a small portion of the body is uncovered

From *The New England Journal of Medicine,* 2005.

at any one time. A nurse, he said, is rarely asked to chaperone: if the doctor is female, it is not necessary, and if male, the family is there to ensure that nothing unseemly occurs.

In Caracas, according to a Venezuelan doctor I met, female patients virtually always have a chaperone for a breast or pelvic exam, whether the physician is male or female. "That way there are no mixed messages," the doctor said. The chaperone, however, must be a medical professional. So the family is sent out of the examination room, and a nurse brought in. If a chaperone is unavailable or has refused to participate, the exam is not done.

A Ukrainian internist told me that she has not heard of doctors in Kiev using a chaperone. If a family member is present, he or she will be asked to leave. Both patient and doctor wear their uniforms— the patient a white examining gown, the doctor a white coat. Last names are always used. There is no effort at informality to muddy the occasion. This practice, she believes, is enough to solidify trust and preclude misinterpretation of the conduct of care.

A doctor, it appears, has a range of options.

In 2003, I set up my clinic hours, and soon people arrived to see me. I was, I realized, for the first time genuinely alone with patients. No attending physician in the room or getting ready to come in; no bustle of emergency room personnel on the other side of a curtain. Just a patient and me. We'd sit down. We'd talk. I'd ask about whatever had occasioned the visit, about past medical problems, medications, the family and social history. Then the time would come to have a look.

There were, I will admit, some awkward moments. I had an instinctive aversion to examination gowns. At our clinic they are made of either thin, ill-fitting cloth or thin, ill-fitting paper. They seem designed to leave patients exposed and cold. I decided to examine my patients while they were in their street clothes. If a patient with gallstones wore a shirt she could untuck for the abdominal exam, this worked fine. But then I'd encounter a patient in stockings and a dress, and the next thing I knew, I had her dress bunched up around her head, her tights around her knees, and both of us wondering what the hell was going on. An exam for a breast lump one could manage, in theory: the woman could unhook her brassiere and lift or unbutton her shirt. But in practice, it just seemed weird. Even checking pulses could be a problem. Pant legs could not be pushed up high enough. Try pulling them down over shoes, however, and... forget it. I finally began to have patients change into the damn gowns. (I haven't, however, asked men to do so nearly as often as women.)

As for having a chaperone present with female patients, I hadn't settled on a firm policy. I found that I always asked a medical assistant to come in for pelvic exams and generally didn't for breast exams. I was completely inconsistent about rectal exams.

I surveyed my colleagues about what they do and received a variety of answers. Many said they bring in a chaperone for all pelvic and rectal exams—"anything below the waist"—but only rarely for breast exams. Others have a chaperone for breast and pelvic exams but not for rectal exams. Some did not have a chaperone at all. Indeed, an obstetrician-gynecologist estimated that about half the male physicians in his department do not routinely use a chaperone. He himself detests the word "chaperone" because it implies that mistrust is warranted, but he offers to bring in an "assistant" for pelvic and breast exams. Few of his patients, however, find the presence of the assistant necessary after the first exam, he said. If the patient prefers to have her sister, boyfriend, or mother stay for the exam, he does not object—but he is under no illusion that a family chaperone offers protection against an accusation of misconduct. Instead, he relies on his reading of a patient to determine whether bringing in a nurse-witness would be wise.

One of our residents, who was trained partly in London, said he found the selectivity here strange. "In Britain, I would never examine a woman's abdomen without a nurse present. But in the emergency room here, when I asked to have a nurse come in when I needed to do a rectal exam or check groin nodes on a woman, they thought I was crazy. 'Just go in there and do it!' they said." In England, he said, "if you need to do a breast or rectal exam or even check femoral pulses, especially on a young woman, you would be either foolish or stupid to do it without a chaperone. It doesn't take much—just one patient complaining, 'I came in with a foot pain and the doctor started diving around my groin,' and you could be suspended for a sexual-harassment investigation."

Britain's standards are stringent: The General Medical Council, the Royal College of Physicians, and the Royal College of Obstetricians and Gynaecologists specify that a chaperone must be offered to all patients who undergo an "intimate exam" (i.e., involving the breasts, genitalia, or rectum), irrespective of the sex of the patient or

254

of the doctor.[1,2] A chaperone must be present when a male physician performs an intimate exam of a female patient. The chaperone should be a female member of the medical team, and her name should be recorded in the notes. If the patient refuses a chaperone and the examination is not urgent, it should be deferred until it can be performed by a female physician.

In the United States, we have no such guidelines. As a result, our patients have little idea of what to expect from us. To be sure, some minimal standards have been established. The Federation of State Medical Boards has spelled out that touching a patient's breasts or genitals for a purpose other than medical care is a disciplinable offense. So are oral contact with a patient, encouraging a patient to masturbate in one's presence, and providing services in exchange for sexual favors. Sexual impropriety—which involves no touching but is no less proscribed—includes asking a patient for a date, criticizing a patient's sexual orientation, making sexual comments about the patient's body or clothing, and initiating discussion of one's own sexual experiences or fantasies.[3] I can't say anyone taught me these boundaries in medical school, but I would like to think that no one needed to.

The difficulty for those of us who do not behave badly is that medical exams remain inherently ambiguous. Any patient can be led to wonder: Did the doctor really need to touch me there? Even when doctors simply inquire about patients' sexual history, can anyone be certain of the intent? The fact that all medical professionals have blushed or found their thoughts straying during a patient visit reveals the potential for impropriety in any encounter.

The tone of an office visit can turn on a single word, a joke, a comment about a tattoo in an unexpected place. One surgeon told me of a young patient who expressed concern about a lump in her "boob." But when he used the same word in response, she became extremely uncomfortable and later made a complaint. Another woman I know left her gynecologist after he made an offhand, probably inadvertent, but admiring comment about her tan lines during a pelvic exam.

The examination itself—the how and where of the touching—is, of course, the most potentially dicey territory. If a patient even begins to doubt the propriety of what a doctor is doing, something is not right. So what then should our customs be?

There are many reasons to consider setting tighter, more uniform professional standards. One is to protect patients from harm. About 4 percent of the disciplinary orders that state medical boards issue against physicians are for sex-related offenses. One of every 200 physicians is disciplined for sexual misconduct with patients sometime during his or her career.[4] Some of these cases involve such outrageous acts as having intercourse with patients during pelvic exams. The vast majority of cases involved male physicians and female patients, and virtually all occurred without a chaperone present.[5] About one third of cases studied in one state involved actual sexual intercourse with patients; two thirds involved sexual impropriety or inappropriate touching short of sexual contact. Another goal might be to reduce false accusations arising from misinterpretation.

Nonetheless, eliminating misconduct and accusations would be the wrong aim to guide medical care. The trouble is not that such acts are rare (though the statistics suggest they are), nor that total prevention—zero tolerance—is impossible. It is that, at some point, the measures required to achieve total prevention will approach the Talibanesque and harm care of patients.

Embracing more explicit standards for medical encounters, however, might actually improve relationships with patients—and that does stand as a worthy goal. The new informality of medicine—with white coats disappearing, and patient and doctor sometimes on a first-name basis—has blurred boundaries that once guided us. If physicians are unsure about what is appropriate behavior for themselves, is it any surprise that patients are, too? Or that misinterpretation can occur? We have jettisoned our old customs but have not bothered to replace them.

My father, a urologist, has thought carefully about how to avert such uncertainties. From the start, he felt the fragility of his standing as an outsider, an Indian immigrant practicing in a rural Ohio town. In the absence of guidelines to reassure patients that what he does as a urologist is routine, he has made painstaking efforts to avoid question.

The process begins before the exam. He always arrives in a tie and white coat. He is courtly. Although he often knows patients socially and doesn't hesitate to speak with them about personal matters (the subjects can range from impotence to sexual affairs), he keeps his language strictly medical. If a female patient must put on a gown, he steps out while she undresses. He makes a point of explaining what he is going to do during the examination and why. If the patient lies down and needs further unzipping or unbuttoning, he is careful not to help. He wears gloves even for abdominal examinations. If the patient is female or under 18 years of age, then he brings in a nurse as a chaperone, whether the exam is "intimate" or not.

His approach has succeeded. I grew up knowing many of his patients, and they trust him completely. I find, however, that some of his practices do not seem quite right for me. My patients are as likely to have problems above the waist as below, and having a chaperone present for a routine abdominal exam or a check of groin pulses feels to me absurd. I don't don gloves for nongenital exams. Nonetheless, I have tried to emulate the spirit of my father's visits—the decorum in language and attire, the respect for modesty, the precision of examination. As I think further about his example, it has also led me to make some changes: I now uniformly use an assistant not just for pelvic exams but also for rectal exams of female patients and as patients desire, for breast exams as well. For the comfort and reassurance of patients, these seem to be reasonable customs, even expectations, for more of us to accept.

A professor once told my medical school class that patients can tell when you've seen a thousand naked patients and when you haven't. I now know that's true. But I have also come to recognize that no patient has seen a thousand doctors. They therefore have little idea, coming to a doctor's office, of what is "normal" and what is not. This we can change.

References

1. Intimate examinations. London: General Medical Council Standards Committee, December 2001.

2. Gynaecological examinations: guidelines for specialist practice. London: Royal College of Obstetricians and Gynaecologists, July 2002.

3. Ad Hoc Committee on Physician Impairment. Report on sexual boundary issues. Dallas: Federation of State Medical Boards of the United States, April 1996.

4. Dehlendorf CE, Wolfe SM. Physicians disciplined for sex-related offenses. JAMA1998; 279: 1883–1888

5. Enbom JA, Thomas CD. Evaluation of sexual misconduct complaints: the Oregon Board of Medical Examiners, 1991 to 1995. Am J Obstet Gynecol 1997;176:1340–1348

The Globalization of Eating Disorders

By Susan Bordo

The young girl stands in front of the mirror. Never fat to begin with, she's been on a no-fat diet for a couple of weeks and has reached her goal weight: 115 lb., at 5'4"—exactly what she should weigh, according to her doctor's chart. But in her eyes she still looks dumpy. She can't shake her mind free of the "Lady Marmelade" video from Moulin Rouge. Christina Aguilera, Pink, L'il Kim, and Mya, each one perfect in her own way: every curve smooth and sleek, lean-sexy, nothing to spare. Self-hatred and shame start to burn in the girl, and envy tears at her stomach, enough to make her sick. She'll never look like them, no matter how much weight she loses. Look at that stomach of hers, see how it sticks out? Those thighs—they actually jiggle. Her butt is monstrous. She's fat, gross, a dough girl.

As you read the imaginary scenario above, whom did you picture standing in front of the mirror? If your images of girls with eating and body image problems have been shaped by *People* magazine and Lifetime movies, she's probably white, North American, and economically secure. A child whose parents have never had to worry about putting food on the family table. A girl with money to spare for fashion magazine and trendy clothing, probably college-bound. If you're familiar with the classic psychological literature on eating disorders, you amy also have read that she's an extreme "perfectionist" with a hyper-demanding mother, and that she suffers from "body-image distortion syndrome" and other severe perceptual and cognitive problems that "normal girls don't share. You probably don't picture her as black, Asian, or Latina.

Read the description again, but this time imagine twenty-something Tenisha Williamson standing in front of the mirror. Tenisha is black, suffers from anorexia, and feels like a traitor to her face. "From an African-American standpoint," she writes, "we as a people are encouraged to embrace our big, voluptuous bodies. This makes me feel terrible because I don't want a big, voluptuous body! I don't ever want to be fat—ever, and I don't ever want to gain weight. I would rather die from starvation than gain a single pound."[1] Tenisha is no

---

From *Unbearable Weight: Feminism, Western Culture, and the Body*, 2003.

longer an anomaly. Eating and body image problems are now not only crossing racial and class lines, but gender lines. They have also become a global phenomenon.

Fiji is a striking example. Because of their remote location, the Fiji islands did not have access to television until 1995, when a single station was introduced. It broadcasts programs from the United States, Great Britian, and Australia. Until that time, Fiji had no reported cases of eating disorders, and a study conducted by anthropologist Anne Becker showed that most Fijian girls and women, no matter how large, were comfortable with their bodies. In 1998, just three years after the station began broadcasting, 11 percent of girls reported vomiting to control weight, and 62 percent of the girls surveyed reported dieting during the previous months.[2]

Becker was surprised by the change; she had thought that Fijian cultural traditions, which celebrate eating and favor voluptuous bodies, would "withstand" the influence of media images. Becker hadn't yet understood that we live in an empire of images, and that there are no protective borders.

In Central Africa, for example, traditional cultures still celebrate voluptuous women. In some regions, brides are sent to fattening farms, to be plumped and massaged into shape for their wedding night. In a country plagued by AIDS, the skinny body has meant—as it used to among Italian, Jewish, and black Americans—poverty, sickness, death. "An African girl must have hips," says dress designer Frank Osodi. "We have hips. We have bums. We like flesh in Africa." For years, Nigeria sent its local version of beautiful to the Miss World competition. The contestants did very poorly. Then a savvy entrepreneur went against local ideals and entered Agbani Darego, a light-skinned, hyper-skinny beauty. (He got his inspiration from M-Net, the South African network seen across Africa on satellite television, which broadcasts mostly American movies and television shows.) Agbani Darego won the Miss World Pageant, the first Black African to do so. Now, Nigerian teenagers fast and exercise, trying to become "lepa"—a popular slang phrase for the thin "it" girls that are all the rage. Said one: "People have realized that slim is beautiful."[3]

How can mere images be so powerful? For one thing, they are never "just pictures," as the fashion magazines continually maintain (disingenuously) in their own defense. They speak to young people not just about how to be beautiful but also about how to become what the dominant culture admires, values, rewards. They tell them how to be cool, "get it together," overcome their shame. To girls who have been abused they may offer a fantasy of control and invulnerability, immunity from pain and hurt. For racial and ethnic groups whose bodies have been deemed "foreign," earthy, and primitive, and considered unattractive by Anglo-Saxon norms, they my cast the lure of being accepted as "normal" by the dominant culture.

In today's world, it is through images—much more than parents, teachers, or clergy—that we are taught how to be. And it is images, too, that teach us how to see, that educate our vision in what's a defect and what Is normal, that give us the models against which our own bodies and the bodies of others are measured. Perceptual pedagogy: "How to Interpret Your Body 101." It's become a global requirement.

I was intrigued, for example, when my articles on eating disorders began to be translated, over the past few years, into Japanese and Chinese. Among the members of audiences at my talks, Asian women had been among the most insistent that eating and body image weren't problems for their people, and indeed, my initial research showed that eating disorders were virtually unknown in Asia. But when, this year, a Korean translation of *Unbearable Weight* was published, I felt I needed to revisit the situation. I discovered multiple reports on dramatic increases in eating disorders in China, South Korea, and Japan. "As many Asian countries become Westernized and infused with the Western aesthetic of a tall, thin, lean body, a virtual tsunami of eating disorders has swamped Asian countries," writes Eunice Park in *Asian Week* magazine. Older people can still remember when it was very different. In China, for example, where revolutionary ideals once condemned and focus on appearance and there have been several disastrous famines, "little fatty" was a term of endearment for children. Now, with fast food on every corner, childhood obesity is on the rise, and the cultural meaning of fat and thin has changed. "When I was young," says Li Xiaojing, who manages a fitness center in Beijing, "people admired and were even jealous of fat people since they thought they had a better life... But now, most of us see a fat person and think 'He looks awful.'"[4]

Clearly, body insecurity can be exported, imported, and marketed—just like any other profitable commodity. In this respect, what's happened with men and boys is illustrative. Ten years ago men tended, if anything, to see themselves as better looking than they (perhaps) actually were. And then (as I chronicle in detail in my book,

260

The Male Body) the menswear manufacturers, the diet industries, and the plastic surgeons "discovered" the male body. And now, young guys are looking in their mirrors, finding themselves soft and ill defined, no matter how muscular they are. Now they are developing the eating and body image disorders that we once thought only girls had. Now they are abusing steroids, measuring their own muscularity against the oiled and perfected images of professional athletes, body-builders, and *Men's Health* models. Now the industries in body-enhancement—cosmetic surgeons, manufacturers of anti-aging creams, spas and salons—are making huge bucks off men, too.

What is to be done/ I have no easy answers. But I do know that we need to acknowledge, finally and decisively, that we are dealing here with a cultural problem. If eating disorders were biochemical, as some claim, how can we account for their gradual "spread" across race, gender, and nationality? And with mass media culture increasingly proving the dominant "public education" in our children's lives—and those of children around the globe—how can we blame families? Families matter, of course, and so do racial and ethnic traditions. But families exist in cultural tie and space—and so do racial groups. In the empire of images, no one lives in a bubble of self-generated "dysfunction" or permanent immunity. The sooner we recognize that—and start paying attention to the culture around us and what it is teaching our children—the sooner we can begin developing some strategies for change.

Notes

1. From the Colours of Ana website (http://coloursofana.com//ss8.asp). [This and subsequent notes in the selection are the author's.]

2. Reported in Nancy Snyderma, *The Girl in the Mirror* (New York: Hyperion, 2002), p. 84.

3. Norimitsu Onishi, "Globalization of Beauty Makes Slimness Trendy," *The New York Times*, Oct. 3, 2002.

4. Reported in Elizabeth Rosenthal, "Beijing Journal: China's Chic Waistline: Convex to Concave," *The New York Times*, Dec. 9, 1999.

Part Six
Nature and the Environment

The American Indian Wilderness (Burning the Shelter)

By Louis Owens

In the center of the Glacier Peak Wilderness in northern Washington, a magnificent, fully glaciated white volcano rises over a stunningly beautiful region of the North Cascades. On maps, the mountain is called Glacier Peak, To the Salishan people who have always lived in this part of the Cascades, however, the mountain is Dakobed, or the Great Mother, the place of emergence. For more than eighty years, a small, three-sided log shelter stood in a place called White Pass just below one shoulder of the great mountain, tucked securely into a meadow between thick stands of mountain hemlock and alpine fir.

In the early fall of 1976, while working as a seasonal ranger for the U.S. Forest Service, I drew the task of burning the White Pass shelter. After all those years, the shelter roof had collapsed like a broken bird wing under the weight of winter snow, and the time was right for fire and replanting. It was part of a Forest Service plan to remove all human-made objects from wilderness areas, a plan of which I heartily approved. So I backpacked eleven miles to the pass and set up camp, and for five days, while a bitter early storm sent snow driving horizontally out of the north, I dismantled the shelter and burned the old logs, piling and burning and piling and burning until nothing remained. The antique, hand-forged spikes that had held the shelter together I put into gunny sacks and cached to be packed out later by mule. I spaded up the earth beaten, hard for nearly a century by boot and hoof, and transplanted plugs of vegetation from hidden spots on the nearby ridge.

At the end of those five days, not a trace of the shelter remained, and I felt good, very smug in fact, about returning the White Pass meadow to its "original" state. As I packed up my camp, the snowstorm had subsided to a few flurries and a chill that felt bone deep with the promise of winter. My season was almost over, and as I started the steep hike down to the trailhead my mind was on the winter I was going to spend in sunny Arizona.

A half mile from the pass I saw the two old women, At first they were dark, hunched forms far down on the last long switchback up the snowy ridge. But as we drew closer to one another, I began to feel

From *The American Nature Writing Newsletter*, 1994.

a growing amazement that, by the time we were face-to-face, had become awe. Almost swallowed up in their baggy wool pants, heavy sweaters, and parkas, silver braids hanging below thick wool caps, they seemed ancient, each weighted with at least seventy years as well as a small backpack. They paused every few steps to lean on their staffs and look out over the North Fork drainage below, a deep, heavily forested river valley that rose on the far side to the glaciers and sawtoothed black granite of the Monte Cristo Range. And they smiled hugely upon seeing me, clearly surprised and delighted to find another person in the mountains at such a time.

We stood and chatted for a moment, and as I did with all backpackers, I reluctantly asked them where they were going. The snow quickened a little, obscuring the view, as they told me that they were going to White Pass.

"Our father built a little house up here," one of them said, "when he worked for the Forest Service like you. Way back before we was born, before this century."

"We been coming up here each year since we was little," the other added. "Except last year when Sarah was not well enough."

"A long time ago, this was all our land," the one called Sarah answered. "All Indi'n land everywhere you can see. Our people had houses up in the mountains, for gathering berries every year."

As they took turns speaking, the smiles never leaving their faces, I wanted to excuse myself, to edge around these elders and flee to the trailhead and my car, drive back to the district station, and keep going south. I wanted to say, "I'm Indian too. Choctaw from Mississippi; Cherokee from Oklahoma"—as if mixed blood could pardon me for what I had done. Instead, I said, "The shelter is gone." Cravenly I added, "It was crushed by snow, so I was sent up to burn it. It's gone now."

I expected outrage, anger, sadness, but instead the sisters continued to smile at me, their smiles changing only slightly. They had a plastic tarp and would stay dry, they said, because a person always had to be prepared in the mountains. They would put up their tarp inside the hemlock grove above the meadow, and the scaly hemlock branches would turn back the snow. They forgave me without saying it—my ignorance and my part in the long pattern of loss which they knew so well.

Hiking out those eleven miles, as the snow of the high country became a drumming rain in the forests below, I had long hours to ponder my encounter with the sisters. Gradually, almost painfully, I began to understand that what I called "wilderness" was an absurdity, nothing more than a figment of the European imagination. Before the European invasion, there was no wilderness in North America; there was only the fertile continent where people lived in a hard-learned balance with the natural world. In embracing a philosophy that saw the White Pass shelter—and all traces of humanity—as a shameful stain upon the "pure" wilderness, I had succumbed to a five-hundred-year-old pattern of deadly thinking that separates us from the natural world. This is not to say that what we call wilderness today does not need careful safeguarding. I believe that White Pass really is better off now that the shelter doesn't serve as a magnet to backpackers and horsepackers who compact the soil, disturb and kill the wildlife, cut down centuries-old trees for firewood, and leave their litter strewn about. And I believe the man who built the shelter would agree. But despite this unfortunate reality, the global environmental crisis that sends species into extinction daily and threatens to destroy all life surely has its roots in the Western pattern of thought that sees humanity and "wilderness" as mutually exclusive.

In old-growth forests in the North Cascades, deep inside the official Wilderness Area, I have come upon faint traces of log shelters build by Suiattle and Upper Skagit people for berry harvesting a century or more ago—just as the sisters said. Those human-made structures were as natural a part of the Cascade ecosystem as the burrows of marmots in the steep scree slopes. Our native ancestors all over this continent lived within a complex web of relations with the natural world, and in doing so they assumed a responsibility for their world that contemporary Americans cannot even imagine. Unless Americans, and all human beings, can learn to imagine themselves as intimately and inextricably related to every aspect of the world they inhabit, with the extraordinary responsibilities such relationship entails—unless they can learn what the indigenous people of the Americas knew and often still know—the earth simply will not survive. A few square miles of something called wilderness will become the sign of failure everywhere.

Why I Hunt

by Rick Bass

I was a hunter before I came far up into northwest Montana, but not to the degree I am now. It astounds me sometimes to step back, particularly at the end of autumn, the end of the hunting season, and take both mental and physical inventory of all that was hunted and all that was gathered from this life in the mountains. The woodshed groaning tight, full of firewood. The fruits and herbs and vegetables from the garden, canned or dried or frozen; the wild mushrooms, huckleberries, thimbleberries, and strawberries. And most precious of all, the flesh of the wild things that share with us these mountains and the plains to the east—the elk, the whitetail and mule deer; the ducks and geese, grouse and pheasant and Hungarian partridge and dove and chukar and wild turkey; the trout and whitefish. Each year the cumulative bounty seems unbelievable. What heaven is this into which we've fallen?

How my wife and I got to this valley—the Yaak—15 years ago is a mystery, a move that I've only recently come to accept as having been inevitable. We got in the truck one day feeling strangely restless in Mississippi, and we drove. What did I know? Only that I missed the West's terrain of space. Young and healthy, and not coincidentally new-in-love, we hit that huge and rugged landscape in full stride. We drove north until we ran out of country—until the road ended, and we reached Canada's thick blue woods—and then we turned west and traveled until we ran almost out of mountains: the backside of the Rockies, to the wet, west-slope rainforest.

We came over a little mountain pass—it was August and winter was already fast approaching—and looked down on the soft hills, the dense purples of the spruce and fir forests, the ivory crests of the ice-capped peaks, and the slender ribbons of gray thread rising from the chimneys of the few cabins nudged close to the winding river below, and we fell in love with the Yaak Valley and the hard-logged Kootenai National Forest—the way people in movies fall with each other, star and starlet, as if a trap door has been pulled out from beneath them: tumbling through the air, arms windmilling furiously, and suddenly

From *Sierra Magazine*, 2001.

no other world but each other, no other world but this one, and eyes for no one, or no place, else.

Right from the beginning, I could see that there was extraordinary bounty in this low-elevation forest, resting as it does in a magical seam between the Pacific Northwest and the northern Rockies. Some landscapes these days have been reduced to nothing but dandelions and fire ants, knapweed and thistle, where the only remaining wildlife are sparrows, squirrels, and starlings. In the blessed Yaak, however, not a single mammal has gone extinct since the end of the Ice Age. This forest sustains more types of hunters—carnivores—than any valley in North America. It is a predator's showcase, home not just to wolves and grizzlies, but wolverines, lynx, bobcat, marten, fisher, black bear, mountain lion, golden eagle, bald eagle, coyote, fox, weasel. In the Yaak, everything is in motion, either seeking its quarry, or seeking to avoid becoming quarry.

The people who have chosen to live in this remote valley—few phones, very little electricity, and long, dark winters—possess a hardness and a dreaminess both. They—we—can live a life of deprivation, and yet are willing to enter the comfort of daydreams and imagination. There is something mysterious happening here between the landscape and the people, a thing that stimulates our imagination, and causes many of us to set off deep into the woods in search of the unknown, and sustenance—not just metaphorical or spiritual sustenance, but the real thing.

Only about 5 percent of the nation and 15 to 20 percent of Montanans are hunters. But in this one valley, almost everyone is a hunter. It is not the peer pressure of the local culture that recruits us into hunting, nor even necessarily the economic boon of a few hundred pounds of meat in a cash-poor society. Rather, it is the terrain itself, and one's gradual integration into it, that summons the hunter. Nearly everyone who has lived here for any length of time has ended up—sometimes almost against one's conscious wishes—becoming a hunter. This wild and powerful landscape sculpts us like clay. I don't find such sculpting an affront to the human spirit, but instead, wonderful testimony to our pliability, our ability to adapt to a place.

I myself love to hunt the deer, the elk, and the grouse—to follow them into the mouth of the forest, to disappear in their pursuit—to get lost following their snowy tracks up one mountain and down the next. One sets out after one's quarry with senses fully engaged, wildly alert:

entranced, nearly hypnotized. The tiniest of factors can possess the largest significance—the crack of a twig, the shift of a breeze, a single stray hair caught on a piece of bark, a fresh-bent blade of grass.

Each year during such pursuits, I am struck more and more by the conceit that people in a hunter-gatherer culture might have richer imaginations than those who dwell more fully in an agricultural or even post-agricultural environment. What else is the hunt but a stirring of the imagination, with the quarry, or goal, or treasure lying just around the corner or over the next rise? A hunter's imagination has no choice but to become deeply engaged, for it is never the hunter who is in control, but always the hunted, in that the prey directs the predator's movements.

The hunted shapes the hunter; the pursuit and evasion of predator and prey are but shadows of the same desire. The thrush wants to remain a thrush. The goshawk wants to consume the thrush and in doing so, partly become the thrush—to take its flesh into its flesh. They weave through the tangled branches of the forest, zigging and zagging, the goshawk right on the thrush's tail, like a shadow. Or perhaps it is the thrush that is the shadow thrown by the light of the goshawk's fiery desire.

Either way, the escape maneuvers of the thrush help carve and shape and direct the muscles of the goshawk. Even when you are walking through the woods seeing nothing but trees, you can feel the unseen passage of pursuits that might have occurred earlier that morning, precisely where you are standing—pursuits that will doubtless, after you are gone, sweep right back across that same spot again and again.

As does the goshawk, so too do human hunters imagine where their prey might be, or where it might go. They follow tracks hinting at not only distance and direction traveled, but also pace and gait and the general state of mind of the animal that is evading them. They plead to the mountain to deliver to them a deer, an elk. They imagine and hope that they are moving toward their goal of obtaining game.

When you plant a row of corn, there is not so much unknown. You can be fairly sure that, if the rains come, the corn is going to sprout. The corn is not seeking to elude you. But when you step into the woods, looking for a deer—well, there's nothing in your mind, or in your blood, or in the world, but imagination.

270

Most Americans neither hunt nor gather nor even grow their own food, nor make, with their own hands, any of their other necessities. In this post-agricultural society, too often we confuse anticipation with imagination. When we wander down the aisle of the supermarket searching for a chunk of frozen chicken, or cruise into Dillard's department store looking for a sweater, we can be fairly confident that grayish wad of chicken or that sweater is going to be there, thanks to the vigor and efficiency of a supply-and-demand marketplace. The imagination never quite hits second gear. Does the imagination atrophy, from such chronic inactivity? I suspect that it does.

All I know is that hunting—beyond being a thing I like to do—helps keep my imagination vital. I would hope never to be so blind as to offer it as prescription; I offer it only as testimony to my love of the landscape where I live—a place that is still, against all odds, its own place, quite unlike any other. I don't think I would be able to sustain myself as a dreamer in this strange landscape if I did not take off three months each year to wander the mountains in search of game; to hunt, stretching and exercising not just my imagination, but my spirit. And to wander the mountains, too, in all the other seasons. And to be nourished by the river of spirit that flows, shifting and winding, between me and the land.

Parkinson's Alley

By Joy Horowitz

Bruce McDermott tosses me the keys to his pickup, and I hoist his chrome walker into the truck's bed. "You need to see this," he tells me as he angles his torso and braced leg into the cab, then slams the door.

It's a rainy fall day in the Central Valley town of Visalia, California, and McDermott wants to show me some of the houses of people here who've been diagnosed with Parkinson's disease, the incurable neurodegenerative affliction that, coupled with a recent car crash, has left him unable to drive. I've never been at the wheel of such a behemoth truck before—or one with shotgun shells in the door well, for that matter—but I know better than to argue. McDermott was once the city's chief of police; when he makes suggestions, people tend to say, "Yes, sir."

A big, friendly bear of a man who likes to joke that his doctor calls him "fat boy," McDermott wears khaki shorts, sandals, and a crisply pressed polo shirt. Diagnosed with early-onset Parkinson's, he was forced to retire from the police force in 1997, at age 46, after he tried to place his right hand on the Bible to swear in a new officer but his arm shook so uncontrollably that people thought he was waving hello.

As we near his boyhood home on Border Links Drive, McDermott points to the house next door, where his godfather, a prominent attorney, died three years ago from complications of Parkinson's. Nearby, he shows me a field where crop dusters once landed their planes and routinely dumped their tanks. In a half-mile stretch, McDermott points to four homes where residents have been diagnosed with the disease.

Some neurologists dub the 300-mile-long string of Central Valley farm towns between Bakersfield and Sacramento "Parkinson's Alley," and recently released statistics back them up. A study published last year by researchers at the University of California, Los Angeles, found that Central Valley residents under age 60 who lived near fields where the pesticides paraquat and maneb had been used between 1974 and 1999 had a Parkinson's rate nearly five times higher than other residents in the region.

From *Sierra Magazine,* 2012.

I steer McDermott's truck into the driveway of his friend Margaret Haworth, a former tennis player and expert skier. Like McDermott, Haworth suffers from early-onset Parkinson's; she was diagnosed 16 years ago, at age 49.

Our visit is a surprise, but Haworth welcomes McDermott as if he's family. As he slowly makes his way up her front steps, she says of his walker, "I see you got a new hot rod."

Haworth tells us her mother was also afflicted by Parkinson's but never spoke of it. McDermott nods; it's a familiar story. "A lot of people in the valley won't tell you they have Parkinson's disease if they do," he says. "I know doctors who would lose their license if their insurance carriers knew they had it."

Research into the link between pesticides and Parkinson's in the Central Valley dates back to 2000, when UCLA epidemiologist Beate Ritz began comparing mortality records with pesticide-application reports. She discovered that California counties reporting the highest pesticide use also had the highest rates for Parkinson's-related deaths. Examining agricultural records from 1989 to 1994, Ritz found that when insecticides were applied to more than a third of a county's acreage, the risk of its residents' dying from Parkinson's disease increased 2.5-fold. She also found studies that revealed that as many as 40 percent of the area's Parkinson's cases are never mentioned on death certificates, possibly because many migrant workers fail to report the disease, or move on before symptoms arise.

Ritz and her research team found that Central Valley residents who consumed private well water and lived within 500 feet of farmland with documented long-term pesticide use were almost twice as likely to get Parkinson's disease. Their 2009 report, produced under the auspices of the federally funded Parkinson's Environment and Genes Study, was the first to quantify residents' exposure to such chemicals by comparing land-use maps with state-mandated pesticide-application records. "We're seeing effects not just on people in their homes but also on farms and in workplaces," Ritz told me in Los Angeles before I traveled 200 miles north to meet with McDermott.

Visalia, a 160-year-old gold rush town, has grown by more than a third to about 120,000 people in the past decade. It's in the heart of the Central Valley—the vast farm belt west of the Sierra Nevada where about 7 percent of the nation's crops are grown, producing $20 billion in annual revenues. Growers here use about 115 million pounds of pesticides every year.

Some of those pesticides are finding their way into residential water supplies in accumulations that surpass government safety standards, according to a number of studies—including tests of private-well samples gathered exclusively for this article. More than 1 million people in the region have tap water that isn't safe to drink because of nitrate contamination from manure, fertilizers, and leaking septic tanks, according to a collaborative report by the Pacific Institute, Visalia's Community Water Center, the Clean Water Fund, and California Rural Legal Assistance Foundation. Most of those residents are from low-income and Spanish-speaking households.

More than half of Central Valley communities rely on water stored underground for their drinking supply, the Community Water Center reports. Recent groundwater sampling found that the water in 75 percent of the private domestic wells in Tulare County, of which Visalia is the seat, contains unsafe levels of nitrates.

"We pay twice for water each month," says Susana DeAnda, the center's co-executive director. "Once for contaminated well water and once for bottled water."

Nitrates can also be a sign of pesticide contamination, but testing for pesticides in drinking water is expensive and not mandated. Some testing is done, however, and last year the State Water Resources Control Board released the results of a domestic-well-water survey in Tulare County; pesticides turned up in 13 of 19 wells sampled.

By the time I park McDermott's truck in his driveway, the rain has stopped. Gripping his walker, he shuffles back inside his home. The walk leaves him breathless. A lifelong Republican who favors Fox News, McDermott says he had long assumed that, in America, if something was wrong, it would be fixed. Now he's not so sure.

"It's an ugly thing when you look at it and think maybe something could be done to prevent this," he says. "I'm convinced it's exposure to the environment. Something's going on here."

Currently, no federal or state water quality standards regulate domestic well water in California, even though private wells are the primary source of drinking water for 1.6 million people in the state and more than 43 million, or 15 percent of the population, nationwide.

The federal Safe Drinking Water Act covers public water supplies, but Congress never extended the law to include private wells, which can be more susceptible to contamination because they tend to draw from shallower aquifers and often are close to farms that use pesticides.

The federal Clean Water Act largely exempts normal agricultural activities from regulation. California's Safe Drinking Water Act monitors water coming out of the tap but doesn't regulate the source. Although statutes are in place mandating the state to monitor and regulate agricultural pollution in drinking water, the program has yet to be implemented, according to Community Water Center co-founder Laurel Firestone. In California, the state Department of Pesticide Regulation conducts an annual survey of some domestic wells. Last year, for example, state regulators tested 136 wells and found pesticides in 103 of them. But the agency keeps the location of its testing confidential, citing concerns about terrorism.

"Nobody is testing domestic wells in any systematic way," says Robert J. Gilliom, a hydrologist and the head of pesticide studies for the U.S. Geological Survey's water quality assessment program.

Since Ritz's UCLA research was based on historical data, I wanted to know what pesticides are in the water now. But no one could tell me. So, I ordered some water-testing kits and set out to answer two simple questions: What pesticides are present in Central Valley well water and are any of them implicated for Parkinson's disease? The lab results revealed a potentially harmful mix of herbicides in tap water from 6 of the 10 private wells I tested.

Of course, not everyone wants to know what's in his or her water. When I arrived at a walnut farm in Visalia to take water samples, I asked the grower—whose hand shook from Parkinson's—what pesticides he used on his property. He said, "Whatever the gestapo lets us use."

"I'm dying to know, but I also am afraid to find out," the widow of a Parkinson's victim told me when I asked if I could test her drinking water. Her husband had worked for a program that advises farmers on how to use pesticides, and the couple had lived on a citrus ranch for more than 40 years. He sometimes came home "up to his elbows in the stuff." She told me I could take water samples on the ranch, but only if I didn't reveal her identity.

Off a country road outside Hanford, about 20 miles west of Visalia, I dropped by the home of Peggy and Jim Greaser to take a water sample from their kitchen sink. Their living room window has a view of the cornfield next door. Both Peggy and Jim, a former Sears technician, complained that the "drift" from crop dusters often burns their eyes and has ruined the paint job on their car.

Jim, now a part-time DJ known as Jim Dee on K6RGZ, suffers from Parkinson's disease. He drives a motorized cart from his front door to a nearby shack that houses his radio studio. Leather straps hang from shelves crammed with tape decks and vinyl records, so he has something to grasp.

"You start losing your walking ability," he said. "I've fallen so many times I've lost track."

Parkinson's, one of the most intractable of all neurological diseases, afflicts 500,000 to 1.5 million people in the United States. It's caused when nerve cells die in the area of the brain that produces dopamine, a neurotransmitter that's essential to everything from moving muscles to feeling pleasure. As dopamine levels decrease, messages that control motor function are blocked.

Although symptoms have been mentioned in texts dating back to biblical times, the disease was officially "discovered" in 1817, when British physician James Parkinson first described the "shaking palsy." But it wasn't until the mid-1980s that scientists stumbled on a link between pesticide exposure and Parkinson's disease, thanks to a bizarre outbreak among heroin addicts and an astute young San Francisco Bay Area neurologist named J. William Langston.

Langston, now scientific director at the Parkinson's Institute in Sunnyvale, California, had been asked to examine a cluster of young patients who looked like living statues; they could neither move nor speak and appeared to be in the advanced stages of Parkinson's disease. He learned that all of them had injected a new form of synthetic heroin. Alarmed, he called a press conference to alert the public to his "frozen addicts" and warn of bad drugs on the streets. When he prescribed levodopa, which is used to treat Parkinson's, the addicts, whose faces were so stiffened that they drooled uncontrollably, soon found that their symptoms abated.

The illicit drug they'd taken contained a compound known as MPTP, which has a similar chemical structure to that of paraquat—one of the most widely used herbicides in the world. Paraquat is of particular concern to Parkinson's researchers because of its synergistic effect, particularly when used with the fungicide maneb.

Taking their cues from Langston's earlier work, Ritz and her team discovered that long-term exposures to paraquat and maneb caused an eightfold increase in the development of Parkinson's for people under age 60. Paraquat was banned by the European Union in 2007 but is still widely used in the United States; about 75,000 pounds of it are applied annually to alfalfa, grapes, and other crops in Tulare County. The EPA banned maneb for use on corn, grapes, and apples in 2005 but continues to allow its use on almonds, which are abundant in the Central Valley.

Another chemical of particular concern to Parkinson's researchers is the fungicide ziram. When the EPA proposed prohibiting ziram use on 35 crops in 2003, a plant pathologist with the U.S. Department of Agriculture insisted that the pesticide had a "clean bill of health" and said workers could protect themselves by wearing "long pants and long sleeves." But cell studies by the UCLA researchers and others have shown that ziram kills certain brain cells whose absence leads to Parkinson's, and the UCLA team found that people exposed to the fungicide for 25 years or longer have a three-times-greater chance of developing the disease.

In 2008, California regulators placed ziram on their risk-assessment "priority" list. Four years later, no one's followed up.

"We have no estimated date for the assessment," Lea Brooks, communications director with California's Department of Pesticide Regulation, told me. "Our work schedule is behind due to furloughs, retirements, and a hiring freeze. It's on the priority list for a risk assessment, but there is no timeline."

Once a Month for the past 10 years, neurologist Jeff Bronstein has left his hillside home in Los Angeles at four a.m. to drive more than 150 miles north to the Central Valley, where he meets with Parkinson's patients before they take their daily medications, which mask symptoms. As part of the UCLA Parkinson's research team, Bronstein, a professor of neurology and molecular toxicology at the university's David Geffen School of Medicine and director of its Movement Disorders Program, needs to make sure that patients enrolled in the Parkinson's Environment and Genes Study have been correctly diagnosed (since it's easy to mistake other neurological symptoms for those of Parkinson's disease) and to chart their progress.

Over the years, Bronstein has met with farmworkers, corporate executives, police officers, college professors, and, of course, pesticide applicators. Although he lacks irrefutable evidence, he is convinced that pesticides are the culprit behind his patients' affliction.

"It's worth it," he told me of his five- to seven-hour round-trip commutes. During one of them, he spoke to me on his car phone as a crop duster roared overhead. "How many years did it take to prove smoking causes lung cancer? That's where we are with pesticides. The onus is on us to prove this stuff is bad. And what's really goofy is that what's considered an 'acceptable' level is completely arbitrary. They come up with numbers based on acute toxicity. But it's years and years of low-level exposure that matter, not acute toxicity. You need to look at chronic exposure before any meaningful discussion can take place."

In 2007 the U.S. Department of Agriculture partnered with the EPA to begin testing for pesticides at extremely low concentration levels in domestic well water. In 2009, the agencies took samples from 278 domestic, school, and farm wells in 16 states and detected pesticides in 152, or 45 percent, of them. "In the future, we'll see more and more pesticides in groundwater," said hydrologist Terry Councell, who runs the USDA's water monitoring program. "A lot of these pesticides haven't even hit the water table yet."

One morning I meet over coffee with Donna DeVries, former president of the Central Valley Parkinson's Disease Support Group. DeVries, a 57-year-old dental office manager, tells me she spends the first Friday of every month at the local Methodist church, with the Visalia-based support group, which ranks second in the United States in fundraising. She spent years caring for her father and father-in-law, both of whom died after battling the disease.

"All of our doctors have told us, 'Move. Get out of the valley. It's not a healthy place to be,' " she says. As she speaks, she sits on her right hand to control its shaking. She suspects she has Parkinson's too. "My doctor told me not to worry about it, but how can I not?"

Several dozen people attend the support group's Friday-morning meeting, and the conversation ranges from sharing medication tips to dealing with the inevitable depression that accompanies the disease. "I told my wife, 'Put the guns in the safe,' " says a man in his 40s who has driven several hours to be here.

Not everyone is keen on such frank talk, though. Bruce McDermott, for one, swore off the group after he sat through a downer of a discussion about morticians. He likes to think of Visalia as a "roll-up-your-sleeves kind of town" where people who share his disease can live a normal life, and where he and others can change the future for the better by verifying—and publicizing—a link between pesticides and Parkinson's.

"If I can help one person," McDermott says, "I feel good."

278

The Environmental Issue from Hell: Global Warming Is the Great Moral Crisis of Our Time

By Bill McKibben

When global warming first emerged as a potential crisis in the late 1980s, one academic analyst called it "the public policy problem from hell." The years since have only proven him more astute: Fifteen years into our understanding of climate change, we have yet to figure out how we're going to tackle it. And environmentalists are just as clueless as anyone else: Do we need to work on lifestyle or on lobbying, on photovoltaics or on politics? And is there a difference? How well we handle global warming will determine what kind of century we inhabit—and indeed what kind of planet we leave behind. The issue cuts close to home and also floats off easily into the abstract. So far it has been the ultimate "can't get there from here" problem, but the time has come to draw a road map—one that may help us deal with the handful of other issues on the list of real, world-shattering problems.

Typically, when you're mounting a campaign, you look for self-interest, you scare people by saying what will happen to us if we don't do something: All the birds will die, the canyon will disappear beneath a reservoir, we will choke to death on smog. But in the case of global warming, that doesn't exactly do the trick, at least in the time frame we're discussing. In temperate latitudes, climate change will creep up on us. Severe storms already have grown more frequent and more damaging. The progression of seasons is less steady. Some agriculture is less reliable. But face it: Our economy is so enormous that it takes those changes in stride. Economists who work on this stuff talk about how it will shave a percentage or two off the GNP over the next few decades. And most of us live lives so divorced from the natural world that we hardly notice the changes anyway. Hotter? Turn up the air-conditioning. Stormier? Well, an enormous percentage of Americans commute from remote-controlled garage to office parking garage—it may have been some time since they got good and wet in a rainstorm. By the time the magnitude of the change is truly in our faces, it will be too late to do much about it: There's such a lag time to increased levels of carbon dioxide in the atmosphere that we need

---

From *In These Times*, 2001.

to be making the switch to solar and wind and hydrogen power right now to prevent disaster decades away. Yesterday, in fact.

So maybe we should think of global warming in a different way—as the great moral crisis of our time, the equivalent of the civil rights movement of the 1960s. Why a moral question? In the first place, no one's ever figured out a more effective way to screw the marginalized and poor of this planet than climate change. Having taken their dignity, their resources, and their freedom under a variety of other schemes, we now are taking the very physical stability on which their already difficult lives depend. Our economy can absorb these changes for a while, but consider Bangladesh for a moment. In 1998 the sea level in the Bay of Bengal was higher than normal, just the sort of thing we can expect to become more frequent and severe. The waters sweeping down the Ganges and the Brahmaputra rivers from the Himalayas could not drain easily into the ocean—they backed up across the country, forcing most of its inhabitants to spend three months in thigh-deep water. The fall rice crop didn't get planted. We've seen this same kind of disaster over the past few years in Mozambique and Honduras and Venezuela and other places.

And global warming is a moral crisis, too, if you place any value on the rest of creation. Coral reef researchers indicate that these spectacularly intricate ecosystems are also spectacularly vulnerable. Rising water temperatures are likely to bleach them to extinction by mid-century. In the Arctic, polar bears are 20 percent scrawnier than they were a decade ago: As pack ice melts, so does the opportunity for hunting seals. All in all, the 21st century seems poised to see extinctions at a rate not observed since the last big asteroid slammed into the planet. But this time the asteroid is us.

It's a moral question, finally, if you think we owe any debt to the future. No one ever has figured out a more thoroughgoing way to strip-mine the present and degrade what comes after—all the people who will ever be related to you. Ever. No generation yet to come will ever forget us—we are the ones present at the moment when the temperature starts to spike, and so far we have not reacted. If it had been done to us, we would loathe the generation that did it, precisely as we will one day be loathed. But trying to launch a moral campaign is no easy task. In most moral crises, there is a villain—some person or class or institution that must be overcome. Once the villain is identified, the battle can commence. But you can't really get angry at carbon dioxide, and the people responsible for its production are, well, us.

So perhaps we need some symbols to get us started, some places to sharpen the debate and rally ourselves to action. There are plenty to choose from: our taste for ever bigger houses and the heating and cooling bills that come with them, our penchant for jumping on airplanes at the drop of a hat. But if you wanted one glaring example of our lack of balance, you could do worse than point the finger at sport utility vehicles. SUVS are more than mere symbols. They are a major part of the problem—we emit so much more carbon dioxide now than we did a decade ago in part because our fleet of cars and trucks actually has gotten steadily less fuel efficient for the past 10 years. If you switched today from the average American car to a big SUV, and drove it for just one year, the difference in carbon dioxide that you produced would be the equivalent of opening your refrigerator door and then forgetting to close it for six years. SUVs essentially are machines for burning fossil fuel that just happen to also move you and your stuff around.

But what makes them such a perfect symbol is the brute fact that they are simply unnecessary. Go to the parking lot of the nearest suburban supermarket and look around: The only conclusion you can draw is that to reach the grocery, people must drive through three or four raging rivers and up the side of a canyon. These are semi-military machines, armored trucks on a slight diet. While they do not keep their occupants appreciably safer, they do wreck whatever they plow into, making them the perfect metaphor for a heedless, supersized society.

That's why we need a much broader politics than the Washington lobbying that's occupied the big environmental groups for the past decade. We need to take all the brilliant and energetic strategies of local grassroots groups fighting dumps and cleaning up rivers and apply those tactics in the national and international arenas. That's why some pastors are starting to talk with their congregations about what cars to buy, and why some college seniors are passing around petitions pledging to stay away from the Ford Explorers and Excursions, and why some auto dealers have begun to notice informational picketers outside their showrooms on Saturday mornings urging customers to think about gas mileage when they look at cars.

The point is not that such actions by themselves—any individual actions—will make any real dent in the levels of carbon dioxide pouring into our atmosphere. Even if you got 10 percent of Americans really committed to changing their energy use, their solar homes wouldn't make much of a difference in our national totals. But 10 percent would be enough to change the politics around the issue, enough to pressure politicians to pass laws that would cause us all to shift our habits. And so we need to begin to take an issue that is now the province of technicians and turn it into a political issue, just as bus boycotts began to make public the issue of race, forcing the system to respond. That response is likely to be ugly—there are huge companies with a lot to lose, and many people so tied in to their current ways of life that advocating change smacks of subversion. But this has to become a political issue—and fast. The only way that may happen, short of a hideous drought or monster flood, is if it becomes a personal issue first.

The Obligation to Endure

By Rachel Carson

The history of life on earth has been a history of interaction between living things and their surroundings. To a large extent, the physical form and the habits of the earth's vegetation and its animal life have been molded by the environment. Considering the whole span of earthly time, the opposite effect, in which life actually modifies its surroundings, has been relatively slight. Only within the moment of time represented by the present century has one species—man—acquired significant power to alter the nature of his world.

283

During the past quarter century this power has not only increased to one of disturbing magnitude but it has changed in character. The most alarming of all man's assaults upon the environment is the contamination of air, earth, rivers, and sea with dangerous and even lethal materials. This pollution is for the most part irrecoverable; the chain of evil it initiates not only in the world that must support life but in living tissues is for the most part irreversible. In this now universal contamination of the environment, chemicals are the sinister and little-recognized partners of radiation in changing the very nature of the world—the very nature of its life. Strontium 90, released through nuclear explosions into the air, comes to earth in rain or drifts down as fallout, lodges in soil, enters into the grass or corn or wheat grown there, and in time takes up its abode in the bones of a human being, there to remain until his death. Similarly, chemicals sprayed on croplands or forests or gardens lie long in soil, entering into living organisms, passing from one to another in a chain of poisoning and death. Or they pass mysteriously by underground streams until they emerge and, through the alchemy of air and sunlight, combine into new forms that kill vegetation, sicken cattle, and work unknown harm on those who drink from once pure wells. As Albert Schweitzer has said, "Man can hardly even recognize the devils of his own creation."

It took hundreds of millions of years to produce the life that now inhabits the earth—eons of time in which that developing and evolving and diversifying life reached a state of adjustment and balance with its surroundings. The environment, rigorously shaping and directing the life it supported, contained elements that were

---

From *Silent Spring*, 1962.

hostile as well as supporting. Certain rocks gave out dangerous radiation; even within the light of the sun, from which all life draws its energy, there were short-wave radiations with power to injure. Given time—time not in years but in millennia—life adjusts, and a balance has been reached. For time is the essential ingredient; but in the modern world there is no time.

The rapidity of change and the speed with which new situations are created follow the impetuous and heedless pace of man rather than the deliberate pace of nature. Radiation is no longer merely the background radiation of rocks, the bombardment of cosmic rays, the ultraviolet of the sun that have existed before there was any life on earth; radiation is now the unnatural creation of man's tampering with the atom. The chemicals to which life is asked to make its adjustment are no longer merely the calcium and silica and copper and all the rest of the minerals washed out of the rocks and carried in rivers to the sea; they are the synthetic creations of man's inventive mind, brewed in his laboratories, and having no counterparts in nature.

To adjust to these chemicals would require time on the scale that is nature's; it would require not merely the years of a man's life but the life of generations. And even this, were it by some miracle possible, would be futile, for the new chemicals come from our laboratories in an endless stream; almost five hundred annually find their way into actual use in the United States alone. The figure is staggering and its implications are not easily grasped—500 new chemicals to which the bodies of men and animals are required somehow to adapt each year, chemicals totally outside the limits of biologic experience.

Among them are many that are used in man's war against nature. Since the mid-1940's over 200 basic chemicals have been created for use in killing insects, weeds, rodents, and other organisms described in the modern vernacular as "pests"; and they are sold under several thousand different brand names.

These sprays, dusts, and aerosols are now applied almost universally to farms, gardens, forests, and homes— nonselective chemicals that have the power to kill every insect, the "good" and the "bad," to still the song of birds and the leaping of fish in the streams, to coat the leaves with a deadly film, and to linger on in soil—all this though the intended target may be only a few weeds or insects. Can anyone believe it is possible to lay down such a barrage of poisons on the surface of the earth without making it unfit for all life? They should not be called "insecticides," but "biocides."

The whole process of spraying seems caught up in an endless spiral. Since DDT was released for civilian use, a process of escalation has been going on in which ever more toxic materials must be found. This has happened because insects, in a triumphant vindication of Darwin's principle of the survival of the fittest, have evolved super races immune to the particular insecticide used, hence a deadlier one has always to be developed—and then a deadlier one than that. It has happened also because, for reasons to be described later, destructive insects often undergo a "flareback," or resurgence, after spraying, in numbers greater than before. Thus the chemical war is never won, and all life is caught in its violent crossfire.

Along with the possibility of the extinction of mankind by nuclear war, the central problem of our age has therefore become the contamination of man's total environment with such substances of incredible potential for harm—substances that accumulate in the tissues of plants and animals and even penetrate the germ cells to shatter or alter the very material of heredity upon which the shape of the future depends.

Some would-be architects of our future look toward a time when it will be possible to alter the human germ plasm by design. But we may easily be doing so now by inadvertence, for many chemicals, like radiation, bring about gene mutations. It is ironic to think that man might determine his own future by something so seemingly trivial as the choice of an insect spray.

All this has been risked—for what? Future historians may well be amazed by our distorted sense of proportion. How could intelligent beings seek to control a few unwanted species by a method that contaminated the entire environment and brought the threat of disease and death even to their own kind? Yet this is precisely what we have done. We have done it, moreover, for reasons that collapse the moment we examine them. We are told that the enormous and expanding use of pesticides is necessary to maintain farm production. Yet is our real problem not one of overproduction? Our farms, despite measures to remove acreages from production and to pay farmers not to produce, have yielded such a staggering excess of crops that the American taxpayer in 1962 is paying out more than one billion dollars a year as the total carrying cost of the surplus-food storage program.

And is the situation helped when one branch of the Agriculture Department tries to reduce production while another states, as it did in 1958, "It is believed generally that reduction of crop acreages under provisions of the Soil Bank will stimulate interest in use of chemicals to obtain maximum production on the land retained in crops."

All this is not to say there is no insect problem and no need of control. I am saying, rather, that control must be geared to realities, not to mythical situations, and that the methods employed must be such that they do not destroy us along with the insects.

The problem whose attempted solution has brought such a train of disaster in its wake is an accompaniment of our modern way of life. Long before the age of man, insects inhabited the earth—a group of extraordinarily varied and adaptable beings. Over the course of time since man's advent, a small percentage of the more than half a million species of insects have come into conflict with human welfare in two principal ways: as competitors for the food supply and as carriers of human disease.

Disease-carrying insects become important where human beings are crowded together, especially under conditions where sanitation is poor, as in time of natural disaster or war or in situations of extreme poverty and deprivation. Then control of some sort becomes necessary. It is a sobering fact, however, as we shall presently see, that the method of massive chemical control has had only limited success, and also threatens to worsen the very conditions it is intended to curb.

Under primitive agricultural conditions the farmer had few insect problems. These arose with the intensification of agriculture—the devotion of immense acreages to a single crop. Such a system set the stage for explosive increases in specific insect populations. Single-crop farming does not take advantage of the principles by which nature works; it is agriculture as an engineer might conceive it to be. Nature has introduced great variety into the landscape, but man has displayed a passion for simplifying it. Thus he undoes the built-in checks and balances by which nature holds the species within bounds. One important natural check is a limit on the amount of suitable habitat for each species. Obviously then, an insect that lives on wheat can build up its population to much higher levels on a farm devoted to wheat than on one in which wheat is intermingled with other crops to which the insect is not adapted.

The same thing happens in other situations. A generation or more ago, the towns of large areas of the United States lined their streets with the noble elm tree. Now the beauty they hopefully created is threatened with complete destruction as disease sweeps through the elms, carried by a beetle that would have only limited chance to build up large populations and to spread from tree to tree if the elms were only occasional trees in a richly diversified planting.

Another factor in the modern insect problem is one that must be viewed against a background of geologic and human history: the spreading of thousands of different kinds of organisms from their native homes to invade new territories. This worldwide migration has been studied and graphically described by the British ecologist Charles Elton in his recent book The Ecology of Invasions. During the Cretaceous Period, some hundred million years ago, flooding seas cut many land bridges between continents and living things found themselves confined in what Elton calls "colossal separate nature reserves." There, isolated from others of their kind, they developed many new species. When some of the land masses were joined again, about 15 million years ago, these species began to move out into new territories—a movement that is not only still in progress but is now receiving considerable assistance from man.

The importation of plants is the primary agent in the modern spread of species, for animals have almost invariably gone along with the plants, quarantine being a comparatively recent and not completely effective innovation. The United States Office of Plant Introduction alone has introduced almost 100,000 species and varieties of plants from all over the world. Nearly half of the 180 or so major insect enemies of plants in the United States are accidental imports from abroad, and most of them have come as hitchhikers on plants.

In new territory, out of reach of the restraining hand of the natural enemies that kept down its numbers in its native land, an invading plant or animal is able to become enormously abundant. Thus it is no accident that our most troublesome insects are introduced species.

These invasions, both the naturally occurring and those dependent on human assistance, are likely to continue indefinitely. Quarantine and massive chemical campaigns are only extremely expensive ways of buying time. We are faced, according to Dr. Elton, "with a life-and-death need not just to find new technological means of suppressing this plant or that animal"; instead we need the basic knowledge of animal populations and their relations to their surroundings that will "promote an even balance and damp down the explosive power of outbreaks and new invasions."

Much of the necessary knowledge is now available but we do not use it. We train ecologists in our universities and even employ them in our governmental agencies but we seldom take their advice. We allow the chemical death rain to fall as though there were no alternative, whereas in fact there are many, and our ingenuity could soon discover many more if given opportunity.

Have we fallen into a mesmerized state that makes us accept as inevitable that which is inferior or detrimental, as though having lost the will or the vision to demand that which is good? Such thinking, in the words of the ecologist Paul Shepard, "idealizes life with only its head out of water, inches above the limits of toleration of the corruption of its own environment... Why should we tolerate a diet of weak poisons, a home in insipid surroundings, a circle of acquaintances who are not quite our enemies, the noise of motors with just enough relief to prevent insanity? Who would want to live in a world which is just not quite fatal?"

Yet such a world is pressed upon us. The crusade to create a chemically sterile, insect-free world seems to have engendered a fanatic zeal on the part of many specialists and most of the so-called control agencies. On every hand there is evidence that those engaged in spraying operations exercise a ruthless power. "The regulatory entomologists... function as prosecutor, judge and jury, tax assessor and collector and sheriff to enforce their own orders," said Connecticut entomologist Neely Turner. The most flagrant abuses go unchecked in both state and federal agencies.

It is not my contention that chemical insecticides must never be used. I do contend that we have put poisonous and biologically potent chemicals indiscriminately into the hands of persons largely or wholly ignorant of their potentials for harm. We have subjected enormous numbers of people to contact with these poisons, without their consent and often without their knowledge. If the Bill of Rights contains no guarantee that a citizen shall be secure against lethal poisons distributed either by private individuals or by public officials, it is surely only because our forefathers, despite their considerable wisdom and foresight, could conceive of no such problem.

I contend, furthermore, that we have allowed these chemicals to be used with little or no advance investigation of their effect on soil, water, wildlife, and man himself. Future generations are unlikely to condone our lack of prudent concern for the integrity of the natural world that supports all life.

There is still very limited awareness of the nature of the threat. This is an era of specialists, each of whom sees his own problem and is unaware of or intolerant of the larger frame into which it fits. It is also an era dominated by industry, in which the right to make a dollar at whatever cost is seldom challenged. When the public protests, confronted with some obvious evidence of damaging results of pesticide applications, it is fed little tranquilizing pills of half truth. We urgently need an end to these false assurances, to the sugar coating of unpalatable facts. It is the public that is being asked to assume the risks that the insect controllers calculate. The public must decide whether it wishes to continue on the present road, and it can do so only when in full possession of the facts. In the words of Jean Rostand, "The obligation to endure gives us the right to know."

289

To Really Save the Planet, Stop Going Green

By Mike Tidwell

As President Obama heads to Copenhagen next week for global warming talks, there's one simple step Americans back home can take to help out: Stop "going green." Just stop it. No more compact fluorescent light bulbs. No more green wedding planning. No more organic toothpicks for holiday hors d'oeuvres.

December should be national Green-Free Month. Instead of continuing our faddish and counterproductive emphasis on small, voluntary actions, we should follow the example of Americans during past moral crises and work toward large-scale change. The country's last real moral and social revolution was set in motion by the civil rights movement. And in the 1960s, civil rights activists didn't ask bigoted Southern governors and sheriffs to consider "10 Ways to Go Integrated" at their convenience.

Green gestures we have in abundance in America. Green political action, not so much. And the gestures ("Look honey, another *Vanity Fair* Green Issue!") lure us into believing that broad change is happening when the data shows that it isn't. Despite all our talk about washing clothes in cold water, we aren't making much of a difference.

For eight years, George W. Bush promoted voluntary action as the nation's primary response to global warming—and for eight years, aggregate greenhouse gas emissions remained unchanged. Even today, only 10 percent of our household light bulbs are compact fluorescents. Hybrids account for only 2.5 percent of U.S. auto sales. One can almost imagine the big energy companies secretly applauding each time we distract ourselves from the big picture with a hectoring list of "5 Easy Ways to Green Your Office."

As America joins the rest of the world in finally fighting global warming, we need to bring our battle plan up to scale. If you believe that astronauts have been to the moon and that the world is not flat, then you probably believe the satellite photos showing the Greenland ice sheet in full-on meltdown. Much of Manhattan and the Eastern Shore of Maryland may join the Atlantic Ocean in our lifetimes. Entire Pacific island nations will disappear. Hurricanes will bring untold

---

From *The Washington Post,* 2009.

destruction. Rising sea levels and crippling droughts will decimate crops and cause widespread famine. People will go hungry, and people will die.

Morally, this is sort of a big deal. It would be wrong to let all this happen when we have the power to prevent the worst of it by adopting clean-energy policies.

But how do we do that? Again, look to the history of the civil rights struggle. After many decades of public denial and inaction, the civil rights movement helped Americans to see Southern apartheid in moral terms. From there, the movement succeeded by working toward legal change. Segregation was phased out rapidly only because it was phased out through the law. These statutes didn't erase racial prejudice from every American heart overnight. But through them, our country made staggering progress. Just consider who occupies the White House today.

All who appreciate the enormity of the climate crisis still have a responsibility to make every change possible in their personal lives. I have, from the solar panels on my roof to the Prius in my driveway to my low-carbon-footprint vegetarian diet. But surveys show that very few people are willing to make significant voluntary changes, and those of us who do create the false impression of mass progress as the media hypes our actions.

Instead, most people want carbon reductions to be mandated by laws that will allow us to share both the responsibilities and the benefits of change. Ours is a nation of laws; if we want to alter our practices in a deep and lasting way, this is where we must start. After years of delay and denial and green half-measures, we must legislate a stop to the burning of coal, oil and natural gas.

Of course, all this will require congressional action, and therein lies the source of Obama's Copenhagen headache. To have been in the strongest position to negotiate a binding emissions treaty with other world leaders this month, the president needed a strong carbon-cap bill out of Congress. But the House of Representatives passed only a weak bill riddled with loopholes in June, and the Senate has failed to get even that far.

So what's the problem? There's lots of blame to go around, but the distraction of the "go green" movement has played a significant role. Taking their cues from the popular media and cautious politicians, many Americans have come to believe that they are personally to blame for global warming and that they must fix it, one by one, at home. And so they either do as they're told—a little of this, a little of that—or they feel overwhelmed and do nothing.

We all got into this mess together. And now, with treaty talks underway internationally and Congress stalled at home, we need to act accordingly. Don't spend an hour changing your light bulbs. Don't take a day to caulk your windows. Instead, pick up a phone, open a laptop, or travel to a U.S. Senate office near you and turn the tables: "What are the 10 green statutes you're working on to save the planet, Senator?"

Demand a carbon-cap bill that mandates the number 350. That's the level of carbon pollution scientists say we must limit ourselves to: 350 parts per million of CO_2 in the air. If we can stabilize the atmosphere at that number in coming decades, we should be able to avoid the worst-case scenario and preserve a planet similar to the one human civilization developed on. To get there, America will need to make deep but achievable pollution cuts well before 2020. And to protect against energy price shocks during this transition, Congress must include a system of direct rebates to consumers, paid for by auctioning permit fees to the dirty-energy companies that continue to pollute our sky.

Obama, too, needs to step up his efforts; it's not just Congress and the voters who have been misguided. Those close to the president say he understands the seriousness of global warming. But despite the issue's moral gravity, he's been paralyzed by political caution. He leads from the rear on climate change, not from the front.

Forty-five years ago, President Lyndon B. Johnson faced tremendous opposition on civil rights from a Congress dominated by Southern leaders, yet he spent the political capital necessary to answer a great moral calling. Whenever key bills on housing, voting and employment stalled, he gave individual members of congress the famous "Johnson treatment." He charmed. He pleaded. He threatened. He led, in other words, in person, and from the front.

Does anyone doubt that our charismatic current president has the capacity to turn up the heat? Imagine the back-room power of a full-on "Obama treatment" to defend America's flooding coastlines and burning Western forests. Imagine a two-pronged attack on the fickle, slow-moving Senate: Obama on one side and a tide of tweets and letters from voters like you.

So join me: Put off the attic insulation job till January. Stop searching online for recycled gift wrapping paper and sustainably farmed Christmas trees. Go beyond green fads for a month, and instead help make green history.

293

Part Seven

Sports

Will Genetics Destroy Sports?

A new age of biotechnology promises bigger, faster, better bodies—
and blood, urine, and saliva tests can't stop the cheating

By Michael Behar, Amy Guip

The chime on H. Lee Sweeney's laptop dings again—another e-mail.
He doesn't rush to open it. He knows what it's about. He knows what
they are all about. The molecular geneticist gets dozens every week,
all begging for the same thing—a miracle. Ding. A woman with
carpal tunnel syndrome wants a cure. Ding. A man offers $100,000,
his house, and all his possessions to save his wife from dying of a
degenerative muscle disease. Ding, ding, ding. Jocks, lots of jocks,
plead for quick cures for strained muscles or torn tendons. Weight
lifters press for larger deltoids. Sprinters seek a split second against
the clock. People volunteer to be guinea pigs.

Gene therapy could do for athletes what photo manipulation has done
for this runner. But performance-enhancing drugs would undermine
amateur athletics, which by definition are supposed to show how far
natural skills can be advanced, says Richard Pound, president of the
World Anti-Doping Agency. "I want athletes," he says, "not gladiators."

Sweeney has the same reply for each ding: "I tell them it's illegal and
maybe not safe, but they write back and say they don't care. A high
school coach contacted me and wanted to know if we could make
enough serum to inject his whole football team. He wanted them to
be bigger and stronger and come back from injuries faster, and he
thought those were good things."

The coach was wrong. Gene therapy is risky. In one recent experiment,
a patient died. In another the therapy worked, but 2 of the 10 human
subjects—infants—got leukemia. To some, such setbacks are minor
hiccups, nothing to worry about if you want to cure the incurable
or win big. In the last few years, Sweeney, a professor of physiology
and medicine at the University of Pennsylvania, and a small cadre of
other researchers have learned how to create genes that repair weak,
deteriorating, or damaged muscles, bones, tendons, and cartilage in
a relatively short period of time. They can also significantly increase

From *Discover Magazine,* 2004.

the strength and size of undamaged muscles with little more than an injection. So far, they have worked with only small laboratory rodents—mice and rats. Clinical trials on larger animals, like dogs and cats, are currently not being funded. Human testing is years away, but gene therapy has already become a controversy in professional and amateur sports, where steroids, human growth hormones, and other performance-enhancing drugs have been a problem for years. With the Olympics opening in Athens on August 13, the subject is only going to get hotter. "It's the natural evolution of medicine, and it's inevitable that people will use it for athletics," Sweeney says. "It's not clear that we will be able to stop it."

Sweeney became interested in gene therapy in 1988, shortly after scientists pinpointed the gene responsible for Duchenne muscular dystrophy. He decided to find out if there was a way to counteract the disease genetically. Children with muscular dystrophy lack the gene required to regulate dystrophin, a protein for muscle growth and stability. Without dystrophin, muscle cells atrophy, wither, and die. Sweeney's plan was to introduce the dystrophin gene by hitching it to the DNA of a virus that can transport genes into cells. As it turned out, viruses were too small to carry that gene. So Sweeney began searching for a smaller gene that would fit inside a virus and at least mimic dystrophin. He settled on a gene that produces insulin-like growth factor (IGF-I), a powerful hormone that drives muscle growth and repair. The IGF-I gene fit nicely inside a virus and was more appealing because it could potentially treat several kinds of dystrophies. In a series of experiments beginning in 1998, Sweeney and his team at Penn injected IGF-I genes into mice and rats and watched in wonder as damaged muscle tissue repaired itself.

Today Sweeney spends much of his time scrutinizing the rats and mice he has injected with IGF-I genes. He puts them through a rigorous exercise program, strapping weights to their hind legs and repeatedly prodding them up a three-foot-high ladder. After two months, the rodents can lift 30 percent more weight, and their muscle mass has swollen by a third—double what his control group of mice (those without IGF-I) can achieve with weight training alone. In another experiment Sweeney gives IGF-I to mice but curbs their exercise. They too bulk up, jumping 15 percent in muscle volume and strength.

On a recent visit to Penn, I asked Sweeney to show me the mice. He led me to a cramped lab where a bubbling tank of liquid nitrogen spewed a cold fog across the floor. Rows of transparent plastic shoebox-size containers were stacked on a chrome pushcart, a pungent, musky odor emanating from each box. Inside were several chocolate-colored mice. Sweeney pointed out two groups in neighboring pens and asked, "Which set do you think we've given IGF-I?" I lean in for a closer look. The mice in the left box no doubt have been watching Buns of Steel videos. Each mouse boasts a rock-hard rump and shockingly large and perfectly chiseled gastrocnemius and soleus muscles (which, in humans, make up the calf). In the adjacent cage, two control mice look scrawny by comparison. The results are impressive and make me wonder just how easy it would be for someone to reproduce Sweeney's results in a human. "I wouldn't be surprised if someone was actively setting up to do it right now," he says. "It's not that expensive, especially if you are just going to do it to a small population of athletes."

That is exactly what worries officials at the World Anti-Doping Agency and the U.S. Anti-Doping Agency. The world agency has put gene doping on the International Olympic Committee's 2004 list of prohibited substances, which includes everything from cough syrup to cocaine. The prohibition defines gene doping as "the non-therapeutic use of genes, genetic elements and/or cells that have the capacity to enhance athletic performance." But no one thinks for a minute that gene doping isn't happening. "Sport is supposed to be fun," says former Olympic swimmer Richard Pound, now president of the world agency and chancellor of McGill University in Montreal. "But it is surrounded by people who are conspiring to destroy the athlete and the game."

Gene doping is different from other performance-enhancing techniques. Human growth hormone, for example, occurs naturally in the body and will accelerate cell division in many types of tissue. Taken in high doses, it can provide a head-to-toe muscle boost and can even add a few extra inches of height. Anabolic steroids, which President Bush attacked in his State of the Union address in January, are chemical relatives of testosterone. They are believed to be in wide use in professional sports such as baseball, football, basketball, and hockey—although most players deny it. They are also popular with weight lifters because they foster new muscle growth in the upper body. Synthetic erythropoietin, or EPO, a chemical naturally produced by the kidneys, is a favorite of cyclists, triathletes, marathon runners, and people who engage in long periods of aerobic activity. EPO flushes fatigued muscles with oxygen to stave off exhaustion.

These and other substances can be detected in blood and urine tests because they drift through the circulatory system for hours, days, or months. But gene doping is not as easy to spot. Genetic modifications become an indistinguishable element of DNA in targeted muscles. The only way to prove that someone has experimented with gene doping is to biopsy a suspicious muscle and look for signs of DNA tampering. It's not hard to imagine that most athletes will object to having bits of flesh sliced from the very muscles they've spent years honing. "Athletes aren't going to say, 'Hey, take a muscle biopsy before my 100-meter run,'" quips Johnny Huard, who developed his own set of muscle-building genes as professor of molecular genetics, biochemistry, and bioengineering at the University of Pittsburgh School of Medicine.

Gene doping involves incorporating healthy growth-factor genes with the DNA in a viral carrier. The virus is then injected into the muscle, where it readily infects the target cell and delivers growth-factor genes to the nucleus. After integrating with chromosomes, the genes exit the nucleus via messenger RNA (mRNA). These strands serve as templates for the production of growth-factor proteins, and ribosomes assist in the conversion. The proteins affect surrounding muscle tissues, helping them to strengthen and to heal.

Lack of detection makes gene doping extremely attractive to athletes. But its muscle-building powers are the big draw. Sweeney predicts gene-doped athletes would readily surpass their personal best and could even smash world records. Sprinters and weight lifters would see the most benefits, their peak speeds and maximum strength amplified. "Athletes could push their muscles harder than ever before because their muscles will repair themselves so much faster," he says. "And they won't have to retire when they're 32."

The anti-doping agency officials are convinced that athletes will try gene doping, despite its dangers. "In the current climate there is even more pressure than when I was competing," says Norway's 1994 Olympic speed skating gold medalist Johann Koss, a physician and former member of the world agency's executive board. "People will take shortcuts. The reward at being the best in the world offers huge financial gains." Pound cites a poll of American athletes who said they would take any drug that would help them win, even if they knew the drug would eventually kill them.

"Nobody ever said athletes are the smartest people in the world," Pound says. "This is why there has to be parentalism. This is why I don't let my kids drive the car at age 13, even though they tell me they can do it safely."

Pound has good reason to worry. The newest therapies work on mice and rats with no apparent adversity. Until clinical trials, however, it's impossible to know exactly what the effects will be on humans. Sweeney acknowledges that IGF-I could make precancerous cells grow faster and stronger.

Huard says "we have absolutely no clue" about side effects, but he and others are worried about an immunologic reaction to the virus that serves as a carrier. That is what killed 18-year-old Jesse Gelsinger, who had a rare liver disease and was participating in gene therapy research at the University of Pennsylvania. The Food and Drug Administration immediately terminated all gene therapy trials at Penn, and the incident prompted federal regulators to establish new rules for human gene therapy research. Another concern is that the vector virus might run amok. Scientists believe that's what happened during a 1999 French gene therapy trial on a group of 10 infants with X-SCID, an immune deficiency disorder known as boy-in-the-bubble syndrome. Researchers engineered a virus to carry a replacement gene to repair the immune systems of the sick children. The technique cured nine of the children, and scientists deemed the trial an overwhelming success. Nearly three years later, however, doctors diagnosed two boys in the study with T-cell leukemia. Somehow the virus carrier—not the replacement gene—had managed to touch off the blood disease. In future tests doctors will either modify or change the carrier.

Like all mammals, including humans, mice lose up to a third of their muscle mass and power as they get older. But gene therapy can arrest this loss. The aging mouse on the right increased its body strength by 27 percent after injections of the IGF-I gene, which fosters muscle growth and repair. The smaller mouse on the left is a control.

Those two incidents sparked widespread condemnation that stifled nascent research initiatives. Today some clinical gene therapy trials on humans are under way with tighter safeguards, but most experiments are confined to rodents. Despite the medical and regulatory setbacks, the largest roadblock to commercializing the technology is money. "We've been struggling with getting dog studies [under way] because of the cost," says Sweeney. But once he gets funding, he's ready to go. His team has already made a version of the IGF-I vector to test on dogs with muscular dystrophy. If successful, he'll begin trials on children with muscular dystrophy sometime before the end of the decade. Sweeney keeps a list of telephone numbers from desperate parents who've contacted him.

Meanwhile, amateur athletics is trying to come to grips with gene doping. In March 2002, Theodore Friedmann, who directs the program in human gene therapy at the University of California at San Diego and has advised the National Institutes of Health and congressional leaders on gene-related issues, organized a three-day workshop for the world agency. Scientists, regulatory officials, and athletes gathered in Cold Spring Harbor on Long Island to discuss gene doping. "People intent on subverting the gene therapy will do so," says Friedmann. "The technology is too easy. It's just graduate student science."

That bothers Arne Ljungqvist, the world agency's health, medical, and research committee chairman, who doles out several million dollars in grant money every year to research groups looking at gene doping and its detection. Additionally, Friedmann, who serves on the agency's anti-doping commission, is working to establish testing protocols. "So far the results are sitting in the form of research advances," he says, "but not in the form of real detection methods." One concept is to hunt for what Friedmann calls physiological fingerprints. Introducing foreign genes into muscles, he says, "is going to produce changes in the way muscles secrete things into the blood and, therefore, into the urine." In the same way breast and colon cancer alter the pattern of proteins in the bloodstream, genes linked to IGF-I or EPO will, in theory, leave traces. Surveillance organizations like the U.S. and world agencies "will look for those signatures and patterns that can be tied, with confidence, to the existence of a foreign gene," Friedmann says. Although it may be years yet in development, Friedmann envisions a noninvasive imaging device akin to an X-ray that detects bits and pieces of leftover viruses used to introduce performance-enhancing genes.

Ironically, the misuse of gene doping in sports is more clearly defined than its proper use. When physicians begin curing athletic injuries with gene therapy, the boundaries of healing and enhancement will blur. "There will be a fuzzy line between what is a medically justifiable treatment of injuries and what is performance enhancement," says Friedmann. "There is nothing terribly noble about an athlete destroying a career with an injury if one can medically prevent or correct it. I would be hard-pressed to say that athletes are not eligible for this or that manipulation. It has always been obvious that there are therapeutic-use exceptions. There is no reason to think that therapeutic-use exceptions would be disallowed for genetic tools."

That, of course, opens the door for abuse. In some instances, athletes would require only minuscule improvements to nudge them into the winner's circle. "For Olympic athletes, they don't need to see a drastic change," says Johnny Huard. "Sometimes the gold medalist is only a fraction of a second over the silver." It would be very easy for a team physician to let therapeutic genes continue working for a few hours, days, or weeks after an officially sanctioned treatment ends.

With no viable testing mechanism on the horizon, the possibility remains that at least one of the 10,000-plus Olympic competitors in Athens this summer will have experimented with gene doping. By the 2006 Winter Games in Turin, Italy, it's even more likely. And by the time Beijing 2008 rolls around, it could easily be a sure thing.

The Shame of College Sports

by Taylor Branch

"I'M NOT HIDING," Sonny Vaccaro told a closed hearing at the Willard Hotel in Washington, D.C., in 2001. "We want to put our materials on the bodies of your athletes, and the best way to do that is buy your school. Or buy your coach."

Vaccaro's audience, the members of the Knight Commission on Intercollegiate Athletics, bristled. These were eminent reformers— among them the president of the National Collegiate Athletic Association, two former heads of the U.S. Olympic Committee, and several university presidents and chancellors. The Knight Foundation, a nonprofit that takes an interest in college athletics as part of its concern with civic life, had tasked them with saving college sports from runaway commercialism as embodied by the likes of Vaccaro, who, since signing his pioneering shoe contract with Michael Jordan in 1984, had built sponsorship empires successively at Nike, Adidas, and Reebok. Not all the members could hide their scorn for the "sneaker pimp" of schoolyard hustle, who boasted of writing checks for millions to everybody in higher education.

"Why," asked Bryce Jordan, the president emeritus of Penn State, "should a university be an advertising medium for your industry?"

Vaccaro did not blink. "They shouldn't, sir," he replied. "You sold your souls, and you're going to continue selling them. You can be very moral and righteous in asking me that question, sir," Vaccaro added with irrepressible good cheer, "but there's not one of you in this room that's going to turn down any of our money. You're going to take it. I can only offer it."

William Friday, a former president of North Carolina's university system, still winces at the memory. "Boy, the silence that fell in that room," he recalled recently. "I never will forget it." Friday, who founded and co-chaired two of the three Knight Foundation sports initiatives over the past 20 years, called Vaccaro "the worst of all" the witnesses ever to come before the panel.

From *The Atlantic,* 2011.

But what Vaccaro said in 2001 was true then, and it's true now: corporations offer money so they can profit from the glory of college athletes, and the universities grab it. In 2010, despite the faltering economy, a single college athletic league, the football-crazed Southeastern Conference (SEC), became the first to crack the billion-dollar barrier in athletic receipts. The Big Ten pursued closely at $905 million. That money comes from a combination of ticket sales, concession sales, merchandise, licensing fees, and other sources—but the great bulk of it comes from television contracts.

Educators are in thrall to their athletic departments because of these television riches and because they respect the political furies that can burst from a locker room. "There's fear," Friday told me when I visited him on the University of North Carolina campus in Chapel Hill last fall. As we spoke, two giant construction cranes towered nearby over the university's Kenan Stadium, working on the latest $77 million renovation. (The University of Michigan spent almost four times that much to expand its Big House.) Friday insisted that for the networks, paying huge sums to universities was a bargain. "We do every little thing for them," he said. "We furnish the theater, the actors, the lights, the music, and the audience for a drama measured neatly in time slots. They bring the camera and turn it on." Friday, a weathered idealist at 91, laments the control universities have ceded in pursuit of this money. If television wants to broadcast football from here on a Thursday night, he said, "we shut down the university at 3 o'clock to accommodate the crowds." He longed for a campus identity more centered in an academic mission.

The United States is the only country in the world that hosts big-time sports at institutions of higher learning. This should not, in and of itself, be controversial. College athletics are rooted in the classical ideal of *Mens sana in corpore sano*—a sound mind in a sound body— and who would argue with that? College sports are deeply inscribed in the culture of our nation. Half a million young men and women play competitive intercollegiate sports each year. Millions of spectators flock into football stadiums each Saturday in the fall, and tens of millions more watch on television. The March Madness basketball tournament each spring has become a major national event, with upwards of 80 million watching it on television and talking about the games around the office water cooler. ESPN has spawned ESPNU, a channel dedicated to college sports, and Fox Sports and other cable outlets are developing channels exclusively to cover sports from specific regions or divisions.

With so many people paying for tickets and watching on television, college sports has become Very Big Business. According to various reports, the football teams at Texas, Florida, Georgia, Michigan, and Penn State—to name just a few big-revenue football schools—each earn between $40 million and $80 million in profits a year, even after paying coaches multimillion-dollar salaries. When you combine so much money with such high, almost tribal, stakes—football boosters are famously rabid in their zeal to have their alma mater win—corruption is likely to follow.

Scandal after scandal has rocked college sports. In 2010, the NCAA sanctioned the University of Southern California after determining that star running back Reggie Bush and his family had received "improper benefits" while he played for the Trojans. (Among other charges, Bush and members of his family were alleged to have received free airfare and limousine rides, a car, and a rent-free home in San Diego, from sports agents who wanted Bush as a client.) The Bowl Championship Series stripped USC of its 2004 national title, and Bush returned the Heisman Trophy he had won in 2005. Last fall, as Auburn University football stormed its way to an undefeated season and a national championship, the team's star quarterback, Cam Newton, was dogged by allegations that his father had used a recruiter to solicit up to $180,000 from Mississippi State in exchange for his son's matriculation there after junior college in 2010. Jim Tressel, the highly successful head football coach of the Ohio State Buckeyes, resigned last spring after the NCAA alleged he had feigned ignorance of rules violations by players on his team. At least 28 players over the course of the previous nine seasons, according to Sports Illustrated, had traded autographs, jerseys, and other team memorabilia in exchange for tattoos or cash at a tattoo parlor in Columbus, in violation of NCAA rules. Late this summer, Yahoo Sports reported that the NCAA was investigating allegations that a University of Miami booster had given millions of dollars in illicit cash and services to more than 70 Hurricanes football players over eight years.

The list of scandals goes on. With each revelation, there is much wringing of hands. Critics scold schools for breaking faith with their educational mission, and for failing to enforce the sanctity of "amateurism." Sportswriters denounce the NCAA for both tyranny and impotence in its quest to "clean up" college sports. Observers on all sides express jumbled emotions about youth and innocence, venting against professional mores or greedy amateurs.

For all the outrage, the real scandal is not that students are getting illegally paid or recruited, it's that two of the noble principles on which the NCAA justifies its existence—"amateurism" and the "student-athlete"—are cynical hoaxes, legalistic confections propagated by the universities so they can exploit the skills and fame of young athletes. The tragedy at the heart of college sports is not that some college athletes are getting paid, but that more of them are not.

Don Curtis, a UNC trustee, told me that impoverished football players cannot afford movie tickets or bus fare home. Curtis is a rarity among those in higher education today, in that he dares to violate the signal taboo: "I think we should pay these guys something."

Fans and educators alike recoil from this proposal as though from original sin. Amateurism is the whole point, they say. Paid athletes would destroy the integrity and appeal of college sports. Many former college athletes object that money would have spoiled the sanctity of the bond they enjoyed with their teammates. I, too, once shuddered instinctively at the notion of paid college athletes.

But after an inquiry that took me into locker rooms and ivory towers across the country, I have come to believe that sentiment blinds us to what's before our eyes. Big-time college sports are fully commercialized. Billions of dollars flow through them each year. The NCAA makes money, and enables universities and corporations to make money, from the unpaid labor of young athletes.

Slavery analogies should be used carefully. College athletes are not slaves. Yet to survey the scene—corporations and universities enriching themselves on the backs of uncompensated young men, whose status as "student-athletes" deprives them of the right to due process guaranteed by the Constitution—is to catch an unmistakable whiff of the plantation. Perhaps a more apt metaphor is colonialism: college sports, as overseen by the NCAA, is a system imposed by well-meaning paternalists and rationalized with hoary sentiments about caring for the well-being of the colonized. But it is, nonetheless, unjust. The NCAA, in its zealous defense of bogus principles, sometimes destroys the dreams of innocent young athletes.

The NCAA today is in many ways a classic cartel. Efforts to reform it—most notably by the three Knight Commissions over the course of 20 years—have, while making changes around the edges, been largely fruitless. The time has come for a major overhaul. And whether the powers that be like it or not, big changes are coming. Threats loom on multiple fronts: in Congress, the courts, breakaway athletic conferences, student rebellion, and public disgust. Swaddled in gauzy clichés, the NCAA presides over a vast, teetering glory.

Founding Myths

From the start, amateurism in college sports has been honored more often in principle than in fact; the NCAA was built of a mixture of noble and venal impulses. In the late 19th century, intellectuals believed that the sporting arena simulated an impending age of Darwinian struggle. Because the United States did not hold a global empire like England's, leaders warned of national softness once railroads conquered the last continental frontier. As though heeding this warning, ingenious students turned variations on rugby into a toughening agent. Today a plaque in New Brunswick, New Jersey, commemorates the first college game, on November 6, 1869, when Rutgers beat Princeton 6–4.

Walter Camp graduated from Yale in 1880 so intoxicated by the sport that he devoted his life to it without pay, becoming "the father of American football." He persuaded other schools to reduce the chaos on the field by trimming each side from 15 players to 11, and it was his idea to paint measuring lines on the field. He conceived functional designations for players, coining terms such as quarterback. His game remained violent by design. Crawlers could push the ball forward beneath piles of flying elbows without pause until they cried "Down!" in submission.

In an 1892 game against its archrival, Yale, the Harvard football team was the first to deploy a "flying wedge," based on Napoleon's surprise concentrations of military force. In an editorial calling for the abolition of the play, *The New York Times* described it as "half a ton of bone and muscle coming into collision with a man weighing 160 or 170 pounds," noting that surgeons often had to be called onto the field. Three years later, the continuing mayhem prompted the Harvard faculty to take the first of two votes to abolish football. Charles Eliot, the university's president, brought up other concerns. "Deaths and injuries are not the strongest argument against football," declared Eliot. "That cheating and brutality are profitable is the main evil." Still, Harvard football persisted. In 1903, fervent alumni built Harvard Stadium with zero college funds. The team's first paid head coach,

Bill Reid, started in 1905 at nearly twice the average salary for a full professor.

A newspaper story from that year, illustrated with the Grim Reaper laughing on a goalpost, counted 25 college players killed during football season. A fairy-tale version of the founding of the NCAA holds that President Theodore Roosevelt, upset by a photograph of a bloodied Swarthmore College player, vowed to civilize or destroy football. The real story is that Roosevelt maneuvered shrewdly to preserve the sport—and give a boost to his beloved Harvard. After McClure's magazine published a story on corrupt teams with phantom students, a muckraker exposed Walter Camp's $100,000 slush fund at Yale. In response to mounting outrage, Roosevelt summoned leaders from Harvard, Princeton, and Yale to the White House, where Camp parried mounting criticism and conceded nothing irresponsible in the college football rules he'd established. At Roosevelt's behest, the three schools issued a public statement that college sports must reform to survive, and representatives from 68 colleges founded a new organization that would soon be called the National Collegiate Athletic Association. A Haverford College official was confirmed as secretary but then promptly resigned in favor of Bill Reid, the new Harvard coach, who instituted new rules that benefited Harvard's playing style at the expense of Yale's. At a stroke, Roosevelt saved football and dethroned Yale.

For nearly 50 years, the NCAA, with no real authority and no staff to speak of, enshrined amateur ideals that it was helpless to enforce. (Not until 1939 did it gain the power even to mandate helmets.) In 1929, the Carnegie Foundation made headlines with a report, "American College Athletics," which concluded that the scramble for players had "reached the proportions of nationwide commerce." Of the 112 schools surveyed, 81 flouted NCAA recommendations with inducements to students ranging from open payrolls and disguised booster funds to no-show jobs at movie studios. Fans ignored the uproar, and two-thirds of the colleges mentioned told The New York Times that they planned no changes. In 1939, freshman players at the University of Pittsburgh went on strike because they were getting paid less than their upperclassman teammates.

Embarrassed, the NCAA in 1948 enacted a "Sanity Code," which was supposed to prohibit all concealed and indirect benefits for college athletes; any money for athletes was to be limited to transparent scholarships awarded solely on financial need. Schools that violated this code would be expelled from NCAA membership and thus exiled from competitive sports.

This bold effort flopped. Colleges balked at imposing such a drastic penalty on each other, and the Sanity Code was repealed within a few years. The University of Virginia went so far as to call a press conference to say that if its athletes were ever accused of being paid, they should be forgiven, because their studies at Thomas Jefferson's university were so rigorous.

The Big Bluff

In 1951, the NCAA seized upon a serendipitous set of events to gain control of intercollegiate sports. First, the organization hired a young college dropout named Walter Byers as executive director. A journalist who was not yet 30 years old, he was an appropriately inauspicious choice for the vaguely defined new post. He wore cowboy boots and a toupee. He shunned personal contact, obsessed over details, and proved himself a bureaucratic master of pervasive, anonymous intimidation. Although discharged from the Army during World War II for defective vision, Byers was able to see an opportunity in two contemporaneous scandals. In one, the tiny College of William and Mary, aspiring to challenge football powers Oklahoma and Ohio State, was found to be counterfeiting grades to keep conspicuously pampered players eligible. In the other, a basketball point-shaving conspiracy (in which gamblers paid players to perform poorly) had spread from five New York colleges to the University of Kentucky, the reigning national champion, generating tabloid "perp" photos of gangsters and handcuffed basketball players. The scandals posed a crisis of credibility for collegiate athletics, and nothing in the NCAA's feeble record would have led anyone to expect real reform.

But Byers managed to impanel a small infractions board to set penalties without waiting for a full convention of NCAA schools, which would have been inclined toward forgiveness. Then he lobbied a University of Kentucky dean—A. D. Kirwan, a former football coach and future university president—not to contest the NCAA's dubious legal position (the association had no actual authority to penalize the university), pleading that college sports must do something to restore public support. His gambit succeeded when Kirwan reluctantly accepted a landmark precedent: the Kentucky basketball team would be suspended for the entire 1952–53 season. Its legendary coach, Adolph Rupp, fumed for a year in limbo.

The Kentucky case created an aura of centralized command for an NCAA office that barely existed. At the same time, a colossal misperception gave Byers leverage to mine gold. Amazingly in retrospect, most colleges and marketing experts considered the advent of television a dire threat to sports. Studies found that broadcasts reduced live attendance, and therefore gate receipts, because some customers preferred to watch at home for free. Nobody could yet imagine the revenue bonanza that television represented. With clunky new TV sets proliferating, the 1951 NCAA convention voted 161–7 to outlaw televised games except for a specific few licensed by the NCAA staff.

All but two schools quickly complied. The University of Pennsylvania and Notre Dame protested the order to break contracts for home-game television broadcasts, claiming the right to make their own decisions. Byers objected that such exceptions would invite disaster. The conflict escalated. Byers brandished penalties for games televised without approval. Penn contemplated seeking antitrust protection through the courts. Byers issued a contamination notice, informing any opponent scheduled to play Penn that it would be punished for showing up to compete. In effect, Byers mobilized the college world to isolate the two holdouts in what one sportswriter later called "the Big Bluff."

Byers won. Penn folded in part because its president, the perennial White House contender Harold Stassen, wanted to mend relations with fellow schools in the emerging Ivy League, which would be formalized in 1954. When Notre Dame also surrendered, Byers conducted exclusive negotiations with the new television networks on behalf of every college team. Joe Rauh Jr., a prominent civil-rights attorney, helped him devise a rationing system to permit only 11 broadcasts a year—the fabled Game of the Week. Byers and Rauh selected a few teams for television exposure, excluding the rest. On June 6, 1952, NBC signed a one-year deal to pay the NCAA $1.14 million for a carefully restricted football package. Byers routed all contractual proceeds through his office. He floated the idea that, to fund an NCAA infrastructure, his organization should take a 60 percent cut; he accepted 12 percent that season. (For later contracts, as the size of television revenues grew exponentially, he backed down to 5 percent.) Proceeds from the first NBC contract were enough to rent an NCAA headquarters, in Kansas City.

Only one year into his job, Byers had secured enough power and money to regulate all of college sports. Over the next decade, the

NCAA's power grew along with television revenues. Through the efforts of Byers's deputy and chief lobbyist, Chuck Neinas, the NCAA won an important concession in the Sports Broadcasting Act of 1961, in which Congress made its granting of a precious antitrust exemption to the National Football League contingent upon the blackout of professional football on Saturdays. Deftly, without even mentioning the NCAA, a rider on the bill carved each weekend into protected broadcast markets: Saturday for college, Sunday for the NFL. The NFL got its antitrust exemption. Byers, having negotiated the NCAA's television package up to $3.1 million per football season—which was higher than the NFL's figure in those early years—had made the NCAA into a spectacularly profitable cartel.

"We Eat What We Kill"

The NCAA's control of college sports still rested on a fragile base, however: the consent of the colleges and universities it governed. For a time, the vast sums of television money delivered to these institutions through Byers's deals made them willing to submit. But the big football powers grumbled about the portion of the television revenue diverted to nearly a thousand NCAA member schools that lacked major athletic programs. They chafed against cost-cutting measures— such as restrictions on team size—designed to help smaller schools. "I don't want Hofstra telling Texas how to play football," Darrell Royal, the Longhorns coach, griped. By the 1970s and '80s, as college football games delivered bonanza ratings—and advertising revenue—to the networks, some of the big football schools began to wonder: Why do we need to have our television coverage brokered through the NCAA? Couldn't we get a bigger cut of that TV money by dealing directly with the networks?

Byers faced a rude internal revolt. The NCAA's strongest legions, its big football schools, defected en masse. Calling the NCAA a price-fixing cartel that siphoned every television dollar through its coffers, in 1981 a rogue consortium of 61 major football schools threatened to sign an independent contract with NBC for $180 million over four years.

With a huge chunk of the NCAA's treasury walking out the door, Byers threatened sanctions, as he had against Penn and Notre Dame three decades earlier. But this time the universities of Georgia and Oklahoma responded with an antitrust suit. "It is virtually impossible to overstate the degree of our resentment ... of the NCAA," said William Banowsky, the president of the University of Oklahoma.

In the landmark 1984 *NCAA* v. *Board of Regents of the University of Oklahoma* decision, the U.S. Supreme Court struck down the NCAA's latest football contracts with television—and any future ones—as an illegal restraint of trade that harmed colleges and viewers. Overnight, the NCAA's control of the television market for football vanished. Upholding Banowsky's challenge to the NCAA's authority, the Regents decision freed the football schools to sell any and all games the markets would bear. Coaches and administrators no longer had to share the revenue generated by their athletes with smaller schools outside the football consortium. "We eat what we kill," one official at the University of Texas bragged.

A few years earlier, this blow might have financially crippled the NCAA—but a rising tide of money from basketball concealed the structural damage of the Regents decision. During the 1980s, income from the March Madness college basketball tournament, paid directly by the television networks to the NCAA, grew tenfold. The windfall covered—and then far exceeded—what the organization had lost from football.

Still, Byers never forgave his former deputy Chuck Neinas for leading the rebel consortium. He knew that Neinas had seen from the inside how tenuous the NCAA's control really was, and how diligently Byers had worked to prop up its Oz-like façade. During Byers's tenure, the rule book for Division I athletes grew to 427 pages of scholastic detail. His NCAA personnel manual banned conversations around water coolers, and coffee cups on desks, while specifying exactly when drapes must be drawn at the NCAA's 27,000-square-foot headquarters near Kansas City (built in 1973 from the proceeds of a 1 percent surtax on football contracts). It was as though, having lost control where it mattered, Byers pedantically exerted more control where it didn't.

After retiring in 1987, Byers let slip his suppressed fury that the ingrate football conferences, having robbed the NCAA of television revenue, still expected it to enforce amateurism rules and police every leak of funds to college players. A lethal greed was "gnawing at the innards of college athletics," he wrote in his memoir. When Byers renounced the NCAA's pretense of amateurism, his former colleagues would stare blankly, as though he had gone senile or, as he wrote, "desecrated my sacred vows." But Byers was better positioned than anyone else to argue that college football's claim to amateurism was unfounded. Years later, as we will see, lawyers would seize upon his words to do battle with the NCAA.

Meanwhile, reformers fretted that commercialism was hurting college sports, and that higher education's historical balance between academics and athletics had been distorted by all the money sloshing around. News stories revealed that schools went to extraordinary measures to keep academically incompetent athletes eligible for competition, and would vie for the most-sought-after high-school players by proffering under-the-table payments. In 1991, the first Knight Commission report, "Keeping Faith With the Student Athlete," was published; the commission's "bedrock conviction" was that university presidents must seize control of the NCAA from athletic directors in order to restore the preeminence of academic values over athletic or commercial ones. In response, college presidents did take over the NCAA's governance. But by 2001, when the second Knight Commission report ("A Call to Action: Reconnecting College Sports and Higher Education") was issued, a new generation of reformers was admitting that problems of corruption and commercialism had "grown rather than diminished" since the first report. Meanwhile the NCAA itself, revenues rising, had moved into a $50 million, 116,000-square-foot headquarters in Indianapolis. By 2010, as the size of NCAA headquarters increased yet again with a 130,000-square-foot expansion, a third Knight Commission was groping blindly for a hold on independent college-athletic conferences that were behaving more like sovereign pro leagues than confederations of universities. And still more money continued to flow into NCAA coffers. With the basketball tournament's 2011 television deal, annual March Madness broadcast revenues had skyrocketed 50-fold in less than 30 years.

The Myth of the "Student-Athlete"

Today, much of the NCAA's moral authority—indeed much of the justification for its existence—is vested in its claim to protect what it calls the "student-athlete." The term is meant to conjure the nobility of amateurism, and the precedence of scholarship over athletic endeavor. But the origins of the "student-athlete" lie not in a disinterested ideal but in a sophistic formulation designed, as the sports economist Andrew Zimbalist has written, to help the NCAA in its "fight against workmen's compensation insurance claims for injured football players."

"We crafted the term student-athlete," Walter Byers himself wrote, "and soon it was embedded in all NCAA rules and interpretations." The term came into play in the 1950s, when the widow of Ray Dennison, who had died from a head injury received while playing football in Colorado for the Fort Lewis A&M Aggies, filed for workmen's-compensation death benefits. Did his football scholarship make the fatal collision a "work-related" accident? Was he a school employee, like his peers who worked part-time as teaching assistants and bookstore cashiers? Or was he a fluke victim of extracurricular pursuits? Given the hundreds of incapacitating injuries to college athletes each year, the answers to these questions had enormous consequences. The Colorado Supreme Court ultimately agreed with the school's contention that he was not eligible for benefits, since the college was "not in the football business."

The term *student-athlete* was deliberately ambiguous. College players were not students at play (which might understate their athletic obligations), nor were they just athletes in college (which might imply they were professionals). That they were high-performance athletes meant they could be forgiven for not meeting the academic standards of their peers; that they were students meant they did not have to be compensated, ever, for anything more than the cost of their studies. *Student-athlete* became the NCAA's signature term, repeated constantly in and out of courtrooms.

Using the "student-athlete" defense, colleges have compiled a string of victories in liability cases. On the afternoon of October 26, 1974, the Texas Christian University Horned Frogs were playing the Alabama Crimson Tide in Birmingham, Alabama. Kent Waldrep, a TCU running back, carried the ball on a "Red Right 28" sweep toward the Crimson Tide's sideline, where he was met by a swarm of tacklers. When Waldrep regained consciousness, Bear Bryant, the storied Crimson Tide coach, was standing over his hospital bed. "It was like talking to God, if you're a young football player," Waldrep recalled.

Waldrep was paralyzed: he had lost all movement and feeling below his neck. After nine months of paying his medical bills, Texas Christian refused to pay any more, so the Waldrep family coped for years on dwindling charity.

Through the 1990s, from his wheelchair, Waldrep pressed a lawsuit for workers' compensation. (He also, through heroic rehabilitation efforts, recovered feeling in his arms, and eventually learned to drive a specially rigged van. "I can brush my teeth," he told me last year, "but I still need help to bathe and dress.") His attorneys haggled with TCU and the state worker-compensation fund over what constituted employment. Clearly, TCU had provided football players with equipment for the job, as a typical employer would—but did the university pay wages, withhold income taxes on his financial aid, or control work conditions and performance? The appeals court finally rejected Waldrep's claim in June of 2000, ruling that he was not an employee because he had not paid taxes on financial aid that he could have kept even if he quit football. (Waldrep told me school officials "said they recruited me as a student, not an athlete," which he says was absurd.)

The long saga vindicated the power of the NCAA's "student-athlete" formulation as a shield, and the organization continues to invoke it as both a legalistic defense and a noble ideal. Indeed, such is the term's rhetorical power that it is increasingly used as a sort of reflexive mantra against charges of rabid hypocrisy.

Last Thanksgiving weekend, with both the FBI and the NCAA investigating whether Cam Newton had been lured onto his team with illegal payments, Newton's Auburn Tigers and the Alabama Crimson Tide came together for their annual game, known as the Iron Bowl, before 101,821 fans at Bryant-Denny Stadium. This game is always a highlight of the football season because of the historic rivalry between the two schools, and the 2010 edition had enormous significance, pitting the defending national champion Crimson Tide against the undefeated Tigers, who were aiming for their first championship since 1957. I expected excited fans; what I encountered was the throbbing heart of college sports. As I drove before daybreak toward the stadium, a sleepless caller babbled over WJOX, the local fan radio station, that he "couldn't stop thinking about the coin toss." In the parking lot, ticketless fans were puzzled that anyone need ask why they had tailgated for days just to watch their satellite-fed flat screens within earshot of the roar. All that morning, pilgrims packed the Bear Bryant museum, where displays elaborated the misery of Alabama's 4–24 run before the glorious Bryant era dawned in 1958.

Finally, as Auburn took the field for warm-ups, one of Alabama's public-address-system operators played "Take the Money and Run" (an act for which he would be fired). A sea of signs reading $CAM taunted Newton. The game, perhaps the most exciting of the season, was unbearably tense, with Auburn coming from way behind to win 28–27, all but assuring that it would go on to play for the national championship. Days later, Auburn suspended Newton after the NCAA found that a rules violation had occurred: his father was alleged to have marketed his son in a pay-for-play scheme; a day after that, the NCAA reinstated Newton's eligibility because investigators had not found evidence that Newton or Auburn officials had known of his father's actions. This left Newton conveniently eligible for the Southeastern Conference championship game and for the postseason BCS championship bowl. For the NCAA, prudence meant honoring public demand.

"Our championships," NCAA President Mark Emmert has declared, "are one of the primary tools we have to enhance the student-athlete experience."

"Whoremasters"

NCAA v. Regents left the NCAA devoid of television football revenue and almost wholly dependent on March Madness basketball. It is rich but insecure. Last year, CBS Sports and Turner Broadcasting paid $771 million to the NCAA for television rights to the 2011 men's basketball tournament alone. That's three-quarters of a billion dollars built on the backs of amateurs—on unpaid labor. The whole edifice depends on the players' willingness to perform what is effectively volunteer work. The athletes, and the league officials, are acutely aware of this extraordinary arrangement. William Friday, the former North Carolina president, recalls being yanked from one Knight Commission meeting and sworn to secrecy about what might happen if a certain team made the NCAA championship basketball game. "They were going to dress and go out on the floor," Friday told me, "but refuse to play," in a wildcat student strike. Skeptics doubted such a diabolical plot. These were college kids—unlikely to second-guess their coaches, let alone forfeit the dream of a championship. Still, it was unnerving to contemplate what hung on the consent of a few young volunteers: several hundred million dollars in television revenue, countless livelihoods, the NCAA budget, and subsidies for sports at more than 1,000 schools. Friday's informants exhaled when the suspect team lost before the finals.

Cognizant of its precarious financial base, the NCAA has in recent years begun to pursue new sources of revenue. Taking its cue from member schools such as Ohio State (which in 2009 bundled all its promotional rights—souvenirs, stadium ads, shoe deals—and outsourced them to the international sports marketer IMG College for a guaranteed $11 million a year), the NCAA began to exploit its vault of college sports on film. For $29.99 apiece, NCAA On Demand offers DVDs of more than 200 memorable contests in men's ice hockey alone. Video-game technology also allows nostalgic fans to relive and even participate in classic moments of NCAA Basketball. NCAA Football, licensed by the NCAA through IMG College to Electronic Arts, one of the world's largest video-game manufacturers, reportedly sold 2.5 million copies in 2008. Brit Kirwan, the chancellor of the Maryland university system and a former president at Ohio State, says there were "terrible fights" between the third Knight Commission and the NCAA over the ethics of generating this revenue.

All of this money ultimately derives from the college athletes whose likenesses are shown in the films or video games. But none of the profits go to them. Last year, Electronic Arts paid more than $35 million in royalties to the NFL players union for the underlying value of names and images in its pro football series—but neither the NCAA nor its affiliated companies paid former college players a nickel. Naturally, as they have become more of a profit center for the NCAA, some of the vaunted "student-athletes" have begun to clamor that they deserve a share of those profits. You "see everybody getting richer and richer," Desmond Howard, who won the 1991 Heisman Trophy while playing for the Michigan Wolverines, told USA Today recently. "And you walk around and you can't put gas in your car? You can't even fly home to see your parents?"

Some athletes have gone beyond talk. A series of lawsuits quietly making their way through the courts cast a harsh light on the absurdity of the system—and threaten to dislodge the foundations on which the NCAA rests. On July 21, 2009, lawyers for Ed O'Bannon filed a class-action antitrust suit against the NCAA at the U.S. District Court in San Francisco. "Once you leave your university," says O'Bannon, who won the John Wooden Award for player of the year in 1995 on UCLA's national-championship basketball team, "one would think your likeness belongs to you." The NCAA and UCLA continue to collect money from the sales of videos of him playing. But by NCAA rules, O'Bannon, who today works at a Toyota dealership near Las Vegas, alleges he is still not allowed to share the revenue the NCAA generates from his own image as a college athlete. His suit quickly gathered co-plaintiffs from basketball and football, ex-players featured in NCAA videos and other products. "The NCAA does not license student-athlete likenesses," NCAA spokesperson Erik Christianson told The New York Times in response to the suit, "or prevent former student-athletes from attempting to do so. Likewise, to claim the NCAA profits off student-athlete likenesses is also pure fiction."

The legal contention centers on Part IV of the NCAA's "Student-Athlete Statement" for Division I, which requires every athlete to authorize use of "your name or picture ... to promote NCAA championships or other NCAA events, activities or programs." Does this clause mean that athletes clearly renounce personal interest forever? If so, does it actually undermine the NCAA by implicitly recognizing that athletes have a property right in their own performance? Jon King, a lawyer for the plaintiffs, expects the NCAA's core mission of amateurism to be its "last defense standing."

In theory, the NCAA's passion to protect the noble amateurism of college athletes should prompt it to focus on head coaches in the high-revenue sports—basketball and football—since holding the top official accountable should most efficiently discourage corruption. The problem is that the coaches' growing power has rendered them, unlike their players, ever more immune to oversight. According to research by Charles Clotfelter, an economist at Duke, the average compensation for head football coaches at public universities, now more than $2 million, has grown 750 percent (adjusted for inflation) since the Regents decision in 1984; that's more than 20 times the cumulative 32 percent raise for college professors. For top basketball coaches, annual contracts now exceed $4 million, augmented by assorted bonuses, endorsements, country-club memberships, the occasional private plane, and in some cases a negotiated percentage of ticket receipts. (Oregon's ticket concessions netted former football coach Mike Bellotti an additional $631,000 in 2005.)

The NCAA rarely tangles with such people, who are apt to fight back and win. When Rick Neuheisel, the head football coach of the Washington Huskies, was punished for petty gambling (in a March Madness pool, as it happened), he sued the NCAA and the university for wrongful termination, collected $4.5 million, and later moved on to UCLA. When the NCAA tried to cap assistant coaches' entering salary at a mere $16,000, nearly 2,000 of them brought an antitrust suit, Law v. NCAA, and in 1999 settled for $54.5 million. Since then, salaries for assistant coaches have commonly exceeded $200,000, with the top assistants in the SEC averaging $700,000. In 2009, Monte Kiffin, then at the University of Tennessee, became the first assistant coach to reach $1 million, plus benefits.

The late Myles Brand, who led the NCAA from 2003 to 2009, defended the economics of college sports by claiming that they were simply the result of a smoothly functioning free market. He and his colleagues deflected criticism about the money saturating big-time college sports by focusing attention on scapegoats; in 2010, outrage targeted sports agents. Last year *Sports Illustrated* published "Confessions of an Agent," a firsthand account of dealing with high-strung future pros whom the agent and his peers courted with flattery, cash, and tawdry favors. Nick Saban, Alabama's head football coach, mobilized his peers to denounce agents as a public scourge. "I hate to say this," he said, "but how are they any better than a pimp? I have no respect for people who do that to young people. None."

Saban's raw condescension contrasts sharply with the lonely penitence from Dale Brown, the retired longtime basketball coach at LSU. "Look at the money we make off predominantly poor black kids," Brown once reflected. "We're the whoremasters."

"Picayune Rules"

NCAA officials have tried to assert their dominion—and distract attention from the larger issues—by chasing frantically after petty violations. Tom McMillen, a former member of the Knight Commission who was an All-American basketball player at the University of Maryland, likens these officials to traffic cops in a speed trap, who could flag down almost any passing motorist for prosecution in kangaroo court under a "maze of picayune rules." The publicized cases have become convoluted soap operas. At the start of the 2010 football season, A. J. Green, a wide receiver at Georgia, confessed that he'd sold his own jersey from the Independence Bowl the year before, to raise cash for a spring-break vacation. The NCAA sentenced Green to a four-game suspension for violating his amateur status with the illicit profit generated by selling the shirt off his own back. While he served the suspension, the Georgia Bulldogs store continued legally selling replicas of Green's No. 8 jersey for $39.95 and up.

A few months later, the NCAA investigated rumors that Ohio State football players had benefited from "hook-ups on tatts"—that is, that they'd gotten free or underpriced tattoos at an Ohio tattoo parlor in exchange for autographs and memorabilia—a violation of the NCAA's rule against discounts linked to athletic personae. The NCAA Committee on Infractions imposed five-game suspensions on Terrelle Pryor, Ohio State's tattooed quarterback, and four other players (some of whom had been found to have sold their Big Ten championship rings and other gear), but did permit them to finish the season and play in the Sugar Bowl. (This summer, in an attempt to satisfy NCAA investigators, Ohio State voluntarily vacated its football wins from last season, as well as its Sugar Bowl victory.) A different NCAA committee promulgated a rule banning symbols and messages in players' eyeblack—reportedly aimed at Pryor's controversial gesture of support for the pro quarterback Michael Vick, and at Bible verses inscribed in the eyeblack of the former Florida quarterback Tim Tebow.

320

The moral logic is hard to fathom: the NCAA bans personal messages on the bodies of the players, and penalizes players for trading their celebrity status for discounted tattoos—but it codifies precisely how and where commercial insignia from multinational corporations can be displayed on college players, for the financial benefit of the colleges. Last season, while the NCAA investigated him and his father for the recruiting fees they'd allegedly sought, Cam Newton compliantly wore at least 15 corporate logos—one on his jersey, four on his helmet visor, one on each wristband, one on his pants, six on his shoes, and one on the headband he wears under his helmet—as part of Auburn's $10.6 million deal with Under Armour.

"Restitution"

Obscure NCAA rules have bedeviled Scott Boras, the preeminent sports agent for Major League Baseball stars, in cases that may ultimately prove more threatening to the NCAA than Ed O'Bannon's antitrust suit. In 2008, Andrew Oliver, a sophomore pitcher for the Oklahoma State Cowboys, had been listed as the 12th-best professional prospect among sophomore players nationally. He decided to dismiss the two attorneys who had represented him out of high school, Robert and Tim Baratta, and retain Boras instead. Infuriated, the Barattas sent a spiteful letter to the NCAA. Oliver didn't learn about this until the night before he was scheduled to pitch in the regional final for a place in the College World Series, when an NCAA investigator showed up to question him in the presence of lawyers for Oklahoma State. The investigator also questioned his father, Dave, a truck driver.

Had Tim Baratta been present in their home when the Minnesota Twins offered $390,000 for Oliver to sign out of high school? A yes would mean trouble. While the NCAA did not forbid all professional advice—indeed, Baseball America used to publish the names of agents representing draft-likely underclassmen—NCAA Bylaw 12.3.2.1 prohibited actual negotiation with any professional team by an adviser, on pain of disqualification for the college athlete. The questioning lasted past midnight.

Just hours before the game was to start the next day, Oklahoma State officials summoned Oliver to tell him he would not be pitching. Only later did he learn that the university feared that by letting him play while the NCAA adjudicated his case, the university would open not only the baseball team but all other Oklahoma State teams to broad punishment under the NCAA's "restitution rule" (Bylaw 19.7), under which the NCAA threatens schools with sanctions if they obey any temporary court order benefiting a college athlete, should that order eventually be modified or removed. The baseball coach did not even let his ace tell his teammates the sad news in person. "He said, 'It's probably not a good idea for you to be at the game,'" Oliver recalls.

The Olivers went home to Ohio to find a lawyer. Rick Johnson, a solo practitioner specializing in legal ethics, was aghast that the Baratta brothers had turned in their own client to the NCAA, divulging attorney-client details likely to invite wrath upon Oliver. But for the next 15 months, Johnson directed his litigation against the two NCAA bylaws at issue. Judge Tygh M. Tone, of Erie County, came to share his outrage. On February 12, 2009, Tone struck down the ban on lawyers negotiating for student-athletes as a capricious, exploitative attempt by a private association to "dictate to an attorney where, what, how, or when he should represent his client," violating accepted legal practice in every state. He also struck down the NCAA's restitution rule as an intimidation that attempted to supersede the judicial system. Finally, Judge Tone ordered the NCAA to reinstate Oliver's eligibility at Oklahoma State for his junior season, which started several days later.

The NCAA sought to disqualify Oliver again, with several appellate motions to stay "an unprecedented Order purporting to void a fundamental Bylaw." Oliver did get to pitch that season, but he dropped into the second round of the June 2009 draft, signing for considerably less than if he'd been picked earlier. Now 23, Oliver says sadly that the whole experience "made me grow up a little quicker." His lawyer claimed victory. "Andy Oliver is the first college athlete ever to win against the NCAA in court," said Rick Johnson.

Yet the victory was only temporary. Wounded, the NCAA fought back with a vengeance. Its battery of lawyers prepared for a damages trial, ultimately overwhelming Oliver's side eight months later with an offer to resolve the dispute for $750,000. When Oliver and Johnson accepted, to extricate themselves ahead of burgeoning legal costs, Judge Tone was compelled to vacate his orders as part of the final settlement. This freed NCAA officials to reassert the two bylaws that Judge Tone had so forcefully overturned, and they moved swiftly to ramp up rather than curtail enforcement. First, the NCAA's Eligibility Center devised a survey for every drafted undergraduate athlete who sought to stay in college another year. The survey asked whether an agent had conducted negotiations. It also requested a signed release waiving privacy rights and authorizing professional teams to disclose details of any interaction to the NCAA Eligibility Center. Second, NCAA enforcement officials went after another Scott Boras client.

The Toronto Blue Jays had made the left-handed pitcher James Paxton, of the University of Kentucky, the 37th pick in the 2009 draft. Paxton decided to reject a reported $1 million offer and return to school for his senior year, pursuing a dream to pitch for his team in the College World Series. But then he ran into the new NCAA survey. Had Boras negotiated with the Blue Jays? Boras has denied that he did, but it would have made sense that he had—that was his job, to test the market for his client. But saying so would get Paxton banished under the same NCAA bylaw that had derailed Andrew Oliver's career. Since Paxton was planning to go back to school and not accept their draft offer, the Blue Jays no longer had any incentive to protect him—indeed, they had every incentive to turn him in. The Blue Jays' president, by telling reporters that Boras had negotiated on Paxton's behalf, demonstrated to future recruits and other teams that they could use the NCAA's rules to punish college players who wasted their draft picks by returning to college. The NCAA's enforcement staff raised the pressure by requesting to interview Paxton.

Though Paxton had no legal obligation to talk to an investigator, NCAA Bylaw 10.1(j) specified that anything short of complete cooperation could be interpreted as unethical conduct, affecting his amateur status. Under its restitution rule, the NCAA had leverage to compel the University of Kentucky to ensure obedience.

As the 2010 season approached, Gary Henderson, the Kentucky coach, sorely wanted Paxton, one of Baseball America's top-ranked players, to return. Rick Johnson, Andrew Oliver's lawyer, filed for a declaratory judgment on Paxton's behalf, arguing that the state constitution—plus the university's code of student conduct—barred arbitrary discipline at the request of a third party. Kentucky courts deferred to the university, however, and Paxton was suspended from the team. "Due to the possibility of future penalties, including forfeiture of games," the university stated, it "could not put the other 32 players of the team and the entire UK 22-sport intercollegiate athletics department at risk by having James compete." The NCAA appraised the result with satisfaction. "When negotiations occur on behalf of student-athletes," Erik Christianson, the NCAA spokesperson, told The New York Times in reference to the Oliver case, "those negotiations indicate that the student-athlete intends to become a professional athlete and no longer remain an amateur."

Paxton was stranded. Not only could he not play for Kentucky, but his draft rights with the Blue Jays had lapsed for the year, meaning he could not play for any minor-league affiliate of Major League Baseball. Boras wrangled a holdover job for him in Texas with the independent Grand Prairie AirHogs, pitching against the Pensacola Pelicans and Wichita Wingnuts. Once projected to be a first-round draft pick, Paxton saw his stock plummet into the fourth round. He remained unsigned until late in spring training, when he signed with the Seattle Mariners and reported to their minor-league camp in Peoria, Arizona.

"You Might As Well Shoot Them in the Head"

"When you dream about playing in college," Joseph Agnew told me not long ago, "you don't ever think about being in a lawsuit." Agnew, a student at Rice University in Houston, had been cut from the football team and had his scholarship revoked by Rice before his senior year, meaning that he faced at least $35,000 in tuition and other bills if he wanted to complete his degree in sociology. Bereft of his scholarship, he was flailing about for help when he discovered the National College Players Association, which claims 7,000 active members and seeks modest reforms such as safety guidelines and better death benefits for college athletes. Agnew was struck by the NCPA scholarship data on players from top Division I basketball teams, which showed that 22 percent were not renewed from 2008 to 2009—the same fate he had suffered.

In October 2010, Agnew filed a class-action antitrust suit over the cancellation of his scholarship and to remove the cap on the total number of scholarships that can be awarded by NCAA schools. In his suit, Agnew did not claim the right to free tuition. He merely asked the federal court to strike down an NCAA rule, dating to 1973, that prohibited colleges and universities from offering any athletic scholarship longer than a one-year commitment, to be renewed or not, unilaterally, by the school—which in practice means that coaches get to decide each year whose scholarships to renew or cancel. (After the coach who had recruited Agnew had moved on to Tulsa, the new Rice coach switched Agnew's scholarship to a recruit of his own.) Agnew argued that without the one-year rule, he would have been free to bargain with all eight colleges that had recruited him, and each college could have decided how long to guarantee his scholarship.

Agnew's suit rested on a claim of an NCAA antitrust violation combined with a laudable academic goal—making it possible for students to finish their educations. Around the same time, lawyers from President Obama's Justice Department initiated a series of meetings with NCAA officials and universities in which they asked what possible educational rationale there was for allowing the NCAA—an organization that did not itself pay for scholarships—to impose a blanket restriction on the length of scholarships offered by colleges. Tidbits leaked into the press. In response, the NCAA contended that an athletic scholarship was a "merit award" that should be reviewed annually, presumably because the degree of "merit" could change. Justice Department lawyers reportedly suggested that a free market in scholarships would expand learning opportunities in accord with the stated rationale for the NCAA's tax-exempt status—that it promotes education through athletics. The one-year rule effectively allows colleges to cut underperforming "student-athletes," just as pro sports teams cut their players. "Plenty of them don't stay in school," said one of Agnew's lawyers, Stuart Paynter. "They're just gone. You might as well shoot them in the head."

Agnew's lawsuit has made him a pariah to former friends in the athletic department at Rice, where everyone identified so thoroughly with the NCAA that they seemed to feel he was attacking them personally. But if the premise of Agnew's case is upheld by the courts, it will make a sham of the NCAA's claim that its highest priority is protecting education.

"They Want to Crush These Kids"

Academic performance has always been difficult for the NCAA to address. Any detailed regulation would intrude upon the free choice of widely varying schools, and any academic standard broad enough to fit both MIT and Ole Miss would have little force. From time to time, a scandal will expose extreme lapses. In 1989, Dexter Manley, by then the famous "Secretary of Defense" for the NFL's Washington Redskins, teared up before the U.S. Senate Subcommittee on Education, Arts, and Humanities, when admitting that he had been functionally illiterate in college.

Within big-time college athletic departments, the financial pressure to disregard obvious academic shortcomings and shortcuts is just too strong. In the 1980s, Jan Kemp, an English instructor at the University of Georgia, publicly alleged that university officials had demoted and then fired her because she refused to inflate grades in her remedial English courses. Documents showed that administrators replaced the grades she'd given athletes with higher ones, providing fake passing grades on one notable occasion to nine Bulldog football players who otherwise would have been ineligible to compete in the 1982 Sugar Bowl. (Georgia lost anyway, 24–20, to a University of Pittsburgh team led by the future Hall of Fame quarterback Dan Marino.) When Kemp filed a lawsuit against the university, she was publicly vilified as a troublemaker, but she persisted bravely in her testimony. Once, Kemp said, a supervisor demanding that she fix a grade had bellowed, "Who do you think is more important to this university, you or Dominique Wilkins?" (Wilkins was a star on the basketball team.) Traumatized, Kemp twice attempted suicide.

In trying to defend themselves, Georgia officials portrayed Kemp as naive about sports. "We have to compete on a level playing field," said Fred Davison, the university president. During the Kemp civil trial, in 1986, Hale Almand, Georgia's defense lawyer, explained the university's patronizing aspirations for its typical less-than-scholarly athlete. "We may not make a university student out of him," Almand told the court, "but if we can teach him to read and write, maybe he can work at the post office rather than as a garbage man when he gets through with his athletic career." This argument backfired with the jurors: finding in favor of Kemp, they rejected her polite request for $100,000, and awarded her $2.6 million in damages instead. (This was later reduced to $1.08 million.) Jan Kemp embodied what is ostensibly the NCAA's reason for being—to enforce standards fairly and put studies above sports—but no one from the organization ever spoke up on her behalf.

The NCAA body charged with identifying violations of any of the Division I league rules, the Committee on Infractions, operates in the shadows. Josephine Potuto, a professor of law at the University of Nebraska and a longtime committee member who was then serving as its vice chair, told Congress in 2004 that one reason her group worked in secret was that it hoped to avoid a "media circus." The committee preferred to deliberate in private, she said, guiding member schools to punish themselves. "The enforcement process is cooperative, not adversarial," Potuto testified. The committee consisted of an elite coterie of judges, athletic directors, and authors of legal treatises. "The committee also is savvy about intercollegiate athletics," she added. "They cannot be conned."

In 2009, a series of unlikely circumstances peeled back the veil of secrecy to reveal NCAA procedures so contorted that even victims marveled at their comical wonder. The saga began in March of 2007, shortly after the Florida State Seminoles basketball team was knocked out of the NIT basketball tournament, which each spring invites the best teams not selected for the March Madness tournament. At an athletic-department study hall, Al Thornton, a star forward for the team, completed a sports-psychology quiz but then abandoned it without posting his written answers electronically by computer. Brenda Monk, an academic tutor for the Seminoles, says she noticed the error and asked a teammate to finish entering Thornton's answers onscreen and hit "submit," as required for credit. The teammate complied, steaming silently, and then complained at the athletic office about getting stuck with clean-up chores for the superstar Thornton (who was soon to be selected by the Los Angeles Clippers in the first round of the NBA draft). Monk promptly resigned when questioned by FSU officials, saying her fatigue at the time could not excuse her asking the teammate to submit the answers to another student's completed test.

Monk's act of guileless responsibility set off a chain reaction. First, FSU had to give the NCAA preliminary notice of a confessed academic fraud. Second, because this would be its seventh major infraction case since 1968, FSU mounted a vigorous self-investigation to demonstrate compliance with NCAA academic rules. Third, interviews with 129 Seminoles athletes unleashed a nightmare of matter-of-fact replies about absentee professors who allowed group consultations and unlimited retakes of open-computer assignments and tests. Fourth, FSU suspended 61 of its athletes in 10 sports. Fifth, the infractions committee applied the byzantine NCAA bylaws to FSU's violations. Sixth, one of the penalties announced in March of 2009 caused a howl of protest across the sports universe.

Twenty-seven news organizations filed a lawsuit in hopes of finding out how and why the NCAA proposed to invalidate 14 prior victories in FSU football. Such a penalty, if upheld, would doom coach Bobby Bowden's chance of overtaking Joe Paterno of Penn State for the most football wins in Division I history. This was sacrosanct territory. Sports reporters followed the litigation for six months, reporting that 25 of the 61 suspended FSU athletes were football players, some of whom were ruled ineligible retroactively from the time they had heard or yelled out answers to online test questions in, of all things, a music-appreciation course.

When reporters sought access to the transcript of the infractions committee's hearing in Indianapolis, NCAA lawyers said the 695-page document was private. (The NCAA claimed it was entitled to keep all such records secret because of a landmark Supreme Court ruling that it had won in 1988, in *NCAA v. Tarkanian,* which exempted the organization from any due-process obligations because it was not a government organization.) Media outlets pressed the judge to let Florida State share its own copy of the hearing transcript, whereupon NCAA lawyers objected that the school had never actually "possessed" the document; it had only seen the transcript via a defendant's guest access to the carefully restricted NCAA Web site. This claim, in turn, prompted intercession on the side of the media by Florida's attorney general, arguing that letting the NCAA use a technical loophole like this would undermine the state's sunshine law mandating open public records. After tumultuous appeals, the Florida courts agreed and ordered the NCAA transcript released in October of 2009.

News interest quickly evaporated when the sports media found nothing in the record about Coach Bowden or the canceled football victories. But the transcript revealed plenty about the NCAA. On page 37, T. K. Wetherell, the bewildered Florida State president, lamented that his university had hurt itself by cooperating with the investigation. "We self-reported this case," he said during the hearing, and he later complained that the most ingenuous athletes—those who asked "What's the big deal, this happens all the time?"—received the harshest suspensions, while those who clammed up on the advice of lawyers went free. The music-appreciation professor was apparently never questioned. Brenda Monk, the only instructor who consistently cooperated with the investigation, appeared voluntarily to explain her work with learning-disabled athletes, only to be grilled about her credentials by Potuto in a pettifogging inquisition of remarkable stamina.

In January of last year, the NCAA's Infractions Appeals Committee sustained all the sanctions imposed on FSU except the number of vacated football victories, which it dropped, ex cathedra, from 14 to 12. The final penalty locked Bobby Bowden's official win total on retirement at 377 instead of 389, behind Joe Paterno's 401 (and counting). This carried stinging symbolism for fans, without bringing down on the NCAA the harsh repercussions it would have risked if it had issued a television ban or substantial fine.

Cruelly, but typically, the NCAA concentrated public censure on powerless scapegoats. A dreaded "show cause" order rendered Brenda Monk, the tutor, effectively unhirable at any college in the United States. Cloaking an old-fashioned blackball in the stately language of law, the order gave notice that any school hiring Monk before a specified date in 2013 "shall, pursuant to the provisions of Bylaw 19.5.2.2(l), show cause why it should not be penalized if it does not restrict the former learning specialist [Monk] from having any contact with student-athletes." Today she works as an education supervisor at a prison in Florida.

The Florida state verdict hardly surprised Rick Johnson, the lawyer who had represented the college pitchers Andrew Oliver and James Paxton. "All the NCAA's enforcements are random and selective," he told me, calling the organization's appeals process a travesty. (Johnson says the NCAA has never admitted to having wrongly suspended an athlete.) Johnson's scalding experience prompted him to undertake a law-review article on the subject, which in turn sent him trawling through NCAA archives. From the summary tax forms required of nonprofits, he found out that the NCAA had spent nearly $1 million chartering private jets in 2006. "What kind of nonprofit organization leases private jets?," Johnson asks. It's hard to determine from tax returns what money goes where, but it looks as if the NCAA spent less than 1 percent of its budget on enforcement that year. Even after its plump cut for its own overhead, the NCAA dispersed huge sums to its 1,200 member schools, in the manner of a professional sports league. These annual payments are universal—every college gets something—but widely uneven. They keep the disparate shareholders (barely) united and speaking for all of college sports. The payments coerce unity within the structure of a private association that is unincorporated and unregulated, exercising amorphous powers not delegated by any government.

Searching through the archives, Johnson came across a 1973 memo from the NCAA general counsel recommending the adoption of a due-process procedure for athletes in disciplinary cases. Without it, warned the organization's lawyer, the association risked big liability claims for deprivation of rights. His proposal went nowhere. Instead, apparently to limit costs to the universities, Walter Byers had implemented the year-by-year scholarship rule that Joseph Agnew would challenge in court 37 years later. Moreover, the NCAA's 1975 convention adopted a second recommendation "to discourage legal actions against the NCAA," according to the minutes. The members voted to create Bylaw 19.7, Restitution, to intimidate college athletes in disputes with the NCAA. Johnson recognized this provision all too well, having won the temporary court judgment that the rule was illegal if not downright despotic. It made him nearly apoplectic to learn that the NCAA had deliberately drawn up the restitution rule as an obstacle to due process, contrary to the recommendation of its own lawyer. "They want to crush these kids," he says.

The NCAA, of course, has never expressed such a desire, and its public comments on due process tend to be anodyne. At a congressional hearing in 2004, the infractions-committee vice chair, Josephine Potuto, repeatedly argued that although the NCAA is "not bound by any judicial due process standards," its enforcement, infractions, and hearing procedures meet and "very likely exceed" those of other public institutions. Yet when pressed, Potuto declared that athletes would have no standing for due process even if the Supreme Court had not exempted the NCAA in the 1988 Tarkanian decision. "In order to reach due-process issues as a legal Constitutional principle, the individual challenging has to have a substantive property or liberty interest," she testified. "The opportunity to play intercollegiate athletics does not rise to that level."

To translate this from the legal jargon, Potuto used a circular argument to confine college athletes beneath any right to freedom or property in their own athletic effort. They have no stake to seek their rights, she claimed, because they have no rights at stake.

Potuto's assertion might be judged preposterous, an heir of the Dred Scott dictum that slaves possessed no rights a white person was bound to respect. But she was merely being honest, articulating assumptions almost everyone shares without question. Whether motivated by hostility for students (as critics like Johnson allege), or by noble and paternalistic tough love (as the NCAA professes), the denial of fundamental due process for college athletes has stood unchallenged in public discourse. Like other NCAA rules, it emanates naturally from the premise that college athletes own no interest in sports beyond exercise, character-building, and good fun. Who represents these young men and women? No one asks.

The debates and commissions about reforming college sports nibble around the edges—trying to reduce corruption, to prevent the "contamination" of athletes by lucre, and to maintain at least a pretense of concern for academic integrity. Everything stands on the implicit presumption that preserving amateurism is necessary for the well-being of college athletes. But while amateurism—and the free labor it provides—may be necessary to the preservation of the NCAA, and perhaps to the profit margins of various interested corporations and educational institutions, what if it doesn't benefit the athletes? What if it hurts them?

"The Plantation Mentality"

"Ninety percent of the NCAA revenue is produced by 1 percent of the athletes," Sonny Vaccaro says. "Go to the skill positions"—the stars. "Ninety percent African Americans." The NCAA made its money off those kids, and so did he. They were not all bad people, the NCAA officials, but they were blind, Vaccaro believes. "Their organization is a fraud."

Vaccaro retired from Reebok in 2007 to make a clean break for a crusade. "The kids and their parents gave me a good life," he says in his peppery staccato. "I want to give something back." Call it redemption, he told me. Call it education or a good cause. "Here's what I preach," said Vaccaro. "This goes beyond race, to human rights. The least educated are the most exploited. I'm probably closer to the kids than anyone else, and I'm 71 years old."

Vaccaro is officially an unpaid consultant to the plaintiffs in *O'Bannon v. NCAA*. He connected Ed O'Bannon with the attorneys who now represent him, and he talked to some of the additional co-plaintiffs who have joined the suit, among them Oscar Robertson, a basketball Hall of Famer who was incensed that the NCAA was still selling his image on playing cards 50 years after he left the University of Cincinnati.

Jon King, an antitrust lawyer at Hausfeld LLP in San Francisco, told me that Vaccaro "opened our eyes to massive revenue streams hidden in college sports." King and his colleagues have drawn on Vaccaro's vast knowledge of athletic-department finances, which include off-budget accounts for shoe contracts. Sonny Vaccaro and his wife, Pam, "had a mountain of documents," he said. The outcome of the 1984 Regents decision validated an antitrust approach for O'Bannon, King argues, as well as for Joseph Agnew in his continuing case against the one-year scholarship rule. Lawyers for Sam Keller—a former quarterback for the University of Nebraska who is featured in video games—are pursuing a parallel "right of publicity" track based on the First Amendment. Still other lawyers could revive Rick Johnson's case against NCAA bylaws on a larger scale, and King thinks claims for the rights of college players may be viable also under laws pertaining to contracts, employment, and civil rights.

Vaccaro had sought a law firm for O'Bannon with pockets deep enough to withstand an expensive war of attrition, fearing that NCAA officials would fight discovery to the end. So far, though, they have been forthcoming. "The numbers are off the wall," Vaccaro says. "The public will see for the first time how all the money is distributed."

Vaccaro has been traveling the after-dinner circuit, proselytizing against what he sees as the NCAA's exploitation of young athletes. Late in 2008, someone who heard his stump speech at Howard University mentioned it to Michael Hausfeld, a prominent antitrust and human-rights lawyer, whose firm had won suits against Exxon for Native Alaskans and against Union Bank of Switzerland for Holocaust victims' families. Someone tracked down Vaccaro on vacation in Athens, Greece, and he flew back directly to meet Hausfeld. The shoe salesman and the white-shoe lawyer made common cause.

Hausfeld LLP has offices in San Francisco, Philadelphia, and London. Its headquarters are on K Street in Washington, D.C., about three blocks from the White House. When I talked with Hausfeld there not long ago, he sat in a cavernous conference room, tidy in pinstripes, hands folded on a spotless table that reflected the skyline. He spoke softly, without pause, condensing the complex fugue of antitrust litigation into simple sentences. "Let's start with the basic question," he said, noting that the NCAA claims that student-athletes have no property rights in their own athletic accomplishments. Yet, in order to be eligible to play, college athletes have to waive their rights to proceeds from any sales based on their athletic performance.

"What right is it that they're waiving?," Hausfeld asked. "You can't waive something you don't have. So they had a right that they gave up in consideration to the principle of amateurism, if there be such." (At an April hearing in a U.S. District Court in California, Gregory Curtner, a representative for the NCAA, stunned O'Bannon's lawyers by saying: "There is no document, there is no substance, that the NCAA ever takes from the student-athletes their rights of publicity or their rights of likeness. They are at all times owned by the student-athlete." Jon King says this is "like telling someone they have the winning lottery ticket, but by the way, it can only be cashed in on Mars." The court denied for a second time an NCAA motion to dismiss the O'Bannon complaint.)

The waiver clause is nestled among the paragraphs of the "Student-Athlete Statement" that NCAA rules require be collected yearly from every college athlete. In signing the statement, the athletes attest that they have amateur status, that their stated SAT scores are valid, that they are willing to disclose any educational documents requested, and so forth. Already, Hausfeld said, the defendants in the Ed O'Bannon case have said in court filings that college athletes thereby transferred their promotional rights forever. He paused. "That's ludicrous," he said. "Nobody assigns rights like that. Nobody can assert rights like that." He said the pattern demonstrated clear abuse by the collective power of the schools and all their conferences under the NCAA umbrella—"a most effective cartel."

The faux ideal of amateurism is "the elephant in the room," Hausfeld said, sending for a book. "You can't get to the bottom of our case without exposing the hypocrisy of amateurism, and Walter Byers says it eloquently." An assistant brought in Byers's memoir. It looked garish on the shiny table because dozens of pink Post-its protruded from the text. Hausfeld read to me from page 390:

> The college player cannot sell his own feet (the coach does that) nor can he sell his own name (the college will do that). This is the plantation mentality resurrected and blessed by today's campus executives.

He looked up. "That wasn't me," he said. "That was the NCAA's architect." He found a key recommendation on page 388:

> Prosecutors and the courts, with the support of the public, should use antitrust laws to break up the collegiate cartel—not just in athletics but possibly in other aspects of collegiate life as well.

Could the book become evidence? Might the aged Byers testify? (He is now 89.) Was that part of the plaintiffs' strategy for the O'Bannon trial? Hausfeld smiled faintly. "I'd rather the NCAA lawyers not fully understand the strategy," he said.

He put the spiny book away and previewed what lies ahead. The court soon would qualify his clients as a class. Then the Sherman Antitrust Act would provide for thorough discovery to break down exactly what the NCAA receives on everything from video clips to jerseys, contract by contract. "And we want to know what they're carrying on their books as the value of their archival footage," he concluded. "They say it's a lot of money. We agree. How much?"

The work will be hard, but Hausfeld said he will win in the courts, unless the NCAA folds first. "Why?" Hausfeld asked rhetorically. "We know our clients are foreclosed: neither the NCAA nor its members will permit them to participate in any of that licensing revenue. Under the law, it's up to them [the defendants] to give a pro-competitive justification. They can't. End of story."

In 2010 the third Knight Commission, complementing a previous commission's recommendation for published reports on academic progress, called for the finances of college sports to be made transparent and public—television contracts, conference budgets, shoe deals, coaches' salaries, stadium bonds, everything. The recommendation was based on the worthy truism that sunlight is a proven disinfectant. But in practice, it has not been applied at all. Conferences, coaches, and other stakeholders resisted disclosure; college players still have no way of determining their value to the university.

"Money surrounds college sports," says Domonique Foxworth, who is a cornerback for the NFL's Baltimore Ravens and an executive-committee member for the NFL Players Association, and played for the University of Maryland. "And every player knows those millions are floating around only because of the 18-to-22-year-olds." Yes, he told me, even the second-string punter believes a miracle might lift him into the NFL, and why not? In all the many pages of the three voluminous Knight Commission reports, there is but one paragraph that addresses the real-life choices for college athletes. "Approximately 1 percent of NCAA men's basketball players and 2 percent of NCAA football players are drafted by NBA or NFL teams," stated the 2001 report, basing its figures on a review of the previous 10 years, "and just being drafted is no assurance of a successful professional career." Warning that the odds against professional athletic success are "astronomically high," the Knight Commission counsels college athletes to avoid a "rude surprise" and to stick to regular studies. This is sound advice as far as it goes, but it's a bromide that pinches off discussion. Nothing in the typical college curriculum teaches a sweat-stained guard at Clemson or Purdue what his monetary value to the university is. Nothing prods students to think independently about amateurism—because the universities themselves have too much invested in its preservation. Stifling thought, the universities, in league with the NCAA, have failed their own primary mission by providing an empty, cynical education on college sports.

The most basic reform would treat the students as what they are—adults, with rights and reason of their own—and grant them a meaningful voice in NCAA deliberations. A restoration of full citizenship to "student-athletes" would facilitate open governance, making it possible to enforce pledges of transparency in both academic standards and athletic finances. Without that, the NCAA has no effective checks and balances, no way for the students to provide informed consent regarding the way they are governed. A thousand questions lie willfully silenced because the NCAA is naturally afraid of giving "student-athletes" a true voice. Would college players be content with the augmented scholarship or allowance now requested by the National College Players Association? If a player's worth to the university is greater than the value of his scholarship (as it clearly is in some cases), should he be paid a salary? If so, would teammates in revenue sports want to be paid equally, or in salaries stratified according to talent or value on the field? What would the athletes want in Division III, where athletic budgets keep rising without scholarships or substantial sports revenue? Would athletes seek more or less variance in admissions standards? Should non-athletes also have a voice, especially where involuntary student fees support more and more of college sports? Might some schools choose to specialize, paying players only in elite leagues for football, or lacrosse? In athletic councils, how much would high-revenue athletes value a simple thank you from the tennis or field-hockey players for the newly specified subsidies to their facilities?

University administrators, already besieged from all sides, do not want to even think about such questions. Most cringe at the thought of bargaining with athletes as a general manager does in professional sports, with untold effects on the budgets for coaches and every other sports item. "I would not want to be part of it," North Carolina Athletic Director Dick Baddour told me flatly. After 44 years at UNC, he could scarcely contemplate a world without amateur rules. "We would have to think long and hard," Baddour added gravely, "about whether this university would continue those sports at all."

I, too, once reflexively recoiled at the idea of paying college athletes and treating them like employees or professionals. It feels abhorrent—but for reasons having to do more with sentiment than with practicality or law. Not just fans and university presidents but judges have often found cursory, non-statutory excuses to leave amateur traditions intact. "Even in the increasingly commercial modern world," said a federal-court judge in *Gaines v. NCAA* in 1990, "this Court believes there is still validity to the Athenian concept of a complete education derived from fostering the full growth of both mind and body." The fact that "the NCAA has not distilled amateurism to its purest form," said the Fifth Circuit Court of Appeals in 1988, "does not mean its attempts to maintain a mixture containing some amateur elements are unreasonable."

But one way or another, the smokescreen of amateurism may soon be swept away. For one thing, a victory by the plaintiffs in O'Bannon's case would radically transform college sports. Colleges would likely have to either stop profiting from students or start paying them. The NCAA could also be forced to pay tens, if not hundreds, of millions of dollars in damages. If O'Bannon and Vaccaro and company win, "it will turn college sports on its ear," said Richard Lapchick, the president of the National Consortium for Academics and Sports, in a recent interview with *The New York Times.*

Though the O'Bannon case may take several years yet to reach resolution, developments on other fronts are chipping away at amateurism, and at the NCAA. This past summer, *Sports Illustrated* editorialized in favor of allowing college athletes to be paid by non-university sources without jeopardizing their eligibility. At a press conference last June, Steve Spurrier, the coach of the South Carolina Gamecocks football team (and the winner of the 1966 Heisman Trophy as a Florida Gator), proposed that coaches start paying players $300 a game out of their own pockets. The coaches at six other SEC schools (Alabama, Florida, Ole Miss, Mississippi State, LSU, and Tennessee) all endorsed Spurrier's proposal. And Mark Emmert, the NCAA president, recently conceded that big changes must come. "The integrity of collegiate athletics is seriously challenged today by rapidly growing pressures coming from many directions," Emmert said in July. "We have reached a point where incremental change is not sufficient to meet these challenges. I want us to act more aggressively and in a more comprehensive way than we have in the past. A few new tweaks of the rules won't get the job done."

Threats to NCAA dominion also percolate in Congress. Aggrieved legislators have sponsored numerous bills. Senator Orrin Hatch, citing mistreatment of his Utah Utes, has called witnesses to discuss possible antitrust remedies for the Bowl Championship Series. Congressional committees have already held hearings critical of the NCAA's refusal to follow due process in disciplinary matters; other committees have explored a rise in football concussions. Last January, calls went up to investigate "informal" football workouts at the University of Iowa just after the season-ending bowl games—workouts so grueling that 41 of the 56 amateur student-athletes collapsed, and 13 were hospitalized with rhabdomyolysis, a life-threatening kidney condition often caused by excessive exercise.

The greatest threat to the viability of the NCAA may come from its member universities. Many experts believe that the churning instability within college football will drive the next major change. President Obama himself has endorsed the drumbeat cry for a national playoff in college football. This past spring, the Justice Department questioned the BCS about its adherence to antitrust standards. Jim Delany, the commissioner of the Big Ten, has estimated that a national playoff system could produce three or four times as much money as the existing bowl system does. If a significant band of football schools were to demonstrate that they could orchestrate a true national playoff, without the NCAA's assistance, the association would be terrified—and with good reason. Because if the big sports colleges don't need the NCAA to administer a national playoff in football, then they don't need it to do so in basketball. In which case, they could cut out the middleman in March Madness and run the tournament themselves. Which would deprive the NCAA of close to $1 billion a year, more than 95 percent of its revenue. The organization would be reduced to a rule book without money—an organization aspiring to enforce its rules but without the financial authority to enforce anything.

Thus the playoff dreamed of and hankered for by millions of football fans haunts the NCAA. "There will be some kind of playoff in college football, and it will not be run by the NCAA," says Todd Turner, a former athletic director in four conferences (Big East, ACC, SEC, and Pac-10). "If I'm at the NCAA, I have to worry that the playoff group can get basketball to break away, too."

This danger helps explain why the NCAA steps gingerly in enforcements against powerful colleges. To alienate member colleges would be to jeopardize its own existence. Long gone are television bans and the "death penalty" sentences (commanding season-long shutdowns of offending teams) once meted out to Kentucky (1952), Southwestern Louisiana (1973), and Southern Methodist University (1987). Institutions receive mostly symbolic slaps nowadays. Real punishments fall heavily on players and on scapegoats like literacy tutors.

A deeper reason explains why, in its predicament, the NCAA has no recourse to any principle or law that can justify amateurism. There is no such thing. Scholars and sportswriters yearn for grand juries to ferret out every forbidden bauble that reaches a college athlete, but the NCAA's ersatz courts can only masquerade as public authority. How could any statute impose amateur status on college athletes, or on anyone else? No legal definition of amateur exists, and any attempt to create one in enforceable law would expose its repulsive and unconstitutional nature—a bill of attainder, stripping from college athletes the rights of American citizenship.

For all our queasiness about what would happen if some athletes were to get paid, there is a successful precedent for the professionalization of an amateur sports system: the Olympics. For years, Walter Byers waged war with the NCAA's older and more powerful nemesis, the Amateur Athletic Union, which since 1894 had overseen U.S. Olympic athletes. Run in high-handed fashion, the AAU had infamously banned Jesse Owens for life in 1936—weeks after his four heroic gold medals punctured the Nazi claim of Aryan supremacy—because instead of using his sudden fame to tour and make money for the AAU at track meets across Europe, he came home early. In the early 1960s, the fights between the NCAA and the AAU over who should manage Olympic athletes become so bitter that President Kennedy called in General Douglas MacArthur to try to mediate a truce before the Tokyo Olympic Games.

Ultimately, Byers prevailed and effectively neutered the AAU. In November 1978, President Jimmy Carter signed the bipartisan

337

Amateur Sports Act. Amateurism in the Olympics soon dissolved—and the world did not end. Athletes, granted a 20 percent voting stake on every Olympic sport's governing body, tipped balances in the United States and then inexorably around the world. First in marathon races, then in tennis tournaments, players soon were allowed to accept prize money and keep their Olympic eligibility. Athletes profited from sponsorships and endorsements. The International Olympic Committee expunged the word *amateur* from its charter in 1986. Olympic officials, who had once disdained the NCAA for offering scholarships in exchange for athletic performance, came to welcome millionaire athletes from every quarter, while the NCAA still refused to let the pro Olympian Michael Phelps swim for his college team at Michigan.

This sweeping shift left the Olympic reputation intact, and perhaps improved. Only hardened romantics mourned the amateur code. "Hey, come on," said Anne Audain, a track-and-field star who once held the world record for the 5,000 meters. "It's like losing your virginity. You're a little misty for awhile, but then you realize, Wow, there's a whole new world out there!"

Without logic or practicality or fairness to support amateurism, the NCAA's final retreat is to sentiment. The Knight Commission endorsed its heartfelt cry that to pay college athletes would be "an unacceptable surrender to despair." Many of the people I spoke with while reporting this article felt the same way. "I don't want to pay college players," said Wade Smith, a tough criminal lawyer and former star running back at North Carolina. "I just don't want to do it. We'd lose something precious."

"Scholarship athletes are already paid," declared the Knight Commission members, "in the most meaningful way poss-ible: with a free education." This evasion by prominent educators severed my last reluctant, emotional tie with imposed amateurism. I found it worse than self-serving. It echoes masters who once claimed that heavenly salvation would outweigh earthly injustice to slaves. In the era when our college sports first arose, colonial powers were turning the whole world upside down to define their own interests as all-inclusive and benevolent. Just so, the NCAA calls it heinous exploitation to pay college athletes a fair portion of what they earn.

The Case Against High-School Sports

By Amanda Ripley

Every year, thousands of teenagers move to the United States from all over the world, for all kinds of reasons. They observe everything in their new country with fresh eyes, including basic features of American life that most of us never stop to consider.

One element of our education system consistently surprises them: "Sports are a big deal here," says Jenny, who moved to America from South Korea with her family in 2011. Shawnee High, her public school in southern New Jersey, fields teams in 18 sports over the course of the school year, including golf and bowling. Its campus has lush grass fields, six tennis courts, and an athletic Hall of Fame. "They have days when teams dress up in Hawaiian clothes or pajamas just because— 'We're the soccer team!,'" Jenny says. (To protect the privacy of Jenny and other students in this story, only their first names are used.)

By contrast, in South Korea, whose 15-year-olds rank fourth in the world (behind Shanghai, Singapore, and Hong Kong) on a test of critical thinking in math, Jenny's classmates played pickup soccer on a dirt field at lunchtime.

They brought badminton rackets from home and pretended there was a net. If they made it into the newspaper, it was usually for their academic accomplishments.

Sports are embedded in American schools in a way they are not almost anywhere else. Yet this difference hardly ever comes up in domestic debates about America's international mediocrity in education. (The U.S. ranks 31st on the same international math test.) The challenges we do talk about are real ones, from undertrained teachers to entrenched poverty. But what to make of this other glaring reality, and the signal it sends to children, parents, and teachers about the very purpose of school?

When I surveyed about 200 former exchange students last year, in cooperation with an international exchange organization called AFS, nine out of 10 foreign students who had lived in the U.S. said that

From *The Atlantic*, 2013.

kids here cared more about sports than their peers back home did. A majority of Americans who'd studied abroad agreed.

Even in eighth grade, American kids spend more than twice the time Korean kids spend playing sports, according to a 2010 study published in the *Journal of Advanced Academics*. In countries with more-holistic, less hard-driving education systems than Korea's, like Finland and Germany, many kids play club sports in their local towns—outside of school. Most schools do not staff, manage, transport, insure, or glorify sports teams, because, well, why would they?

When I was growing up in New Jersey, not far from where Jenny now lives, I played soccer from age 7 to 17. I was relieved to find a place where girls were not expected to sit quietly or look pretty, and I still love the game. Like most other Americans, I can rattle off the many benefits of high-school sports: exercise, lessons in sportsmanship and perseverance, school spirit, and just plain fun. All of those things matter, and Jenny finds it refreshing to attend a school that is about so much more than academics. But as I've traveled around the world visiting places that do things differently—and get better results—I've started to wonder about the trade-offs we make.

Nearly all of Jenny's classmates at Shawnee are white, and 95 percent come from middle- or upper-income homes. But in 2012, only 17 percent of the school's juniors and seniors took at least one Advanced Placement test— compared with the 50 percent of students who played school sports.

As states and districts continue to slash education budgets, as more kids play on traveling teams outside of school, and as the globalized economy demands that children learn higher-order skills so they can compete down the line, it's worth reevaluating the American sporting tradition. If sports were not *central* to the mission of American high schools, then what would be?

On October 12, 1900, the Wall School of Honey Grove played St. Matthew's Grammar School of Dallas in football, winning 5–0. The event was a milestone in Texas history: the first recorded football game between two high-school teams. Until then, most American boys had played sports in the haphazard way of boys the world over: ambling onto fields and into alleys for pickup games or challenging other loosely affiliated groups of students to a match. Cheating was rampant, and games looked more like brawls than organized contests.

Schools got involved to contain the madness. The trend started in elite private schools and then spread to the masses. New York City inaugurated its Public Schools Athletic League in 1903, holding a track-and-field spectacular for 1,000 boys at Madison Square Garden the day after Christmas.

At the time, the United States was starting to educate its children for more years than most other countries, even while admitting a surge of immigrants. The ruling elite feared that all this schooling would make Anglo-Saxon boys soft and weak, in contrast to their brawny, newly immigrated peers. Oliver Wendell Holmes Sr. warned that cities were being overrun with "stiff- jointed, soft-muscled, paste-complexioned youth."

Sports, the thinking went, would both protect boys' masculinity and distract them from vices like gambling and prostitution. "Muscular Christianity," fashionable during the Victorian era, prescribed sports as a sort of moral vaccine against the tumult of rapid economic growth. "In life, as in a foot-ball game," Theodore Roosevelt wrote in an essay on "The American Boy" in 1900, "the principle to follow is: Hit the line hard; don't foul and don't shirk, but hit the line hard!"

Athletics succeeded in distracting not just students but entire communities. As athletic fields became the cultural centers of towns across America, educators became coaches and parents became boosters.

From the beginning, though, some detractors questioned whether tax money should be spent on activities that could damage the brain, and occasionally leave students dead on the field. In 1909, New York City superintendents decided to abolish football, and *The New York Times* predicted that soccer would become the sport of choice. But officials reversed course the next year, re-allowing football, with revised rules.

The National Collegiate Athletic Association had emerged by this time, as a means of reforming the increasingly brutal sport of college football. But the enforcers were unable to keep pace with the industry. Once television exponentially expanded the fan base in the mid-20th century, collegiate sports gained a spiritual and economic choke hold on America. College scholarships rewarded high-school athletes, and the search for the next star player trickled down even to grade school. As more and more Americans attended college, growing ranks of alumni demanded winning teams—and university presidents found their reputations shaped by the success of their football and basketball programs.

In 1961, the sociologist James Coleman observed that a visitor entering an American high school would likely be confronted, first of all, with a trophy case. His examination of the trophies would reveal a curious fact: The gold and silver cups, with rare exception, symbolize victory in athletic contests, not scholastic ones ... Altogether, the trophy case would suggest to the innocent visitor that he was entering an athletic club, not an educational institution.

Last year in Texas, whose small towns are the spiritual home of high-school football and the inspiration for *Friday Night Lights*, the superintendent brought in to rescue one tiny rural school district did something insanely rational. In the spring of 2012, after the state threatened to shut down Premont Independent School District for financial mismanagement and academic failure, Ernest Singleton suspended all sports—including football.

To cut costs, the district had already laid off eight employees and closed the middle-school campus, moving its classes to the high-school building; the elementary school hadn't employed an art or a music teacher in years; and the high school had sealed off the science labs, which were infested with mold. Yet the high school still turned out football, basketball, volleyball, track, tennis, cheerleading, and baseball teams each year.

Football at Premont cost about $1,300 a player. Math, by contrast, cost just $618 a student. For the price of one football season, the district could have hired a full-time elementary-school music teacher for an entire year. But, despite the fact that Premont's football team had won just one game the previous season and hadn't been to the playoffs in roughly a decade, this option never occurred to anyone.

"I've been in hundreds of classrooms," says Singleton, who has spent 15 years as a principal and helped turn around other struggling schools. "This was the worst I've seen in my career. The kids were in control. The language was filthy. The teachers were not prepared." By suspending sports, Singleton realized, he could save $150,000 in one year. A third of this amount was being paid to teachers as coaching stipends, on top of the smaller costs: $27,000 for athletic supplies, $15,000 for insurance, $13,000 for referees, $12,000 for bus drivers. "There are so many things people don't think about when they think of sports," Singleton told me. Still, he steeled himself for the town's reaction. "I knew the minute I announced it, it was going to be like the world had caved in on us."

First he explained his decision to Enrique Ruiz Jr., the principal of Premont's only high school: eliminating sports would save money and refocus everyone's attention on academics. Ruiz agreed. The school was making other changes, too, such as giving teachers more time for training and planning, making students wear uniforms, and aligning the curriculum with more-rigorous state standards. Suspending sports might get the attention of anyone not taking those changes seriously.

343

Then Singleton told the school's football coach, a history teacher named Richard Russell, who'd been coaching for two decades. Russell had played basketball and football in high school, and he loved sports. But he preferred giving up the team to shutting down the whole district. He told Singleton to do whatever he needed to do, then walked over to the gym and told the basketball players, who were waiting for practice to begin. At first, the students didn't seem to understand. "What? Why?" asked Nathan, then a junior and a quarterback on the football team. "Would you rather have sports or school?," Russell replied.

Out by the tennis courts, Daniel, a junior who was in line to become a captain of the football team, was waiting for tennis practice to start when a teacher came out and delivered the news. Daniel went home and texted his friends in disbelief, hoping there had been some kind of mistake.

"We were freaking out," says Mariela, a former cheerleader and tennis and volleyball player. American kids expect to participate in school sports as a kind of rite of passage. "We don't get these years back," she told me. "I'm never going to get the experience of cheering as captain under the lights."

As the news trickled out, reporters from all over America came to witness the unthinkable. A photographer followed Nathan around, taking pictures of him not playing football, which the *Corpus Christi Caller-Times* ran in a photo essay titled "Friday Without Football in Premont."

Many observers predicted that Singleton's experiment would end in disaster.

344

Premont was a speck on the map, an hour and a half southwest of Corpus Christi. The town's population had dwindled since the oil fields had dried up, and a majority of the 282 high-school students who remained were from low- income Hispanic families. How many football players would drop out? How many cheerleaders would transfer to the next town's school? How would kids learn about grit, teamwork, and fair play?

Last fall at Premont, the first without football, was quiet—eerily so. There were no Friday-night games to look forward to, no players and their parents cheered onto the field on opening night, no cheerleaders making signs in the hallway, no football practice 10 or more hours a week. Only the basketball team was allowed to play, though its tournament schedule was diminished.

More than a dozen students transferred, including four volleyball players and a football player. Most went to a school 10 miles away, where they could play sports. Two teachers who had been coaches left as well. To boost morale, Principal Ruiz started holding sports-free pep rallies every Friday. Classes competed against each other in drum-offs and team-building exercises in the school gym.

But there was an upside to the quiet. "The first 12 weeks of school were the most peaceful beginning weeks I've ever witnessed at a high school," Singleton says. "It was calm. There was a level of energy devoted to planning and lessons, to after-school tutoring. I saw such a difference."

Nathan missed the adrenaline rush of running out onto the field and the sense of purpose he got from the sport. But he began playing flag football for a club team on the weekends, and he admitted to one advantage during the week: "It did make you focus. There was just all this extra time. You never got behind on your work."

That first semester, 80 percent of the students passed their classes, compared with 50 percent the previous fall. About 160 people attended parent-teacher night, compared with six the year before. Principal Ruiz was so excited that he went out and took pictures of the parking lot, jammed with cars. Through some combination of new leadership, the threat of closure, and a renewed emphasis on academics, Premont's culture changed. "There's been a definite decline in misbehavior," says Desiree Valdez, who teaches speech, theater, and creative writing at Premont. "I'm struggling to recall a fight. Before, it was one every couple of weeks."

Suspending sports was only part of the equation, but Singleton believes it was crucial. He used the savings to give teachers raises. Meanwhile, communities throughout Texas, alarmed by the cancellation of football, raised $400,000 for Premont via fund-raisers and donations—money that Singleton put toward renovating the science labs.

No one knew whether the state would make good on its threat to shut the district down. But for the first time in many years, Premont had a healthy operating balance and no debt. This past spring, the school brought back baseball, track, and tennis, with the caveat that the teams could participate in just one travel tournament a season. "Learning is going on in 99 percent of the classrooms now," Coach Russell told me, "compared to 2 percent before."

In many schools, sports are so entrenched that no one—not even the people in charge—realizes their actual cost. When Marguerite Roza, the author of *Educational Economics*, analyzed the finances of one public high school in the Pacific Northwest, she and her colleagues found that the school was spending $328 a student for math instruction and more than four times that much for cheerleading—$1,348 a cheerleader. "And it is not even a school in a district that prioritizes cheerleading," Roza wrote. "In fact, this district's 'strategic plan' has for the past three years claimed that *math* was the primary focus."

Many sports and other electives tend to have lower student-to-teacher ratios than math and reading classes, which drives up the cost. And contrary to what most people think, ticket and concession sales do not begin to cover the cost of sports in the vast majority of high schools (or colleges).

Football is, far and away, the most expensive high-school sport. Many football teams have half a dozen or more coaches, all of whom typically receive a stipend. Some schools hire professional coaches at full salaries, or designate a teacher as the full-time athletic director. New bleachers can cost half a million dollars, about the same as artificial turf. Even maintaining a grass field can cost more than $20,000 a year. Reconditioning helmets, a ritual that many teams pay for every year, can cost more than $1,500 for a large team. Some communities collect private donations or levy a special tax to fund new school-sports facilities.

Many of the costs are insidious, Roza has found, "buried in unidentifiable places." For example, when teacher-coaches travel for game days, schools need to hire substitute teachers. They also need to pay for buses for the team, the band, and the cheerleaders, not to mention meals and hotels on the road. For home games, schools generally cover the cost of hiring officials, providing security, painting the lines on the field, and cleaning up afterward. "Logistics are a big challenge," says Jared Bigham, until recently the supervising principal of two schools in Copperhill, Tennessee, and a former teacher, coach, and player. "Even though the coaches are in charge of the budgets, I still have to oversee them and approve each expenditure. You're looking at 10 different budgets you have to manage."

That kind of constant, low-level distraction may be the greatest cost of all. During football season in particular, the focus of American principals, teachers, and students shifts inexorably away from academics. Sure, high-school football players spend long, exhausting hours practicing (and according to one study, about 15 percent experience a brain injury each season), but the commitment extends to the rest of the community, from late-night band practices to elaborate pep rallies to meetings with parents. Athletics even dictate the time that school starts each day: despite research showing that later start times improve student performance, many high schools begin before 8 a.m., partly to reserve afternoon daylight hours for sports practice.

American principals, unlike the vast majority of principals around the world, make many hiring decisions with their sports teams in mind—a calculus that does not always end well for students. "Every school in the entire country has done this," Marcia Gregorio, a veteran teacher in rural Pennsylvania, told me. "You hire a teacher, and you sometimes lower the standards because you need a coach."

But here's the thing: most American principals I spoke with expressed no outrage over the primacy of sports in school. In fact, they fiercely defended it. "If I could wave a magic wand, I'd have more athletic opportunities for students, not less," Bigham, the former Tennessee principal, told me. His argument is a familiar one: sports can be bait for students who otherwise might not care about school. "I've seen truancy issues completely turned around once students begin playing sports," he says. "When students have a sense of belonging, when they feel tied to the school, they feel more part of the process."

Premont is not alone. Over the past few years, budget cuts have forced more school districts, from Florida to Illinois, to scale back on sports programs. But in most of these places, even modest cuts to athletics are viewed as temporary—and tragic—sacrifices, not as necessary adaptations to a new reality. Many schools have shifted more of the cost of athletics to parents rather than downsize programs. Others have cut basic academic costs to keep their sports programs intact. Officials in Pasco County, Florida, have considered squeezing athletic budgets for each of the past six years. They've so far agreed to cut about 700 education jobs, and they extended winter break in 2011, but sports have been left mostly untouched.

In these communities, the dominant argument is usually that sports lure students into school and keep them out of trouble—the same argument American educators have made for more than a century. And it remains relevant, without a doubt, for some small portion of students.

But at this moment in history, now that more than 20 countries are pulling off better high-school-graduation rates than we are, with mostly nominal athletic offerings, using sports to tempt kids into getting an education feels dangerously old-fashioned. America has not found a way to dramatically improve its children's academic performance over the past 50 years, but other countries have—and they are starting to reap the economic benefits.

Andreas Schleicher, a German education scientist at the Organization for Economic Cooperation and Development, has visited schools all over the world and is an authority on different regional approaches to education. (I profiled Schleicher for this magazine in 2011.) He is wary of the theory that sports can encourage sustained classroom engagement. "Our analysis suggests that the most engaging environment you can offer students is one of cognitive challenge combined with individualised pedagogical support," he told me in an e-mail. "If you offer boring and poor math instruction and try to compensate that with interesting sport activities, you may get students interested in sports but I doubt it will do much good to their engagement with school."

Though the research on student athletes is mixed, it generally suggests that sports do more good than harm for the players themselves. One 2010 study by Betsey Stevenson, then at the University of Pennsylvania, found that, in a given state, increases in the number of girls playing high-school sports have historically generated higher college-attendance and employment rates among women. Another study, conducted by Columbia's Margo Gardner, found that teenagers who participated in extracurriculars had higher college- graduation and voting rates, even after controlling for ethnicity, parental education, and other factors.

But only 40 percent of seniors participate in high-school athletics, and what's harder to measure is how the overriding emphasis on sports affects everyone who doesn't play. One study of 30,000 students at the University of Oregon found that the grades of men who did not play sports went down as the football team's performance improved. Both men and women reported that the better their football team did, the less they studied and the more they partied.

Exercise, without a doubt, is good for learning and living. But these benefits accrue to the athletes, who are in the minority. What about everyone else?

At Spelman College, a historically black, all-women's college in Atlanta, about half of last year's incoming class of some 530 students were obese or had high blood pressure, Type 2 diabetes, or some other chronic health condition that could be improved with exercise. Each year, Spelman was spending nearly $1 million on athletics—not for those students, but for the 4 percent of the student body that played sports.

Spelman's president, Beverly Daniel Tatum, found the imbalance difficult to justify. She told me that early last year, while watching a Spelman basketball game, "it occurred to me that none of these women were going to play basketball after they graduated. By that I don't mean play professionally—I mean even recreationally. I thought of all the black women I knew, and they did not tend to spend their recreational time playing basketball. So a little voice in my head said, *Well, let's flip it.*"

That April, after getting approval from her board and faculty, she gathered Spelman's athletes and coaches in an auditorium and announced that she was going to cancel intercollegiate sports after the spring of 2013, and begin spending that $1 million on a campus-wide health-and-fitness program.

Many of Spelman's 80 athletes were devastated, needless to say, and it is too early to tell whether the new swim, aerobics, and Zumba classes, among other offerings, will lead to healthier students on campus. But Tatum's signal was clear: lifelong health habits matter more than expensive, elite sporting competitions with rival schools. One priority has real and lasting benefits; the other is a fantasy.

Imagine, for a moment, if Americans transferred our obsessive intensity about high-school sports—the rankings, the trophies, the ceremonies, the pride—to high-school academics. We would look not so different from South Korea, or Japan, or any of a handful of Asian countries whose hypercompetitive, pressure-cooker approach to academics in many ways mirrors the American approach to sports. Both approaches can be dysfunctional; both set kids up for stress and disappointment. The difference is that 93 percent of South Korean students graduate from high school, compared with just 77 percent of American students—only about 2 percent of whom receive athletic scholarships to college.

As it becomes easier and more urgent to compare what kids around the world know and can do, more schools may follow Premont's lead. Basis public charter schools, located in Arizona, Texas, and Washington, D.C., are modeled on rigorous international standards. They do not offer tackle football; the founders deemed it too expensive and all-consuming. Still, Basis schools offer other, cheaper sports, including basketball and soccer. Anyone who wants to play can play; no one has to try out. Arizona's mainstream league is costly to join, so Basis Tucson North belongs to an alternative league that costs less and requires no long-distance travel, meaning students rarely miss class for games. Athletes who want to play at an elite level do so on their own, through club teams—not through school.

Basis teachers channel the enthusiasm usually found on football fields into academic conquests. On the day of Advanced Placement exams, students at Basis Tucson North file into the classroom to "Eye of the Tiger," the *Rocky III* theme song. In 2012, 15-year-olds at two Arizona Basis schools took a new test designed to compare individual schools' performance with that of schools from around the world. The average Basis student not only outperformed the typical American student by nearly three years in reading and science and by four years in math, but outscored the average student in Finland, Korea, and Poland as well. The Basis kid did better even than the average student from Shanghai, China, the region that ranks No. 1 in the world.

"I actually believe that sports are extremely important," Olga Block, a Basis co-founder, told me. "The problem is that once sports become important to the school, they start colliding with academics."

350

In a column published in 1927, Roy Henderson, the athletic director of the University Interscholastic League, a public-school sports organization in Texas, articulated the challenge of keeping sports and academics in balance: "Football cannot be defended in the high school unless it is subordinated, controlled, and made to contribute something definite in the cause of education."

The State of Texas announced in May that the Premont Independent School District could stay open. The district has a lot of work to do before its students can feel the kind of pride in their academics that they once felt in their sports teams. But Ernest Singleton, Enrique Ruiz, the teachers, and the students have proved their ability to adapt. Nathan, the one-time quarterback, started college this fall, as did Mariela, the cheerleader—and, as it turns out, the valedictorian. This fall, Premont brought back a volleyball team and a cross-country team, in addition to basketball, baseball, track, and tennis. But for now, still no football.

The Sports Metaphor in American Cultural Discourse

By Jeffrey O. Segrave

Metaphor is one of the most distinctive and salient features of language. Nietzsche in fact took the metaphor so seriously that he considered it the basic principle of all language: so-called literal talk remained a sort of frozen sediment of metaphor.[1] Ortega y Gasset also valued the metaphor considering it, like Nietzsche, a principle component of reality: far from being the deformation of reality, it was rather its organization.[2] As both Nietzsche and Ortega y Gasset realized, the metaphor is nuclear rather than atomistic, an intellectual device that links rather than isolates the distinctive features of everyday experiences. It is therefore through rhetorical devices like metaphor that we communicate a common set of symbols; language, communication, symbolism and communal life become inseparable and interrelated components of an identifiable cultural perspective. As a result, culture becomes encoded in metaphor.

One of the sources of metaphor, and hence one of the mechanisms by which our communal reality is mediated, is the world of sport. The language of sport—'sportspeak' as Robert Lipsyte[3] once called it—has penetrated our entire national language system. R. Palmatier and H. Ray, in fact, have identified as many as 1700 commonly used sports metaphors, taken from more than 100 games and sports ranging from boxing ('catch someone off guard') to bull-fighting ('take the bull by the horns'), cricket ('shiver my timbers') to rowing ('pull your weight'), polo ('come a cropper') to wrestling ('no holds barred').[4] The idea of sport as a metaphor for life ('life is a game') is so common in America and American literature that it has become a part of our conventional wisdom. But as frequently as we use the sports metaphor, often unwittingly, its omnipresence must be qualified by specificity. Metaphors from particular sports predominate in particular cultural discourses. The purpose of this article is to identify and account for the sports metaphors that dominate particular cultural discourses, often noting a change over time. In my analysis, I will uncover patterns of metaphor use and in so doing I will explore the nexus of shared values and assumptions that undergird our collective way of life. The four discourses I am most concerned with are warfare,

From *Culture, Sport, Society,* 2000.

351

352

politics, business and sexual relations, those discourses that have most readily embraced the sports metaphor.

Warfare

The language of sport has long been incorporated into the language of the military. Shakespeare was one of the first to recognize that natural synergy between sport and war, a synergy grounded in the similarity between the means and ends of both—conquest, glory and victory through courage, aggression, and strength. In what is perhaps the most prominent and well-known example, King Henry, looking for an excuse to attack France, finds one upon receipt of a gift from the Dauphin—a present of 'tennis balls' which serves as an insult to the heroic king, an estimation of Henry's maturity, or lack of it:

> We are glad the Dauphin is so pleasant with us.
> His present and your pains we thank you for.
> When we have matched our rackets to these balls
> We will in France, by God's grace, play a set
> Shall strike his father's crown into the hazard
> Tell him he hath made a match with such a wrangler
> That all the courts of France will be disturbed
> With chaces (1, ii, 258–268)...
> And tell the pleasant Prince this mock of his
> Hath turned his ball into gunstones.[5]

However, while the sport of tennis, a frivolous indulgence among England's aristocratic youth at the time, may well have appealed to Shakespeare's audiences, the modern proclivity has tended toward a more overtly militaristic sport—football. After all, war, as Tom Callahan of the *US News and World Report* has noted with parodic aplomb, is at least 'the moral equivalent of football'.[6] Both football and war share a fundamental structural homology as M. Real's definition of football suggests: 'North American professional football is an aggressive, strictly regulated team game fought between males who use both violence and technology to gain control of property for the economic gain of individuals within a nationalistic entertainment context'.[7]

Conflation of the metaphors and specialized vocabularies of football and war are commonplace. Seeking to disassociate himself from Lyndon Johnson's Vietnam war policy, Presidential hopeful, Hubert Humphrey, once remarked: 'I have not been calling the signals. I have been in the position of a lineman doing some of the downfield blocking'.[8] More recently, General 'Stormin' Norman Schwartzkopf described the final manoeuver in the Gulf War as 'the equivalent of a "Hail Mary" play on a football field[9] and Schwartzkopf, himself, was characterized as having the 'gut of a middle linebacker but a quarterback's brain'.[10] Brian Duffy of the *US News and World Report* wrote that 'a stunning endgame killed Saddam Hussein's army'[11] and one of Schwartzkopf's officers concluded that Operation Desert Storm was 'like the Super Bowl to end Super Bowls'.[12] So prevalent is the football/war metaphor that Fred Mish, editor-in-chief of *Merriam-Webster Dictionary* claimed, in reference to the Gulf War, that George Bush had 'taken football words to war'.[13] Examples of the language of war in the language of football are equally legion: attack, blitz, bombs, ground and air assaults, offence and defence, scouts, and trenches are standard terms in football argot. Football coaches, as Real reminds us, are like 'field marshals directing troops trained in boot camp, aided by scouts, prepared for complex attack and defence maneuvers'.[14]

More recently, and in perfect keeping with the new technological sophistication associated with modern warfare, a new sport metaphor has crept into the national discourse of war—the video game metaphor. Reflecting the pinpoint accuracy and 'info-tech' wizardry of contemporary weaponry, the video game metaphor has appeared most recently in the discourse surrounding Operation Desert Storm. 'We hit the target with video game precision,' George Cheney noted, [15] and the *US News and World Report* described the aerial assault on Baghdad as 'the "Nintendo" videos of bomb attack'.[16]

But if, as several commentators have argued, football/war metaphors serve as crucial rhetorical resources for valorizing and rationalizing the ideological hegemony of white, male elites, as well as for desensitizing us to the horrors of war,[17] then the video game metaphor might suggest something new in the American cultural dialogue—the degendering of war and the escalation of public insensitivity to the realities of war. Unlike football, there is nothing inherently gender-specific about video games or increasingly about the demography of the armed forces. Perhaps the video game metaphor represents a shift away from androcentric forms of discourse, signaling less an intensification or renewal of the language, practices and values of male domination, as S. Jansen and D. Sabo[18] suggest, and more an incipient cultural acknowledgement of the diminishing relevance of gender in the conduct of our military agenda.

On the other hand, the video game metaphor would also appear to operate as an increasingly powerful form of cultural anesthetic, numbing us beyond the language of football to the atrocities of war and duping us into the false consciousness that modern warfare is somehow without human cost and suffering. So we mix our play/war metaphors—'the Nintendo War'—as easily as we mix our medical/war metaphors—'surgical strike'. Both sanitize the cruelties of war and both release us from feelings of remorse, guilt, and responsibility.

354

Politics

Not only did Shakespeare recognize the value of a good sports metaphor in the language of war, he also recognized its value in the language of politics. Exhorting his troops before the siege of Harfleur, King Henry V declared: 'I see you stand like greyhounds in the slips, straining upon the start. The game's afoot ...'[19]

The game's been afoot ever since and metaphors drawn from a wide variety of sports have emerged as an indelible feature of the American political landscape. Early metaphors were often taken from the honourable sport of pugilism. Theodore White wrote: 'Like aging prize-fighters, short of wind and stiffening of muscle, the Southerners were left with no reserve but cunning'.[20] But it was another Theodore, Theodore Roosevelt, who truly popularized the boxing metaphor, announcing his willingness to run as the Republican Presidential nominee with the following statement: 'My hat's in the ring. The fight's on, and I'm stripped to the buff'.[21] The 'hat in the ring' metaphor was to remain both durable and flexible: Harold Ickes once derided young Thomas E. Dewey for 'throwing his diaper in the ring'[22] and in 1967 the *New York Times* noted that Congressional candidate Shirley Temple Black had 'thrown her curls in the ring'.[23]

Over the course of the century the boxing metaphor, reflective in part of the mano-y-mano nature of early political campaigning as well as the ethic of fair play and sportsmanship, has given way to the bombastic football metaphor with its emphasis on teamwork and a win-at-all-cost mentality. Other individual sports metaphors have infiltrated the American political dialogue at one time or another, especially the horse-racing analogy with its references to front-runners and dark horses, long-shots and shoo-ins, also-rans and nose-outs[24]—a metaphor incidentally that reveals the seamier, more disreputable face of politics as well as the affinity of politics to gambling—and other team sports metaphors have proven popular on occasions—FDR, for example, dismissed his failures with 'I have no expectation of making a hit every time I come to bat,'[25] and Sherman Adams discarded the first Soviet sputnik with a refusal to become engaged in 'an outer-space basketball game'[26]—but the football metaphor has emerged as the pre-eminent figure of speech, the root metaphor of American political discourse.

Example are legion, but just to name a few: John F. Kennedy once told his press secretary, Pierre Salinger, 'politics is like football. If you see daylight, go through it;'[27] former Secretary of State, Dean Acheson, once said that 'when the President fumbles, the whole goal line in open';[28] more recently, reporting on the progress of the campaign, one of George Bush's advisors noted that 'We're moving the ball on the ground just fine. Unless they make us put it in the air, why do it?,'[29] and Presidential hopeful, Pat Robertson, charged George Bush with stealing delegates away from him which was 'like trying to take a touchdown back after the game';[30] even more recently, Bill Clinton included the following remarks about the fragile peace in Bosnia in his 1998 State of the Union Address: 'This is like being ahead in the fourth quarter of a football game. Now is not the time to walk off the field and forfeit the victory'.[31] No one, of course, mixed football and political metaphors more frequently or more manipulatively—'public doublespeak' as F. Hardaway called it[32]—than Richard Nixon, whose 'macho jocko' talk,[33] was as Hugh Rank writes, 'akin to verbal locker room swaggering of muscle-flexing *machismo* at the beach'.[34]

The salience of the football metaphor is partly grounded in the construct of teamwork and the concomitant values of loyalty, co-ordination, and unity, and a pious attitude toward hierarchy and authority, and if Nixon accentuated the aggressive dimension of teamwork with metaphors like 'tough it out,' 'zone defense,' and 'bottom line it,'[35] then Ronald Reagan emphasized the disciplinary aspect of teamwork with his constant, restraining references to his administration as 'team players'.[36] Subsequent to a political rebuff from Reagan after his depiction of the Kemp-Roth bill as a 'Trojan Horse,' controller David Stockman was referred to as 'a chastened team player'.[37] Even a contrite Stockman, himself, during his press conference, stated that 'the President asked me to stay on the team'.[38] To Reagan, to be a 'member of the President's team,' as one of his top officials referred to it,[39] clearly presumed and demanded the sublimation of the individual ego for the sake of the team goal.

But there is something more to the football metaphor than the notion of team unity and purpose. I. Balbus, for example, has argued that football both reflects and popularizes the technocratic model of contemporary politics, a model that asserts the neutral 'scientific' character of state economic decisions, the technical expertise of those who make them, and their overall integration in the form of a plan.[40] Football, like politics, becomes increasingly heroic, the preserve of men of mythic dimensions and capabilities, reducing the rest of the electorate to the role of spectator or fan. The danger is obvious—the ritualization and celebration of both football and politics is entertainment spectacles, and the corresponding exclusion, and ultimately the atrophy, of popular political will; citizenship transformed into acclamation. All of which suggests that the ultimate sports metaphor for the *fin de millinaire*—a metaphor often employed predictably by Reagan—is sadly but accurately the 'Monday-morning quarterback'.

Business

According to J. Clancy[41] in a fascinating study based on an analysis of business speeches of 43 business leaders from the past 200 years, the most prominent metaphor in the discourse of business during the first half of the twentieth century was the metaphor of the journey, a metaphor by Clancy's account that spoke to the heritage of American business as a humanitarian endeavor dedicated to the service of society. 'The business of business,' George Draper-Dayton, the founder of Dayton-Hudson, once wrote in 1932, 'is serving society, not just making money'.[42] The journey metaphor also implied peril and the notion of a mission fraught with danger and potential failure.

The journey metaphor, however, with its altruistic connotations gradually made room for the game metaphor, an analogy that more precisely captured the intricacies and complexities of a burgeoning corporate America at the same time as it encapsulated the emergent ethics of instrumentalism, teamwork, and winning. Serving society, in other words, gave way to making a profit, production for consumption to maximizing shareholder wealth. Consequently, while Henry Ford could once write that 'business as a mere money-making game was not worth giving much thought'.[43] Andrew Carnegie could also proclaim that 'the end was money and yet more money ... business is the greatest game in the world'.[44] Walter Winston, once chair of Citicorp, also talked of 'winning the game in the marketplace'[45] and Lee Iacocca, CEO of Chrysler, advocated game principles as directly relevant to business: teach the fundamentals, enforce discipline, and play as a team.[46] In the 1983 study of the top business executives of their day, Donaldson and Lorsch aptly noted that, business leaders 'are fundamentally gamesmen, motivated to win the game they are playing'.[47]

But—and perhaps predictably by now—the generic game metaphor has given way to the more specific, and increasingly ubiquitous football metaphor. 'No figure of speech is as tenth as seductive to the businessman,' writes Whyte.[48] Reflecting a more modern zeitgeist, Ross Perot recently dismissed the 'level playing field' metaphor, attributing US post-war economic domination over Japan rather to American ownership of 'both teams and the stadium'. Perot also advised '"blocking and tackling" instead of buying new uniforms' in our escalating competition with the Japanese.[49] Not unsurprisingly, the language of business—'reverse gobbledygook' as Whyte calls it[50]— is also more than reminiscent of the rhetoric of Republican Presidents like Nixon and Reagan. Harold Green at ITT, for example, speaks of his associates as 'a team,' with a 'game plan' that frequently 'huddles' and occasionally needs 'new players'.[51]

The success of the football metaphor is predicted, according to Whyte, on 'its adaptability to all sorts of situations'.[52] It is, as Whyte argues, a 'satisfying' analogy because football is 'bounded by two goal lines and is thus finite. There is always a solution'.[53] But it is how the solution is reached that is perhaps most telling. Success in business, like success in football, is predicted on aggression, instrumentalism, regimentation, and the zero-sum game that epitomizes corporate capitalism as an ideology. Both football and business require a highly specialized division of labour which, as Clancy puts it, presumes 'precision, analysis, and optimization of each process and the worker's unthinking performance of regimented tasks ... If there is a game, that is not a game, play that is not play, with the focus on regimentation as opposed to spontaneity, it is football'.[54] This is what makes the football analogy so appealing and as Whyte recognizes so 'treacherous';[55] while the lingo of football may serve as a malleable dramaturgical device for motivation and persuasion, it can also serve as a rhetorical subterfuge that falsely clarifies moral complexity with images of ethical simplicity. Human issues are portrayed as strategic dilemmas, moral issues as technical problems.

The truth of the matter of course is that football is not *like* American business; it *is* American business. The metaphor is so complete that it appears incontrovertible, even, ironically, from a feminist perspective. The task of both football and business is unequivocally unimodal, the development of the most efficient means to achieve the predetermined and uncontestable end—success, winning, and making a profit. But football is more than just a caricature of corporate America, it has become a caricature of our entire corporate-military complex, which is why the football metaphor is so commonplace in the languages of war, politics and business, and why it is ultimately so dangerous—'normal problems,' as John Updike so poignantly reminds us, 'have no rules and no end'.[56]

Sexual Relations

As common a rhetorical convention as the sport metaphor is in the language of corporate-*realpolitik*, nowhere do we appear to have developed a more popular affliction for its use than in the language of sexual relations. And, once again, Shakespeare provides us with an historical template; the hunt metaphor, perhaps not surprisingly given Shakespeare's patriarchal and traditional society, is the most prominent metaphor used. Referring to Rosaline, Romeo notes that 'The game was ne'er so fair'.[57] Likewise, Ulysses remarks to Nestor:

> Set them down
> For the sluttish spoils of opportunity
> And daughters of the game.[58]

No doubt in deference to the subtleties and intricacies of romantic interplay, Shakespeare also used the angling metaphor. Having sent Hermione and Polinixes out into the garden alone, Leontes comments: 'I am angling now, Though you perceive me not how I give line'.[59] The often censored French poet, Theophile de Viau also predicted our contemporary proclivity for the sports metaphor when, in 1622, he conscripted the tennis metaphor into service in the infamous lines:

> If you kiss her count fifteen
> If you touch her buds, thirty ...[60]

The hunt and tennis metaphors of medieval and Renaissance Europe, however, have more recently been replaced by a variety of sports metaphors, among the most prominent being 'go all the way,' 'sink the putt,' 'put the puck in the net,' 'get a hole on one,' and 'score'.[61]

But of all the language used this way, baseball jargon is by far the most frequently heard. One can, for example, 'get to first, second, or third base,' 'hit a home run,' 'go to extra innings,' or 'strike out'. In my own informal investigation among a sample of 127 undergraduate students, I found that 47 percent of all sports metaphors used in this way were drawn from the sport of baseball. The four most commonly reported metaphors—'get to first, second, or third base,' 'hit a home run,' 'score,' and 'strike out'—accounted for 57 percent of all sports metaphors reported.[62]

The salience of the baseball metaphor may be because it offers the possibilities of gradation of sexual encounter; that is, one can 'get to first, second, or third base,' before finally 'hitting a home run' or 'striking out'. Here, the sexual interlude is likened to an epic sprint around the bases in which more venturesome levels of physical intimacy are accomplished with every base. Maybe it is simply that 'getting a hit,' especially a 'home run,' is as difficult and as exciting in baseball as it is in sexual relations.

Perhaps, it is that baseball embodies a more primitive, elemental myth, the myth of the man carrying a club. Hercules, the Greek patron of athletics, was often pictured carrying a club, and in Bernard Malamud's *The Natural*,[63] the bat, Roy Hobbs' 'Wonderboy,' the 'foolproof lance,' serves as the archetype symbol of strength and fertility, power and potency, an image reminiscent of Marshall Smelser's description of Babe Ruth as 'the man with the club, primitive but successful, the fundamental man who was victor over everything'.[64]

But perhaps the underlying homology between baseball and sexual relations revolves around the issue of privacy. Baseball is, after all, a more private game than football or field hockey for example. In both football and field hockey, all the players are always visible, on the field or on the bench, under our gaze; in baseball, players are often invisible, in the dugout or in the bullpen, out of sight. Privacy in sport is rare; only in baseball can one find privacy and security of home, as baseball commissioner Bart Giamatti so beautifully reminds us:

Home plate radiates a force no other spot on the field possesses ... even opponents gather at the same curious, unique place called home plate. Catcher and batter, siblings who may see the world differently but share the same sight lines, are backed up and get ruled by the parent figure, the umpire ... This tense family clusters at home, facing the world together, each with separate responsibilities and tasks and perspectives, each with different obligations and instruments.[65]

All literary romance begins—as Odysseus so well knew—with a journey of discovery, a separation from home, a tour around the base paths, and it ends with a rejoicing, a reunion at home. Both baseball and sex are ultimately about romance, about union and reunion; both as Giamatti notes are about the 'restoration of the right relations among things—and going home is where that restoration occurs because that is where it matters most'.[66]

Upon deeper reflection, perhaps the language of baseball is most suitably employed metaphorically to represent sexual relations because both sex and baseball so poignantly reflect the problematic nexus of self-interest and social responsibility. No sport more than baseball symbolically enacts the ontological tensions between domestic, private, and individual concerns, one the one hand, and social, public and communal concerns on the other. After all, baseball reflects a recurrent cultural dilemma: how to reconcile communal values with a powerful tradition of heroic individualism and privatism. Although this tension operates on several different levels—from the clash of two teams each demanding intense social loyalties to the mythic clash between pitcher and batter—it is crystallized in the confrontation between the batter at home play and the opposition arrayed in the field. It is here that the game most vividly and most earnestly seeks to reconcile notions of community and fair play with those of privacy and individual heroism.

Nor, as a matter of fact, is the language of baseball gender specific. It is only by default assumption that we assume it is. The language of baseball is, of course, also the language of softball; there is nothing inherently androcentric about such euphemisms as 'strike out' or 'get to first base'. Given the consensual nature of sexual relations, it is oxymoronic to presuppose that sex is an exclusively male domain, although our default assumption does suggest a cultural perspective that reinforces a traditional masculine sovereignty even in this the most domestic of habits.

The greater danger in all of this parlance is that it functions as a mechanism for transforming a profound and delicate human relations issue into a problem of strategy. It objectifies women linguistically conceiving of them as parts, and it constructs notions of masculine hegemony and hegemonic masculinity, in the end, contributing to a larger cultural discourse through which patterns of empowerment and subordination are socialized into successive generations of men and women. Of all our linguistic proclivities, the athleticization of sexual relations may be our most dangerous, the most threatening to our ongoing sense of humanness—the reduction and transmogrification of the most human of affairs to the level of a game.

Conclusion

Once a mere establishment of language, a rhetorical flourish, the metaphor is now recognized not only for its affective and oratorical efficacy but for its cognitive contribution. Its study, according to P. Ricoeur, is less a matter of semantics and more a matter of hermeneutics.[67] Or as Aristotle once wrote: 'Midway between the unintelligible and the common place, it is a metaphor which most produces knowledge'.[68] Consequently, what I have attempted to do in this essay is to demonstrate the ways in which the sports metaphor is, to borrow a phrase from E. Kittay, 'cognitively meaningful,'[69] the site of many a deep-seated, often unexamined belief or attitude and so a significant factor in the structure of knowledge and experience.

In so doing, however, I have tended to adopt an accuracy or representationalist perspective, one that suggests that any given metaphor validates some authentic and accessible objective reality. This view presumes the possibility of an epitemic position 'outside' of language and reality, a supposedly neutral position. However, within post-structuralist and anti-representationalist positions, the metaphor is viewed as more than just reflective of reality but actually constitutive of it. Metaphors, as Lakoff and Johnson put it, 'create realities' and therefore serve as 'a guide for future action'.[70] Or to steal a term from Althusser and Marxist cultural studies, the metaphor 'interpellates' its subjects; it beckons subjects to be certain kinds of people.[71] Consequently, as Rorty points out: 'It is useless to ask whether one vocabulary rather than another is close to reality. For different vocabularies serve different purposes, and there is no such thing as a purpose that is closer to reality than another purpose'.[72] The better question to ask about the sports metaphor then becomes not whether any one particular metaphor provides a better picture of a knowable reality than another, but since any way of talking about war, politics, business and sexual relations will inevitably and in fact necessarily elevate one set of human purposes over another, what objectives and whose agenda will be furthered by mediating cultural life through certain sports metaphors rather than others.

Several studies have fruitfully adopted this approach. Jansen and Sabo, for example, have demonstrated that the sport/war metaphors during the Persian Gulf War were used as powerful rhetorical devices for mobilizing the patriarchal values that construct, mediate and maintain hegemonic forms of masculinity.[73] Similarly, S. Walk has shown how Lyndon Johnson and Ronald Reagan differentially employed the footrace metaphor to frame basic assumptions about public policy in keeping with their own party ideologies.[74] Finally, Bineham has argued that the deployment of team sport metaphors in the discourse surrounding David Stockman's offer of resignation as Reagan's Director of the Office of Management and Budget constituted subjects with a particular range of expectations, including the public's orientation to the situation as well as the form of Stockman's response.[75]

As each of these studies suggest, the sports metaphor has so thoroughly colonized our cultural discourse that the guiding logics and ethical dimensions of sports are now routinely employed in the form of language as frames for not only commenting upon and understanding a vast complexity of issues but for interpellating us as cultural beings who are a part of the complexity. Explaining who or what agenda is best served by the deployment of sports metaphors in a wide array of cultural arenas and settings remains the ongoing challenge for future research on the topic.

Skidmore College, Saratoga Springs

(Endnotes)

[1] F. Nietzsche, 'On Truth and Lies in the Nonmoral Sense,', in D. Breazeale (ed.), *Philosophy and Truth: Selections from Nietzsche's Notebooks of the Early 1870s* (Atlantic Highlands, NJ: Humanities Press, 1979), pp. 79–97.

[2] J. Lukacs, *Historical Consciousness* (New York: Harper Row, 1968), p. 7.

[3] R. Lipsyte, *Sportsworld: An American Dreamland* (New York: Quadrangle Books, 1975), p. 1.

[4] R.A. Palmatier and H.L. Ray, *Sports Talk: A Dictionary of Sports Metaphors* (New York: Greenwood Press, 1989).

[5] *King Henry V*, 1, ii, 281–2.

6 Quoted in L. Berkow, 'Once Again, It's the Star-Spangled Super Bowl,' *New York Times*, 27 January 1991, 8.

7 M. Real, 'Super Bowl: Mythic Spectacle,' *Journal of Communications*, 25 (1975), 43.

8 M.D. Tullai, 'Football and Politics,' *Scholastic Coach*, 58 (1989), 34.

9 B. Duffy, 'The 100-Hour War,' *U.S. News & World Report*, 11 March 1986, 14.

10 T. Mathews, C.S. Manegold and T.M. DeFrank, 'A Soldier of Conscious,' *Newsweek*, 11 March 1991, 34.

11 Duffy, 'The 100-Hour War,' 11.

12 Quoted in R. Wilkinson, 'Anatomy of a Cakewalk', *Newsweek*, 11 March 1991, 48.

13 Quoted in M. Capuzzo, *Philadelphia Inquirer*, 19 Jan. 1991, D2.

14 Real, 'Super Bowl: Mythic Spectacle', 36.

15 G. Cheney, '"We're Talking War": Symbols, Strategies, and Images,' in B.S. Greenberg and W. Gantz (eds.), *Desert Storm and the Mass Media* (Cresskill, NJ: Hampton Press, 1993), p. 63.

16 'The Fury of Desert Storm,' *U.S. News & World Report*, 11 March 1981, 67.

17 S.C. Jansen and D. Sabo, 'The Sport/War Metaphor: Hegemonic Masculinity, the Persian Gulf War, and the New World Order' (hereafter 'The Sport/War Metaphor'), *Sociology of Sport Journal*, 11 (1994), 1–17; M.J. Shapiro, 'Representing World Politics: The Sport/War Intertext,' in J.D. Derian and M.J. Shapiro (eds.), *International/Intertextual Relations: Postmodern Readers of World Politics* (Lexington, MA: D.C. Heath, 1989), pp. 69–96.

18 Jensen and Sabo, 'The Sport/War Metaphor', 7.

19 *King Henry V*, 3, i, 31–2.

20 Quoted in W. Safire, *The New Language of Politics: An Anecdotal Dictionary of Catchwords, Slogans, and Political Usage* (New York: Random House, 1968), p. 421.

21 Ibid., p. 185.

22 Ibid.

23 Ibid.

24 Ibid., p. 101.

25 Ibid., p. 421.

26 Ibid.

27 Tullai, 'Football and Politics', 34.

28 Ibid.

29 Ibid., 35.

30 Ibid.

[31] 'President Clinton's State of the Union Address', *New York Times*, 28 Jan. 1998, A19-20.

[32] F. Hardaway, 'Foul Play: Sports Metaphors as Public Doublespeak,' *College English*, 38 (1976), 78-82.

[33] Nicholas Von Hoffman quoted in H. Rank (ed.), 'Watergate and Language,' *Language and Public Policy* (Urbana, IL: National Council of Teachers of English, 1974), p. 7.

[34] Rank, 'Watergate and Language', p. 7.

[35] Ibid.

[36] J. Bineham, 'Some Ethical Implications of Team Sports Metaphors in Politics' (hereafter 'Some Ethical Implications'), *Communication Reports*, 4 (1991), 35-42.

[37] E. Cowen, 'Chastened Team Player,' *New York Times*, 13 Nov. 1981, 39.

[38] Quoted in Bineham, 'Some Ethical Implications,' 39.

[39] Ibid., 38.

[40] I. Balbus, 'Politics as Sports: The Political Ascendancy of the Sports Metaphor in America,' *Monthly Review*, 26 (1989), 26-39.

[41] J.J. Clancy, *The Invisible Powers: The Language of Business* (hereafter *The Invisible Powers*) (Lexington, MA: D.C. Heath, 1989).

[42] Quoted in J. O'Toole, *Vanguard Management: Redesigning the Corporate Future* (Garden City, NY: Doubleday, 1986), p. 147.

[43] H. Ford, *My Life and Works* (New York: Doubleday, 1923), p. 41.

[44] Quoted in J.K. Winkler, *Incredible Carnegie* (New York: Vanguard Press, 1931), p.95.

[45] Quoted in H. Levinson and S. Rosenthal, *CEO: Corporate Leadership in Action* (New York: Basic Books, 1984), p. 69.

[46] L. Iacocca, *Iacocca* (New York: Bantam Books, 1986).

[47] G. Donaldson and J.E. Lorsch, *Decision Making at the Top* (New York: Basic Books, 1983), p. 25.

[48] W.H. Whyte, 'The Language of Business,' in H.A. Estrin (ed.), *Technical and Professional Writing: A Practical Anthology* (New York: Harcourt, Brace and World, 1983), p. 82.

[49] Quoted in D.P. Levin and P. Ingrassia, 'New on the Inside: Ross Perot Tells GM and its Rivals How They Must Change,' *Wall Street Journal*, 8 Nov. 1986, 7.

[50] Whyte, 'The Language of Business,' p. 82.

[51] Quoted in H. Geneen and A Moscow, *Managing* (Garden City, NY: Doubleday, 1984), p. 99.

[52] Whyte, 'The Language of Business,' p. 82.

[53] Ibid., p. 83.

[54] Clancy, *The Invisible Powers*, p. 47.

364

55 Whyte, 'The Language of Business,' p. 83.
56 Quoted in J. Reston, 'Sports and Politics in America,' *New York Times*, 12 Sept. 1969, 42.
57 *Romeo and Juliet*, 1, iv, 39.
58 *Troilus and Cressida*, 4, vi, 61–3.
59 *The Winter's Tale*, 1, ii, 180.
60 Quoted in Alexander, 'The Birth of Tennis,' *Lingua Franca* (Dec./Jan. 1999), 18–20.
61 J.O. Segrave, 'The Perfect 10: "Sportspeak" in the Language of Sexual Relations,' *Sociology of Sport Journal*, 11 (1994), 95–113.
62 Ibid.
63 B. Malamud, *The Natural* (New York: Avon Books, 1952).
64 M. Smelser, 'The Babe on Balance,' *American Scholar*, 44 (1975), 301.
65 A.B. Giammati, *Take Time for Paradise: Americans and Their Games* (New York: Summit Books, 1989), pp. 87–8.
66 Ibid., p. 92.
67 P. Ricouer, 'The Metaphorical Process as Cognition, Imagination, and Feeling,' in S. Sacks (ed.), *On Metaphor* (Chicago: University of Chicago Press, 1979).
68 *Rhetoric*, III, 1410b.
69 E.F. Kittay, *Metaphor: Its Cognitive Force and Linguistic Structure* (Oxford: Claredon Press, 1987), p. 2.
70 G. Lakoff and M. Johnson, *Metaphors We Live By* (Chicago: University of Chicago Press), p. 156.
71 L. Althusser, *Lenin and Philosophy* (New York: Basic Books, 1970), pp. 170–7.
72 R. Rorty, *Objectivity, Relativism, and Truth: Philosophical Papers Volume 1* (Cambridge: Cambridge University Press, 1990), p. 3.
73 Jansen and Sabo, 'The Sport/War Metaphor'.
74 S.R. Walk, 'The Footrace Metaphor in American Presidential Rhetoric,' *Sociology of Sport Journal*, 12 (1995), 36–55.
75 Bineham, 'Some Ethical Implications'.

Just How Much Is Sports Fandom Like Religion?

by Michael Serazio

Pro sports teams are like what religion and sociology scholars call "totems"—symbols of greater entities that communities gather around for identity and unity.

The Super Bowl, professional sports' highest holy day, is again upon us. As fans paint their faces and torsos, pile on licensed apparel, and quixotically arrange beer cans in the shape of team logos, the question must, again, be asked: Why exactly do we do this for our teams?

Why, in my own case, do I feel the need to sport a Chargers cap on fall Sundays sitting in front of the television when decades of futility, not to mention common sense, suggests it has little effect on outcome?

The answer—and the secret of fandom—might just be found in a context far removed from professional football.

Almost precisely a century ago, Emile Durkheim pondered along similar lines. Durkheim, a pioneering sociologist, began digging through accounts of "primitive" cultures like the Arunta tribe of Australia, hoping to excavate the ancient source of ties that bind. His conclusion—as revealed in *The Elementary Forms of the Religious Life*—remains as profound and relevant today as it is elegantly simple: Whenever a society (or, here, sports subculture) worships a divine form, it is, in fact, also simultaneously worshipping itself.

For Durkheim, this all hinged on what he called "the totem." As he wrote, "On the one hand, [the totem] is the external and tangible form of what we have called the... god. But on the other, it is the symbol of that particular society we call the clan. It is its flag; it is the sign by which each clan distinguishes itself from others, the visible mark of its personality."

In other words, our religious totems, while "officially" symbolizing deities, also implicitly offer vessels for fellowship; licenses to congregate together. As social creatures, there is something universal—and still enduring—in that tribal yearning. Yet community is often more abstract and imagined than concrete and identifiable.

From *The Atlantic,* 2013.

The totem, then, gives believers a physical representation of that need for identity and unity: a Star of David hung from the neck; a Ganesh figurine placed on the dashboard; a St. Christopher medal tucked in the wallet. Theological justifications are really just incidental; what matters is that through our faith in these common artifacts, community is forged.

Alas, formal, organized religion in America today seems but a shell of its former self. A recent Pew study noted that the percentage of the U.S. public declaring themselves religiously "unaffiliated" had grown to one-fifth, including one-third of those under 30—the highest figures in the poll's history. Faith in other institutions—family, one's employer, political entities—is equally dwindling, though such institutions once also rooted the individual in something larger.

What totems, therefore, still survive in this culture of ours? The Red Sox. The Packers. The Lakers. And so on. The notion that sports remain our civic religion is truer than we often let on: In fandom, as in religious worship, our social connections are brought to life, in the stands as in the pews. It serves as a reminder of our interconnectedness and dependency; it materially indexes belonging. Like others, I indulge the royal "we" when speaking of my team, though there is little evidence they need me much beyond ticket sales, merchandise, and advertising impressions. Nonetheless, as Durkheim long ago noticed, "Members of each clan try to give themselves the external appearance of their totem ... When the totem is a bird, the individuals wear feathers on their heads." Ravens fans surely understand this.

In short, if you look hard at sports, you can't help but see contours of religion.

Others have gestured to these parallels over the years. Some have highlighted how both preserve revered spaces (e.g., Sistine Chapel, Wrigley Field) and observe seasonal rhythms and orderly ceremonial frameworks. Elsewhere, it has been claimed that with its religious metaphors, regular invocations of good and evil, and sacred vestments (The Shroud of Schilling!), sports channel a natural religious impulse—driving one, somehow, "Godward."

The notion that sports remain our civic religion is truer than we often let on: In fandom, as in religious worship, our social connections are brought to life, in the stands as in the pews.

Writing about British soccer fans, one sociologist observed that: "Just as Durkheim suggested aboriginal tribes worship their society through the totem, so do the lads reaffirm their relations with other lads through the love of the team."

The sports totem therefore gives me reason to strike up a conversation with a stranger; better still, it offers phone fodder for calls to Grandpa. We routinely speak of being "born" into a particular fandom and treat those who change allegiances to rival teams with the same alienation familiar to heretics and apostates.

And should the Chargers ever reward my faith with a Super Bowl win—and, having lived through the Ryan Leaf years, I'm not holding my breath here—I'll finally have recourse to revel riotously, just as we'll see for one lucky, exhilarated fan base in a few days' time.

Durkheim had a name for this, too. He called it "collective effervescence," that social "electricity" that gets generated when groups gather to exalt in epic rituals. In that, the post-game celebration and day-after parades, with its feverish outpouring of emotion—all that hugging and high-fiving, those deafening howls and blubbery weeping—might look like chaotic disorder but it is actually a rare moment of social order: a glimpse of spontaneous solidarity, an interlude of uninhibited integration. This is not to excuse the excess of vandalism or violence that often accompanies the effervescence; the same social norms that maintain chilly anonymity in day-to-day modern life also serve to uphold law and decorum.

Yet that anonymity can inevitably be an unsettling thing; just ask anyone who's ever moved far from home. It doesn't really matter whether our teams win or lose on the field. As long as the totem survives, so do we. Turns out, that's what I'm really rooting for and why I'm still wearing that Chargers cap every Sunday afternoon.

Acknowledgments

Alloway, Tracy, Rachel Runac, Mueez Qureshi, and George Kemp. "Is Facebook Linked to Selfishness?" from *Social Networking*, 3, 150-158. Copyright © 2014 by the authors and Scientific Research Publishing Inc. This work is licensed under the Creative Commons Attribution International License (CC BY).

Armstrong, Karen. "Religion: What's God Got to Do with It" from *New Statesman*, April 10, 2006. Reprinted with permission of New Statesman Media Group. All rights reserved.

Bass, Rick. "Why I Hunt" from *Sierra Magazine*, July 2001. Reprinted with permission of Sierra Club and the author. All rights reserved.

Bazelon, Emily. "The Next Kind of Integration" from *The New York Times*, Apr. 20, 2008. Copyright © 2008 *The New York Times/* PARS International Corp. Reprinted with permission. All rights reserved.

Begley, Sharon and Jeneen Interlandi. "The Dumbest Generation?" from *Newsweek*, May 24, 2008. Reprinted with permission. All rights reserved.

Behar, Michael and Amy Guip. "Will Genetics Destroy Sports?" from *Discover Magazine*. Copyright © 2004 by Michael Behar. All rights reserved.

Bordo, Susan. "The Globalization of Eating Disorders" from *Unbearable Weight: Feminism, Western Culture*. Copyright © 1993 by the Regents of the University of California. Reprinted with permission. All rights reserved.

Branch, Taylor. "The Shame of College Sports" from *The Atlantic*, Sept. 7, 2011. All rights reserved.

Carr, Nicolas. "Is Google Making Us Stupid?" from *The Atlantic*, July/ August 2008. Copyright © 2008 by Nicholas Carr. Reprinted with permission of the author. All rights reserved.

Carson, Claybourne. "Two Cheers for *Brown v Board of Education*" from the *Journal of American History*, Jun. 2004. Reprinted with permission. All rights reserved.

Carson, Rachel. "The Obligation to Endure" from *Silent Spring*. Copyright © 1962 by Rachel L. Carson. Reprinted with permission of Houghton Mifflin Harcourt Co. All rights reserved.

Christina, Greta. "Grief Beyond Belief: How Atheists are Dealing with Death" from Freethoughtsblog.com (2011). All rights reserved.

Ferguson, Niall. "America's *Oh Sh*t* Moment: How American Civilization Can Avoid Collapse" by Niall Ferguson. Copyright © 2011 Newsweek LLC. All rights reserved.

Gawande, Atul. "Naked" from *The New England Journal of Medicine*, Vol. 353, No. 7. Copyright © 2005 by Massachusetts Medical Society. Reprinted with permission. All rights reserved.

Gelertner, David. "Unplugged: The Myth of Computers in the Classroom" from *The New Republic,* 1994. All rights reserved.

Gitlin, Todd. "Supersaturation, or, The Media Torrent and Disposable Feeling" from *Media Unlimited: How the Torrent of Images and Sounds Overwhelms Our Lives.* Copyright © 2002 by Todd Gitlin. Reprinted with permission of Picador, a division of MacMillan Publishers. All rights reserved.

Hitchens, Christopher. "Topic of Cancer" from *Vanity Fair.* Copyright © 2010 Condé Nast. Reprinted with permission. All rights reserved.

Hoagland, Edward. "1776 and All That" from *The Nation.* Copyright © 2002 Agence Global. Reprinted with permission. All rights reserved.

Horowitz, Joy. "Parkinson's Alley" from *Sierra Magazine.* Reprinted with permission of Sierra Club and the author. All rights reserved.

Jacoby, Susan. "When Bright Girls Decide that Math is 'A Waste of Time'" from *The New York Times.* Copyright © 1983 *The New York Times*/PARS International Corp. Reprinted with permission. All rights reserved.

Kilbourne, Jean. "Jesus is a Brand of Jeans" from *New Internationalist,* Sept. 2006. Copyright © 1973-2016 by New Internationalist and licensed under Creative Commons Attribution International License.

Lepore, Jill. "It's Spreading: Outbreaks, Media Scares, and the Parrot Panic of 1930" from *The New Yorker.* Copyright © 2009 Condé Nast. Reprinted with permission. All rights reserved.

Lewis, Bernard. "I'm Right, You're Wrong, Go to Hell" from *The Atlantic,* May 2003. All rights reserved.

Lewis, C.S. "The Rival Conceptions of God" from *Mere Christianity.* Copyright © 1952 by C.S. Lewis. Reprinted with permission of C.S. Lewis Co. All rights reserved.

McKibben, Bill. "The Environmental Issue from Hell: Global Warming is the Great Moral Crisis of our Time" from *In These Times*, April 30, 2001. Copyright © 2001 by *In These Times* and the Institute for Public Affairs. All rights reserved.

Mendoza, Martha. "Between a Woman and Her Doctor: A Story About Abortion You Will Never Forget" from *Ms. Magazine*. Copyright © 2004 by Martha Mendoza. Reprinted with permission of the author. All rights reserved.

Ortiz Cofer, Judith. "The Myth of the Latin Woman: I Just Met a Girl Named Maria" from *The Latin Deli*. Copyright © 1996 by Judith Ortiz Cofer. Reprinted with permission of the University of Georgia Press. All rights reserved.

Owens, Louis. "The American Indian Wilderness (Burning the Shelter)" originally appeared in *The American Nature Writing Newsletter* 6, no. 2 (Fall 1994). All rights reserved.

Quindlen, Anna. "Sex Ed" from *Living Out Loud*. Copyright © 1987 by Anna Quindlen. Used by permission of Ballantine Books, an imprint of Penguin Random House LLC. All rights reserved.

Reed, Ishmael. "America: The Multinational Society" from *Writin' is Fightin': Thirty-Seven Years of Boxing on Paper*. Copyright © 1988 by Ishmael Reed. Reprinted with permission of Simon and Schuster. All rights reserved.

Ripley, Amanda. "The Case Against High-School Sports" from *The Atlantic*, Oct. 2013. All rights reserved.

Rose, Mike. "What College Can Mean to the Other America" from *The Chronicle of Higher Education*. Copyright © 2011 The Chronicle of Higher Education. Reprinted with permission. All rights reserved.

Ross, Deborah. "Escape from Wonderland: Disney and the Female Imagination" from *Marvels and Tales: Journal of Fair-Tale Studies*, Vol.18, No. 1 (2004). Copyright © 2004 by Wayne State University Press. Reprinted with permission. All rights reserved.

Rushdie, Salman. "Yes, This is about Islam" from *The New York Times*, Nov. 2, 2001. Reprinted with permission. All rights reserved.

Sachs, Jeffrey. "A Nation of Vidiots" from *Project Syndicate*, Oct. 28, 2011. Reprinted with permission. All rights reserved.

Seagrave, Jeffrey O. "The Sports Metaphor in American Cultural Discourse" from *Culture, Sport, Society*, 3.1 (2000). Reprinted with permission of Taylor and Francis. All rights reserved.

Sen, Amartya. "A World Not Neatly Divided" from *The New York Times.* Copyright © 2001 *The New York Times*/PARS International Corp. Reprinted with permission. All rights reserved.

Serazio, Michael. "Just How Much is Sports Fandom Like Religion?" from *The Atlantic,* Jan 29, 2013. All rights reserved.

Staples, Brent. "Just Walk on by: Black Men and Public Space" originally appeared in *Ms. Magazine.* Copyright © 1986 by Brent Staples. Reprinted with permission. All rights reserved.

Tidwell, Mike. "To Fix Climate Change, Stop Going Green All Alone" from *The Washington Post,* Dec. 4, 2009. Reprinted with permission. All rights reserved.

Tuchman, Barbara. Excerpt(s) from *A Distant Mirror: The Calamitous 14th Century.* Copyright © 1978 by Barbara W. Tuchman. Used by permission of Alfred A. Knopf, an imprint of the Knopf Doubleday Publishing Group, a division of Penguin Random House LLC. All rights reserved.